GUIDE TO LATIN IN INTERNATIONAL LAW

GUIDE TO LATIN IN INTERNATIONAL LAW

AARON X. FELLMETH & MAURICE HORWITZ

OXFORD
UNIVERSITY PRESS

OXFORD
UNIVERSITY PRESS

Oxford University Press, Inc., publishes works that further Oxford University's objective of excellence in research, scholarship, and education.

OXFORD NEW YORK
Auckland Cape Town Dar es Salaam Hong Kong Karachi
Kuala Lumpur Madrid Melbourne Mexico City Nairobi
New Delhi Shanghai Taipei Toronto

WITH OFFICES IN
Argentina Austria Brazil Chile Czech Republic France Greece
Guatemala Hungary Italy Japan Poland Portugal Singapore
South Korea Switzerland Thailand Turkey Ukraine Vietnam

Published by Oxford University Press, Inc.
198 Madison Avenue, New York, New York 10016

www.oup.com

Library of Congress Cataloging-in-Publication Data
Fellmeth, Aaron Xavier.
Guide to latin in international law / Aaron X. Fellmeth & Maurice Horwitz.
p. cm.
Includes bibliographical references.
ISBN 978–0–19–536938–0 (hardback : alk . paper)
1. Law—Dictionaries—Latin. 2. Latin language—Law Latin—Dictionaries—English
3. Latin language—Dictionaries—English. 4. Latin language—Terms and phrases.
I. Horwitz, Maurice. II. Title.
K52.L37F45 2009
340.03—dc22 2008055215

9 8 7 6 5 4 3 2 1

Printed in the United States of America on acid-free paper

CONTENTS

PREFACE

Maurice and I created this guidebook to assist international lawyers and law students seeking to master, or at least to decipher, the Latin recurrently injected into our profession's already arcane argot. It may seem strange that a reference book-sized niche remains in the twenty-first century given the profusion of legal reference works, but the fact remains that recognizing the need for a guidebook like this one is a little uncomfortable. The use of Latin in international legal writing is supposed to appear natural, if not inevitable. We typically pepper our writings with Latin as if the dead language were cayenne in a jambalaya—the more the better. Yet, at some level we are all aware that we often obscure rather than clarify our meaning when we use it instead of plain English. And when we get the Latin right, which we frequently do, and pronounce the words without butchering them beyond all hope of recognition, which we occasionally do, the practice nonetheless tends to baffle law students and even experienced international lawyers unschooled in the vernacular of Cicero.

Aspiring international lawyers may wonder about the ubiquity of Latin in international legal discourse in the first place. It may seem that the esoterism of such a prevalent practice can only be intentional. The official explanation is that much early international law was developed by the Roman Empire, and the much admired Roman civil law has found its way by analogy into public international law wherever a lacuna or ambiguity in the principles of international law arose.[1] When combined with the fact that Latin was the scholarly *lingua franca* of most of Europe during international law's early development, international lawyers have inherited an even better stocked arsenal of Latin phrases and terms than other lawyers.

1 For a classic discussion of this practice, *see* Hersch Lauterpacht, PRIVATE LAW SOURCES AND ANALOGIES OF INTERNATIONAL LAW (1970).

The historical reasons for the recurrence of Latin in legal writing, however, do not explain why international lawyers continue the practice with English equivalents so readily available. There are, indeed, modern instances of authors inventing new Latin terms for well-known concepts previously expressed perfectly adequately in English, presumably in quest of immortality as the originator of a neologism. Clearly, the official explanation for Latin's prevalence in international legal usage tells only part of the story.

W. Michael Reisman has offered an alternative explanation: "I warn my students that if they confront something in Latin, it is usually a signal that jurists are unsure of what they are talking about and are trying to conceal their confusion behind a solemn and pretentious Latin phrase."[2] Peter Tiersma has suggested a complementary theory: "[A] great majority of legal maxims are indeed in Latin, partly for historical reasons, but sometimes also to mask the fact that many of these maxims are self-evident banalities made to seem more impressive by being expressed in a dead language."[3] Another perspective, supported by the more frequent usage of Latin in European legal writing than in U.S. writing, is that the authors are trying to justify their years of doggedly memorizing Latin conjugations and declensions by putting it to some plausible use.

Whatever the true explanation, the important point is that a facility with at least some Latin assists international lawyers to understand the sources of law and each other. An excellent example of prolific Latin usage may be found in the World Trade Organization Agreement on Trade–Related Aspects of Intellectual Property Rights (TRIPs Agreement). In only twelve articles of the TRIPs Agreement (Articles 50 through 62), we find the following Latin terms:

Inaudita altera parte
Ex officio
Prima facie
Mutatis mutandis
De minimis
Inter partes

Elsewhere in the TRIPs Agreement we find such terms as *inter alia*, *sui generis*, and the adoption—seemingly idiosyncratic to international and civil lawyers—of *bis*, *ter*, and so forth, which are used to insert articles between other articles of consecutive numbering. A listing of such articles in a table, for example, might appear as follows:

2 W. Michael Reisman, *Jonathan I. Charney: An Appreciation*, 36 Vand. J. Transnat'l L. 23, 23 (2003).
3 Peter Tiersma, *The New* Black's, 55 J. Legal Educ. 386, 397 (2005).

Article 1
Article 2
Article 3
Article 3*bis*
Article 4
Article 4*bis*
Article 4*ter*
Article 5
...

This practice makes an appearance in greater or lesser proliferation in many amended treaties, such as the 1967 Paris Convention on the Protection of Industrial Property, which occasionally counts up to "*septies*" (after the serendipitously/offensively named "*sexies*"). For ease of reference, the Appendix to this guide contains a listing of such ordinals up to fifteen (beyond which treaties rarely go even after numerous emendations).

The prevalence of Latin in judicial and arbitral decisions is still more striking. Some judges of the International Court of Justice have used Latin so promiscuously as to call into question their comfort with the English or French languages. One judge, for example, recently invoked close on one hundred different Latin phrases in a single separate opinion. He then presumably stepped back into his time machine and returned to drafting the Magna Carta.

Given the current reality of profligate Latin usage, *Guide to Latin in International Law* was written for those who wish to understand the language of international lawyers, not so much for those seeking to boost their bombasticity quotient. For this reason, this guide defines Latin terms and phrases, but does not provide Latin translations for common English terms and phrases. Nor does the guidebook organize the terms and phrases by topic or keyword to facilitate the use of Latin. If the latter book were published, knowledge of its existence would be strictly controlled by a secretive cartel of international lawyers and academics, jealously guarding it with a password such as *do ut des*.

A second intended function of the guidebook is to assist in correcting the wayward usages of Latin in the international law discourse. The modern international lawyer's fondness for Latin is nearly matched by his inability to reproduce properly its orthography, grammar, and pronunciation. We have seen *ius denegare* transformed into *ius denagata*; we have seen *ius fetiale* become *ius feciale*, *male captus* turned into *mala captus*, and the nonexistent term *in extenso* used *extense* in academic writings, judicial opinions, and even reference works. Latin is so commonly mangled in the literature that correcting every mistake appearing there would be a mammoth and profitless task, but we have tried to include references to the most common mistaken Latin spellings and grammar in hopes of encouraging proper usage.

While the preceding explanations may convey less than unadulterated appreciation of the modern use of Latin in legal writing, our irreverence hardly stems from any failure to appreciate the language's elegance or historical significance—Maurice is, after all, a trained classics scholar. Its source is, rather, an equal appreciation for the genius of the English language. Having already absorbed words from a huge variety of languages, modern English has proved winningly flexible and only rarely stands in real need of further assistance from its foreign brethren, ancient or modern. Few foreign words or phrases are significantly more helpful than their English counterparts. This is not to deny that the occasional foreign word or phrase captures a complex idea more succinctly than is possible in English. Tiersma has offered a helpful example: "The Supreme Court of Utah once invented a new maxim: 'Equity will not relieve one who could have relieved himself.'...The court should have said it in Latin."[4] Similarly, perhaps there is no tersely eloquent English translation for *Zeitgeist*, *Weltanschauung*, *éminence grise*, *vice versa*, or *voilà*, but is it really necessary to say *vel non* when we mean "or not," or *a fortiori* when we mean "all the more," or perhaps most egregious of all, *primo* instead of "first"? There is, of course, always a risk that a foreign phrase will lose some of its color or connotation in the translation. The objection is not to the occasional use of Latin, but to its uncontrolled proliferation, resulting from its status as a shibboleth among legal scholars and especially international lawyers. If this volume contributes to the demystification of international law scholarship, we have done our most important job. If not, at least the accuracy of the Latin used might be improved.

Speaking of other foreign languages, a reader might wonder why we have not included terms in foreign languages other than Latin in this guidebook. International lawyers certainly do make frequent use of French (*e.g.*, *chargé d'affaires*, *compromis*, *dispositif*, *procès-verbal*, *hors de combat*, *nonrefoulement*, *tracé parallele*, *travaux préparatoires*), German (*e.g.*, *Fremdenrecht*, *Grundnorm*, *Kompetenz-Kompetenz*), Italian (*e.g.*, *copia vera*), and sometimes other languages. The temptation to include such terms was great, but we refrained on the theory that these languages, unlike Latin, are commonly spoken by international lawyers and, when not, translations can be easily be obtained from any of the conveniently available dictionaries of international law, foreign language dictionaries, or translation software. And a guidebook of this kind is not nearly as necessary for living languages, not only because they are more readily accessible, but because presumably lawyers rarely use living languages in order to be

[4] Tiersma, *supra* note 3, at 397 n.27 (citation omitted).

deliberately obscure, when a far more cryptic dead language has made itself available.

Finally, regarding the selection of the terms and phrases translated and defined in this work, although we aimed at providing a comprehensive reference work, we are lawyers rather than professional lexicographers. As such, we are primarily concerned with providing a useful reference for any Latin an international lawyer is likely to happen upon, and this means that most of our source material for the Latin defined here is the typical fodder of international lawyers—treaties, decisions, and opinions of international tribunals, resolutions and work documents produced by international organizations, and the works of publicists in the field. But the uses of Latin in international law are so varied that, whatever our aspirations for comprehensiveness, some readers will no doubt happen upon the occasional term or phrase not included here. We hope the user of this work will view it in the same light that its authors do—as an ongoing project. To that end, we have made available a Web site (http://www.fellmeth.net/latinguide/) where you may submit Latin terms and phrases that you have encountered in the study of international law but that are nonetheless absent from this work. We, the authors, will do our best to supply you with a translation and to include it, if appropriate, in any future edition of this work.

ACKNOWLEDGMENTS

The authors owe a debt of gratitude to Prof. Dawn Bates of the Arizona State University for her advice on phonological matters and to Beth DiFelice for her research assistance. The authors also appreciate the useful assistance of the Oxford University Press staff. Aaron Fellmeth especially thanks Linda Demaine for her advice and patience in the process of compiling, writing, and editing this work. All errors are attributable to the authors alone.

AARON X. FELLMETH
Scottsdale, Arizona
April 1, 2009

PRONUNCIATION

Two pronunciations are always given in this guide. The first is classical (properly, restored) Latin. The second is the pronunciation commonly used by Americans in general and American lawyers in particular. Restored pronunciation, used mostly by classics experts, attempts to reproduce the sounds used by Romans between approximately 50 BCE and 50 CE. Restored Latin is only rarely used in legal discourse but is presented here for the purist and in the admittedly quixotic hope of providing some basis for a more elegant substitute to the unpredictable and belabored pronunciation commonly used by English speakers since about the fourteenth century. Although A.P. Herbert has insisted that proper Latin pronunciation "is dead and must be buried," we agree with H.A. Kelly's verdict that "it is undead rather than dead, and it has left its mark everywhere, destroying all semblance of consistency and tradition."[5]

On the other hand, one may be well advised, or one may prefer, to speak Latin in the most discreet and unobtrusive possible manner, which in the United States usually means mispronouncing it in the way most American English speakers do. Unfortunately, the American English pronunciations of Latin that we provide do not and cannot purport to establish a single authoritative pronunciation for each entry included here. There is no single wrong way to speak Latin. Language is organic, and a variety of pronunciations may successfully convey the speaker's meaning in terms of content and possibly even style. There is, indeed, something anomalous in offering an "authoritative" pronunciation of terms that are so diversely mispronounced by speakers of a language with significant regional variations.

The absence of uniformity is greater still when one considers pronunciations outside the United States. European, Australian, and British speakers pronounce Latin terms in ways that differ significantly from American pronunciations. This baffling diversity is the main reason, other than the love of pedantry,

5 H.A. Kelly, *Lawyers' Latin: Loquenda ut Vulgus?*, 38 J. Legal Educ. 195, 203 (1988).

for preferring restored Latin pronunciations. Nonetheless, common American pronunciations for the terms are provided here for those in search of a more or less accepted vulgar pronunciation.

Before presenting the alternative keys to pronunciation for restored and English pronunciations, it is important to note the following common markings:

- ´ An accent mark follows the syllable on which the accent falls. For example, in *sub poe´na,* the accent falls on the "*poe*" syllable.
- \- A hyphen is sometimes used purely for clarity where multiple adjacent vowels may be confused with diphthongs. For example, the pronunciation of the word "*tertii*" is written tär´tē-ē to make clear that the first "e" and second "e" are each separately pronounced, not combined into a single "ee" sound.

The remaining rules of pronunciation depend on whether the restored or American English system is used.

Regarding the phonemic alphabet offered for these pronunciations, we note the divergence in practices among lexicographers and the relative obscurity of the symbols used in the widely accepted International Phonetic Alphabet (IPA) for English. The IPA uses the unfamiliar "ʃ" mark for the "sh" sound in "*sh*ould," for example, and chooses "j" to represent the sound "y" in "*y*earn." The less arcane alternative, the American Phonetic Alphabet (APA), offers more intuitive consonant phonemes for the American audience, but its vowel phonemes are often surprising. The APA uses the letter "i," for example, to represent the sound of "ea" in "b*ea*t" instead of the more intuitive "e" or "ē," and it uses "e" to represent the sound of "a" in "st*a*te" instead of "a" or "ā." In preference to these conventions, we have adopted a key that is unique, but, we hope, more universally appealing to an American audience. This key is based loosely on a combination of some of the IPA's vowel phonemes and some of the APA's consonant phonemes. Occasionally we choose idiosyncratic symbols for diphthongs for the sake of clarity and ease of use. Some scrupulous phonologists may be offended by the unorthodoxy of our approach, but our goal here is accuracy and clarity for the benefit of the user of this work, not phonemic purity for the linguist.

CLASSICAL (RESTORED) PRONUNCIATION

From what classics scholars know of Ciceronian Latin, it was pronounced with vowels generally more open than in English and consonants always hard. The following chart will aid in pronunciation as a general matter when the sound differs from the English.

LETTER/DIPHTHONG	PRONOUNCED	SYMBOL	AS IN...
a	*ah*	a	T*a*ll; C*o*p
ae or æ	*ai*	ī	*Eye*; T*ie*
au	*ow*	ô	H*ow*; Pr*ou*d
c	*k*	k	*C*ow; Sa*ck*
ch	*k-h*	kh	Bla*ck* *h*eather
e	*ay*	ā	S*ay*; *A*ce
ei	*ayee*	āē	Gr*ay* *ee*l
eu	*ayoo*	āū	L*ay* *u*sage
g	*gh*	g	*G*ate; Ta*g* (never like "j")
i or j	*ee* or *y*	ē or y	Tr*ee*; K*ey*; *Y*es
ii	*ee-ee*	ē-ē	Fr*ee* *ee*ls
o	*oh*	ō	T*oe*; Sn*ow*
oe or œ	*oy*	œ	B*oy*; M*oi*st
ph	*p-h*	p-h	Sla*p* *h*ard (never like "f")
s	*s*	s	*S*ip; Ta*s*k (never like "z")
th	*t-h*	t-h	Caugh*t* *h*er (never like "th")
u or v	*oo*	ū or w	Tr*ue*; *W*est
ui	*oo-ee*	ūē	D*ewy*; Gl*uey*
x	*ks*	ks	Tric*ks* (never like "z" or "gz")
y	*ew*	ü	L*ew*d

Vowels can be spoken for a short or long duration (*e.g.*, *pater* versus *mater*, respectively) depending on their position in the word. But this level of technicality goes well beyond the call of duty except insofar as it is necessary to understand where the accent falls in words of three syllables or more. The accent always falls on the first syllable in two-syllable words. In words of more than two syllables, the accent always falls on the penultimate syllable if that syllable's vowel is long (as in *ami´cus*) and on the *antepenultimate* syllable if the *penultimate* syllable's vowel is short (as in *æ´quitas*).

It will be noted that two pairs of letters are pronounced identically: (1) i and j; and (2) u and v. The Latin alphabet does not contain the letter "j." To ease pronunciation for English speakers, the classical Latin "i" sometimes became "j" in European and English Latin. Wherever either letter appears, however, the same sound is represented. This is equally true for "u" and "v." Technically, the classical Latin alphabet does not contain a "u." Instead, the Romans used "v" to represent something akin to the "ooh" sound. European and English Latin differentiated the two in order to avoid long strings of vowels (just as with the "i" and "j" distinction). Finally, other letters are missing from the Latin alphabet, specifically, "k," "w," "y," and "z." These letters did not exist as such in classical Latin. This guidebook does not distinguish between "i" and "j" organizationally, but it does distinguish between "u" and "v" because the latter pair is more often distinguished than the former and, in any case, they are pronounced differently by American speakers.

Classical pronunciation is always presented in the Gotham-Bold open type as boxed text.

AMERICAN ENGLISH PRONUNCIATION

Throughout Europe and in the United States, what you usually hear when people try to speak Latin is an attempt at vulgar, also known as ecclesiastical, Latin. Knowing approximately how to pronounce classical Latin is nice, but the important thing is to make your meaning plain. That of course usually argues for eschewing Latin altogether, but one is more likely to be understood and to understand others if he or she is familiar with the English pronunciation that is far more common in the United States than the classical. Due to variations in the way Latin is pronounced by Americans, the pronunciations will merely be those most common and consistent with other American English conventions. As noted above, there is no one "correct" way to mispronounce Latin, so these pronunciations are (as they must be) more in the way of suggestions or guidelines than iron laws. The following chart will aid in pronunciation of Latin as spoken in the United States.

LETTER/DIPHTHONG	PRONOUNCED	SYMBOL	AS IN...
a	*ah*	a	T*a*ll; C*o*p
	ay	ā	S*ay*; *A*ce
	a (mouth wide)	â	*A*pple; St*a*nd
	uh	u	Min*us*; Sec*o*nd
ae or æ	*ay*	ā	S*ay*; *A*ce
	ee	ē	Tr*ee*; K*ey*
au	*ow*	ô	H*ow*; Pr*ou*d
	auw	ă	*Au*dience; H*o*llow
c (before æ, e, i or œ)	*s*	s	*S*ort; Cla*ss*
c (before other letters)	*c*	k	*C*ow (*not* like "s")
ch	*ch*	č	*Ch*ase; *Ch*arge

e	*eh*	e	J*e*t; P*e*nt
	ee	ē	Tr*ee*; K*ey*
	e(r)	ɜ	*U*rge; T*e*rm; B*i*rd
	uh	u	Min*u*s; Sec*o*nd
g	*g*	g	*G*ate; Ta*g*
	zh	ž	Vi*s*ion; Mira*g*e
	j	j	*J*ust; *G*esture
h	*h*	h	*H*eart; Pan*h*andle
i	*ai*	ī	*Eye*; T*ie*
	ee	ē	Tr*ee*; K*ey*
	ih	i	*I*n; F*i*g
	e(r)	ɜ	*U*rge; T*e*rm; B*i*rd
	uh	u	Min*u*s; Sec*o*nd
ii	*ai*	ī	*Eye*; T*ie*
	ee	ē	Tr*ee*; K*ey*
j	*j*	j	*J*ust; *G*esture
	zh	ž	Vi*s*ion; Mira*g*e
ng	*ng*	ɲ	Ba*ng*
o	*oh*	ō	T*o*te; *O*ats
	ah	a	B*o*x; T*au*t
	ow	ô	H*o*w; Pr*ou*d
	uh	u	Min*u*s; Sec*o*nd
oe or œ	*eh*	e	J*e*t; P*e*nt
	ee	ē	Tr*ee*; K*ey*
ph	*f*	f	Tele*ph*one; *F*airy
s	*s*	s	*S*ort; Cla*ss*
	z	z	Cho*s*e; *Z*oo
	zh	ž	Vi*s*ion; Mira*g*e
sh	*sh*	š	*Sh*ort; Crea*t*ion
t	*t*	t	*T*aut; Rou*t*e
	sh	š	*Sh*ort; Crea*t*ion
	ch	č	Fu*t*ure; Na*t*ural
th	*th* fortis	θ	*Th*in; E*th*er
	th lenis	ð	*Th*is; Clo*th*es
u	*oo*	ū	F*oo*l; T*oo*
	oe	ŭ	P*u*t; C*ou*ld
	e(r)	ɜ	*U*rge; T*e*rm; B*i*rd
	yoo	yū	Pop*u*lar; *U*se
	uh	u	Min*u*s; Sec*o*nd; *U*p
v	*v*	v	*V*ice; Stri*v*e

x	*ks*	ks	Tric*ks*; O*x*ygen
	gz	gz	E*x*it; Au*x*iliary
y	*y*	y	*Y*ou; La*y*er
z	*z*	z	*X*ylophone; *X*enon

There appears to be no uniform practice in the pronunciation of diphthongs in English. The entries accordingly vary on a case-by-case basis.

English pronunciations are presented in Gotham-Bold open type with no box and always immediately follow the classical pronunciation.

ETYMOLOGY AND GRAMMAR KEY

acc.	Accusative (direct object) declension
adj.	Adjective or adjectival phrase
adv.	Adverb or adverbial phrase
B.C.E.	Before the Common Era (formerly BC—Before Christ)
C.E.	Common Era (formerly AD—*Anno Domini*)
conj.	Conjunction
fem.	Feminine gender
ger.	Gerund form of verb
imp.	Imperative form of verb
inf.	Infinitive form of verb
masc.	Masculine gender
n.	Noun or nominal phrase
N.	Proper noun
pl.	Plural
prep.	Preposition
pro.	Pronoun
s.	Singular
v.	Verb or verbal phrase
Ecc.	Originating in ecclesiastical Latin
Faux	False or recently invented, as opposed to proper, Latin
Cel.	Originating in ancient Celtic rather than Latin
Gr.	Originating in ancient Greek rather than Latin
Ital.	Originating in modern Italian rather than Latin
Med.	Originating in late or medieval, rather than classical, Latin
Neo.	Neo-Latin originating in the Renaissance or later
( )	Parenthetical words may sometimes be excluded for the sake of brevity

GUIDE TO LATIN IN INTERNATIONAL LAW

A

A.R. An abbreviation of **Anno regni.**

A communi observantia non est recedendum. a kōmmū´nē ōbsārwan´tē-a nōn āst rākādān´dūm. ā- OR a kamyū´nī abs3rvân´tē-u nan est reseden´dum. "A common practice must not to be abandoned." A maxim meaning that a customary practice, once well established, creates an obligation of continued observance. *See* 1 Edward Coke, INSTITUTES OF THE LAWES OF ENGLAND 186 (1628).

A contrario. a kōntra´rēō. ā- OR a kantra´rēō. *adj.* or *adv.* "On the contrary." (1) Contrary; contrarily; in the opposite sense. *E.g.*, "There cannot be an obligation to extradite someone you choose not to try unless that person is within your reach.…These sensible realities are critical for the obligatory exercise of *aut dedere aut prosequi* jurisdiction, but cannot be interpreted *a contrario* so as to exclude a voluntary exercise of a universal jurisdiction." *Arrest Warrant of 11 April 2000* (Congo v. Belg.), 2002 I.C.J. Rep. 3, 80, ¶ 57 (separate opinion of Judges Higgins, Kooijmans, and Buergenthal). (2) In opposition. (3) Arrived at by negative reasoning or inference. *E.g.*, "[I]n May 1983 the assessment of the Intelligence Committee…was that the Contras 'constitute[d] an independent force' and that the 'only element of control that could be exercised by the United States' was the 'cessation of aid.' Paradoxically this assessment serves to underline, *a contrario*, the potential for control inherent in the degree of the Contras' dependence on aid." *Military and Paramilitary Activities in and Against Nicaragua* (Nicar. v. U.S.), 1986 I.C.J. Rep. 14, ¶ 109. *Contrast with* **A pari.** *See also* **Argumentum a contrario.**

A contrario sensu. a kōntra´rēō sān´sū. ā- OR a kantra´rēō sen´sū. *adj.* or *adv.* "In the contrary sense." (1) In the opposite sense or meaning. (2) Arriving at a contrary or opposite conclusion based on similar reasoning. A person reasons *a contrario sensu* when he or she infers that a scenario opposite to one addressed by a rule should accordingly be addressed by an opposite rule. *E.g.*, "Similarly, a study of the domestic laws of various States—although most of them make a distinction between simple passage, sojourn in territorial waters and entry into ports—does not convey an impression clearly in favour of freedom of passage for warships, even if a large margin is allowed for the always dangerous argument *a contrario sensu.*" *Corfu Channel Case* (U.K. v. Alb.), 1949 I.C.J. Rep. 4, 100, ¶ 30 (Judge Azevedo, dissenting). *See also* **Argumentum a contrario.**

A datu. a da´tū. ā- OR a dā´tū. *adv.* "From the date." Beginning from a specified date and continuing therefrom.

A fortiori. a fōrtēō´rē. ā- OR a fōršō´rī. *adv.* "From the stronger." Even more so; by the same logic, to an even greater degree. *E.g.*, "The fact that in this particular case the Parties could not even agree upon the applicable legal rules shows that *a fortiori* they could not agree on any particular [maritime delimitation] line which might follow from the application of appropriate rules." *Barbados v. Republic of Trinidad & Tobago*, Permanent Ct. of Arb., Award of Apr. 11, 2006, ¶ 198, 45 I.L.M. 800, 833 (2006). *Compare with* **A multo fortiori.**

A gratia. a gra´tē-a. ā- OR a grā´šu. *adv.* or *adj.* "From kindness." An alternative formulation of **Ex gratia.**

A limine. a lē´mēnā. ā- OR a li´minē. *adv.* "From the threshold." From or at the beginning; from inception. A motion or pleading *a limine* is one made at the beginning of a litigation, such as an objection to the tribunal's jurisdiction. *E.g.*, "[T]he crime of genocide implies the cumulation of two elements—the material (the commission of the acts indicated *a limine* in Article II of the Convention) and the subjective (the intention (*dolus specialis*) to 'destroy, in whole or in part, a national, ethnical, racial or religious group, as such')." *Application of the Convention on the Prevention and Punishment of the Crime of Genocide* (Bosn. & Herz. v. Yugo.), 1993 I.C.J. Rep. 325, 460 (Judge *ad hoc* Kreća, dissenting). *Compare with* **Ab initio, In initio,** and **In limine.**

A maiore ad minus. a mayō´rā ad mē´nūs. ā- OR a mâjō´rē âd mī´nus. "From the greater scale to the lesser." From the larger or more general to the smaller or more specific. This is a type of reasoning based on the proposition that what is true in general, for a larger quantity, or for a more important consequence, must also be true specifically, for a smaller quantity, or for a less important consequence. *E.g.*, "[T]he interpretation in question may be regarded as also following from reasoning *a majore ad minus*. Since the termination of contracts for an indefinite period, with the period of notice stipulated in the contract and in accordance with Article 47(2) of the CEOS, falls within the discretion of the competent authority, no provision of the CEOS prohibits that authority from restricting its power to terminate contracts, in the interests of the staff, by means of contractual provisions." *Karatzoglou v. European Agency for Reconstruction*, E.C.J. Case No. T-471/04, Celex No. 604A0471, ¶ 42. *See* **Argumentum a maiore ad minus**. *See also* **A fortiori**.

A maxima. a ma´ksēma. ā- OR a mâ´ksimu. *adv.* "From the maximum." To the highest or outer boundary. A limit *a maxima* is the greatest extent allowed. Treaties, for example, typically do not limit the obligations of the parties *a maxima* with respect to each other, meaning that a state performing its duties more generously or vigorously than required by the treaty would generally not violate its legal obligations unless the performance acted contrary to the intent or spirit of the treaty. *Contrast with* **A minima**.

A mensa (et thoro). a mān´sa (āt t-hō´rō). ā- OR a men´su (et θō´rō). *adj.* "From table and hearth." Relating to or authorizing the separation of spouses. A divorce *a mensa et thoro* does not technically dissolve the marriage, but merely proclaims that the spouses are not legally obligated to live together. *Contrast with* **A vinculo (matrimonii)**.

A minima. a mē´nēma. ā- OR a mi´nimu. *adv.* "From the minimum." To the lowest or least boundary; to the minimal extent. *E.g.*, "Acting *a minima*, the Court could in effect have avoided seeking to call into question the underlying reasoning of the Weightman report…; it could instead simply have sought to draw all the conclusions necessarily flowing therefrom, rather than only certain of them, as the British Government had already done." *Maritime Delimitation and Territorial Questions* (Qatar v. Bahr.), 2001 I.C.J. Rep. 40, 164, ¶ 53 (Judges Bedjaoui *et al.*, dissenting). *Contrast with* **A maxima**.

A minore ad maius. a mēnō´rā ad ma´yūs. ā- OR a mīnō´rē âd mâ´jus OR -ma´yus. "From the lesser scale to the greater." From the smaller or more specific to the larger or more general. This is a type of reasoning based on the proposition that what is true in a specific case or for a smaller quantity must also be true in general or for a large quantity. *E.g.*, "If in the case of the profession of hospital administrator the Court regards university education and training lasting three years and additional post-secondary education and training lasting two years as a diploma as defined in the directive on higher-education diplomas, this would have to apply *a minore ad maius* in the case of the profession of director of voluntary sales of chattels by public auction since the education and training for this profession requires, in addition to a post-secondary training period, not only one but two university qualifications (education in law and history or archaeology or art) and consequently this education and training would *a fortiori* have to constitute a diploma...." *Price v. Conseil des Ventes Volontaires de Meubles Aux Enchères Publiques*, E.C.J. Case No. C-149/05, [2006] E.C.R. I-7691, ¶ 53. *See* **Argumentum a minore ad maius.**

A

A multo fortiori. a mūl´tō fōrtēō´rē. ā- OR a mзl´tō fōršō´rī. *adv.* "From the much stronger." Even more so to a much greater degree; by the same reasoning leading to a much more compelling argument. *Compare with* **A fortiori.**

A pari. a pa´rē. ā- OR a pa´rī. *adv.* "Equally." (1) Equally; in equal measure. (2) Similarly; based on similarity. When used with respect to reasoning or an argument, the term means that one kind of reasoning or argument, or the facts upon which it is based, applies to another reasoning or argument, or its facts, because of their similarity. *E.g.*, "[T]he differences in the legal regime and in the texts of Articles 62 and 63 are so clear and significant that it does not seem possible to treat them as complementary, nor is it a convincing method of interpretation to invoke the text of one of these articles by arguments *a pari* or *a contrario* in order to reach a certain conclusion in respect of the other provision." *Continental Shelf Case* (Libya v. Malta), 1984 I.C.J. Rep. 3, 58, ¶ 10 (separate opinion of Judge Jiménez de Aréchaga). *Compare with* **Ex pari.** *Contrast with* **A contrario.** *See also* **Pari passu.**

A pari passu. a pa´rē pas´sū. ā- OR a pa´rī pâ´sū. *adv.* "From equal pace." An alternative formulation of **In pari passu.**

A piratis (et latronibus) capta dominium non mutant. a pēra´tēs (ăt latrō´nēbūs) kap´ta dōmē´nē-ūm nōn mū´tant. ā- OR a pirâ´tis (et lâtra´nibus) kâp´tu dumi´nē-um nan myū´tant. "The ownership of things captured by pirates (and thieves) does not change." An alternative formulation of **Pirata non mutat dominium.**

A posteriori. a pōstārēō´rē. ā- OR a pastērēō´rī. *adj.* or *adv.* "From what follows." (1) A kind of inductive reasoning by which one derives theories or principles from the empirical observation. In positive law practice, *a posteriori* reasoning is used to generate predictions of general legal rules from specific judicial decisions in various cases. *E.g.*, "In drawing into international law the benefits of the insights available from other cultures, and in looking to the past for inspiration, international environmental law would not be departing from the traditional methods of international law, but would, in fact, be following in the path charted out by Grotius. Rather than laying down a set of principles *a priori* for the new discipline of international law, he sought them also *a posteriori* from the experience of the past, searching through the whole range of cultures available to him for this purpose." *The*

Gabcikovo-Nagymaros Project (Hung. v. Slovak.), 1997 I.C.J. Rep. 7, 96 (separate opinion of Judge Weeramantry). (2) Relating to something that can only be derived from practical experience; relating to actual consequences, as opposed to theory. *E.g.*, "The methods used involve both the *a priori* use of equity to work forwards towards a possible result and the *a posteriori* use of equity to test a result thus reached." *Maritime Delimitation in Area Between Greenland and Jan Mayen* (Den. v. Norway), 1993 I.C.J. Rep. 38, 181, ¶ 10 (separate opinion of Judge Weeramantry). (3) This term is often mistakenly used in place of **Ex post** or **Ex post facto**. *Contrast with* **A priori.**

A priori. a prēō´rē. ā prīō´rī. *adj.* or *adv.* "From the former." (1) Derived by deductive reasoning from self-evident or assumed propositions; derived by a chain of reasoning starting at general propositions to deduce specific conclusions. (2) Presumptive(ly) and definite(ly), without examination or further consideration or attention to consequences or evidence. *E.g.*, "Trinidad and Tobago argues, 'There is no indication in the *travaux* of the [France-Dominica maritime boundary delimitation] agreement that the line stopped because of some *a priori* rule of international that you cannot go within 200 nm of another State.'" *Barbados v. Republic of Trinidad & Tobago*, Permanent Ct. of Arb., Award of Apr. 11, 2006, ¶ 177, 45 I.L.M. 800, 830 (2006). *Contrast with* **A posteriori.**

A quo. a kwō. a kwō. *adv.* "From which." From which an appeal is made. A tribunal *a quo* is the tribunal from whose judgment the parties are appealing. *See also* **Dies a quo** and **Terminus a quo.** *Contrast with* **Ad quem.**

A scintilla iuris. a skēntēl´la yū´rēs. ā- OR a sinti´lu j3´ris. *adv.* "From the glimmer of right." (1) A legal right of uncertain existence or small force. *E.g.*, "[I]f subsequent conduct can disqualify the waiver, the conduct must either be assessed at the moment (*a scintilla juris*) after the delivery of the waiver, or at some other time." *Waste Management, Inc. v. Mexico*, ICSID Case No. ARB (AF)/98/2, Award of June 2, 2000, ¶ 54 (K. Highet, dissenting). (2) A right arising from a legal fiction. In medieval English law, *scintilla juris* was a specific kind of legal fiction applicable to the transferee of an estate in fee simple.

A vinculo (matrimonii). a wēn´kūlō (matrēmō´nē-ē). ā- OR a vin´kyūlō (mâtrimō´nī). "From the chains of marriage." Relating to or authorizing the dissolution of a marriage. A divorce *a vinculo matrimonii* terminates the marriage and empowers the spouses to remarry. *Contrast with* **A mensa (et thoro).**

Ab abusu ad usum non valet consequentia. ab abū´sū ad ū´sūm nōn wa´lāt kōnsākwān´tē-a. âb âbyū´zū âd yū´zum nan vâ´let kansekwen´šu. "A progression from abuse to use is ineffective." A maxim meaning that the use or application of a principle or other thing or idea may lead to invalid or undesirable consequences if the principle or thing is not used or applied judiciously and with adequate discrimination.

A

Ab ante. ab an´tā. âb ân´tē. *adv.* "From before." Done in advance or prior to a relevant event. An alternative formulation is **Ab antecedente.** *See also* **Ex ante.**

Ab antecedente. ab antākādān´tā. âb ântēseden´tē. *adv.* "From the preceding." An alternative formulation of **Ab ante.**

Ab antiquo. ab antē´kwō. âb ân´tikwō. *adv. Neo.* "From antiquity." Having been so since ancient times; having a temporally distant origin. *E.g.*, "As regards the claim of the Jews to be allowed to bring appurtenances to the Wall, such as benches, chairs, a screen, etc., that is not based on any established custom still less on a habit *ab antiquo*, for the Arabs, they say, and before them the Turks, have always protested against such innovations as appears from the above-mentioned documents of the years 1840 and 1911." *Report of the U.K. Comm'n on the Wailing Wall*, Dec. 1930, UN Doc. A/7057Add.1—S/8427/Add.1 (1968). *Compare with* **Ab initio mundi** and **Ab olim.** *See also* **Ab initio.**

Ab extra. ab āks´tra. âb eks´tru. *adv.* "From outside." Originating from an outside source; originating from a third party. *E.g.*, "The [UN General] Assembly can only exercise powers conferred upon it or derived *aliunde* or *ab extra* provided it keeps within the limits of its constitutional role under the structure of the Charter." *Advisory Opinion on Legal Consequences for States of the Continued Presence of South Africa in Namibia (South West Africa) Notwithstanding Security Council Resolution 276 (1970)*, 1971 I.C.J. Rep. 16, 284, ¶ 97 (Judge Fitzmaurice, dissenting). *Compare with* **Aliunde.**

Ab identitate rationis. ab ēdāntēta´tā ratēō´nēs. âb īden´titātē râšō´nis. *adv.* "By the same reasoning." Using the same kind or method of reasoning.

Ab inconvenienti. ab ēnkōnwānē-ān´tē. âb inkunvēnyen´tī. *adj.* "From what is inconvenient." Due to inconvenience. The judicial doctrine of *forum non conveniens* is based on considerations *ab inconvenienti*, because it relies on the inconvenience of the forum to the parties as a basis for referring the case to a different jurisdiction. *See also* **Argumentum ab inconvenienti** and **Forum non conveniens.**

Ab initio. ab ēnē´tēō. âb ini´šō. *adv.* "From the beginning." From or at the beginning; originally; from inception. The term does not imply that the situation existing *ab initio* continues into the present or has terminated. *E.g.*, "[T]he Congo claims that the arrest warrant was issued in violation of the immunity of its Minister for Foreign Affairs, that that warrant was unlawful *ab initio*, and that this legal defect persists despite the subsequent changes in the position occupied by the individual concerned." *Arrest Warrant of 11 April 2000* (Congo v. Belg.), 2002 I.C.J. Rep. 3, 12, ¶ 25. *Compare with* **A limine**, **In initio**, and **In principio**. *See also* **Ab antiquo** and **Ab initio mundi**.

Ab initio mundi. ab ēnē´tēō mūn´dē. âb ini´šyō mun´dī. *adv.* "From the beginning of the world." (1) Always, as when a state or practice always existed and has always existed. (2) Beginning in ancient or very early times. *Compare with* **Ab antiquo**. *See also* **Ab initio**.

Ab invito. ab ēnwē´tō. âb invī´tō. *adv.* "By the unwilling person." (1) Involuntarily; unwillingly. (2) Done or performed by an unwilling party. For example, a treaty signed *ab invito* may still be binding if the objecting party was not coerced through threat of force.

Ab novo. ab nō´wō. âb nō´vō. *adv.* "Newly." An alternative term for **De novo**.

Ab olim. ab ō´lēm. âb ō´lim. *adv.* "Of old; formerly." (1) In distant times. (2) By long tradition. *Compare with* **Ab antiquo**.

Aberratio ictus. abärra´tēō ēk´tūs. âbɜrā´šō ik´tus. *n.* "Diversion of the blow." A harm accidentally inflicted on a party as a result of an action directed at a different party. *E.g.*, "Criminal law does not admit of a reduction of sentence in the case of *aberratio ictus*." *The Corfu Channel Case* (U.K. v. Alb.), 1949 I.C.J. Rep. 4, 95, ¶ 23 (Judge Azevedo, dissenting).

Ablegatus. ablāga´tūs. ablegā´tus. *n.* "Envoy." An envoy or other diplomatic representative ranked below the level of ambassador.

Abrogatio legis. abrōga´tēō lā´gēs. âbrōgā´šō le´jis. *n.* "Abrogation of law." A law that has been repealed or is otherwise no longer in force.

Absente reo. absān´tā rā´ō. âbsen´tē rā´ō or -rē´ō. *adv.* "The defendant being absent." The defendant not being present at the proceeding. *E.g.*, "On 18 September 1992, the District Court of Metz sentenced DZ *absente reo* to one year's imprisonment for failing to return the children and issued a warrant for his arrest." *Ignaccolo-Zenide v. Romania*, 31 E.H.R.R. 7, 218, ¶ 20 (2001).

Absit verbo invidia. ab´sēt wār´bō ēnwē´dē-a. âb´sit vɜr´bō invi´dē-u. "May hostility be absent from my words." An imprecation that the listener or reader take the speaker's or writer's words as an expression without hostile intent. *E.g.*, "[S]ubjects, in as far as their obedience is a matter of private benefit to the sovereign, may, without any real impropriety (*absit verbo invidia*,) be considered as subjects of his property." Jeremy Bentham, *The Principles of*

International Law: Essay II, *in* 2 THE WORKS OF JEREMY BENTHAM 542 (John Bowring ed., 1843).

Absoluta sententia expositore non indiget. absōlū´ta sāntān´tē-a ākspōsētō´rā nōn ēn´dēgāt. âbsōlū´tu senten´šu ekspazitō´rē nan in´dijet. "A complete statement requires no interpreter." A maxim meaning that clear and unambiguous text should be read according to its plain meaning rather than with reference to secondary sources of interpretation. *See* the Vienna Convention on the Law of Treaties art. 31, May 23, 1969, 1155 U.N.T.S. 331.

Absque. ab´skwā. âb´skwā. *prep.* "Without." Without; in the absence of.

Absque dubio. ab´skwā dū´bēō. âb´skwā dū´byō. *adv.* "Without doubt." (1) Most probably. (2) Indubitably; unquestionably.

Absque iniuria. ab´skwā ēnyū´rē-a. âb´skwā injз´rē-u. *adv.* "Without wrong." Without a violation of a legally recognized right. Something done *absque iniuria* does not violate international law and can give rise to no liability. *See also* **Damnum absque iniuria.**

Absque iniuria damnum. ab´skwā ēnyū´rē-a dam´nūm. âb´skwā injз´rē-u dâm´num. *n.* "Injury without a wrong." An alternative formulation of **Damnum absque iniuria.**

Abstinentia guerrarum. abstēnān´tē-a gwārra´rūm. abstinen´šu gwera´rum. *n. Neo.* "Abstention from war." The state of immunity from attack and absence of any duty to attack, usually conferred by treaty. *Abstinentia guerrarum* differs from true neutrality in that it may allow deviations from customary neutral duties and rights while nonetheless guaranteeing that the state in question will not be attacked. Note that "*guerrarum*" is not a proper Latin term. *E.g.*, "[S]tates recognised a condition of abstention from hostilities, whether these were deemed justly or unjustly undertaken, as a possible position for other states to adopt in such cases as were covered by the signature of an *abstinentia guerrarum* on their part with other contractants." Geoffrey Butler and Simon Maccoby, THE DEVELOPMENT OF INTERNATIONAL LAW 231 (1928).

Abundans cautela non nocet. abūn´dans kôtā´la nōn nō´kāt. abun´dânz kă´telu nan na´set. "Abundant caution does no harm." A maxim counseling that great caution or care, or an excess of it, is preferable to an insufficiency of it. *See also* **Ad abundantiorem cautelam** and **Ob maiorem cautelam.**

Accessio. akkās´sēō. âkse´syō. *n.* "Approach." (1) Accession. (2) Lawful inheritance of a right or thing. (3) In Roman civil law, the increase in size of an existing property by the addition of a smaller property. *See also* **Accessio cedit principali.**

A

Accessio cedit principali. akkās´sēō kā´dēt prēnkēpa´lē. âkse´syō sē´dit prinsupâ´lī. "An addition to the principle thing becomes part of it." A maxim meaning that a subordinate thing that is attached to a principal thing loses its independence or identity by merger with the principal thing. *E.g.*, "[A]nnexes to an application are accessories to that application and follow the general legal principle of *accessio cedit principali*." Opinion of Advocate General Trstenjak, *Ingenieurburo Michael Weiss & Partner GbR v. Industrie- & Handelskammer Berlin*, E.C.J. Case No. C-14/07, Celex No. 607C0014, ¶ 58.

Accessorium non ducit, sed sequitur principalem. akkāssō´rē-ūm nōn dū´kēt, sād sā´kwētūr prēnkēpa´lām. âksesō´rē-um nan dū´sit, sed se´kwitɜr prinsipâ´lem. "The accessory does not lead, but rather follows, the principal." A maxim, originating in the Roman doctrine of *accessio*, meaning that an accessory thing (*res accessoria*) follows or is treated similarly to the principal thing (*res principalis*). The maxim has broad application in the fields of liability, property, and elsewhere. Sometimes abbreviated **Accessorium principali sequitur.**

Accessorium principali sequitur. akkāssō´rē-ūm prēnkēpa´lē sā´kwētūr. âksesō´rē-um prinsipâ´lē se´kwitɜr. "The accessory follows the principal." An abbreviated form of **Accessorium non ducit, sed sequitur principalem.**

Accomenda. akkōmān´da. âkōmen´du. *n. Med.* "Commitment [of money or goods]." In maritime law, the *accomenda* was a set of two contracts between a cargo exporter and shipmaster to split the net profits earned from the sale of the cargo at the port of destination. The first agreement (the *mandatum*) authorized the shipmaster to sell the cargo on the exporter's behalf; the second (the contract of partnership) was a profit-sharing agreement. The Statutes of the City of Genoa of 1678 authorized the use of the *accomenda*. This form of contract is no longer used with any frequency. *See also* **Mandatum.**

Accommodatum. akkōmmōda´tūm. âkōmōdā´tum. *n.* "That which is suitable." An alternative term for **Commodatum.**

Acta. ak´ta. âk´tu. *n. pl.* "Transactions." *See* **Actum.**

Acta publica. ak´ta pūb´lēka. âk´tu pub´liku. *n. pl.* "Public records." (1) In Roman law, a public register (*e.g.*, of land records, of transactions before the courts, or of popular assemblies). (2) In modern civil law, matters of general or public interest; official governmental matters.

Actio. ak´tēō. âk´tyō. *n.* "Action at law." (1) A right to initiate a lawsuit. (2) A lawsuit. (3) In Roman law, a charge, indictment or accusation, or the spoken or written pleadings in a case.

Actio bonae fidei. ak´tēō bō´nī fē´dāē. âk´tyō bō´nā fī´dē. *n.* [*pl.* **Actiones bonae fidei.** aktēō´nās bō´nī fē´dāē. âkšō´nēz bō´nā fī´dē.] "Action at law in good faith." In Roman law, a kind of lawsuit in which the judge (*arbiter*) is authorized to consider equity and need not strictly apply the law in deciding the outcome of the dispute. *Contrast with* **Actio stricti iuris.** *See also* **Ex aequo et bono.**

A

Actio contraria. ak´tēō kōntra´rē-a. âk´tyō kantra´rē-u. *n.* "Contrary action at law." A counterclaim. *Contrast with* **Actio directa.**

Actio criminalis. ak´tēō krēmēna´lēs. âk´tyō kriminâ´lis. *n.* "Criminal action at law." A criminal action or prosecution.

Actio damni iniuria. ak´tēō dam´nē ēnyū´rē-a. âk´tyō dâm´nī inj3´rē-u. *n.* "Action at law for damages from wrongdoing." An action seeking recovery of damages caused by an illegal or wrongful act resulting in some harm to the claimant.

Actio de iudicato. ak´tēō dā yūdēka´tō. âk´tyō dā jūdikā´tō. *n.* "Action at law for a judgment." A lawsuit seeking a binding judgment to resolve an existing dispute, as opposed to one seeking an advisory opinion. *E.g.*, "[A]s procedure has developed, the existence of purely declaratory awards has come to be admitted, especially in Germany and the United States: the applicant is content—for some reason—to have his right declared, without desiring that it shall subsequently be rendered effective; at the same time, however, he retains the right to bring another action of a purely executory nature: *actio de judicato.*" *Corfu Channel Case* (U.K. v. Alb.), 1949 I.C.J. Rep. 4, 97, ¶ 26 (Judgment) (Judge Azevedo, dissenting).

Actio directa. ak´tēō dērāk´ta. âk´tyō direk´tu. *n.* "Direct action at law." (1) A direct claim or action at law. *Contrast with* **Actio contraria.** (2) A claim or lawsuit based on a formal or well-defined law. *Compare with* **Actio stricti iuris.** *See also* **De rigore iuris, Stricto iure,** and **Strictissimi iuris.**

Actio ex contractu. ak´tēō āks kōntrak´tū. âk´tyō eks kantrâk´tū. *n.* "Action at law from contract." A claim or lawsuit based on a cause of action arising under contract. *Contrast with* **Actio ex delicto.**

Actio ex delicto. ak´tēō āks dālēk´tō. âk´tyō eks dulik´tō. *n.* "Action at law from wrongdoing." A claim or lawsuit based on a cause of action arising from illegal conduct, tort, or other wrongdoing. *Contrast with* **Actio ex contractu.**

Actio exercitoria. ak´tēō āksārkētō´rē-a. âk´tyō eks3rsitō´rē-u. *n.* "Action at law relating to the business." A lawsuit against the owner or lessee of a vessel, usually relating to contracts for the transportation of goods or carriage of persons.

Actio finium regundorum. ak´tēō fē´nē-ūm rāgūndō´rūm. âk´tyō fi´nyum rejundō´rum. *n.* "Action at law for the definition of boundaries." In Roman law, a lawsuit brought to delimit the borders between neighboring properties having a disputed boundary.

Actio in aequum et bonum concepta. ak´tēō ēn ī´kwūm āt bō´nūm kōnkāp´ta. âk´tyō in e´kwum et bō´num kansep´tu. *n.* [*pl.* **Actiones in aequum et bonum conceptae.** aktēō´nās ēn ī´kwūm āt bō´nūm kōnkāp´tī. âkšō´nēz in e´kwum et bō´num kansep´tā.] "An action grounded on what is fair and just." In Roman law, a lawsuit brought based on a tort, following which the aggrieved party and the tortfeasor agreed to allow the court to resort to principles of justice and fairness. The term appears in Justinian's *Digest* (1.1.11) and the *Institutes of Gaius*.

Actio indicati. ak´tēō ēndēka´tē. âk´tyō indikā´tī. *n.* "The action at law of a convicted person." A judgment, award, or conviction originating in one state that is presented to the courts of another state for recognition or enforcement.

Actio iudicati. ak´tēō yūdēka´tē. âk´tyō jūdikā´tī. *n.* "Action at law for judgment." In Roman law, a lawsuit to enforce a judgment by execution on the defendant's property.

Actio non datur non damnificato. ak´tēō nōn da´tūr nōn damnēfēka´tō. âk´tyō nan dâ´tɜr nan dâmnifikā´tō. "An action at law is not given to one who is uninjured." A maxim meaning that an injury must meet certain legal criteria to give rise to a right of recovery against the alleged wrongdoer. If this condition is not satisfied, a *damnum absque iniuria* is deemed to have occurred. *E.g.*, "[The Claimant] has suffered no damage. Pursuant to the principle of *actio non datur non damnificato* the Tribunal therefore finds that [the Claimant] no longer has a cause of action." *Futura Trading Inc. and The National Iranian Oil Co.*, Award No. 263–324–3 (Oct. 30, 1986), 13 Iran-U.S. Cl. Trib. Rep. 99, 116. *See also* **Damnum absque iniuria.**

Actio personalis. ak´tēō pārsōna´lēs. âk´tēō pɜrsunâ´lis. *n.* [*pl.* **Actiones personales.** aktēō´nās pārsōna´lās. âkšō´nēz pɜrsunâ´lus.] "Personal action at law." A private right of action, as opposed to one invoking a state or governmental interest. *Contrast with* **Actio popularis.**

Actio personalis moritur cum persona. ak´tēō pārsōna´lēs mō´rētūr kūm pārsō´na. âk´tēō pɜrsōnâ´lus mō´ritɜr kum pɜrsō´nu. "A person's action at law dies with the person." A doctrine under which the rights and liabilities incurred by a person during his life are extinguished with his death. This rule of civil law has never been recognized in international law as depriving a successor state of the right of standing to represent the nationals of its predecessor state.

A

Actio popularis. ak´tēō pōpūla´rēs. âk´tēō papyūle´rus. *n.* [*pl.* **Actiones populares.** aktēō´nās pōpūla´rās. âkšō´nus papyūla´rus.] "Action at law of the people." (1) A public or universal right to initiate a lawsuit or prosecution. In domestic law, this term is often used to refer to a right of private citizens to bring a legal action on behalf of the state, such as a *qui tam* action. *E.g.*, "Belgian law does not provide an *actio popularis*, but only allows victims and their relatives to trigger criminal investigations through the procedure of a formal complaint." *Arrest Warrant of 11 April 2000* (Congo v. Belg.), 2002 I.C.J. Rep. 3, 130 n.96 (separate opinion of Judge Bula-Bula). (2) A right of action belonging to the international community as a whole or to any person, usually arising from a violation of a duty *erga omnes*. *E.g.*, "Although we recognize that the existence of a so-called *actio popularis* in international law is a matter of controversy, the observations of this Court in the *Barcelona Traction, Light, and Power Company, Limited* case...suffice to show that the question is one that may be considered as capable of rational legal argument and a proper subject of litigation before this Court." *Nuclear Tests* (N.Z. v. Fr.), 1974 I.C.J. Rep. 457, 521, ¶ 52 (Judgment) (Judges Onyeama *et al.*, dissenting). *Contrast with* **Actio personalis.** *See also* **Erga omnes.**

Actio stricti iuris. ak´tēō strēk´tē yū´rēs. âk´tēō strik´tī jɜ´ris. *n.* "Action at law in strict right." A lawsuit invoking a formal positive right to a remedy based on a literal legal authority, without reference to equity or public policy, as when seeking a remedy clearly defined in an applicable agreement or statute. *Contrast with* **Actio bonae fidei.** *See also* **Ius strictum, De rigore iuris, Stricto iure,** and **Strictissimi iuris.**

Actor allegans probat. ak´tōr al´lāgans prō´bat. âk´tɜr â´lejunz prō´bât. "The plaintiff provides the proof." The plaintiff bears the burden of showing that he has stated a valid claim at law. *E.g.*, "Not only has [the Applicant] chosen the wrong forum—this Court not being one dealing with matters of substance relating to possible individual criminal responsibility—it has failed, moreover, to provide proof of such responsibility. It should be remembered that *actori incumbit probatio*, but also that *allegans probat*." *Arrest Warrant of 11 April 2000* (Congo v. Belg.), 2002 I.C.J. Rep. 3, 124, ¶ 73 (separate opinion of Judge *ad hoc* Bula-Bula).

Actor forum rei sequitur. ak´tōr fō´rūm rā´ē sā´kwētūr. âk´tɜr fō´rum rā se´kwitɜr. "The plaintiff follows the matter's forum." An alternative formulation of **Actor sequitur forum rei.**

Actor sequitur forum rei. ak´tōr sā´kwētūr fō´rūm rā´ē. âk´tɜr se´kwitɜr fō´rum rā. "The plaintiff follows the matter's forum." A maxim meaning that a claimant must seek redress before a tribunal having competent jurisdiction over the matter or respondent at issue, usually meaning at the domicile or place of business of the respondent. *E.g.*, "The provision embodies the adage *actor sequitur forum rei*, commonly accepted in comparative law, which favours the protection of the rights of the defendant for whom it is more difficult to mount a defence in the courts of a foreign country." Opinion of Advocate General Colomer, *Reisch Montage AG v. Kiesel Baumaschinen Handels GmbH*, E.C.J. Case C-103/05, [2006] E.C.R. I-6827, ¶ 21. An alternative formulation is **Actor forum rei sequitur.**

Actori incumbit (onus) probandi. aktō´rē ēnkūm´bēt (ō´nūs) prōba´ndē. âktō´rī inkum´bit (ō´nus) prōbân´dī. "The (burden of) proving weighs on the plaintiff." An alternative formulation of **Actori incumbit (onus) probatio.**

Actori incumbit (onus) probatio. aktō´rē ēnkūm´bēt (ō´nūs) prōba´tēō. âktō´rī inkum´bit (ō´nus) prōbā´šō. "The (burden of) proof weighs on the plaintiff." A doctrine allocating the burden of proof to the party bringing a charge or instigating a legal action. *E.g.*, "Not only has [the Applicant] chosen the wrong forum—this Court not being one dealing with matters of substance relating to possible individual criminal responsibility—it has failed, moreover, to provide proof of such responsibility. It should be remembered that *actori incumbit probatio*, but also that *allegans probat.*" *Arrest Warrant of 11 April 2000* (Congo v. Belg.), 2002 I.C.J. Rep. 3, 124, ¶ 73 (separate opinion of Judge *ad hoc* Bula-Bula). An alternative formulation is **Actori incumbit (onus) probandi.**

Actori incumbit (onus) probatio, reus in excipiendo fit actor. aktō´rē ēnkūm´bēt (ō´nūs) prōba´tēō, rā´ūs ēn āks-kēpē-ān´dō fēt ak´tōr. âktō´rī inkum´bit (ō´nus) prōbā´šō, res in eksipyen´dō fit âk´tɜr. "The (burden of) proof weighs on the plaintiff, but the defendant in objecting becomes a plaintiff." A maxim meaning that, when the respondent denies a claimant's offer of proof, the burden of proof shifts to the respondent to refute the claimant's evidence.

Actum. ak´tūm. âk´tum. *n.* [*pl.* **Acta.** ak´ta. âk´tu.] "Transaction." (1) A transaction. (2) The official record of a transaction, such as a deed or decree.

Actum gestionis. ak´tūm gāstēō´nēs. âk´tum jestēō´nus. *n.* [*pl.* **Acta gestionis.** ak´ta gāstēō´nēs. âk´tu jestēō´nus.] "Act of behavior." A private act; an act of the kind performable by private citizens. *E.g.*, "[T]he use of a car in ordinary traffic belonged to the sphere of private law, so that an *actum gestionis* and not an *actum imperii* was concerned." Paul Abel, *State Immunity*, 11 INT'L & COMP. L.Q. 840, 841 (1962). *Compare with* **Actum iure gestionis.** *Contrast with* **Actum imperii.**

Actum imperii. ak´tūm ēmpā´rē-ē. âk´tum impɜ´rī. *n.* [*pl.* **Acta imperii.** ak´ta ēmpā´rē-ē. âk´tu impɜ´rī.] "Act of the sovereign." An act of state manifesting its power as sovereign; a public act. *E.g.*, "An *actum imperii* is to be assumed if the organ of the state and the other party do not stand on the same level [because the other party is a private person]." Paul Abel, *State Immunity*, 11 INT'L & COMP. L.Q. 840, 841 (1962). *Compare with* **Actum iure imperii.** *Contrast with* **Actum gestionis.**

A

Actum iure gestionis. ak´tūm yū´rā gāstēō´nēs. âk´tum j3´rē jestēō´nus. *n.* [*pl.* **Acta iure gestionis.** ak´ta yū´rā gāstēō´nēs. âk´tu j3´rē jestēō´nus.] "Act of the right of behavior." An act of the kind performable by private citizens, which under a restrictive theory of sovereign immunity can give rise to a cause of action in a foreign court even if undertaken by a sovereign. *E.g.*, "The original concept of absolute [state] immunity, based on status…has been replaced by that of restrictive immunity; within the latter a distinction was made between *acta jure imperii* and *acta jure gestionis* but immunity is granted only for the former. The meaning of these two notions is not carved in stone, however; it is subject to a continuously changing interpretation which varies with time reflecting the changing priorities of society." *Arrest Warrant of 11 April 2000* (Congo v. Belg.), 2002 I.C.J. Rep. 3, 84–85, ¶ 72 (separate opinion of Judge Higgins). *Contrast with* **Actum iure imperii.** *See also* **Iure gestionis** and **De iure gestionis.**

Actum iure imperii. ak´tūm yū´rā ēmpā´rē-ē. âk´tum j3´rē imp3´rī. *n.* [*pl.* **Acta iure imperii.** ak´ta yū´rā ēmpā´rē-ē. âk´tu j3´rē imp3´rī.] "Act of sovereign right." An act of the kind that only a sovereign may undertake, which generally cannot give rise to a cause of action in a foreign court under principles of foreign sovereign immunity. *Compare with* **Actum imperii.** *See example of usage under,* and *contrast with,* **Actum iure gestionis.** *See also* **Iure imperii, De iure imperii,** and **Par in parem non habet imperium.**

Actus. ak´tūs. âk´tus. *n.* "Act." An act; something accomplished or in the process of being accomplished by activity.

Actus non facit reum, nisi mens sit rea. ak´tūs nōn fa´kēt rā´ūm, nē´sē māns sēt rā´a. âk´tus nan fâ´sit rā´um, ni´zē menz sit rā´u. "The act does not make evil unless the spirit is evil." A doctrine providing that an act is not culpable (*e.g.*, criminal) unless performed with malignant intent. In international law, this doctrine applies most commonly to the crime of genocide, which is said to require a specific intent (*mens rea*) to extinguish a defined group. *See also* **Dolus specialis** and **Mens rea.**

Actus reus. ak´tūs rā´ūs. âk´tus rā´us. *n.* "Guilty act." The physical conduct element of a criminal offense. Most crimes have both a conduct component (*actus reus*) and a mental or intent component (*mens rea*). *E.g.*, "Members of the joint criminal enterprise used or cooperated with others, including those under their command or effective control, to facilitate or carry out the *actus reus* of crimes against the Serbian civilian population and civilian property." *Prosecutor v. Markac*, ICTY Case No. IT-06-90-T, Indictment of Mar. 12, 2008, ¶ 16. *See also* **Mens rea.**

A

Ad abundantiam. ad abūndan´tē-am. âd âbundân´tyum. *adj.* "To abundance." (1) To a great degree; in great measure. (2) For the purpose of showing a great profusion. *E.g.*, "The European Communities…maintains that…, *ad abundantiam*, it submitted and will submit as further evidence additional contextual documentation and information…." *United States—Sections 301–310 of the Trade Act of 1974*, Panel Report of Dec. 22, 1999, WTO Doc. WT/DS152/R, at 32, ¶ 4.93.

Ad abundantiorem cautelam. ad abūndantēō´rām kôtā´lam. âd âbundântyō´rum kă´telum. *adv.* "For a great abundance of caution." Done with exceeding care to prevent possible, if unlikely, negative consequences. *Compare with* **Ob maiorem cautelam.** *See also* **Abundans cautela non nocet.**

Ad adiuvandum. ad adyūwan´dūm. âd âdjūvân´dum. *adj.* "For the encouragement." Intervening in support of the position of a party to the case currently pending before a tribunal. *Contrast with, and see the example of usage in,* **Ad excludendum.**

Ad aliud examen. ad a´lē-ūd āksa´mān. âd â´lyud egzâ´men. *adv.* "To another examination." To a different tribunal; to consideration by a different tribunal. *E.g.*, "I apprehend it is not in the power of one of the parties, by leaving the place, to draw the question of the marriage or contract, *ad aliud examen*, to be tried by different laws than those of the place where the parties contracted. They may change the forum, but they must be tried by the laws of the country which they left." D. Mendes da Costa, *The Formalities of Marriage in the Conflict of Laws*, 7 INT'L & COMP. L.Q. 217 (1958) (quoting *Scrimshire v. Scrimshire*, [1752] 2 Hag. Con. 395, 412). Sometimes abbreviated **Aliud examen.**

Ad alium diem. ad a´lē-ūm dē´ām. âd â´lyum dē´um. *adv.* "To another day." To the future; to be delayed for some time. In a treaty negotiation, for example, parties might agree to delay consideration of the troublesome issues *ad alium diem* in order to conclude negotiations of the less problematic aspects of the treaty immediately.

Ad casum. ad ka´sūm. âd kâ´zum. *adv.* "For the case." Relating to the case or cause of action. *E.g.*, "[C]an a reservation be made to the provision that the boundary of the continental shelf 'shall be determined by agreement between' the States concerned?....Obviously not, [because] this stipulation should be read as the application *ad casum* of a general obligation of States." *North Sea Continental Shelf Case* (F.R.G. v. Den. & Neth.), 1969 I.C.J. Rep. 3, 223 (Judge Lachs, dissenting).

A

Ad coelum (et ad inferos). ad kœ´lūm (āt ad ēn´fārōs). âd sē´lum (et âd in´fɜrōz). *adv.* "To the heavens (and to the depths)." Upward (and downward) to a great distance or without limit. The term is most commonly used to refer to the jurisdiction of a state over its territory, which theoretically includes the airspace above that territory and the soil and substrate of the territory to the center of the Earth. An alternative formulation is **Usque ad coelum.** *See also* **Ad inferos** and **Cuius est solum eius est usque ad coelum (et ad inferos).**

Ad confirmandam iurisdictionem. ad kōnfērman´dūm yūrēsdēktēō´nām. âd kanfɜr-mân´dum jɜrisdikšō´nem. *adv.* "For confirmation of jurisdiction." For the purpose of confirming jurisdiction. *E.g.*, "On June 30 Bouygues issued a writ *in rem* in the Supreme Court of South Africa against the tug....The Supreme Court on July 25 made an attachment order *ad fundandam jurisdictionem* or *ad confirmandam jurisdictionem* in *in personam* proceedings brought by Bouygues against the tug-owners and Ultisol." *Ultisol Transport Contracting Ltd. v. Bouygues Offshore SA*, [1996] 2 Lloyd's Rep. 140, 140 QBD (Adm.) (U.K.). *Compare with* **Ad fundandam iurisdictionem.**

Ad consimiles casus. ad kōnsē´mēlēs ka´sūs. âd kansi´milēz kâ´zus. *adv.* "To similar cases." With reference to analogous or similar positions, situations, or constellations of facts. Sometimes abbreviated **Consimili casu.** *Compare with* **In consimili casu.**

Ad crumenam. ad krūmā´nam. âd krū´menum. *adj.* "To the purse." Relating to wealth. *See also* **Argumentum ad crumenam.**

Ad curiam. ad kū´rē-am. âd kyū´rē-um. *adv.* "To the court." Regarding or directed to the court or tribunal.

Ad damnum. ad dam´nūm. âd dâm´num. *adj.* "For the injury." Relating to a loss caused by an injurious act. An *ad damnum* clause in a claim or petition states the amount of damages sought by the claimant. *E.g.*, "[T]he petitioner filed a motion to dismiss, assigning the following grounds, amongst others:...the court is without jurisdiction because the...sum named in the *ad damnum* clause of the complaint is not a true statement of complainant's damages and is not alleged in good faith...." *KVOS, Inc. v. Associated Press*, 299 U.S. 269, 274 (1936).

Ad diem. ad dē´ām. âd dē´um. *adv.* "To the day." On a specific date; on the date expected. *E.g.*, "The [insurance] policy having been renewed and continued in force by the company for a year...when the note in question was given,... mere non-payment *ad diem* was not alone sufficient to effect an absolute forfeiture of the insurance." *Thompson v. Knickerbocker Life Ins. Co.*, 104 U.S. 252, 253 (1881). *See also* **Ad horam**.

Ad effectum (sequentem). ad ăffāk´tūm (sākwān´tām). âd ēfek´tum (sē´kwentem). *adv.* "To the (following) effect." Having the effect or outcome to be described.

Ad effectum videndi. ad ăffāk´tūm wēdān´dē. âd efek´tum viden´dī. *adv.* "To have the effect of seeing." (1) Having an effect that remains to be seen. (2) In Latin American legal practice, according to due process of law. *E.g.*, "In addition to the writ of *habeas corpus*, the Government mentioned various remedies that might possibly be invoked, such as appeal, cassation, extraordinary writ of *amparo*, *ad effectum videndi*, criminal complaints against those ultimately responsible and a presumptive finding of death." *Velasquez Rodriguez Case*, Inter-Am. Ct. Hum. Rts., Judgment of July 29, 1988, 28 I.L.M. 291, 304, ¶ 52 (1989).

Ad excludendum. ad āks-klūdān´dūm. âd eks-klūden´dum. *adj.* "For the exclusion." Intervening in opposition to the position of a party to the case currently pending before a tribunal. *E.g.*, "Thus, what Italy will be submitting to the Court is something described in municipal law as a principal or 'competing' intervention, or, as the Latin has it more aptly, an intervention *ad excludendum*, since Italy wants the Court to exclude or reject Maltese and Libyan claims with respect to certain sectors of the area in dispute in the case. An intervention *ad excludendum* is to be distinguished from an intervention *ad adjuvandum* such as the one filed by Fiji in the *Nuclear Tests* cases, in support of Australia and New Zealand against France. To a greater extent even than this latter type of supporting intervention, a competing intervention *ad excludendum* of the kind sought by Italy has the inevitable consequence that not just one, but both original parties would automatically become respondent States *vis-à-vis* Italy." *Continental Shelf Case* (Libya v. Malta), 1984 I.C.J. Rep. 3, 67, ¶ 34 (separate opinion of Judge Jiménez de Aréchaga).*Contrast with* **Ad adiuvandum**.

Ad fin. *adv.* An abbreviation of **Ad finem**.

Ad finem. ad fē´nām. âd fī´num. *adv.* "To the end." Up to the end of the cited material. *Ad finem* is a rarely used citation signal denoting that the referenced material is to be found either on the page cited (meaning up to the end of the page) or through and up to the end of the cited range of pages. Commonly abbreviated **Ad fin**.

Ad fundandam (iurisdictionem). ad fūndan´dam (yūrēsdēktēō´nām). âd fundân´dum (ʒrisdikšō´nem). *adv.* "For the foundation (of jurisdiction)." Relating to or for purposes of creating the basis for the assertion of jurisdiction. *Compare with, and see the example of usage under*, **Ad confirmandam iurisdictionem**.

Ad hoc. ad hōk. âd hak. *adj. Neo.* "For this." For the specific purpose at hand, without reference to wider application or use. An *ad hoc* committee is one formed to address a specific issue and without any intent to remain permanently constituted. An *ad hoc* judge is appointed solely for a specific case; he or she does not sit permanently on the tribunal. Similarly, *ad hoc* arbitration is arbitration agreed upon to resolve a specific dispute rather than to govern an ongoing treaty, contractual or other relationship between the parties. *E.g.*, "Article 281 [of the UN Convention on the Law of the Sea] applies where Parties 'have agreed' to seek settlement of their dispute by a peaceful means of their own choice. Since it appears that Article 282 applies where the Parties have a standing bilateral or multilateral dispute settlement agreement which could cover the UNCLOS dispute which has arisen between them, it would appear that Article 281 is intended primarily to cover the situation where the Parties have come to an *ad hoc* agreement as to the means to be adopted to settle the particular dispute which has arisen." *Barbados v. Republic of Trinidad & Tobago*, Permanent Ct. Arb., Award of Apr. 11, 2006, ¶ 200(ii), 45 I.L.M. 800, 833 (2006).

A

Ad hominem. ad hō´mēnām. âd ha´minum. *adj.* "To the man." Directed to an individual personally, especially made with insulting intent or without relevance to the issue under consideration. *E.g.*, "The EC has also made play of the fact that one of the companies in the US industry was Australian owned and is also an importer of wheat gluten from Australia. As we pointed out in our submission, these facts are irrelevant to the matters before the Panel. The EC's points amount to no more than an *ad hominem* argument." *United States—Definitive Safeguard Measures on Imports of Wheat Gluten from the European Communities*, Panel Report of July 31, 2000, WTO Doc. WT/DS166/R, Attach. 3-1-2, at 381, ¶ 6. *See also* **Argumentum ad hominem**.

Ad horam. ad hō´ram. âd hō´rum. *adv.* "To the hour." (1) Punctually; on time. (2) At a specific hour. *See also* **Ad diem**.

Ad horum. A common misspelling of **Ad horam**.

Ad hunc diem. ad hūnk dē´ām. âd hunk dē´um. *adv.* "To this day." Up to the present day, as when a condition or state of affairs has continued to present (at which point it may continue currently or may terminate).

Ad idem. ad ē´dām. âd ī´dum. *adj.* "To the same." (1) Relating to the same matter. (2) Having the same opinion, belief, or view of a matter. *E.g.*,

"[T]he fact that the parties are *ad idem* with regard to the normative element, that is, the subject of their reciprocal obligations, is not in itself sufficient to characterize this mutual and concordant manifestation of a common intent." *Fisheries Jurisdiction Case* (Sp. v. Can.), 1988 I.C.J. Rep. 432, 566–67, ¶ 33 (Jurisdiction) (Judge Ranjeva, dissenting).

Ad impossibilia nemo tenetur. ad ēmpōssēbē´lē-a nā´mō tānā´tūr. âd impasibi´lyu nē´mō te´netɜr. "Nobody is held to the impossible." An alternative formulation of **Impossibilium nulla obligatio est.**

Ad inferos. ad ēn´fārōs. âd in´fɜrōz. *adv.* "To the depths." Downward to a great distance or without limit. The term is most commonly used to refer to the jurisdiction of a state over its territory, which theoretically includes the soil and substrate of the territory to the center of the Earth. *See also* **Ad coelum (et ad inferos).**

Ad infinitum. ad ēnfēnē´tūm. âd infinī´tum. *adj.* or *adv.* "To infinity." To an infinite degree, distance, duration, etc. This term can be used in either a literal or figurative sense. *E.g.*, "National regulations often lay down restrictions as to the number and tonnage of ships, the repetition of visits, etc.; this is evidence of the menacing character of warships, and serves to controvert the erroneous argument that if one ship is admitted, a second must also be allowed and then a third and a fourth, *ad infinitum*." *Corfu Channel Case* (U.K. v. Alb.), 1949 I.C.J. Rep. 4, 109, ¶ 39 (Merits) (Judge Azevedo, dissenting). An alternative formulation is **In infinitum.**

Ad instantiam partis. ad ēnstan´tē-am par´tēs. âd instân´šum par´tis. *adv.* "By the inducement of a party." At the request of a party to a case pending before a tribunal. For example, a motion to dismiss a case brought *ad instantiam partis* means that one of the parties to the case moved for the dismissal. *Contrast with* **Sua sponte.**

Ad interim. ad ēn´tārēm. âd in´tɜrim. *adj.* or *adv.* "For the moment." (1) Temporary; temporarily. *E.g.*, "[F]rom the viewpoint of the Court's adjudication, whether *ad interim* or final, what is vital is the positive pleading of Pakistan that Bangla-Desh and not India is contesting Pakistan's claim to exclusive jurisdiction for the holding of trials of 195 prisoners of war." *Trial of Pakistani Prisoners of War* (Pak. v. India), 1973 I.C.J. Rep. 328, 332 (Interim Measures) (separate opinion of Judge Singh). (2) During the intermission or intervening time. Between the tenures of officials, an official may be appointed to serve *ad interim* until a new appointment can be made. The appointment of a *chargé d'affaires ad interim* is a common international practice when a special diplomatic representative is needed on an *ad hoc* basis.

Ad largum. ad lar´gūm. âd lar´jum. *adj.* or *adv.* "At large." Unconfined; free and unrestrained; at large; at liberty.

Ad lib. An abbreviation of **Ad libitum.**

A

Ad libita. ad lē´bēta. âd li´bitu. *adj.* or *adv.* "To one's wishes." An alternative formulation of **Ad libitum.**

Ad libitum. ad lē´bētūm. âd li´bitum. *adj.* or *adv.* "To one's wishes." (1) In the manner that appeals best to one's taste or preference. *E.g.*, "Lewald rightly emphasizes the dangers that arise, once *ordre public* is upheld in respect of State conventions. This would enable any State practically to restrict the application of the convention *ad libitum* and, in such manner, to divest the convention of practically its entire value." Martin Wolff, DAS INTERNATIONALE PRIVATRECHT DEUTSCHLANDS 70 (1949) (translated to English). (2) Extemporaneous; extemporaneously. Commonly abbreviated **Ad lib.** An alternative formulation is **Ad libita.** *Compare with* **Ad voluntatem.** *See also* **Ex tempore.**

Ad litem. ad lē´tām. âd li´tum OR -lī´tum. *adj.* "To/for the lawsuit." For purposes of and during the specific lawsuit. When a guardian or representative is appointed *ad litem* to represent the interests of those unable to represent themselves, such as children or the mentally handicapped, that person does not assume the role of guardian generally, but rather with respect to the litigation only. *E.g.*, "On April 19, 2002 in the main proceedings concerning parental responsibility and access rights, the Münster District Court appointed a lawyer of the Münster Bar as curator *ad litem* to represent the children's interests in the proceedings." *Haase v. Germany*, 46 E.H.R.R. SE20, 243 (2008). *Compare with* **Pendente lite.**

Ad loc. An abbreviation of **Ad locum.**

Ad locum. ad lō´kūm. âd lōk´um. *adv.* "To the place." At the source or place. This term is usually used as a citation signal to indicate that the source cited is the same as one previously cited. *E.g.*, The author argues in his book that Grotius maintained a theocentric view of international law, and draws a connection *ad locum* to Kant's essay, *Toward Eternal Peace.* Sometimes abbreviated **Ad loc.**

Ad manum. ad ma´nūm. âd mâ´num. *adj.* or *adv.* "At hand." On hand; conveniently situated for immediate use.

Ad modum. ad mō´dūm. âd mō´dum. *adv.* "In the manner." (1) Using the same method as. (2) In the manner of.

Ad nauseam. ad nô´sä-am. âd nă´zē-um. *adv.* "To nausea." To the point that the subject matter under consideration provokes physical sickness. Usually used as a hyperbolic substitute for *ad infinitum*, often for comical or sardonic effect. *E.g.*, "The Canadian argument about 'the integrity of the legislation' has been invoked *ad nauseam* during the present incidental proceedings, yet neither Canada nor the Judgment took the trouble to examine the issue." *Fisheries Jurisdiction Case* (Sp. v. Can.), 1998 I.C.J. Rep. 432, 652, ¶ 184 (Jurisdiction) (Judge Bernárdez, dissenting).

A

Ad opus. ad ō´pūs. âd ō´pus. *adv.* "To the work." On behalf of or for the benefit of another person.

Ad perpetuam rei memoriam. ad pārpā´tūam rā´ē māmō´rē-am. âd pɜrpe´čūum rā memō´rē-um. *adv.* "For a permanent record of the matter." To serve as a permanent documentary record of a fact, settlement of a dispute, etc. *E.g.*, "The grant of asylum thus constitutes an admitted fact the circumstances of which must be fixed, once and for all, *ad perpetuam rei memoriam*, in view of any appreciation which may have to be made in the future." *The Asylum Case* (Colom. v. Peru), 1950 I.C.J. Rep. 266, 345.

Ad personam. ad pārsō´nam. âd pɜrsō´num. *adv.* "To a person." Relating to an individual person. *E.g.*, "[W]hile the expropriation law in issue in *Ruiz-Mateos* could be considered as *ad personam* legislation, in the present case the Autonomous Community Law of 1996 was of general application and did not concern the applicants alone." *Lizarraga v. Spain*, 45 E.H.R.R. 45, ¶ 58 (2007).

Ad quem. ad kwām. âd kwem. *adv.* "To which." To which an appeal is made. A tribunal *ad quem* is the tribunal to which a lower tribunal's award or judgment is appealed. *See also* **Dies ad quem** and **Terminus ad quem.** *Contrast with* **A quo.**

Ad referendum. ad rāfārān´dūm. âd refɜren´dum. *adv.* "For making a reference." For further consideration or ratification. When a state representative executes a legal instrument *ad referendum*, it is understood that, while the signature may authenticate the text of the instrument, it does not bind the state until the state has duty ratified the treaty (subject to any provisional obligations). *E.g.*, "[T]he signature *ad referendum* of a treaty by a representative, if confirmed by his State, constitutes a full signature to the treaty." Vienna Convention on the Law of Treaties, May 23, 1969, art. 12(2)(b), 1155 U.N.T.S. 331. *See also id.* art. 10(b). *Compare with* **Sub spe rati.**

Ad rem. ad rām. âd rem. *adv.* "To the thing." (1) Pertinently; germanely. (2) To the point. (3) Relating to a matter or to property, as opposed to a person, as in *ius ad rem*, a "right respecting property." *See also* **Nihil ad rem.**

A

Ad singulorum utilitatem. ad sēngūlōr´ūm ūtēlēta´tām. âd sēŋyūlō´rum yūtilitā´tum. *adj.* "For the use of each individual." Concerning or relating to the individual. According to Ulpian, this is the defining character of private law, as opposed to public law. *Contrast with* **Ad statum rei publicae spectat.**

Ad statum rei publicae spectat. ad stat´ūm rā´ē pūb´lēkī spāk´tat. âd stâ´tum rā pub´likā spek´tât. "It concerns the status of a public thing/the state." The subject concerns the state or the public as a whole. According to Ulpian, this is the defining character of public law, as opposed to private law. *Contrast with* **Ad singulorum utilitatem.**

Ad valorem. ad walōr´ām. âd vulō´rum. *adv.* "For the value." Based upon or proportional to the monetary value of goods, technology, or services. Often used in tax law as a basis for assessing taxes owed. In international practice, customs duties are often calculated based on a percentage of the value of the imported goods. *E.g.*, "Whenever an article is entered for sale under heading 9706 ["Antiques of an age exceeding 100 years"], and thereafter determined to be not over 100 years of age, a duty of 6.6 percent *ad valorem*...shall be assessed thereon in addition to any other duty or penalty imposed on such articles under the tariff schedule." Harmonized Tariff Schedule of the United States ch. 97, Additional U.S. Note 2 (2007).

Ad voluntatem. ad wōlūnta´tām. âd valuntā´tem. *adv.* "At will." According to one's discretion or whim; without external constraint. *Compare with* **Ad libitum.**

Admiralitas. admēra´lētas. âdmurâ´litus. *n.* "Admiralty." An alternative term for **Societas navalis.**

Adventurae maris. adwāntū´rī ma´rēs. âdven´č3rā ma´ris. *n. pl. Med.* "Adventures of the sea." Ship wreckage washed ashore (flotsam) or material cast overboard from a distressed ship (jetsam and lagan) to lighten the cargo and thereby avoid sinking. *See also* **Levandae navis causa.**

Adversus. adwār´sūs. âdv3r´sus. *prep.* "Contrary to." Against. *Compare with* **Versus.**

Adversus bonos mores. adwār´sūs bō´nōs mō´rās. âdv3r´sus bō´nus mō´rēz. *adj.* "Contrary to good morals." An alternative formulation of **Contra bonos mores (et decorum).**

Adversus omnes. adwār´sūs ōm´nās. âdv3r´sus am´nēz. *adj.* or *adv.* "Contrary to all." Against the opinions or interests of all others.

Adversus omni. A misspelling of **Adversus omnes.**

Aedificare in tuo proprio solo non licet quod alteri noceat. īdēfēka´rā ēn tū´ō prōp´rēō sō´lō nōn lē´kāt kwōd al´tārē nō´kā-at. edifika´rē in tū´ō pra´prēō sō´lō nan lī´set kwad âl´t3rī nō´sē-ât. "It is impermissible to build within your own land that which would harm another's." A maxim meaning that one must refrain from using one's territory or property in such a manner as to harm another (such as a neighboring property owner or state). By extension, it is sometimes argued that one must refrain from allowing others to make a similarly noxious use of one's property against a neighboring state or property owner. *See Corfu Channel Case* (U.K. v. Alb.), 1949 I.C.J. Rep. 4, 22.

Aequitas. ī´kwētas. e´kwitus. *n.* "Equity." (1) Equity; fairness; impartiality. (2) A system of law developed by courts to supplement the incomplete or sometimes harsh consequences of a strict application of law with considerations of justice or fairness.

Aequitas contra legem. ī´kwētas kōn´tra lā´gām. e´kwitus kan´tru le´jum. "Equity in opposition to the law." A maxim justifying the use of equity in derogation of a legal rule to avoid an unintended or unjust result. *Compare with* **Aequitas praeter legem.** *Contrast with* **Aequitas intra legem.** *See also* **Aequitas sequitur legem** and **Aequitas nunquam contravenit legem.**

Aequitas est correctio legis generaliter latae qua parte deficit. ī´kwētas āst kōrrāk´tēō lā´gēs gānāra´lētār la´tī kwa par´tā dā´fēkēt. e´kwitus est kurek´tyō le´jis jen3râ´ lit3r lâ´tā kwā par´tē de´fisit. "Equity is the correction of law that has been legislated broadly in that part where it is defective." A maxim meaning that a tribunal may use equity to create an exception to an overbroad law to fulfill the intent of the law drafter or the needs of justice, although the exception may not technically conform to the literal terms of the law.

Aequitas infra legem. ī´kwētas ēn´fra lā´gām. e´kwitus in´fru le´jum. *n.* "Equity under the law." Equity used to interpret the law in a manner that achieves a most just result without violating or exceeding the scope of the law itself. *E.g.*, "Equity may be applied only to fill in a gap. It could be *aequitas infra legem* or *aequitas secundum legem* but not *aequitas praeter legem* or *contra legem*." *Territorial Dispute* (Libya v. Chad), 1994 I.C.J. Rep. 6, 59, ¶ 29 (separate opinion of Judge Ajibola). *Contrast with* **Aequitas contra legem** and **Aequitas praeter legem.**

Aequitas legem sequitur. ī´kwētas lā´gām sā´kwētūr. e´kwitus le´jum se´kwit3r. "Equity follows the law." An alternative formulation of **Aequitas sequitur legem.**

Aequitas non facit ius, sed iuri auxiliatur. ī´kwētas nōn fa´kēt yūs, sād yū´rē ôksēlē-a´tūr. e´kwitus nan fâ´sit jus, sed j3´rī ăkzi´lyut3r. "Equity creates no right, but aids right." A maxim meaning that equity cannot be invoked to create a new right, but rather to supplement or give meaning to an existing legal right.

A

Aequitas nunquam contravenit legem. ī´kwētas nūn´kwam kōntrawā´nēt lā´gām. e´kwitus nun´kwum kantruve´nit le´jum. "Equity never contravenes the law." A maxim meaning that equity supplements the law rather than overruling it. *Compare with* **Aequitas sequitur legem.** *Contrast with* **Aequitas contra legem** and **Aequitas praeter legem.**

Aequitas praeter legem. ī´kwētas prī´tār lā´gām. e´kwitus prā´tɜr le´jum. *n.* "Equity apart from the law." Principles of equity used to fill in a gap or vagueness in the law, without directly contravening any established legal principle. *Compare with* **Aequitas contra legem.** *Contrast with, and see the example of usage in,* **Aequitas infra legem.** *See also* **Aequitas sequitur legem** and **Aequitas nunquam contravenit legem.**

Aequitas sequitur legem. ī´kwētas sā´kwētūr lā´gām. e´kwitus se´kwitɜr le´jum. "Equity follows the law." A maxim meaning that a tribunal sitting in equity conforms equity to general rules and supplements (as opposed to supplants) the law when necessary to arrive at a just decision. An alternative formulation is **Aequitas legem sequitur.** *Compare with* **Aequitas nunquam contravenit legem** and **Lex respicit aequitatem.** *Contrast with* **Aequitas contra legem** and **Aequitas praeter legem.**

Affectio coniugalis. affāk´tēō kōnyūga´lēs. ufek´šō kanjūgâ´lis. *n.* "Conjugal affection." The love that spouses bear for one another. Traditionally, one of the expected attributes of a married couple.

Affirmanti (non neganti) incumbit probatio. affērman´tē (nōn nāgan´tē) ēnkūm´bēt prōba´tēō. âfɜrmân´tī (nan negân´tī) inkum´bit prōbā´šō. "The claimant (not the respondent) bears the proof." A maxim meaning that a party asserting a claim bears the burden of persuasion rather than the party denying the claim. *E.g.*, "The Court has also recognised that Convention proceedings do not in all cases lend themselves to a rigorous application of the principle *affirmanti incumbit probatio*....In certain circumstances, where the events in issue lie wholly, or in large part, within the exclusive knowledge of authorities, the burden of proof may be regarded as resting on the authorities to provide a satisfactory and convincing explanation." *D.H. v. Czech Rep.*, Eur. Ct. Hum. Rts. App. No. 57325/00, Judgment of Nov. 13, 2007, ¶ 179, 47 I.L.M. 38.

Affirmatio unius (est) exclusio alterius. affērma´tēō ūnē´ūs (āst) āks-klū´sēō altār-ē´ūs. âfɜrmā´šō ū´nē-us (est) eks-klū´zēō altɜ´rē-us. "The affirmation of one is the exclusion of the other." An alternative formulation of **Expressio unius (est) exclusio alterius.**

Aliamenta. alē-amān´ta. âlē-umen´tu. *n. Neo.* "Freedom of transit." In common law, a freedom of transit, passage, or access to or through a territory or its natural resources, usually for the accommodation of a tenant. By analogy, an equitable servitude to transit through or access the land, water, or air of a foreign state. This term is not attested in classical Latin.

Alieni generis. alē-ā´nē gā´nārēs. ālye´nī je´nɜris. *adj.* "Of another kind." Of a kind different than that previously discussed or referenced; of a foreign kind.

A

Alieni iuris. alē-ā´nē yū´rēs. ālye´nī jɜ´ris. *adj.* "Subject to another's jurisdiction." Subject to the authority or law of a foreign power or sovereign. *Contrast with* **Sui iuris.**

Alio intuitu. a´lēō ēntū´ētū. â´lēō intū´itū. *adv.* "In another respect." From another point of view.

Aliquis non debet esse iudex in propria sua causa (quia non potest esse iudex et pars). a´lēkwēs nōn dā´bāt ās´sā yū´dāks ēn prōp´rē-a sū´a kô´sa (kwē´a nōn pō´tāst ās´sā yū´dāks āt pars). â´likwis nan de´bet e´sā jū´deks in prō´prē-u sū´u kă´zu (kwē´u nan pō´test e´sā jū´deks et parz). "A person should not be a judge in his own matter (because one cannot be a judge and a party)." An alternative formulation of **Nemo debet esse iudex in (propria) sua causa.**

Aliter. a´lētār. â´litɜr. *adv.* "Otherwise." (1) Alternatively. (2) In a different manner; with different characteristics. (3) Elsewhere. *E.g.*, "But Article 22 did not itself confer any Mandates, appoint any Mandatories, or define the terms of any Mandates. This was done *aliter*, as will be seen." *South West Africa Cases* (Eth. v. S. Afr.; Liber. v. S. Afr.), 1962 I.C.J. Rep. 319, 479 (Preliminary Objections). *See also* **Aliter et aliunde.**

Aliter et aliunde. a´lētār āt alē-ūn´dā. â´litɜr et âlē-un´dē. *adv.* "Otherwise and from elsewhere." In some other manner and with reference to (or in reliance on) some other source of authority. *E.g.*, "Parties are in disagreement…as to whether India's action in relation to Pakistan overflights was such as not to involve the Treaties, but to be justifiable *aliter et aliunde*…." *Aerial Incident of 10 August 1999* (Pak. v. India), 2000 I.C.J. Rep. 12, 88 (2000). An alternative formulation is **Aliunde vel aliter.** *See also* **Aliter** and **Aliunde.**

Aliud examen. a´lē-ūd āksa´mān. â´lē-ud egzâ´men. *adv.* "To another examination." An abbreviation of **Ad aliud examen.**

Aliunde. alē-ūn´dā. âlē-un´dē. *adv.* "From elsewhere." From a different source of authority. *E.g.*, "The [UN General] Assembly can only exercise powers conferred upon it or derived *aliunde* or *ab extra* provided it keeps within the limits of its constitutional role under the structure of the Charter." *Advisory Opinion on Legal Consequences for States of the Continued Presence of South Africa in Namibia (South West Africa) Notwithstanding Security*

Council Resolution 276 (1970), 1971 I.C.J. Rep. 16, 285. *Compare with* **Ab extra.** *See also* **Aliter et aliunde.**

Aliunde vel aliter. alē-ūn´dā wāl a´lētār. âlē-un´dē vel â´litɜr. *adv.* "From elsewhere or otherwise." An alternative formulation of **Aliter et aliunde.** *E.g.*, "The Court can see nothing in it that would take the clause outside the normal rule that, in a dispute causing the activation of a jurisdictional clause, the substantive rights themselves which the dispute is about, must be sought for elsewhere than in this clause, or in some element apart from it—and must therefore be established *aliunde vel aliter*." *South West Africa Cases* (Eth. v. S. Afr.; Liber. v. S. Afr.), 1966 I.C.J. Rep. 6, ¶ 65 (Second Phase).

Alius acta. alē´ūs ak´ta. ā´lē-us âk´tu. *n. pl.* "The acts of another." Acts by a third party; the acts of a natural person, organization, or state other than the parties currently before a tribunal.

Allegans contraria non audiendus est. allā´gans kōntra´rē-a nōn ôdē-ān´dūs āst. â´legunz kantra´rē-u nan ădē-en´dus est. "A person adducing to the contrary is not to be heard." An alternative formulation of **Allegans contraria non est audiendus.**

Allegans contraria non est audiendus. allā´gans kōntra´rē-a nōn āst ôdē-ān´dūs. â´lejunz kantra´rē-u nan est ădē-en´dus. "A person adducing to the contrary is not to be heard." A maxim meaning that a tribunal will not entertain contradictory claims by the same party, or claims by a party contradictory to the party's own conduct, in a single case. *E.g.*, "Whatever term or terms be employed to designate this principle such as it has been applied in the international sphere, its substance is always the same: inconsistency between claims or allegations put forward by a State, and its previous conduct in connection therewith, is not admissible (*allegans contraria non audiendus est*)." *Temple of Preah Vihear* (Camb. v. Thail.), 1962 I.C.J. Rep. 6, 41 (Merits) (separate opinion of Vice President Alfaro). An alternative formulation is **Allegans contraria non audiendus est.**

Allegans probat. *See* **Actor allegans probat.**

Allegatum. allāga´tūm. âlegā´tum. *n.* "That which is adduced." An allegation; a fact alleged to be true in a complaint, petition, response, or other pleading.

Alluvio maris. allū´wēō ma´rēs. alū´vēō ma´ris. *n.* "Flood of the sea." Clay, silt, sand, gravel, or similar material deposited by oceanic waters (as opposed to river or other fresh waters), thereby building upon existing land by accretion. Over time, such accretion may reduce the size of a river delta or extend a coastal region, which in turn may change the distribution of a state's land

and sea. Such geographic alterations have possible consequences for the state's international land and sea boundaries.

Alma mater. al´ma ma´tär. al´mu ma´tɜr. *n.* [*pl.* **Almae matres.** al´mī mat´rās. al´mu māt´rēz.] "Nourishing mother." An institution, especially a school, that one has attended; an educational institution from which one has graduated.

Alter ego. al´tär ā´gō. al´tɜr ē´gō. *n.* "Another I." A second name or identity of a legal or natural person, or of a state. In international practice, the term sometimes expresses the control that a state exercises over, or the representative capacity in which a state acts on behalf of, its citizens or entities incorporated in or formed by the state. It may also describe a foreign state or government over which a principal state exercises control or influence. *E.g.*, "From the viewpoint of functional differentiation a question arises when shares are owned by two persons: the one, a nominee, whose name is entered in the share register and who exercises rights as *alter ego* of the real owner; the other, the beneficial owner, who enjoys rights as the real or economic owner of the shares." *Barcelona Traction, Light, and Power Co., Ltd.* (Belg. v. Sp.), 1970 I.C.J. Rep. 3, 135 (separate opinion of Judge Tanaka).

Alternatim. altärna´tēm. altɜrnā´tim. *adv.* "Alternately." In turns; by alternation.

Alterum tantum. al´tärūm tan´tūm. alt´ɜrum tân´tum. *n.* "Another as great." A rule of Roman law, sometimes held applicable in international law, that an award of interest may not exceed the amount of principal due regardless of the period during which the interest runs.

Alteruter. altärū´tär. altɜryū´tɜr. *adj.* "One or the other; both." (1) Either of. (2) One or another of.

Altum mare. al´tūm ma´rā. al´tum ma´rē. *n.* "The high seas." The high seas generally, being the area of an ocean or sea beyond any state's territorial waters. In modern practice under the UN Convention on the Law of the Sea (UNCLOS), the *altum mare* ends at the territorial sea, which usually extends to 12 nautical miles from the state's baseline, although in earlier times the territorial sea had a lesser reach and the *altum mare* was accordingly more extensive. Part VII of the UNCLOS defines state rights and obligations on "the high seas," but includes in this definition only oceanic waters outside of any state's exclusive economic zone (an area beyond and adjacent to the territorial sea up to 200 nautical miles from the coastal state's baseline) or archipelagic waters. In modern international law, the high seas are an area closed off from claims of state sovereignty and dedicated to the freedom of navigation, overflight, fishing, scientific research, and other rights, although seabed mining rights on the high seas are not unrestricted. *See* UNCLOS pt. VII, Dec. 10, 1982, 21

I.L.M. 1245 (1982). An alternative formulation is **Mare altum**. *See also* **Super altum mare.**

Alumna. alūm´na. ulum´nu. *n. fem.* [*pl.* **Alumnae.** alūm´nī. ulum´nā.] "Pupil." (1) A person who has graduated from a specific educational institution. (2) A person who is a former member or employee of an organization. The term *alumna* applies only to a woman; *alumnae* applies to a group of two or more women only. *Compare with* **Alumnus.**

Alumnae. *See* **Alumna.**

Alumni. *See* **Alumnus.**

Alumnus. alūm´nūs. ulum´nus. *n. masc.* [*pl.* **Alumni.** alūm´nē. ulum´nī.] "Pupil." (1) A person who has graduated from a specific educational institution. (2) A person who is a former member or employee of an organization. The term *alumnus* applies only to a man. The term *alumni* applies only to a group of two or more, of which at least one must be a man. *Compare with* **Alumna.**

Alvei mutatio. al´wā-ē mūta´tēō. âl´vē myūtā´šō. *n.* "Change of streambed." An alteration in the flow of a watercourse such as a river or stream. Such alterations may have consequences for international water rights, or for the borders of states where a river defines an international land boundary.

Ambiguitas contra stipulatorem est. ambē´gū-ētas kōn´tra stēpūlatō´rām āst. âmbigyū´itus kan´tru stipyūlutō´rem est. "An ambiguity is construed against the drafter." A canon of contract construction that dictates that vague or ambiguous terms or provisions should be interpreted in the manner most favorable to the position of the party other than the one who drafted the document.

Ambiguitas latens. ambē´gū-ētas la´tāns. âmbigyū´itus lā´tenz. *n.* "Latent ambiguity." An ambiguity in a legal instrument that may not be readily apparent from a superficial inspection but that becomes manifest upon an attempt to interpret or apply a rule set forth in the instrument to unexpected facts. For example, if a treaty provides for the sharing of water rights between Freedonia and Ruritania with respect to all rivers and lakes crossing the borders of the two states, and a Freedonian river formerly flowing into Ruritania naturally changes course so that it remains entirely in Freedonia, the *ambiguitas latens* becomes evident as to whether the relevant watercourses are (a) those existing at the time the treaty was adopted regardless of whether they change course in the future, or (b) the watercourses as they exist at the time of the claim. *Contrast with* **Ambiguitas patens.**

Ambiguitas patens. ambē´gū-ētas pa´tāns. âmbigyū´itus pā´tenz. *n.* "Evident ambiguity." An ambiguity in the language of a legal instrument that is readily apparent from a plain reading. For example, a treaty providing for arbitration of all disputes between the parties that specifies that the arbitral authority will be the "International Chamber of Stockholm" suffers from an *ambiguitas patens* as to whether the authority is to be the International Chamber of Commerce or the Stockholm Chamber of Commerce. *Contrast with* **Ambiguitas latens.**

A

Ambiguum pactum contra venditorem interpretandum est. ambē´gū-ūm pak´tūm kōn´tra wāndētō´rām ēntārprātan´dūm āst. âmbi´gyū-um pâk´tum kan´tru venditō´rum int3rpretân´dum est. "An ambiguous agreement is construed against the seller." A canon of private contract construction providing that vague or ambiguous terms or provisions should be interpreted in the manner most favorable to the position of the buyer. This canon is based upon the (often erroneous) assumption that the seller has greater bargaining power than the buyer. In modern private international law, this doctrine has usually given way to the canon **Ambiguitas contra stipulatorem est.**

Amicus. amē´kūs. â´mikus OR umē´kus. *n.* [*pl.* **Amici.** amē´kē. â´mēkē OR umē´kē.] "Friend." Friend, meant literally or figuratively in the sense of an advocate or ally. This term is sometimes used as an abbreviation of **Amicus curiae.**

Amicus curiae. amē´kūs kū´rē-ī. â´mikus- OR umē´kus kyū´rē-ē OR -kyū´rē-ā. *n.* "Friend of the court." A nonparty to a litigation who contributes a written submission or oral argument to a tribunal for the tribunal's information, either *sua sponte* with the tribunal's consent or specifically at the request of the tribunal, depending on the procedural rules in effect. *E.g.*, "For its part, Indonesia argues that 'the objective of the Philippines is not to inform [the] Court of its interests in the case before [it], but to draw the Court's attention to another dispute, speculating that this might, perhaps, be of interest. At best, the Philippines might appear as *amicus curiae*.'" *Sovereignty over Pulau Ligitan and Pulau Sipadan* (Indon. v. Malay.), 2001 I.C.J. Rep. 575, 604, ¶ 85. Sometimes abbreviated **Amicus.** *Compare with* **Amicus publici.**

Amicus publici. amē´kūs pūb´lēkē. â´mikus- OR umē´kus pub´likī. *n.* "Friend of the public." An advocate on behalf of the public interest. *E.g.*, "A matter of conscience can impel the lawyer into a public arena. If he occupies a prominent place in the community, his explanations as *amicus publici* further close the gap [between the legal and popular views of a case]." W. Michael Reisman, NULLITY AND REVISION 77 (1971). *Compare with* **Amicus curiae.**

Analogia proportionis. analō´gē-a prōpōrtēō´nēs. ânulō´jyu prupōršō´nis. *n. Med.* "An analogy of proportion." Analogy that is appropriate based on the similarity or comparability of the key characteristic of the analogized subject.

A

Ancipitis usus. ankē´pētēs ū´sūs. ânsi´pitis yū´zus. *n. pl.* "Double use." Dual-use items; goods having both potential military and civilian uses, such as oil, metal ore, and radar. Historically, some belligerent states in armed conflicts aggressively claimed the right to intercept neutral ships bound for their enemies and confiscate *ancipitis usus* as contraband. The notion of *ancipitis usus* as contraband has never, however, developed into rule of the customary international law of war. *E.g.*, "For it being impossible to ascertain the final use of an article *ancipitis usus*, it is not an injurious rule which deduces both ways the final use from the immediate destination." *The Jonge Margaretha*, 1 Rob. 189 (High Ct. Adm. 1799) (Lord Stowell) (U.K.). *See also* **Usus bellici.**

Animus. a´nēmūs. â´nimus. *n.* "Intention." (1) Spirit; disposition. (2) Intention to do something (such as claim sovereignty over or abandon a territory). *E.g.*, "There is no reason to suppose that France has subsequently lost her right by *derelictio*, since she never had the *animus* of abandoning the island, and the fact that she has not exercised her authority there in a positive manner does not imply the forfeiture of an acquisition already definitively perfected." *Sovereignty over Clipperton Island Case* (Fr. v. Mex.), Award of Jan. 28, 1931, 26 AM. J. INT'L L. 390, 394 (1932). (3) Dislike; hatred. *E.g.*, "Underlying much discrimination law is the notion that *animus* can lead to false and unjustified stereotypes, and *vice versa*." *Olmstead v. L.C. ex rel. Zimring*, 527 U.S. 581, 611 (1999). *Compare with* **Causa.**

Animus aggressionis. a´nēmūs aggrāssēō´nēs. â´nimus ugrešō´nis. *n. Neo.* "Intention to attack." The intention to commit an act of aggression against another. A harmful act directed against a state may not furnish a *casus belli* to the aggrieved state in the absence of *animus aggressionis*.

Animus adiuvandi. a´nēmūs adyūwan´dē. â´nimus âdjūvân´dī. *n.* "Intention to assist." The intention of a neutral state to assist a belligerent, either directly or indirectly, in violation of its neutrality obligations under the international law of war.

Animus belligerendi. a´nēmūs bāllēgārān´dē. â´nimus belijɜren´dī. *n.* "Intention to fight." The intention of a state to engage in armed action against another. *E.g.*, "Cerkez argues that there is no international armed conflict if all belligerent parties deny the existence of it, thus lacking the *animus belligerandi* [*sic*: *belligerendi*]." *Prosecutor v. Kordic & Cerkez*, ICTY Case No. IT-95-14/2-A, Judgment of Dec. 17, 2004, ¶ 346.

Animus belligerandi. A misspelling of **Animus belligerendi.**

Animus capiendi. a´nēmūs kapē-ān´dē. â´nimus kâpē-en´dī. *n.* "Intention to capture." An intention to seize or capture.

Animus commerciandi. a´nēmūs kōmmārkē-an´dē. â´nimus kōmɜršân´dī. *n.* "Intention to trade." The intention to engage in normal trading and other commercial relations with a state. The term is often used in the context of neutral trade with belligerents, when the neutral state has the option of terminating trade with all belligerents equally or of continuing normal trade relations subject to the usual neutral duties under the law of war.

Animus contrahendi. a´nēmūs kōntrahān´dē. â´nimus kantruhen´dī. *n.* "Intent to contract." An intention to be bound by contractual, treaty, or other legal obligations. *E.g.*, "My opposition to the majority is based primarily on theoretical convictions...of the collective wrongfulness embodied in the existence, on the part of both the States involved, of attitudes denoting that the *animus contrahendi* which supposedly united them in the past has now disappeared." *Gabcikovo-Nagymaros Project* (Hung. v. Slovk.), 1997 I.C.J. Rep. 7, 86 ¶ 1 (Judge Rezek, dissenting).

Animus derelinquendi. a´nēmūs dārālēnkwān´dē. â´nimus dārulinkwen´dī. *n.* "Intention to abandon." An intention to abandon something. In international practice, the thing abandoned is often territory, as when a state renounces sovereignty or control over territory. *Compare with* **Animus disponendi.** *Contrast with* **Animus domini, Animus occupandi,** and **Animus possidendi.** *See also* **Derelictio.**

Animus disponendi. a´nēmūs dēspōnān´dē. â´nimus dispōnen´dī. *n.* "Intention to dispose." An intention to abandon something, such as a territory, and renounce sovereignty or control over it. *Compare with* **Animus derelinquendi.** *Contrast with* **Animus domini, Animus occupandi,** and **Animus possidendi.**

Animus domini. a´nēmūs dō´mēnē. â´nimus da´minī. *n.* "Intention of the sovereign." An intention to assert sovereignty or ownership over a territory. *E.g.*, "[T]he possession exercised by the Netherlands was in no way a defective one and was based upon an incontestable legal title....It was a possession exercised in all good faith, with the *animus domini* which characterizes a situation of this kind and which the law protects." *Sovereignty Over Certain Frontier Land* (Belg. v. Neth.), 1959 I.C.J. Rep. 209, 255 (Judge Morena Quintana, dissenting). *Compare with* **Animus occupandi** and **Animus possidendi.** *Contrast with* **Animus disponendi** and **Animus derelinquendi.**

Animus donandi. a´nēmūs dōnan´dē. â´nimus dōnân´dī. *n.* "Intention to give." An intention to give gratuitously; an intention to gift something to another. *E.g.*, "[T]he manager had no intention to act gratuitously—there was no *animus donandi*." *Masdar (UK) Ltd. v. Commission of the Eur. Communities*, [2006] E.C.R. II-4377, ¶ 76.

Animus lucrandi. a´nēmūs lūkran´dē. â´nimus lūkrân´dī. *n.* "Intention to profit." (1) An intention to engage in commerce. (2) An intention to earn profit by some investment or commercial enterprise.

A

Animus malus. a´nēmūs ma´lūs. â´nimus mâ´lus. *n.* "Evil intention." The intention to do harm; the intention to commit an illegal or immoral act. *Compare with* **Animus nocendi, Dolus malus, Mens rea,** and **Scienter.**

Animus manendi. a´nēmūs manān´dē. â´nimus munen´dī. *n.* "Intention to remain." The intention to stay somewhere indefinitely. *Animus manendi* is generally considered a prerequisite in private international law for the establishment of domicile and is sufficient to establish domicile at the moment when the person's residency in a state coincides with *animus manendi. E.g.*, "In the first place, I would point out that, according to the case-law of the court, a person resides in the place in which he has established, with *animus manendi*, the 'permanent' or 'habitual' centre of his interests." Opinion of Advocate General Mancini, *Schaflein v. Commission*, [1988] E.C.R. 4475, ¶ 4. An alternative formulation is **Animus remanendi.**

Animus nocendi. a´nēmūs nōkān´dē. â´nimus nasen´dī. *n.* "Intention to harm." An intention to commit a harmful act against another.

Animus obligandi. a´nēmūs ōblēgan´dē. â´nimus abligân´dī. *n.* "Intention to obligate." An intention to assume an obligation toward another or the international community as a whole.

Animus occupandi. a´nēmūs ōkkūpan´dē. â´nimus akyūpân´dī. *n.* "Intention to occupy." An intention to occupy or control territory and to assert sovereignty over it. In addition to physical occupation or control over a disputed territory, the state must generally demonstrate *animus occupandi* to prove its sovereignty over the territory. *E.g.*, "It is beyond doubt that by immemorial usage having the force of law, besides the *animus occupandi*, the actual, and not the nominal, taking of possession is a necessary condition of occupation." *Sovereignty over Clipperton Island Case* (Fr. v. Mex.), Award of Jan. 28, 1931, 26 AM. J.INT'L L. 390, 393 (1932). An alternative term is **Animus possidendi.** *Compare with* **Animus domini.** *Contrast with* **Animu derelinquendi** and **Animus disponendi.** *See also* **Corporis possessio.**

Animus possidendi. a´nēmūs pōssēdān´dē. â´nimus pasiden´dī. *n.* "Intention to possess." An alternative term for **Animus occupandi.** *E.g.*, "Effective possession, the objective element of a '*corpore possessio*,' should be accompanied by a subjective element consisting of the '*animus possidendi*.'..." *Maritime Delimitation and Territorial Questions* (Qatar v. Bahr.), 2001 I.C.J. Rep. 40, 177, ¶ 100 (Merits) (Judge Bedjaoui, dissenting).

Animus remanendi. a´nēmūs rāmanān´dē. â´nimus remânen´dī. *n.* "Intention to remain." An alternative formulation of **Animus manendi**.

Animus restituendi. a´nēmūs rāstētūān´dē. â´nimus restičūen´dī. *n.* "Intention to restore." (1) An intention to give restitution in compensation for a violation of another's rights. (2) Generally, an intention to restore something to the possession of its former owner or possessor. *See also* **Restitutio in integrum**.

Animus revertendi. a´nēmūs rāwārtān´dē. â´nimus revɜrten´dī. *n.* "Intention to return." (1) The intention to return to a place visited before. *E.g.*, "To be regarded as domiciled in a foreign State, a person must not only be resident there but also have the intention of remaining there permanently and have lost the *animus revertendi*." *Johnston v. Ireland*, 9 E.H.R.R. 203, 208, ¶ 20 (1987). (2) The intention to return something borrowed, taken, annexed, or occupied. *E.g.*, "General principles of maritime and international law dictate that an abandonment constitutes a repudiation of ownership, and that a party taking possession under salvage operations may be considered a finder under the doctrine of '*animus revertendi*,' i.e., the owner has no intention of returning. Ownership in the vessel would then vest in the finder by operation of law." *Treasure Salvors, Inc. v. Abandoned Sailing Vessel Believed to Be Nuestra Señora de Atocha*, 408 F. Supp. 907, 909 (S.D. Fla. 1976) (U.S.). *Compare with* **Animus derelinquendi** and **Animus disponendi**.

Animus revocandi. a´nēmūs rāwōkan´dē. â´nimus revōkân´dī. *n.* "Intent to revoke." An intent to revoke or rescind, usually used in the context of an offeror's intent to rescind a will or an offer to form a contract.

Animus signandi. a´nēmūs sēgnan´dē. â´nimus signân´dī. *n.* "Intention to sign." The intention to execute a legal instrument such as a contract or treaty.

Anno regni. an´nō rāg´nē. â´nō reg´nī. *n.* "In the year of the reign." In a designated year (*e.g.*, the first, second, etc.) of the reign of a specific monarch. *Anno regni* is most commonly used in dating statutes in the monarchical states of Europe. Sometimes abbreviated **A.R.**

Annus. an´nūs. â´nus. *n.* "Year." (1) The year. (2) One calendar year.

Ante. an´tā. ân´tē. *adv.* "Before." Before; earlier. *Ante* is sometimes used as a citation signal in the same manner as *supra* to indicate that the cited source occurs earlier in the same work. *E.g.*, "The Court [majority] acknowledges that its decision [in this case] is contrary to the Federal Government's 'preference for the taxing method adopted by the international community.' *Ante*, at 2952." *Container Corporation of Am. v. Franchise Tax Bd.*, 463 U.S.

159, 202 (1983) (Justice Powell, dissenting). *Compare with* **Opera citato** and **Supra (citatum)**. *Contrast with* **Post**.

Ante factum. an´tā fak´tūm. ân´tē fâk´tum. *adj.* or *adv.* "Before the event." Occurring before the event in question. *E.g.*, "The Court gives an advisory opinion endowed with the limited force proper to it. Such force as provisions, agreements, statutes or rules emanating from States or organizations may bestow on the opinion *ante factum* or *ex post facto* neither diminishes nor enlarges the jurisdiction of the Court." *Advisory Opinion on the Application for Review of Judgement No. 158 of the United Nations Administrative Tribunal*, 1973 I.C.J. Rep. 166, 275 (Judge De Castro, dissenting). *Compare with* **Ante hoc**. *Contrast with* **Ex post facto** and **Post hoc**.

Ante hoc. an´tā hōk. ân´tē hak. *adj.* or *adv.* "Before this." Occurring before the event in question. *Compare with* **Ante factum**. *Contrast with* **Ex post facto** and **Post hoc**.

Apertum factum. apār´tūm fak´tūm. âpɜr´tum fâk´tum. *n.* "Open act." A public act or course of action.

Apocrisarius. apōkrēsa´rē-ūs. âpakriza´rē-us. *n.* [*pl.* **Apocrisarii.** apōkrēsa´rē-ē. âpakriza´rī.] "Delegate." During the late Roman Empire, *Apocrisarii* were envoys of the Pope who took up residence on foreign courts to represent the Holy See. In some early Christian empires, the *Apocrisarius* was granted the rank of a Court Minister. In modern ecclesiastical practice, an *Apocrisarius* may on request advice on matters of religious law or ethics. An alternative spelling is **Apocrisiarius**.

Apocrisiarius. apōkrēsē-a´rē-ūs. âpakrizē-a´rē-us. *n.* [*pl.* **Apocrisiarii.** apōkrēsē-a´rē-ē. âpakrizē-a´rī.] "Delegate." An alternative spelling of **Apocrisarius**.

Appellatio. appālla´tēō. âpelā´šō. *n.* "Appeal." An appeal from a lower tribunal to a higher one.

Aqua. a´kwa. a´kwu. *n.* "Water." (1) Water. (2) A watercourse.

Aqua currens. a´kwa kūr´rāns. a´kwu kɜ´renz. *n.* "Running water." Flowing water, as in a river or stream. An alternative term is **Aqua profluens**.

Aqua currit et debet currere ut currere solebat. a´kwa kūr´rēt āt dā´bāt kūr´rārā ūt kūr´rārā sōlā´bat. â´kwu kɜ´rit et de´but kɜ´rɜrē ut kɜ´rɜrē sō´lubât. "Water runs and ought to run as it was accustomed to run." A maxim meaning that an upstream landowner or state cannot unreasonably interfere with the downstream landowner's or state's use of riparian water or other watercourses.

Aqua dulcis. a´kwa dūl´kēs. a´kwu dɜl´sis. *n.* “Sweet water.” Fresh water. *Contrast with* **Aqua salsa.**

Aqua fontanea. a´kwa fōnta´nā-a. a´kwu fantâ´nē-u. *n.* “Fountain water.” Water from a spring or aquifer.

Aqua frisca. a´kwu fris´ku. *n. Ital.* Freshly drawn water; cold water. Although commonly cited in law dictionaries as a Latin term meaning “fresh water,” this term is not in fact proper Latin. The correct Latin for fresh water is **Aqua dulcis.**

Aqua profluens. a´kwa prō´flūāns. a´kwu prōflū´enz. *n.* “Running water.” An alternative term for **Aqua currens.**

Aqua salsa. a´kwa sal´sa. a´kwu sal´su. *n.* “Salted water.” Salt water; sea water. *Contrast with* **Aqua dulcis.**

Arbiter nihil extra compromissum facere potest. ar´bētār nē´hēl āks´tra kōm-prōmēs´sūm fa´kārā pō´tāst. ar´bītɜr nī´hil eks´tru kamprumī´sum fâ´sɜrē pō´test. “The arbitrator can do nothing beyond the agreement to arbitrate.” A maxim deriving from Roman civil law meaning that in voluntary arbitration, the arbitral tribunal (being an instrument of private dispute settlement) has no power to decide matters outside the scope of the dispute that the parties submitted to the tribunal to resolve. This doctrine follows from the maxim: “Arbitration is a creature of contract.” *E.g.*, “The first ground for annulment listed in the article is that ‘the tribunal has exceeded its powers.’ This is perhaps the oldest and most universally recognized ground for nullity. The maxim of Roman law *arbiter nihil extra compromissum facere potest* has been adopted in international law.” International Law Commission, *Commentary on the Draft Convention on Arbitral Procedure*, at 107, UN Doc. A/CN.4/92 (1955). An alternative formulation is **Extra compromisum arbiter nihil facere potest.**

Arbitramentum aequum tribuit cuique suum. arbētramān´tūm ī´kū-ūm trē´būēt kūē´kwā sū´ūm. arbitrumen´tum e´kwum tri´bwit kwi´kwā sū´um. *Med.* “An equitable arbitration renders each person’s due.” A maxim meaning that an arbitral tribunal should strive to do justice to the parties in applying the law properly.

Arbitrio boni iudicis. arbēt´rēō bō´nē yū´dēkēs. arbit´ryō bō´nī jū´disis. *adv.* (often used as a *n.*) “By the opinion of a good judge.” A judicial act not strictly in conformity with the law but rather according to the judgment and discretion of the judge or tribunal. *E.g.*, “If indeed a Court of Equity in England did possess the unbounded jurisdiction which has been thus generally ascribed to it, of correcting, controlling, moderating, and even superceding the law...[i]t would literally place the whole rights and property of the community under the arbitrary will of the Judge, acting, if you please, *arbitrio boni judicis*, and, it may be, *ex aequo et bono*, according to his own notions and conscience; but still acting with a despotic and sovereign authority." Joseph Story, 1 COMMENTARIES ON EQUITY JURISPRUDENCE AS ADMINISTERED IN ENGLAND AND AMERICA § 19 (1886). *Compare with* **Ex aequo et bono.** *See also* **Ex arbitrio (boni) iudicis.**

A

Arbitrium. arbē´trē-ūm. arbi´trē-um. *n.* "Judgment." The award of an arbitrator or arbitral tribunal.

Arbitrium est iudicium. arbēt´rē-ūm āst yūdē´kē-ūm. arbi´trē-um est jūdi´šum. "The decision of the arbitrator is a judgment." A maxim meaning that the lawful award of an arbitral tribunal, once recognized by a court of competent jurisdiction, is enforceable at law as if it had been an award of the recognizing court itself. *Compare with* **Compromissarii sunt iudices.**

Arcana imperii. arka´na ēmpā´rē-ē. arkâ´nu impe´rī. *n. pl.* "Secrets of the empire." State secrets.

Arguendo. argūān´dō. argyūen´dō. *ger. v.* "Arguing." (1) For the sake of argument only, without admitting the truth of the point asserted. *E.g.*, "[W]ere I to agree with the Court—*arguendo*—that a few turtle eggs and signal lights do, indeed, have greater *gravitas* than the voyage of HNLMS Lynx, that would still not get me across to the other shore. In my opinion, these are token acts of no legal value." *Sovereignty over Pulau Ligitan and Pulau Sipadan* (Indon. v. Malay.), 2002 I.C.J. Rep. 625, 697, ¶ 21 (Judge Franck, dissenting). (2) In the course of making an argument.

Argumento. argūmān´tō. argyūmen´tō. *n.* "By way of argument." *Argumento* is the instrumental ablative of the noun **Argumentum.** Thus, for example, an *argumentum a contrario* ("argument from the opposite"), when expressed as *argumento a contrario*, becomes "by means of argument from the opposite."

Argumentum. argūmān´tūm. argyūmen´tum. *n.* [*pl.* **Argumenta.** argūmān´ta. argyūmen´tu.] "Argument." (1) A claim or contention; a course of reasoning. (2) An argument; a dispute. *See also* **Argumento.**

Argumentum a contrario. argūmān´tūm a kōntra´rēō. argyūmen´tum ā kantra´ryō. *n.* "Argument from the contrary." An argument for different treatment made by negative reasoning from another argument. An *argumentum a contrario* may rely on reasoning *a contrario sensu*. *E.g.*, "The fact that the Applicant's claim is being qualified as the 'principal' claim determines the counter-claim, by the logic of *argumentum a contrario*, as a non-principal claim, a lesser claim." *Application of the Convention on the Prevention and Punishment of the Crime of Genocide* (Bosn. & Herz. v. Yugo.), 1997 I.C.J. Rep. 243, 262, ¶ 1 (declaration of Judge *ad hoc* Kreća). *Contrast with* **Argumentum a simili.** *See also* **A contrario** and **A contrario sensu.**

Argumentum a maiore ad minus. argūmān´tūm a mayō´rā ad mē´nūs. argyūmen´tum ā mâjō´rē âd mī´nus. "From the larger scale argument to the smaller one." A kind of argument reasoning that what is true on a large (or important or consequential) scale is equally true on a smaller (or less important or consequential) scale. A rare alternative spelling sometimes favored by Cicero is *a maiori ad minus*. *E.g.*, "If granting privileges is not a matter of rights, is it not then true that the bestower of privilege is entitled—*argumento a majori ad minus*—not only to discretion but also to discrimination in terms of substance as well as in terms of procedure?" *E.B. v. France*, 47 E.H.R.R. 21, ¶ O-II15 (Judge Zupančič, dissenting). *See also* **Argumentum a minore ad maius.**

Argumentum a minore ad maius. argūmān´tūm a mēnō´rā ad ma´yūs. argyūmen´tum ā mīnō´rē âd mâ´jus. "From the smaller scale argument to the larger one." A kind of argument reasoning that what is true on a small (or specific) scale is equally true on a larger (or more general) scale. *See also* **Argumentum a maiore ad minus.**

Argumentum a simili. argūmān´tūm a sē´mēlē. argyūmen´tum ā si´myūlī. *n.* "Argument from a similar thing." An argument sustained by use of analogy to a comparable scenario or the similarity of one case or the characteristics of one thing to another. *Contrast with* **Argumentum a contrario.** *See also* **Argumentum a simili valet in lege.**

Argumentum a simili valet in lege. argūmān´tūm a sē´mēlē wa´lāt ēn lā´gā. argyūmen´tum ā si´myulī vâ´let in le´jē. "Argument by analogy prevails in law." A maxim meaning that, when no law is directly on point, an argument making an analogy to some law relating to a similar subject or matter is considered persuasive.

Argumentum ab auctoritate est fortissimum (in lege). argūmān´tūm ab ôktōrēta´tā āst fōrtēs´sēmūm (ēn lā´gā). argyūmen´tum âb ăktōritā´tē est fōrti´simum (in le´jē). "Argument from authority is the most forceful (in law)." A maxim meaning that arguments based on positive sources of authority or precedents, or the opinions of respected legal authorities, are considered the most persuasive kind of arguments.

Argumentum ab impossibili. argūmān´tūm ab ēmpōssē´bēlē. argyūmen´tum âb impasi´bilī. *n.* "Argument from impossibility." An argument that draws its force from the impossibility of the alternatives to the position advocated.

Argumentum ab inconvenienti. argūmān´tūm ab ēnkōnwānē-ān´tē. argyūmen´tum âb inkunvēnē-en´tī. *n.* "Argument from inconvenience." An argument that draws its force from the inconvenience or other undesirable consequences of the available alternatives to the position advocated. *Compare with* **Argumentum ad consequentiam.** *See also* **Ab inconvenienti** and **Ex incommodo.**

Argumentum ad baculum. argūmān´tūm ad ba´kūlūm. argyūmen´tum âd bâ´kyūlum. *n.* "Argument to the staff." An argument based on coercion or violence as its dominant reason. An argument that negative consequences such as punishment will follow upon not accepting the argument is an *argumentum ad baculum*. An *argumentum ad baculum* is a special case of the negative form of an **Argumentum ad consequentiam.** An alternative formulation is **Argumentum baculinum.**

Argumentum ad captandum. argūmān´tūm ad kaptan´dūm. argyūmen´tum âd kâptân´dum. *n.* "Argument for the catching." An argument that relies for its force on an appeal to popular beliefs or emotion, or on its ability to win popular approval. *Compare with* **Argumentum ad populum.**

Argumentum ad consequentiam. argūmān´tūm ad kōnsākwān´tē-am. argyūmen´tum âd kansekwen´tē-um. *n.* "Argument to the consequence." An argument that something is true or false based whether it leads to desirable or undesirable consequences. *Compare with* **Argumentum ab inconvenienti.**

Argumentum ad crumenam. argūmān´tūm ad krūmā´nam. argyūmen´tum âd krū´menum. *n.* "Argument to the purse." (1) An argument drawing conclusions based on one's wealth or lack thereof. (2) An argument that appeals to the desire to save money or avoid expense. Generally, the term is used to refer to the logical fallacy of assuming that great wealth gives one special insight or virtue, or that poverty denotes the absence of insight or virtue. An example of an *argumentum ad crumenam* would be a claim that, by virtue of the economic power of the G8 countries, those countries alone should be entrusted with setting monetary policy for the developing world, because wealthy countries are most likely to understand how to achieve economic growth. *Contrast with* **Argumentum ad lazarum.**

Argumentum ad hominem. argūmān´tūm ad hō´mēnām. argyūmen´tum âd ha´minum. *n.* "Argument to the man." An argument that constitutes a personal attack or relates to personal matters instead of addressing the merits of the relevant issue. *See also* **Ad hominem.**

Argumentum ad ignorantiam. argūmān´tūm ad ēgnōran´tē-am. argyūmen´tum âd ignōran´tē-um. *n.* "Argument to ignorance." An argument based on the opponent's ignorance of the subject in dispute. This is a special case of **Argumentum ad hominem.**

Argumentum ad invidiam. argūmān´tūm ad ēnwē´dē-am. argyūmen´tum âd invi´dē-um. *n.* "Argument to hatred." An argument that appeals to popular hatred or prejudice to sustain its rationale. This is a special case of **Argumentum ad captandum.**

A

Argumentum ad lazarum. argūmān´tūm ad la´sarūm. argyūmen´tum âd lâ´zɜrum. *n.* "Argument to Lazarus." An argument drawing conclusions based on poverty. Generally, the term is used to refer to the logical fallacy of assuming that poverty gives one special insight or virtue. An example of an *argumentum ad lazarum* would be a claim that, because developing states have the greatest incentive to understand and seek their own development, lenders should not impose any constraints on loans to such states. *Contrast with* **Argumentum ad crumenam.**

Argumentum ad misericordiam. argūmān´tūm ad mēsārēkōr´dē-am. argyūmen´tum âd mizɜrikōr´dē-um. *n.* "Argument to pity." An argument that derives its force from an appeal to a sense of pity or sympathy.

Argumentum ad populum. argūmān´tūm ad pō´pūlūm. argyūmen´tum âd pa´pyūlum. *n.* "Argument to the people." An argument that derives its force from the popularity of beliefs on which it is based. An argument that, if most people believe something to be true, it therefore must be true, is an *argumentum ad populum. Compare with* **Argumentum ad captandum.**

Argumentum ad rem. argūmān´tūm ad rām. argyūmen´tum âd rem. *n.* "Argument to the matter." An argument directed to the point in dispute.

Argumentum ad verecundiam. argūmān´tūm ad wārākūn´dē-am. argyūmen´tum âd verukun´dē-um. *n.* "Argument to modesty." An argument that appeals to the testimony of an authority speaking or writing outside of his field. The term appears to originate in irony.

Argumentum baculinum. argūmān´tūm bakūlē´nūm. argyūmen´tum bâkyūli´num. *n. Neo.* "Argument of the staff." An alternative formulation of **Argumentum ad baculum.**

Argumentum circulum. argūmān´tūm kēr´kūlūm. argyūmen´tum sɜr´kyūlum. *n.* "Circular argument." A tautology; an argument that proves nothing because it assumes its own necessary premise. An argument, for example, that "treaties that provide they may never be denounced may in fact never be legally denounced due to the binding nature of the treaty" is unproved as an *argumentum circulum.*

Argumentum ex concesso. argūmān´tūm āks kōnkās´sō. argyūmen´tum eks kanse´sō. *n.* "Argument from an admission." An argument based on a prior admission or confession of one's opponent.

Argumentum ex silentio. argūmān´tūm āks sēlān´tēō. argyūmen´tum eks silen´tēō. *n.* "Argument from silence." (1) An argument drawing conclusions from an opponent's failure to respond to a point or allegation. (2) An argument drawing conclusions from the lack of contrary evidence.

Armata vis. arma´ta wēs. arma´tu vis. *n.* "Armed force." An alternative formulation of **Vis armata**.

Arrestatio navium. arrāsta´tēō na´wē-ūm. arestā´šō nâ´vē-um. *n.* "Arrest of seagoing vessels." The seizure of a seagoing vessel. This term is usually used with reference to the law of prize.

Arresto facto super bonis mercatorum alienigenorum. arrās´tō fak´tō sū´pār bō´nēs mārkatō´rūm alē-ānēgānō´rūm. ares´tō fâk´tō sū´pɜr bō´nis mɜrkutō´rum ālē-enijenō´rūm. *n.* "Arrest of the goods of foreign merchants." An English writ authorizing the seizure of the goods of an alien of the nationality of a foreign state that has expropriated goods of an English subject. This writ was a kind of countermeasure designed to compensate the English subject for the unlawful taking when the English subject was denied restitution by the foreign state.

Ars aequi et boni. ars ī´kwē āt bō´nē. arz e´kwī et bō´nī. *n.* "The art of what is equitable and good." The technique of determining what is equitable and fair. This term is used to elaborate on the definition of *ius* in the preamble to Justinian's *Digest* (1.1.pr). *See also* **Ius est ars aequi et boni.**

Assensio mentium. assān´sēō mān´tē-ūm. asen´sēō men´šum. *n.* "Agreement of the minds." Mutual consent or agreement; a meeting of the minds.

Assumpsit. assūmp´sēt. asump´sit. *v.* (commonly used as a *n.*) "He has promised." A basis for the recognition of a legal duty flowing from a promise to perform some action. Formerly in some countries, a formal requirement that the debtor must recognize the claimed debt as a precondition to its enforceability.

Auctoritate iudicis. ôktōrēta´tā yū´dēkēs. ăktōritā´tē jū´disis. *adv.* "By judicial authority." Based on the established authority and jurisdiction of the tribunal.

Audaces fortuna iuvat. ôda´kās fōrtū´na yū´wat. ădâ´sēz fōrtū´nu jū´vut. "Fortune succors the bold." A maxim predicting that those making unexpected or hazardous maneuvers or choices in pursuit of gain thereby increase their chances of success.

Audi alteram partem. ô´dē al´tāram par´tām. ă´dī âl´terum par´tum. *imp. v.* "Listen to the other side." A principle of due process, originating in Augustine of Hippo's views of natural law, under which all parties before an international tribunal must have an opportunity to be heard and are treated equally under the law. *E.g.*, "Although as a judicial body the Court is conscious of the importance of the principle expressed in the maxim *audi alteram partem*, it does not consider that this principle precludes the Court from taking account of statements made subsequently to the oral proceedings. . . ." *Nuclear Test Cases* (Austl. v. Fr.), 1974 I.C.J. Rep. 252, ¶ 33 (Judgment). *Compare with* **Audiatur et altera pars.**

Audiatur et altera pars. ôdē-a´tūr āt al´tāra pars. ădē-ā´tɜr et âl´teru parz. *imp. v.* "May the other side also be heard." A principle of due process according to which parties before an authoritative tribunal must have an equal opportunity to be heard and their arguments considered under the law. *E.g.*, "All these [pleading] rules [of the Hague Conventions and World Court] are merely different methods designed to ensure that the judge should hear and consider what each party may have to say on the dispute as fully as possible—not only on the question at issue, but also on the statements of its opponent. They constitute a more or less elaborate implementation of the fundamental principle: *audiatur et altera pars*." Bin Cheng, General Principles of Law as Applied by International Courts and Tribunals 293 (1953). *Compare with* **Audi alteram partem.**

Aut. ôt. ăt. *conj.* "Either/or." Either; or (disjunctive). *Aut* is used where one or another option is possible, but not both. *Compare with* **Vel.**

Aut dedere aut iudicare. ôt dā´dārā ôt yūdēka´rā. ăt de´dɜrē ăt jūdika´rē. *imp. v.* "Either to deliver or to adjudge." A principle requiring states to extradite or prosecute alleged violators of international criminal laws. Under the principle, if an individual alleged to have violated a national or international criminal law is found in a given state, that state must choose between extraditing that individual for trial in another state or before an international criminal tribunal on one hand, or prosecuting the individual itself on the other. *Aut dedere aut iudicare* may become applicable by treaty obligation, where it is commonly used to deal with the suppression of specific international offenses (*e.g.*, the UN Convention against Torture and Other Cruel, Inhuman, or Degrading Treatment or Punishment arts. 5.2, 8), or, in some cases, under customary international law to punish crimes giving rise to universal jurisdiction. *E.g.*, "In the case of *war crimes*...there is specific conventional international law in support of the proposition that States are entitled to assert jurisdiction over acts committed abroad: the relevant provision is Article 146 of the IVth Geneva Convention, which laws down the principle *aut dedere aut judicare* for war crimes committed against civilians." *Arrest Warrant of 11 April 2000* (Congo v. Belg.), 2002 I.C.J. Rep. 3, 173-74, ¶ 59 (Judge Van den Wyngaert, dissenting). An alternative phrase is **Aut dedere aut prosequi.** *Compare with* **Aut punire aut dedere** and **Primo prosequi, secundo dedere.**

A

Aut dedere aut prosequi. ôt dā´dārā ôt prō´sākwē. ăt de´dɜrē ăt pra´sekwī. "Either to deliver or to prosecute." An alternative phrase for **Aut dedere aut iudicare.** *E.g.*, "There are...certain indications that a universal criminal jurisdiction for certain international crimes is clearly not regarded as unlawful. The duty to prosecute under those treaties which contain the *aut dedere aut prosequi* provisions opens the door to a jurisdiction based on the heinous nature of the crime rather than on links of territoriality or nationality...." *Arrest Warrant of 11 April 2000* (Congo v. Belg.), 2002 I.C.J. Rep. 3, 76, ¶ 46 (separate opinion of Judge Higgins).

Aut punire aut dedere. ôt pūnē´rā ôt dā´dārā. ăt pyūnī´rē ăt de´dɜrē. "Either to punish or to deliver." A principle according to which a state may assume an affirmative obligation (usually by treaty) either to punish a person shown to have violated an applicable principle of law or to extradite the person to another state for punishment. This principle has sometimes been incorporated into treaties and UN Security Council resolutions regarding terrorists and other violators of international law. *Compare with* **Aut dedere aut iudicare.**

Auxiliorum principali sequitur. ôksēlēō´rūm prēnkēpa´lē sā´kwētūr. ăgzilēō´rum prinsipâ´lī se´kwitɜr. "The assistant follows the principal." A phrase meaning that a subsidiary point follows naturally from acceptance of the principal point, as when a tribunal exercises jurisdiction over matters subsidiary to the main issue in dispute as necessarily intertwined with the resolution of that main issue.

B

Bello pacta cedunt republicae. bāl´lō pak´ta kā´dūnt rāpūb´lēkī. be´lō pâk´tu sē´dunt repub´likā. "In war, agreements yield to the state." A maxim meaning that the initiation of a state of war may render some contracts, such as those involving the sale of goods or services to, or purchase from, the opposing belligerent, unenforceable.

Bellum. bāl´lūm. be´lum. *n.* "War." (1) A war, literally or figurative. (2) An armed conflict.

Bellum iniustum. bāl´lūm ēnyūs´tūm. be´lum injus´tum. *n.* "Unjust war." A war believed to have been commenced based on morally unjustifiable and, therefore, in some views illegal, grounds. UN Charter Articles 2(4) and 51 imply that all use of armed force except in cases of individual and collective self-defense is illegal, if not unjust. *Compare with* **Bellum nefarium.** *Contrast with* **Bellum iustum.**

Bellum iustum. bāl´lūm yūs´tūm. be´lum jus´tum. *n.* "Just war." A war believed to have been commenced based on morally justifiable and, therefore, in some views legal, grounds. UN Charter Articles 2(4) and 51 imply that the just war doctrine is limited to the use of force in individual or collective self-defense. However, the doctrine survives in the sense that even a defensive use of armed force must be necessary and proportional to the threat posed in order to qualify as *bellum iustum*. *See also* **Bellum iustum et pium.** *Contrast with* **Bellum iniustum** and **Bellum nefarium.**

Bellum iustum et pium. bāl´lūm yūs´tūm āt pē´ūm. be´lum jus´tum et pī´um. *n.* "Just and pious war." A war believed to have been commenced based on morally and theologically justifiable and, therefore, in some views legal, grounds. *See also* **Bellum iustum.**

Bellum nefarium. bāl´lūm nāfa´rē-ūm. be´lum nefā´rē-um. *n.* "Impious war." A war believed to have been commenced based on morally unjustifiable and, therefore, in some views unlawful, grounds. *Compare with* **Bellum iniustum.** *Contrast with* **Bellum iustum** and **Bellum iustum et pium.**

Bellum omnium in omnia. bäl´lūm ōm´nē-ūm ēn ōm´nē-a. be´lum am´nē-um in am´nē-u. *n.* "War of all against all." An alternative formulation of **Bellum omnium contra omnes.**

B

Bellum omnium contra omnes. bäl´lūm ōm´nē-ūm kōn´tra ōm´näs. be´lum am´nē-um kan´tru am´nēz. *n.* "War of all against all." A state of total or permanent war or hostility, either active or suspended, among all states. In *The Leviathan* (1651), Thomas Hobbes characterized the state of anarchy in these terms. In *Notes on the State of Virginia* (1782), Thomas Jefferson applied this observation to the then-current state of international relations using the alternative formulation **Bellum omnium in omnia.** *E.g.*, "After the proclamation of sovereignty and independence of Bosnia and Herzegovina by the incomplete parliament of Bosnia and Herzegovina, the civil war became, in my opinion, an international armed conflict.... This was *bellum omnium contra omnes.*" *Application of the Convention on the Prevention and Punishment of the Crime of Genocide* (Bosn. & Herz. v. Yugo.), 1996 I.C.J. Rep. 595, 765, ¶ 100 (Preliminary Objections) (Judge *ad hoc* Kreća, dissenting).

Beneficium. bānāfē´kē-ūm. benufi´šum. *n.* "Benefit." A benefit, right, or remedy provided by law.

Beneficium competentiae. bānāfē´kē-ūm kōmpātān´tē-ī. benufi´šum kamputen´šā. *n.* "Benefit of competency." In Roman civil law, a debtor's right to pay his creditors no more than the amount that will leave the debtor a reasonable maintenance for living. By analogy, some measure of forgiveness of an insolvent developing state's international debt in lieu of a strict enforcement of the debt.

Benignius leges interpretandae sunt quo voluntas earum conservetur. bānēg´nē-ūs lā´gās ēntārprātan´dī sūnt kwō wōlūn´tas ā-a´rūm kōnsārwā´tūr. bunig´nē-us le´jēz intɜrpretân´dā sunt kwō va´luntas ē´rum kansɜr´vutɜr. "Laws are to be liberally interpreted to preserve their intent." A maxim meaning that language in a legal instrument such as a statute or treaty should not be read literally if a literal reading would nullify the intent of the drafters, but rather should be read in a manner consistent with that intent.

Billa exonerationis. bēl´la āksōnāratēō´nēs. bi´lu egzanɜrāšō´nis. *n. Neo.* "Bill of lading." A bill of lading; a shipping document issued by a carrier to acknowledge the receipt of goods shipped and that can be used as a document of title (often negotiable) by the intended recipient of the shipped goods to present evidence to the shipper of the right to take delivery. The term *billa* is pseudo-Latin.

Bis. bēs. bis. *adv.* "Secondly." An adverbial number (the second) usually inserted into a consecutively numbered series by way of amendment. In amending an existing treaty, drafters wishing to insert a new article between existing articles might use *bis* to renumber, so that a new article inserted between articles 6 and 7 becomes "article 6*bis*." Article 6 may or may not be renamed article 6*semel*. The next addition after article 6*bis* but prior to article 7 would be named article 6*ter*. *See* the Appendix for a list of Latin adverbial numbers commonly used in international law. *See also* **Semel** and **Ter**.

B

Bis dat qui cito dat. bēs dat kwē kē´tō dat. biz dât kwī sī´tō dât. "He who gives swiftly gives twice." A maxim meaning that something given expeditiously is far preferable to the same thing given belatedly. The maxim is often used in the sense that the highest form of justice or generosity is that given promptly. *E.g.*, "Having used less time than I am entitled to, and as you know, I use Latin a lot, there is another Latin saying I would like to say, to use *bis dat qui cito dat*, who speaks briefly gains double [*sic*]." *Prosecutor v. Kvocka*, ICTY Case No. IT-98-30/1, Trial Transcript of July 18, 2001, at 12592.

Bona confiscata. bō´na kōnfēska´ta. bō´nu kanfiskā´tu. *n. pl.* "Confiscated goods." Personal property that has been expropriated or confiscated by the state.

Bona fide. bō´na fē´dā. bō´nu fid. *adj.* "In good faith." Having sincere or benevolent intent; lacking in deceptive or fraudulent intent. *E.g.*, "In the process of *bona fide* negotiations, concessions are made, facts are accepted, compromises are worked out, admissions and apologies are offered. Documents embodying such acts may well be exchanged. It is important that all this should take place on a footing of openness and equality." *Land and Maritime Boundary Between Cameroon and Nigeria* (Camer. v. Nig.), 1998 I.C.J. Rep. 275, 375 (Preliminary Objections) (Vice President Weeramantry, dissenting). *Compare with* **Optima fide**. *See also* **Bona fides**.

Bona fides. bō´na fē´dās. bō´nu fī´dēz. *n.* "Good faith." Sincere or benevolent intent; intent lacking in deceptive or fraudulent purpose. *E.g.*, "Modern international law does not recognize the survival of a right of sovereignty based solely on historic title; not, in any event, after an exercise of self-determination conducted in accordance with the requisites of international law, the *bona fides* of which has received international recognition by the political organs of the United Nations." *Sovereignty over Pulau Ligitan and Pulau Sipadan* (Indon. v. Malay.), 2001 I.C.J. Rep. 575, 657 (separate opinion of Judge Franck). *Compare with* **Conscientia illaesa**. *Contrast with* **Mala fides**.

Bona mores. A common misspelling of **Boni mores**.

Bona non intelliguntur nisi deducto aere alieno. bō´na nōn ēntēllēgūn´tūr nē´sē dādūk´tō ī´rā alē-ā´nō. bō´nu intelijun´tɜr ni´zē dēduk´tō ā´rē ālē-e´nō. "No goods are recognized unless debts have been removed." A maxim meaning that debts due must be satisfied before a debtor may claim the benefit of its assets.

B

Bona vacantia. bō´na wakan´tē-a. bō´nu vukân´šu. *n. pl.* "Unowned goods." Property (usually, personal property) having no owner definitely determinable by law; unowned property. "It should not be forgotten that, as the Permanent Mandates Commission had declared, the assets transferred by Germany (railways, tramways, ports, etc.) and public assets of all kinds (mines, *bona vacantia*, non-private waterways, etc.) have remained the exclusive property of the Namibian people and, since these are assets in the public domain, there can be no bar of limitation to their restitution." *Advisory Opinion on the Legal Consequences for States of the Continued Presence of South Africa in Namibia (South West Africa) Notwithstanding Security Council Resolution 276 (1970)*, 1971 I.C.J. Rep. 16, 218 (separate opinion of Judge De Castro). An alternative formulation is **Vacantia bona**. *See also* **Res nullius**.

Bonae fidei. bō´nī fē´dāē. bō´nā fi´dē. *adv.* "Of good faith." In good faith; with an intent lacking in deceptive or fraudulent purpose. *See also* **Bona fides**.

Bonae fidei negotium. bō´nī fē´dāē nāgō´tē-ūm. bō´nu fi´dē negō´šum. *n.* "A good faith negotiation." The good faith intent to negotiate to resolve a dispute or conclude a treaty or other agreement.

Boni iudicis est ampliare iurisdictionem. bō´nē yū´dēkēs āst amplē-a´rā yūrēsdēktēō´nām. bō´nī jū´disis est âmplē-a´rē jɜrisdikšō´num. "The quality of a good judge is to expand jurisdiction." A maxim meaning that a court or other tribunal should not hesitate to construe its own jurisdiction expansively to avoid injustice. Several judges of the International Court of Justice have cautioned against applying this maxim to the Court's own jurisdiction. *E.g.*, "[C]are needs to be used not to import the principle *boni judicis est ampliare jurisdictionem*; it is not considered to be applicable to the Court...." *Maritime Delimitation and Territorial Questions* (Qatar v. Bahr.), 1995 I.C.J. Rep. 6, 65-66 (Jurisdiction) (Judge Shahabuddeen, dissenting).

Boni mores. bō´nē mō´rās. bō´nī mō´rēz. *n. pl.* "Good behavior." (1) Virtue; high standards of ethical behavior. (2) A term broadly denoting good public policy, proper moral sentiment, or accepted customary practices that do not by themselves rise to the level of legal obligations. In some states, a contract must evidence *boni mores* to be considered valid or enforceable by, for example, not requiring any party to perform an illegal act. *E.g.*, "Arbitral tribunals have more often based their decisions on universal values in using various formulations such as 'good morals,' '*bonas mores*,' [*sic*] 'ethics of international trade' or 'transnational public policy.'...But it has been rightly stressed that Tribunals must be very cautious in this respect and must carefully check the objective existence of a particular transnational public policy rule in identifying it through international conventions, comparative law and arbitral awards." *World Duty Free Co., Ltd. v. Kenya*, ICSID Case No. ARB/00/7, ¶ 141, 46 I.L.M. 339, 360 (2007). *See also* **Bonos mores** and **Contra bonos mores (et decorum).**

B

Bonos mores. bō´nōs mō´rās. bō´nus mō´rēz. *n. pl. acc.* "Good behavior." The accusative form of **Boni mores.**

Bonum et aequum. bō´nūm āt ī´kwūm. bō´num et e´kwum. *n.* "The good and equitable." That which is just and fair.

Bonus fumus iuris. bō´nūs fū´mūs yū´rēs. bō´nus fyū´mus jɜ´ris. *n.* "Good smoke of law." An alternative formulation of **Fumus boni iuris.** *E.g.*, "At this stage, it is not a question of the effects, but rather of the bases [of the requested provisional measures]. These are: the *bonus fumus juris*, the *prima facie* merit of the Applicant's argument in support of its claim; and the danger in delay...." *Arrest Warrant of 11 April 2000* (Congo v. Belg.), 2000 I.C.J. Rep. 182, 216, ¶ 2 (Preliminary Measures) (Judge Rezek, dissenting).

Bonus paterfamilias. bō´nūs pa´tārfamē´lē-as. bō´nus pa´tɜrfumē´lē-us. *n.* "Good father of the family." A diligent guardian of the rights and interests of his or her ward. *E.g.*, "[T]here is no escaping the dialectical necessity of comparing the responsibility of an authority administering a country placed under its guardianship with that of other authorities entrusted with the administration of their own countries or the interests of their nationals. The latter are expected in public law to provide good government and, in the area of personal rights, to model their conduct on that of the *bonus paterfamilias*; they are for that reason the more to be blamed for any abuse of law or misuse of power." *Advisory Opinion on the Legal Consequences for States of the Continued Presence of South Africa in Namibia (South West Africa) Notwithstanding Security Council Resolution 276 (1970)*, 1971 I.C.J. Rep. 16, 88, ¶ 11 (separate opinion of Vice President Ammoun). *See also* **Paterfamilias.**

Brutum fulmen. brū´tūm fūl´mān. brū´tum fɜl´men OR -ful´men. *n. Med.* "Loud thunder." (1) An empty or ineffective threat. *Brutum Fulmen* was originally the name of a 1681 pamphlet by Thomas Lord Bishop of Lincoln denouncing the Papal Bull of Pius V, by which the Catholic Church excommunicated Queen Elizabeth of England to no serious effect. (2) A judgment, award, or provision of a law or legal document lacking in effect, especially in legal effect. *E.g.*, "It is unthinkable that the Parties, when they drafted this Article and included it in the Treaty, intended to forge a *brutum fulmen*, a provision for judicial review and decision dependent for its effect upon the momentary whim or interest of a defaulting party." *Advisory Opinion on Interpretation of Peace Treaties with Bulgaria, Hungary, and Romania*, 1950 I.C.J. Rep. 221, 237 (Judge Read, dissenting).

C

C.V. An abbreviation of **Curriculum vitae.**

Caeteris paribus. An alternative spelling of **Ceteris paribus.**

Capitula. kapē´tūla. kâpi´čūlu OR kâpi´tyūlu. *n. pl.* "Chapters." A collection of statutes or articles of law organized by heading.

Captio. kap´tēō. kâp´tēō OR kâp´šō. *n.* "Capture." (1) An arrest or capture of a person. (2) A capture or seizure of a vessel, cargo, or other property.

Caput lupinum. ka´pūt lūpē´nūm. kâ´put lū´pinum. *n.* (often used as an *adj.*) "The head of the wolf." In medieval English law, an outlawed felon could be declared *caput lupinum*, often by the pronouncement of a sentence of *Caput gerat lupinum* ("Let him bear the head of a wolf"), meaning that the convicted felon lacked any form of legal protection; anyone who encountered the felon might legally kill him or her as if he or she were a predatory wolf. While no such right exists in international law, the term has sometimes been applied to describe the plight of stateless persons, who have no sovereign from whom to claim protection.

Cardo controversiae. kar´dō kōntrōwār´sē-ī. kar´dō kantruvɜr´sē-ā. *n.* "The hinge of the controversy." The central point of an argument or dispute.

Casu consimili. ka´sū kōnsē´mēlē. kâ´zū- OR kā´sū kansi´milī. *adv.* "In a similar case." An abbreviated form of **In consimili casu.**

Casu quo. ka´sū kwō. kâ´zū- OR kā´sū kwō. *adj.* or *adv.* "In this case." In this case. *E.g.*, "[I]f in general this is the only just standpoint from which to view the right to ask and to grant the means of diplomatical intervention and in consequence *casu quo* of arbitration, how much the more where the recourse to the tribunals of the country was formally pledged and the right to ask for intervention solemnly renounced by contract...." *The Orinoco Steamship*

Company Case, U.S.-Venez. Cl. Comm'n, Award of Feb. 22, 1904, H.C.R. (Series 1), at 266 (Scott, 1916).

Casus. ka´sūs. kâ´zus. *n.* [*pl.* **Casus.** ka´sūs. kâ´zus.] "Event." An occurrence or event.

Casus belli. ka´sūs bāl´lē. kâ´zus be´lī. *n.* "Event of war." An event or action that furnishes a legal justification to a state to resort to armed force against another. *E.g.*, "[I]t must be observed that a State with great experience would not likely risk provoking a *casus belli* with a great Power...." *Corfu Channel Case* (U.K. v. Alb.), 1949 I.C.J. Rep. 4, 89 (Merits) (Judge Azevedo, dissenting). *See also* **Casus foederis** and **Iusta causa.**

Casus foederis. ka´sūs fœ´dārēs. kâ´zus fedē´ris. *n.* "An event in connection with a treaty." (1) An event or act, usually of a hostile kind, by one state toward another that triggers an alliance or other treaty obligation between the offended state and a third state. The third state may, by the *casus foederis*, be called upon to rise to the defense of the offended state. *E.g.*, "*Casus fœderis* is the event upon the occurrence of which it becomes the duty of one of the allies to render the promised assistance to the other. Thus in case of a defensive alliance the *casus foederis* occurs when war is declared or commenced against one of the allies." 1 Lassa Oppenheim, International Law 572, § 573 (1905). (2) A treaty clause specifying the circumstances under which such an alliance is triggered. (3) More generally, any provision of a treaty specifying a condition precedent for a right or duty to arise. *E.g.*, "In view of the clear and compelling terms of [the Exchange of Notes between the parties specifying that, if Iceland extends its fisheries jurisdiction, any resulting dispute may be referred to the ICJ], and of the fact that what is therein expressly specified as constituting the *casus foederis*, namely a further extension of Icelandic waters, has now occurred, it is difficult to make any sense of the contention that the obligation to have recourse to the Court is no longer operative because the 1961 Exchanges of Notes had achieved their purpose...." *Fisheries Jurisdiction Case* (U.K. v. Ice.), 1973 I.C.J. Rep. 3, 30–31, ¶ 12 (separate opinion of Judge Fitzmaurice). *See also* **Casus belli.**

Casus fortuitus. ka´sūs fōrtū-ē´tūs. kâ´zus fōrtū´itus. *n.* "Fortuitous event." (1) An accident or faultless mishap. (2) Any unexpected or fortuitous occurrence. *Compare with* **Casus improvisus** and **Casus insolitus.**

Casus improvisus. ka´sūs ēmprōwē´sūs. kâ´zus impruvī´zus. *n.* "Unforeseen event." (1) Any unforeseen or unexpected occurrence. (2) An event not provided for in an existing treaty, agreement, or law, and that therefore must be considered to fall outside of its scope or to fall within its scope only under a liberal or equitable reading. An alternative phrase is **Casus incogitati**. *Compare with* **Casus fortuitus** and **Casus insolitus**.

C

Casus incogitati. ka´sūs ēnkōgēta´tē. kâ´zus inkajitā´tī. *n. pl.* "Unconsidered events." An alternative (but plural) formulation of **Casus improvisus**.

Casus insolitus. ka´sūs ēnsō´lētūs. kâ´zus insa´litus OR -insōli´tus. *n.* "Unusual event." Any unusual or unexpected occurrence. An alternative phrase is **Casus rarior**. *Compare with* **Casus fortuitus** and **Casus improvisus**.

Casus omissus. ka´sūs ōmēs´sūs. kâ´zus ōmi´sus. *n.* "Omitted cause of action." A matter within the scope of a treaty or other agreement that is not directly addressed in the text, and that must therefore be the subject of interpretation.

Casus rarior. ka´sūs ra´rēōr. kâ´zus re´rēōr. *n.* [*pl.* **Casi rariores**. ka´sē rarēō´rās. kâ´zī rerēō´rēz.] "A rather rare event." An alternative phrase for **Casus insolitus**.

Causa. kô´sa. kă´zu. *n.* [*pl.* **Causae**. kô´sī. kă´zā.] "Cause." (1) Cause; something or someone that brings about some result or effect; an antecedent reason for something. (2) The reason or motivation for which a law or decision was made. (3) An inducement. *Compare with* **Animus**.

Causa causans. kô´sa kô´sans. kă´zu kă´zunz. *n.* "The causing cause." (1) The original, primary, or fundamental cause. (2) The effective or immediate cause.

Causa credendi. kô´sa krădān´dē. kă´zu kruden´dī. *adv.* (commonly used as a *n.*) "For the sake of credit." An obligation assumed because it is thought to furnish consideration for the obligation of another party, thereby creating a binding agreement. In Roman civil law, *causa credendi* referred to the consideration having the specific purpose of a loan. Thus, one who gave another money *causa credendi* was giving a loan. *Compare with* **Causa debendi**.

Causa debendi. kô´sa dābān´dē. kă´zu deben´dī. *n.* "The cause of debt." The consideration for which a debt is incurred. *Compare with* **Causa credendi**.

Causa impotentiae. kô´sa ēmpōtān´tē-ī. kă´zu impōten´šā. *adv.* "By cause of inability." Due to an unforeseen event (usually, a *force majeure*) that prevents a party from performing its obligations under a contract, treaty, or other agreement.

Causa petendi. kô´sa pātān´dē. kă´zu peten´dī. *n.* "The cause of the claims." The factual reason for or legal theory underlying a claimant or petitioner's cause of action or claims; wrongs or injuries giving rise to a claim for relief. *E.g.*, "A judge does not fulfil his judicial duty (*judex decidere debet*) if he fails to give a decision on one of the *causae petendi* of the application (*non est judex minus* *petita partium*)." *Advisory Opinion on the Application for Review of Judgement No. 158 of the United Nations Administrative Tribunal*, 1973 I.C.J. Rep. 166, 291, ¶ 41 (Judge De Castro, dissenting).

C

Causa proxima. kô´sa prō´ksēma. kă´zu pra´ksimu. *n.* "Nearby cause." (1) The immediate cause; the proximate cause. (2) A cause, the effect of which should have reasonably been foreseen. In the tort and criminal law of common law countries, an actor's wrongdoing or omission must be the proximate or foreseeable cause of a harm to trigger the actor's responsibility for the harm. *The International Law Commission's Draft Articles on Responsibility of States for Internationally Wrongful Acts* art. 31, GAOR, 56th Sess., Supp. No. 10, UN Doc. A/56/10, do not expressly adopt a *causa proxima* requirement; they instead provide more generally that a state is responsible to make full reparation for any injury "caused by" an internationally wrongful act. However, Comment 10 to Article 31 states that a proximate causation standard may be appropriate in some circumstances. *Contrast with* **Causa remota.** *See also* **Causa sine qua non.**

Causa proxima non remota inspicitur. kô´sa prō´ksēma nōn rāmō´ta ēnspē´kētūr. kă´zu pra´ksimu nan rēmō´tu inspi´sitɜr. "It is the proximate, not the remote, cause that is considered." A maxim meaning that a state or person is responsible for those harms that follow in a direct chain of causation from the wrongful act, as opposed to consequences that were remote or not reasonably foreseeable. *E.g.*, "[Previous legal expenses] are damages indirectly consequent to the collision; but it is a well known principle of the law of damages that *causa proxima non remota inspicitur*." *China Navigation Co., Ltd. (Great Britain) v. United States*, 6 Rev. Int'l Arb. Awards 64, 68 (1921). An alternative formulation is **Causa proxima non remota spectatur.** *See also* **Causa proxima.**

Causa proxima non remota spectatur. kô´sa prō´ksēma nōn rāmō´ta spākta´tūr. kă´zu pra´ksimu nan rēmō´tu spek´tātɜr. "It is the proximate, not the remote, cause that is considered." An alternative formulation of **Causa proxima non remota inspicitur.**

Causa remota. kô´sa rāmō´ta. kă´zu rēmō´tu. *n.* "Remote cause." (1) A remote or indirect cause. (2) A cause, the effect of which could not have been reasonably foreseen by the actor. *Contrast with* **Causa proxima.** *See also* **Causa proxima non remota inspicitur.**

Causa sine qua non. kô´sa sē´nā kwa nōn. kă´zu si´nē- or -si´nā kwā nan. *n.* "Cause not without which." A factual cause, regardless of the directness or indirectness of the effect produced; a necessary but not necessarily sufficient cause; a cause without which the resulting effect would not have been produced. *See also* **Causa proxima** and **Sine qua non.**

Causa solvendi. kô´sa sōlwān´dē. kă´zu salven´dī. *adv.* "For the sake of discharging." An obligation is assumed *causa solvendi* when it replaces a different, prior obligation owed by either the obligor (usually, a debtor) or another party.

Causae. *See* **Causa.**

Cautio iudicatum solvi. kô´tēō yūdēka´tūm sōl´wē. kă´tēō jūdikā´tum sal´vī. *n.* "A bond for payment of the judgment." A bond deposited with a tribunal to secure payment for the costs of a litigation. The deposit of a *cautio iudicatum solvi* is a prerequisite to filing a complaint in the courts of some states when the plaintiff is not a national of that state. *E.g.*, "*Saldanha* and *MTS* concerned a rule of Austrian civil procedure requiring nationals of other Member States not resident in Austria to lodge a security for costs (*cautio iudicatum solvi*) when bringing legal proceedings." Opinion of Advocate General Cosmas, *Andersson v. Sweden*, E.C.J. Case C-321/97, [1999] E.C.R. I-3551, ¶ 60.

Caveat. ka´wā-at. kâ´vē-ât. *v.* (commonly used as a *n.*) "May he or she be aware." A warning. Often seen in the form of the maxim "*caveat emptor*," meaning "let the buyer beware" (i.e., the buyer bears the risk of having purchased defective goods and, therefore, must be on his or her guard and inspect them purchasing) or "*caveat venditor*," meaning "let the seller beware." *E.g.*, "In this respect the Court would recall the *caveat* it included in its Judgment in the case concerning *Military and Paramilitary Activities in and against Nicaragua*, that 'Widespread reports of a fact may prove on closer examination to derive from a single source, and such reports, however numerous, will in such case have no greater value as evidence than the original source.'" *Oil Platforms Case* (Iran v. U.S.), 2003 I.C.J. Rep. 161, 190, ¶ 60 (Judgment).

Certiorari. kārtēōra´rē. s3ršōra´rī. *inf. v.* "To be apprised." In U.S. federal law, a notice to a lower court that an appellate court will exercise its discretion to review the lower court's decision. *E.g.*, "The Supreme Court declined to grant *certiorari* to hear a recent case...." *Avena and Other Mexican Nationals* (Mex. v. U.S.), 2004 I.C.J. Rep. 12, 110, ¶ 34 (separate opinion of Judge *ad hoc* Sepúlveda).

Cessante ratio, cessat etiam lex. kāssan´tā ra´tēō, kās´sat ā´tē-am lāks. sesan´tē rā´šō, se´sut e´tē-um leks. "When the rationale ceases, the law also ceases." A maxim meaning that, when the precondition, rationale, or policy basis for a law becomes obsolete, the law itself ceases to remain in force. Alternative phrases are **Cessante ratione legis, cessat ipse lex**; **Cessat ratio, cessat ipse lex**; and **Ratione cessante (cessat ipse lex).**

Cessante ratione legis, cessat ipse lex. kāssan´tā ratēō´nā lā´gēs, kās´sat ēp´sā lāks. sesan´tē rāšō´nē le´jis, se´sut ip´sē leks. "When the rationale of the law ceases, the law also ceases." An alternative formulation of **Cessante ratio, cessat etiam lex.**

C

Cessat ratio, cessat ipse lex. kās´sat ra´tēō, kās´sat ēp´sā lāks. se´sât rā´šō, se´sut ip´sē leks. "When the rationale ceases, the law itself ceases." An alternative formulation of **Cessante ratione, cessat etiam lex**.

Cessio bonorum. kās´sēō bōnō´rūm. se´sē-ō bōnō´rum. *n.* "Surrender of the goods." A surrender of assets to a tribunal, usually in the context of bankruptcy or preparatory to satisfying an award of restitution.

Ceteris paribus. kā´tārēs pa´rēbūs. se´tзris pa´ribus. "All else being equal." (1) With everything else being equal; with no other facts considered. (2) In equivalent circumstances. *E.g.*, "[W]henever an offence committed by an accused is deemed to be a 'crime against humanity,' it must be regarded as inherently of greater gravity...*ceteris paribus*...than if it is instead characterised as a 'war crime.' Consequently, it must entail a heavier penalty." *Prosecutor v. Tadic*, I.C.T.Y. Case No. IT-94-1-A (Jan. 26, 2000), 39 I.L.M. 635, 664, ¶ 16 (2000) (Judgment in Sentencing Appeals) (separate opinion of Judge Cassese). Sometimes spelled **Caeteris paribus**.

Cf. *v.* An abbreviation of **Confer**.

Circa. kēr´ka. sзr´ku. "About." Approximately, often used with respect to dates. *E.g.*, "Bahrain has claimed to have demonstrated *effectivités* on the Hawars for a period of almost a century and a half, including the claim that the original Dawasir settlement on Hawars was effected through grant by a Qadi of Zubarah (*circa* 1800) when that town was still under Al-Khalifah rule." *Maritime Delimitation and Territorial Questions Between Qatar and Bahrain* (Qatar v. Bahr.), 2001 I.C.J. Rep. 40, 255, ¶ 21 (separate opinion of Judge Al-Khasawneh). Sometimes abbreviated as **c**.

Circulus inextricabilis. kēr´kūlūs ēnākstrēka´bēlēs. sзr´kyūlus inekstrikâ´bilis. *n.* "A circle that cannot be undone." A vicious circle; a self-perpetuating cycle in which a first disorder causes a second disorder that, in turn, aggravates the first, and so on.

Civilis. kēwē´lēs. si´vilus. *adj.* "Civil." Relating to or according to civil law.

Civiliter. kēwē´lētār. sivi´litзr. *adv.* "Civilly." (1) Done by a civil action or proceeding. (2) Relating to one's civil rights or duties.

Civitas. kē´wētas. si´vitas. *n.* [*pl.* **Civitates**. kēwēta´tās. sivitā´tēz.] "The state." (1) A state or city-state. (2) An organized society, community, or social group. (3) A territorial subdivision of a state.

C

Civitas maxima. kē´wētas ma´ksēma. si´vitas mâ´ksimu. *n.* "Greatest society." A coalition or confederation of diverse social, ethnic, or cultural groups bound together by common legal, moral, and/or cultural ties.

Civitates esse immortales. kēwēta´tās ās´sā ēmmōrta´lās. sivita´tēz e´sē imōrtâ´lēz. "States are immortal." An alternative phrase for **Civitates immortales sunt.**

Civitates immortales sunt. kēwēta´tēs ēmmōrta´lās sūnt. sivita´tēz imōrtâ´lēz sunt. "States are immortal." A maxim meaning that states and their legal obligations persist, although any persons in a state's population may die and governments may change. An alternative phrase is **Civitates esse immortales.**

Civitatis omissio. kēwēta´tēs ōmēs´sēō. sivitā´tis umi´sēō. *n.* "Dismissal of citizenship." The loss of citizenship, whether through renunciation or deprivation by the state. In modern international law, it is considered a violation of human rights to deprive a citizen of his or her citizenship. *See* Universal Declaration of Human Rights art. 15, G.A. res. 217A (III), UN Doc A/810, at 71 (1948).

Claris verbis. kla´rēs wār´bēs. kle´ris vɜr´bis. *adv.* "In clear words." Lucidly and unambiguously stated or written. *E.g.*, "[T]he position of the Prosecutor is not expressed *claris verbis.*" *Prosecutor v. Kayishema and Ruzindana*, Judgment of May 21, 1999, ¶ 614, Case No. ICTR-95-1-T. *Compare with* **Expressis verbis.**

Clausula. klô´sūla. klă´zyūlu. "Clause." A clause or provision of an agreement, treaty, or other legal instrument.

Clausula rebus sic stantibus. klô´sūla rā´būs sēk stan´tēbūs. klă´zyūlu rē´bus sik stân´tibus. "By the clause the situation thus remaining." A condition sometimes argued to be implicit in international instruments to the effect that they cease to be obligatory when the facts that were a necessary precondition to the agreement have fundamentally changed so as to undermine the intent of the parties. The fulfillment of this condition, for example, may be satisfied by an unforeseen *force majeure*. *E.g.*, "According to the French contention…these Treaties [between France and its protectorates], which were concluded for an indefinite period, that is to say, in perpetuity, have lapsed by virtue of the principle known as the *clausula rebus sic stantibus* because the establishment of a legal and judicial regime [in the protectorates] in conformity with French legislation has created a new situation which deprives the capitulatory regime of its *raison d'être*." *Advisory Opinion on the Tunis-Morocco Nationality Decrees* (Fr. v. Gr. Brit.), 1923 P.C.I.J. (Ser. B) No. 4, 7, at 21. *See* Vienna Convention on the Law of Treaties art. 62, May 23, 1969, 1155 U.N.T.S. 331. Sometimes abbreviated **Rebus sic stantibus.** An alternative phrase is **Conventio omnis intelligitur rebus sic stantibus.** *Compare with* **Res noviter (interveniens).**

Clausula si omnes. klô´sūla sē ōm´nās. klă´zyūlu sē am´nēz. "The clause (that states:) If all" A treaty clause providing that if all relevant parties are not bound by the treaty, then the treaty is not binding upon any of the parties.

C

Clausulae inconsuetae semper indicunt suspicionem. klô´sūlī ēnkōnswā´tī sām´pār ēndē´kūnt sūspēkēō´nām. klă´zyūlā inkan´swetā sem´p3r in´dikunt suspišō´num. "Unusual clauses always arouse suspicion." A maxim meaning that, when a provision of a legal instrument such as a contract or treaty contains terms inconsistent with normal customs or drafting techniques, interpretation of the provision should proceed with sensitivity to the intentions of the parties to depart from customary or normal practices.

Codex. kō´dāks. kō´deks. *n.* "Book." A written code or collection of laws, rules, or regulations. The term is sometimes used to refer to the Justinian *Code* (*Codex Iustinianus*) (529 CE), which forms part of the collected *Corpus Iuris Civilis* ("Body of Civil Law") comprising the *Code*, the *Digest*, and the *Institutes*.

Codex Alimentarius. kō´dāks alēmānta´rē-ūs. kō´deks âlimenta´rē-us. *n.* "Alimentary Code." The collection of internationally promoted voluntary standards for foods, food production, and food safety maintained by the Codex Alimentarius Commission, an international organization established by the UN Food and Agriculture Organization and the World Health Organization to protect consumer health and informed choice.

Codex iuris canonici. kō´dāks yū´rēs kanō´nēkē. kō´deks j3´ris kâna´nisī. *n.* "Code of canon laws." The written code of religious or ecclesiastical laws adopted to govern a Christian church or other mystical faith.

Cogitationis poenam nemo meretur. kōgētatēō´nēs pœ´nam nā´mō mārā´tūr. kajitāšō´nis pē´num nē´mō me´ret3r. "Nobody deserves punishment for thought." An alternative phrase for **Cogitationis poenam nemo patitur.**

Cogitationis poenam nemo patitur. kōgētatēō´nēs pœ´nam nā´mō pa´tētūr. kajitāšō´nis pē´num nē´mō pâ´tit3r. "Nobody endures punishment for thought." A maxim, originating in Justinian's *Digest* (48.19.18), meaning that the mere thought of committing an illegal act cannot itself violate the law. In common law, this principle finds expression in the requirement of an *actus reus* in addition to *mens rea* for a criminal violation. International human rights law embodies a version of this principle in guarantees of freedom of thought and conscience. *See, e.g.*, Universal Declaration of Human Rights art. 18, G.A.

Res. 217A(III), UN Doc. A/810, at 71 (1948); International Covenant on Civil and Political Rights art. 18(1), Mar. 23, 1976, 999 U.N.T.S. 171. Alternative formulations are **Cogitationis poenam nemo meretur** and **Nemo cogitationis poenam patitur.**

Collegium fetialum. kōllā´gē-ūm fātē-a´lūm. kulē´jum fetē-â´lum. *n.* "Fetial commission." The Roman imperial agency (composed of *Fetiales*) charged with the conduct of diplomacy and determining and seeking divine authorization for a decision to resort to war or to pursue peace. *Fetiales* were considered inviolate and had duties approximating those of heralds. *See also* **Fetiales** and **Ius fetiale (divinum).**

Collisio obligationum. kōllē´sēō ōblēgatēō´nūm. kōli´zyō abligāšō´num. *n.* "Clash of obligations." A conflict between obligations.

Collisio officiorum. kōllē´sēō ōffēkēō´rūm. kōli´zyō ōfišō´rum. *n.* "Clash of duties." An alternative term for **Collisio obligationum.**

Colorandi causa. kōlōran´dē kô´sa. kulōrân´dī kă´zu. *adj.* or *adv.* "For the purpose of decoration." (1) For the purpose of illustration or example. (2) For the purpose of adding flair or panache. *E.g.*, "[T]he invocation [of fair and equitable principles in international investment disputes] is deemed necessary by claimant's lawyers *colorandi causa*, to present a certain flair of an offense to basic notions of justice to its cause." Rudolf Dolzer, *Fair and Equitable Treatment: A Key Standard in Investment Treaties*, 39 Int'l Law. 87 (2005).

Colore officii. kōlō´rā ōffē´kē-ē. kulō´rē ufi´šī. *adv.* "By color of office." By apparent, claimed, or pretended authority, as when a government official acts within his or her apparent sphere of competence or jurisdiction. An agent's promise made *colore officii* may impose a binding obligation on the principal, and an agent's wrongful act *colore officii* may give rise to liability on the part of the principal, even though the commitment or act was beyond the technical competence of the agent under the terms of the agency. An alternative formulation is **Sub colore officii.** *Compare with* **Intra vires** and **Sub colore iuris.** *See also* **Respondeat superior.**

Comitas (gentium). kō´mētas (gān´tē-ūm). ka´mitas (jen´tē-um). *n.* "Courtesy (of nations)." International comity; equitable consideration for a foreign state's interest in the outcome of a dispute or the observance of its own laws; equitable recognition of a foreign state's legislation, executive acts, or judicial decisions based on respect for the foreign state's sovereign interests. In common law, a court may dismiss a pending action on the principle of *comitas gentium* after determining that a foreign state has a superior interest in the outcome of the dispute or application of its own law, or if a tribunal of the foreign jurisdiction has already been seized of the dispute and has made significant progress toward its resolution. *E.g.*, "The Commission therefore adopted the view that the rules it was drafting on special missions were rules of law and that they were not based on *comitas gentium*." International Law Commission, *Special Missions: Second Report*, UN Doc. A/CN.4/179 (Apr. 21, 1965), 1965 (II) Y.B. INT'L L. COMM'N 113, ¶ 19.

C

Commercia belli. kōmmär´kē-a bäl´lē. kum3r´šu be´lī. *n. pl.* "Commerce of war." An agreement between belligerents on the treatment of commercial or humanitarian activities that might affect the belligerent states themselves or their populations during the course of an armed conflict. *E.g.*, "The usage of civilized nations has…introduced certain *commercia belli*, by which the violence of war may be allayed, so far as is consistent with its object and purposes, and something of a pacific intercourse may be kept up, which may lead, in time, to an adjustment of differences, and ultimately to peace." Henry Wheaton, ELEMENTS OF INTERNATIONAL LAW 270 (1836).

Commercium iure gentium commune esse debet et non in monopolium et privatum paucorum quaestum convertendum. kōmmär´kē-ūm yū´rā gān´tē-ūm kōmmū´nā äs´sā dā´bāt ät nōn ēn mōnōpō´lē-ūm ät prēwa´tūm pôkō´rūm kwī´stūm kōnwärtān´dūm. kum3r´šum j3´rē jen´tē-um kamyū´nē e´sā de´bet et nan in manapō´lē-um et privâ´tum păkō´rum kwes´tum kanv3rten´dum. "Under international law, commerce should be in common and not converted into a monopoly and the private gain of a few." A maxim meaning that it is consistent with international law for a state and its courts to prevent the private citizens and companies of other states from monopolizing its commerce.

Commodatum. kōmmōda´tūm. kamōdā´tum. "Loan." A loan or loan contract. An alternative term is **Accommodatum.**

Commodum ex iniuria non oritur. kōm´mōdūm äks ēnyū´rē-a nōn ōrē´tūr. ka´mōdum eks inj3´rē-u nan ō´rit3r. "Benefit does not arise from wrongdoing." An alternative phrase for **Nullus commodum capere (potest) de sua iniuria propria.**

Commodum ex iniuria sua nemo habere debet. kōm´mōdūm äks ēnyū´rē-a sū´a nā´mō habā´rā dā´bāt. ka´mōdum eks inj3´rē-u sū´u nē´mō hâ´b3rē de´bet. "Nobody should profit from his own wrongdoing." An alternative phrase for **Nullus commodum capere (potest) de sua iniuria propria.**

Commodum ex iniuria sua non habere debet. kōm´mōdūm äks ēnyū´rē-a sū´a nōn ha´bārā dā´bāt. ka´mōdum eks inj3´rē-u sū´u nan hâ´b3rē de´bet. "Nobody should have a profit from his own wrong doing." An alternative phrase for **Nullus commodum capere (potest) de sua iniuria propria.**

Commune bonum. kōmmū´nā bō´nūm. kamyū´nē bō´num. *n.* "Communal good." Something that benefits the public or state in general.

Communi consensu. kōmmū´nē kōnsān´sū. kamyū´nī kansen´sū. *adv.* "By common consent." By general or universal consent.

Communia. kōmmū´nē-a. kamyū´nē-u. *n. pl.* "Common things." (1) Private property in which many people have, or the public in general has, a right of servitude. (2) Publicly owned property or things, such as the air or sea.

Communia praecepta. kōmmū´nē-a prīkāp´ta. kamyū´nē-u prēsep´tu. *n. pl.* "Common precepts." Common rules or laws that are binding universally within their proper jurisdiction.

Communio rei vel iuris. kōmmū´nēō rā´ē wāl yū´rēs. kamyū´nēō rā vel jɜ´ris. *n.* "Joint ownership in fact or law." Accidental community of ownership created by operation law (as opposed to an express agreement between the owners).

Communis error facit ius. kōmmū´nēs ār´rōr fa´kēt yūs. kamyū´nis e´rɜr fâ´sit jus. "A common error makes law." A maxim of Scottish law meaning that an "error" of law, repeated often enough and with sufficient conviction, displaces the former, "correct" legal rule and creates a new legal rule. *Contrast with* **Communis error non facit ius.**

Communis error non facit ius. kōmmū´nēs ār´rōr nōn fa´kēt yūs. kamyū´nis e´rɜr nan fâ´sit jus. "A common error does not make law." A maxim meaning that an "error" of law, no matter how often repeated, cannot change the "correct" legal rule or create a new legal rule. *Contrast with* **Communis error facit ius.**

Communis opinio (doctorum). kōmmū´nēs ōpē´nēō (dōktō´rūm). kamyū´nis upi´nyō (daktō´rum). *n.* "The commonly held opinion (of the educated)." (1) The general opinion of legal experts or scholars on questions of Roman law, compiled by European glossators of Justinian's *Digest* in the late medieval period. (2) A general opinion of legal experts or scholars that a specific act or practice is required or forbidden by international law. *Communis opinio doctorum* is widely considered evidence of the establishment of a rule of customary international law. *E.g.*, "The court had stated in that decision that many States…adhere strictly to the principle of absolute State immunity; and that also the *communis opinio doctorum* is not at all uniform." Paul Abel, *State Immunity*, 11 INT'L & COMP. L.Q. 840, 841 (1962). *Compare with* **Opinio iuris (sive necessitatis).**

Communis scriptura. kōmmū´nēs skrēptū´ra. kamyū´nis skrip´čзru. *n.* "Communal writing." The text of an agreement or treaty.

Compensatio lucri cum damno. kōmpānsa´tēō lūk´rē kūm dam´nō. kampensā´šō lūk´rī kum dâm´nō. *n.* "Compensation of profits with damages." The addition of a claimant's lost profits or the respondent's unjust enrichment to out-of-pocket damages claimed by or awarded to the claimant. *E.g.*, "T. Port maintains...that in paragraph 66 of the contested judgment the Court of First Instance misapplied the principle *compensatio lucri cum damno* by applying it to a situation in which the advantages created [by] the increase in tariff quota and the reduction in customs duties are not a consequence of the breach of law which occasioned the loss in this case, the costs involved in the mandatory purchase of the export licences which it is supposed that those advantages offset." *T. Port GmbH & Co. KG v. Commission*, E.C.J. Case No. C-122/01, ¶ 15, [2003] E.C.R. I-4261.

Compos mentis. kōm´pōs mān´tēs. kam´pus men´tis. *adj.* "Having mastery of the mind." (1) Mentally competent and mature; adequately intelligent. (2) Sane or sound of mind. *Contrast with* **Non compos (mentis).**

Compromissarii sunt iudices. kōmprōmēssa´rē-ē sūnt yū´dēkās. kamprōmisa´rī sunt jū´disēz. "Arbitrators are judges." A maxim meaning that lawfully constituted arbitral tribunals will be treated as having the same authority to resolve the dispute, and the same duty of impartiality, as if they were judges. *Compare with* **Arbitrium est iudicium.**

Compromissum. kōmprōmēs´sūm. kamprōmi´sum. *n.* "Arbitration." A *compromis*; an agreement to submit a dispute or a class of potential disputes to arbitration.

Concordare leges legibus est optimus interpretandi modus. kōnkōrda´rā lā´gās lā´gēbūs āst ōp´tēmūs ēntārprātan´dē mō´dūs. kankōrda´rē le´jēz le´jibus est ap´timus intзrpretân´dī mō´dus. "The best method of interpretation is to harmonize laws with laws." A maxim meaning that whenever possible laws should be interpreted not to conflict with or contradict each other.

Concursus in delicto. kōnkūr´sūs ēn dālēk´tō. kankзr´sus in dulik´tō. *n.* "Cooperation in crime." (1) A conspiracy to commit a criminal act. (2) Cooperation in a criminal enterprise generally.

Condicio. kōndē´kēō. kandi´šō. *n.* "Condition." A condition; a prerequisite. *See also* **Conditio.**

Condicio per quam. kōndē´kēō pār kwam. kandi´šō pзr kwam. *n.* "Condition by means of which." A stipulation or condition that, if fulfilled, causes some specified effect; a causative condition. *E.g.*, "The efficacy of the entire legal order is a necessary condition for the validity of every single norm of the order. A *conditio sine qua non*, but not a *conditio per quam*. The efficacy of the total legal order is a condition, not the reason for the validity of its constituent norms." Hans Kelsen, GENERAL THEORY OF LAW AND STATE 119 (Anders Wedberg trans., 1945).

Condicio praecedens adimpleri debet prius quam sequatur effectus. kōndēˊkēō prīkāˊdāns adēmplāˊrē dāˊbāt prēˊūs kwam sākwaˊtūr āffākˊtūs. kandiˊšō prēsēˊdenz âdimˊplɜrī deˊbet prīˊus kwam seˊkwutɜr efekˊtus. "A condition precedent should be fulfilled before the effect can follow." A maxim meaning that a provision in an agreement or treaty conditioning a right or obligation on some prior event should not be given effect until that event has occurred.

Condicio sine qua non. kōndēˊkēō sēˊnā kwa nōn. kandiˊšō siˊnē kwa nan. *n.* "Condition without which...not." Something that is quintessential, definitional, or indispensable for something else. Commonly used in abbreviated form as **Sine qua non.** *E.g.*, "Since the Court has found that the condition *sine qua non* required for the exercise of the right of collective self-defence by the United States is not fulfilled in this case..., even if the United States activities in question had been carried on in strict compliance with the canons of necessity and proportionality, they would not thereby become lawful." *Military and Paramilitary Activities in and Against Nicaragua* (Nicar. v. U.S.), 1986 I.C.J. Rep. 13, ¶ 237.

Conditio. kōndēˊtēō. kandiˊšō. *n.* "Condition." This is an alternative spelling, which became popular in the medieval era, of the term **Condicio**. The proper classical Latin spelling is *condicio*; for definitions of terms that use the word *conditio* in this guidebook, substitute *condicio*.

Condominium. kōndōmēˊnē-ūm. kandumiˊnē-um. *n.* "Joint dominion." (1) A situation in which two or more states share sovereignty over a territory external to the territory of the sovereign states. *E.g.*, "Given that there is a *condominium* of the waters of the Gulf, it follows that there is a tri-partite presence at the closing line and that Honduras is not locked out from rights in respect of the ocean waters outside the bay." *Land, Island, and Maritime Frontier Dispute* (El Sal. v. Hond.; Nicar. intervening), 1992 I.C.J. Rep. 351, 607, ¶ 418 (Judgment). (2) Generally, common or joint ownership.

Confer. kōnˊfār. kanˊfɜr. *v. imp.* "Compare." Compare with. This term is used in a citation to indicate that the argument made or fact stated should be compared with a different cited source that makes an analogous point or contains related background information. Commonly abbreviated **Cf.**

Confessio in iudicio. kōnfās´sēō ēn yūdē´kēō. kanfe´sēō in jūdi´šō. *n.* "Confession in court." A confession or admission made before an authoritative tribunal while the tribunal is in session.

C

Coniectio. kōnyāk´tēō. kanjek´šō. *n.* [*pl.* **Coniectiones.** kōnyāktēō´nās. kanjekšō´nēz.] "Inference." A conclusion inferred from evidence.

Coniuncta. kōnyūnk´ta. kanjunk´tu. *n. pl.* "Conjoined things." Things or matters connected or joined in fact or law.

Coniunctim et divisim. kōnyūnk´tēm āt dēwē´sēm. kanjunk´tim et divī´zim. *adv.* "Jointly and separately." Both jointly and severally.

Conquisitio. kōnkwēsē´tēō. kankwizi´šō. *n.* "A seeking out." The occupation and annexation of a foreign territory by armed force. Historically, *conquisitio* was considered a valid means by which a state could acquire new territory and expand its dominion. In modern international law, both international custom and Article 2(4) of the UN Charter prohibit territorial aggression.

Conscientia illaesa. kōnskē-ān´tē-a ēllī´sa. kanšē-en´šu ilā´zu. *n.* "Inviolate conscience." (1) Good faith. (2) A clean conscience. *Compare with* **Bona fides.**

Consensus ad idem. kōsān´sūs ad ē´dām. kansen´sus âd ī´dum. *n.* "Agreement to the same." (1) An agreement on the substance (*e.g.*, of a treaty's terms). (2) Generally, a meeting of the minds. An alternative formulation is **Consensus in idem.**

Consensus in idem. kōsān´sūs ēn ē´dām. kansen´sus in ī´dem. *n.* "Agreement into the same." An alternative formulation of **Consensus ad idem.**

Consentire videtur qui tacet. kōnsāntē´rā wēdā´tūr kwē ta´kāt. kansentī´rē vi´det3r kwī tâ´set. "One who remains silent is considered to consent." An abbreviation of **Qui tacet consentire videtur (ubi tractatur de eius commodo).**

Consimili casu. kōnsē´mēlē ka´sū. kansi´milī kā´sū. *adv.* "In a similar case." An abbreviated form of **In consimili casu.**

Consuetudo. kōnswātū´dō. kanswetū´dō. *n.* "Custom." (1) Customary law; norms that have become binding on the relevant parties by long and consistent usage giving rise to a shared expectation of continuation of the practice. (2) Custom or longstanding practice generally.

Consuetudo debet esse certa. kōswātū´dō dā´bāt ās´sā kār´ta. kanswetū´dō de´bet e´sē s3r´tu. "A custom should be settled." A maxim meaning that, to arise to the level of a binding custom, a practice must be enduring, consistent, and no longer subject to serious doubt.

Consuetudo est altera lex. kōnswātū´dō āst al´tāra lāks. kanswetū´dō est al´tɜru leks. "Customs is another law." A maxim meaning that a customary practice of sufficient consistency and longevity becomes binding. *Compare with* **Consuetudo observanda est.**

Consuetudo est optimus interpres legum. kōnswātū´dō āst ōp´tēmūs ēntār´prās lā´gūm. kanswetū´dō est ap´timus intɜr´prez le´jum. "Custom is the best interpreter of law." An alternative formulation of **Optima est legis interpres consuetudo.**

Consuetudo loci observanda est. kōnswātū´dō lō´kē ōbsārwan´da āst. kanswetū´dō lō´sī absɜrvân´du est. "The custom of the place should be observed." A maxim meaning that local customs are generally binding on parties acting or transacting business within the jurisdiction. *Compare with* **Consuetudo observanda est.**

Consuetudo mercatoria. kōnswātū´dō mārkatō´rē-a. kanswetū´dō mɜrkutō´rē-u. *n.* "Mercantile custom." An alternative term for **Lex mercatoria.**

Consuetudo mercatorum. kōnswātū´dō mārkatō´rūm. kanswetū´dō mɜrkutō´rum. *n.* "The custom of merchants." An alternative term for **Lex mercatoria.**

Consuetudo observanda est. kōnswātū´dō ōbsārwan´da āst. kanswātūdō absɜrvân´du est. "Custom is observed." A maxim meaning that customary laws and practices should be enforced even though they may not have been formally enacted or codified. *Compare with* **Consuetudo est altera lex** and **Consuetudo loci observanda est.**

Consules. kōn´sūlās. kan´sɜlēz. *n. pl.* "Consuls." Diplomats beneath the level of ambassador assigned to represent the state in a host state (usually having responsibilities for a specific city or region) for limited matters, such as the protection of the sending state's citizens visiting or residing in the host state, or facilitating international trade or investment. *See* the Vienna Convention on Consular Relations art. 5, Apr. 24, 1963, 596 U.N.T.S. 261.

Consules electi. kōn´sūlās ālāk´tē. kan´sɜlēz elek´tī. *n. pl.* "Elect consuls." Honorary consuls; prominent citizens of a host state chosen by a foreign state to represent that foreign state in the host state for purposes of protecting the foreign state's citizens while in the host state. *But see* the Vienna Convention on Consular Relations art. 22 and ch. III, Apr. 24, 1963, 596 U.N.T.S. 261. *Contrast with* **Consules missi.** *See also* **Consules.**

Consules missi. kōn´sūlās mēs´sē. kan´sɜlēz mi´sī. *n. pl.* "Sent consuls." Official career consuls, usually of the nationality of the sending state. *See also* **Consules.** *Contrast with* **Consules electi.**

C

Contemporanea expositio. *n.* kōntämpōra´nä-a äkspōsē´tēō. kantempōrâ´nē-u ekspōzi´šō. "Contemporaneous exposition." An interpretation of a law or legal instrument based on evidence of the intent of the negotiators or drafters at the time of the law's or instrument's adoption. *See also* **Contemporanea expositio est optima et fortissima in lege.**

Contemporanea expositio est optima et fortissima in lege. kōntämpōra´nä-a äkspōsē´tēō äst ōp´tēma ät fōrtēs´sēma ēn lä´gä. kantempōrâ´nē-u ekspōzi´šō est ap´timu et fōrti´simu in le´jē. "A contemporaneous exposition is the best and strongest in the law." A maxim meaning that evidence of the intent of the drafters of a law or parties to a legal instrument at the time of the law's or instrument's adoption, as well as their understanding of the law as it existed at that time, is the most credible and valid evidence of the meaning of vague, ambiguous, or disputed language. *See also* **Contemporanea expositio.**

Contestatio litis. kōntästa´tēō lē´tēs. kantestā´šō li´tis. *n.* "Contestation of the lawsuit." An alternative formulation of **Litis contestatio.**

Continuum iuris. kōntē´nū-ūm yū´rēs. kantin´yū-um jɜ´ris. *n.* "Continuation of law." (1) The continuation of legal obligations or a code of laws after a change in a state's government or identity. (2) A continuation of laws resulting in the elimination of any gap in legal authority or rules. *E.g.*, "[I]nternational law does not effect any *renvoi* to the law established by the colonizing State, nor indeed to any legal rule unilaterally established by any State whatever; French law—especially legislation enacted by France for its colonies and *territoires d'outre-mer*—may play a role not in itself (as if there were a sort of *continuum juris*, a legal relay between such law and international law), but only as one factual element among others, or as evidence indicative of what has been called the 'colonial heritage,' i.e., the 'photograph of the territory' at the critical date." *Frontier Dispute* (Burk. Faso v. Mali), 1986 I.C.J. Rep. 554, 568, ¶ 30.

Contra. kōn´tra. kan´tru. *prep.* "Against." (1) In opposition. (2) To the contrary. (3) A citation signal meaning that the authority cited takes a position opposing the proposition to which the citation refers. *Compare with* **Secus.**

Contra bonos mores (et decorum). kōn´tra bō´nōs mō´räs (ät dākō´rūm). kan´tru bō´nōs mō´rēz- OR -mōrz (et dekō´rum). *adj.* or *adv.* "Against good (and right) practices." (1) Immoral. (2) Inequitable. (3) Inconsistent with or contrary to preferred or sound practices, customs, public policy, or notions of equity. A court may refuse to enforce a foreign judgment if the law on which the judgment was based is considered *contra bonos mores*. *E.g.*, "The law of that place [where two persons were married and that is the domicile of each] will therefore control in all respects, even when the marriage is called into question elsewhere as being contrary to the law of the forum, unless it be *contra bonos mores*, as polygamous, or universally incestuous." Raleigh C. Minor, CONFLICT OF LAWS; OR, PRIVATE INTERNATIONAL LAW 149–50, § 73 (1901). An alternative phrase is **Adversus bonos mores**. *See also* **Boni mores**.

Contra constitutionem. kōn´tra kōnstētūtēō´nām. kan´tru kanstitūšō´nem. *adj.* or *adv.* "Against the constitution." Contrary to the constitution. *E.g.*, "[B]y its nature [this provision of the Constitution of the Republic of Bosnia and Herzegovina] constitutes a revision of the Constitution carried out *contra constitutionem* in the form of a consolidation of the text of the Constitution...." *Application of the Convention on the Prevention and Punishment of the Crime of Genocide* (Bosn. & Herz. v. Yugo.), 1996 I.C.J. Rep. 595, 700, ¶ 34 (Judge *ad hoc* Kreća, dissenting).

Contra factum proprium. kōn´tra fak´tūm prōp´rē-ūm. kan´tru fâk´tum prap´rē-um. *adj.* or *adv.* "Against one's own deed." In contradiction to oneself; inconsistent(ly); hypocritical(ly). *E.g.*, "A couple of relevant facts regarding the practice of the [United Nations] Organization concerning membership of the Federal Republic of Yugoslavia raise the question of whether the Organization acted *contra factum proprium* [in allowing Yugoslavia to participate in the UN General Assembly while denying it membership]." *Legality of Use of Force* (Yugo. v. Can.), 1999 I.C.J. Rep. 259, 343 (Request for Provisional Measures).

Contra ius belli. kōn´tra yūs bāl´lē. kan´tru jus be´lī. *adj.* or *adv.* "Against the law of war." Contrary to the international law governing the initiation or conduct of an armed conflict. *See also* **Ius ad bellum** and **Ius in bello**.

Contra legem. kōn´tra lā´gām. kan´tru le´jem. *adj.* or *adv.* "Against the law." (1) Contrary to a legal obligation; illegal(ly); based on a principle of equity in contradiction to a rule of positive law. (2) Not rising to the level of a legal obligation; permissible but not required by law. *E.g.*, "[T]he rejection of these...principles [asserted to represent international law] implies that [the rejecting states] consider them as being *contra legem*." *The Caltex Arbitration* (Texaco v. Libya), 53 I.L.R. 87, ¶ 87 (1982).

Contra legem terrae. kōn´tra lā´gām tār´rī. kan´tru le´jem te´rā. *adj.* "Against the law of the land." Against the municipal law of the state.

Contra pacem. kōn´tra pa´kām. kan´tru pâ´kum. *adv.* "Against peace." (1) In municipal law, done in breach of the public peace. (2) By extension to international law, in violation of the rights of another state or the international community in such a manner as to furnish the offended state with justification for resorting to armed force against the violator. *See also* **Casus belli.**

Contra proferentem. kōn´tra prōfārān´tām. kan´tru praf3ren´tum. *adv.* "Against the offeror." A principle of private law suggesting that ambiguity or vagueness in the legal instrument should be construed against the interests of the drafter. Thus, where there are two possible interpretations of contractual language, one of which is less favorable to the drafter and more favorable to the other party or parties, the instrument will be construed in this manner. *Compare with* **In favorem debitoris.** *Contrast with* **In ambiguis orationibus maxime sententia spectanda est eius qui eas protulisset.**

C

Contradictio in adiecto. kōntradēk´tēō ēn adyāk´tō. kantrudik´šō in âdjek´tō. *n.* "A contradiction in what has been added." A self-contradiction. *E.g.,*"[I]t appears that both the scope and the object of killing allow only the interpretation expressed in the *Krstić* case that 'selective genocide' took place, a notion which, in the light of the requirements established in Article II of the Convention, represents no more than *contradictio in adjecto.*" *Application of the Convention on the Prevention and Punishment of the Crime of Genocide* (Bosn. & Herz. v. Yugo.), I.C.J. No. 91, Judgment of Feb. 26, 2007, at 87, ¶ 150 (separate opinion of Judge *ad hoc* Kreća).

Contrarius consensus. kōntra´rē-ūs kōnsān´sūs. kantra´rē-us kansen´sus. *n.* "Agreement to the contrary." (1) Agreement to the contrary. (2) Agreement to renounce or repeal a prior agreement or other legal instrument. *E.g.*, "[I]f tacit abrogation [of a treaty] were recognized, it would be necessary to produce proof of the *facta concludentia* which would have to be relied on to demonstrate the *contrarius consensus* of the parties, and proof of sufficient force to relieve the parties of the obligation undertaken by them under the treaty." *Nuclear Tests* (Austl. v. Fr.), 1974 I.C.J. Rep. 253, 381 (Judge De Castro, dissenting). *See also* **Per facta concludentia.**

Conventio. kōnwān´tēō. kanven´šō. *n.* "Coming together." An agreement, treaty, or convention.

Conventio omnis intelligitur rebus sic stantibus. kōnwān´tēō ōm´nēs ēntāllē´gētūr rā´būs sēk stan´tēbūs. kanven´šō am´nis inteli´jit3r rē´bus sik stân´tibus. "With circumstances being as they are, the entire agreement is understood...." An alternative phrase for **Clausula rebus sic stantibus.**

Convictio iuris (sive necessitatis). kōnwēk´tēō yū´rēs (sē´wā nākās´sētatēs). kanvik´šō j3´ris (si´vē nesesitā´tis). *n.* "Legal conviction (whether necessary)." An alternative formulation of **Opinio iuris (sive necessitatis).**

Coram iudice. kō´ram yū´dēkā. kō´rum jū´disē. *adv.* "Before the judge." (1) Before a tribunal having proper jurisdiction. (2) Generally, in the presence of, or before, a judge or authoritative tribunal. *Contrast with* **Coram non iudice.**

Coram non iudice. kō´ram nōn jū´disē. kō´rum nan jū´disē. *adv.* "Not before the judge." (1) In a tribunal or venue lacking proper jurisdiction. (2) Outside the presence of, or not before, a judge or authoritative tribunal. *Contrast with* **Coram iudice.**

Corpora delicti. kōr´pōra dālēk´tē. kōr´pɜru dulik´tī. *n. pl.* "Objects of the offense." Physical or tangible evidence of wrongdoing. *E.g.*, "According to [the U.K.] Government, the *corpora delicti* must be secured as quickly as possible, for fear they should be taken away, without leaving traces, by the authors of the [unlawful] minelaying...." *The Corfu Channel Case* (U.K. v. Alb.), 1949 I.C.J. Rep. 4, 34 (Merits).

Corpore possessio. A misspelling of **Corporis possessio.**

Corporis possessio. kōr´pōrēs pōssās´sēō. kōr´puris pōze´sēō. *n.* "Possession of the body." Physical occupation of a territory, which is considered important to sustain a claim of sovereignty over inhabited or contested territory. *E.g.*, "Effective possession, the objective element of a '*corpore possessio*,' [*sic*: *corporis possessio*] should be accompanied by a subjective element consisting of the '*animus possidendi*.'..." *Maritime Delimitation and Territorial Questions Between Qatar and Bahrain*, 2001 I.C.J. Rep. 40, ¶ 100 (Merits). *Compare with* **Corpus possessionis.** *See also* **Animus possidendi.**

Corpus. kōr´pūs. kōr´pus. *n.* "Body." (1) A person's physical being. (2) A portion of matter especially distinct from other portions or the totality, as in a "body of cavalry." (3) The totality of something itself, as in a "body of law" (*corpus iuris*). *E.g.*, "The reservations [to jurisdiction] constitute exceptions—in this case *ratione materiae*—to that jurisdiction. They do not constitute exceptions to the ruling principles of the *corpus* of international law." *Fisheries Jurisdiction* (Spain v. U.K.), 1998 I.C.J. Rep. 432, 502, ¶ 24 (Jurisdiction) (Judge Weeramantry, dissenting).

Corpus iuris. kōr´pūs yū´rēs. kōr´pus jɜ´ris. *n.* "Body of law." (1) A body of law, such as the collection of rules relating to a specific subject. (2) A comprehensive collection of the laws of a jurisdiction.

Corpus iuris civilis. kōr´pūs yū´rēs kēwē´lēs. kōr´pus jɜ´ris si´vilus. *n.* "Body of civil law." (1) Generally, the entirety of Roman civil law. (2) Specifically, the comprehensive code of Roman law, compiled by order of Emperor Justinian I between 529 and 535 CE under the supervision of the jurist Tribonian, with the intent of synthesizing and codifying the entirety of Roman civil law.

Corpus iuris gentium. kōr´pūs yū´rēs gān´tē-ūm. kōr´pūs jɜ´ris jen´tē-um. *n.* "Body of the law of nations." (1) The entirety of the rules of international law, both substantive and procedural. (2) The entirety of the rules of international law relating to a specific (named) subject matter. *E.g.*, "In this domain [of treaty interpretation], as elsewhere, the *corpus juris gentium* has been considerably enriched, and this the Court, if it is faithfully to discharge its functions, may not ignore." *Advisory Opinion on the Legal Consequences for States of the Continued Presence of South Africa in Namibia (South West Africa)*, 1971 I.C.J. Rep. 16, ¶ 53.

C

Corpus possessionis. kōr´pūs pōssāssēō´nēs. kōr´pus pōzešō´nis. *n.* "The body of what is occupied." A territory physically occupied by a party. Such occupation is considered important to sustain a claim of sovereignty over inhabited or contested territory. *Compare with* **Corporis possessio.** *See also* **Animus occupandi.**

Corrigendum. kōrrēgān´dūm. kōrijen´dum. *n.* [*pl.* **Corrigenda.** kōrrēgān´da. kōrijen´du.] "Thing to be corrected." An error, usually typographical, needing to be or having been corrected. *See also* **Erratum.**

Crimen. krē´mān. krī´men. *n.* [*pl.* **Crimina.** krē´mēna. kri´minu.] "Crime." (1) Crime. (2) A charge against someone of having committed a crime.

Crimen contra omnes. krē´mān kōn´tra ōm´nās. krī´men kan´tru am´nēz. *n.* "Crime against all." A crime against humanity as a whole, such as piracy, slavery, genocide, or terrorism.

Crimen laesae maiestatis. krē´mān lī´sī mayāsta´tēs. krī´men lā´zā mâjestā´tis. *n.* "The crime of injured sovereignty." High treason against a sovereign. A *crimen laesae maiestatis* could include such acts as espionage against one's own state of nationality on behalf of a foreign sovereign or waging war against one's own sovereign. An alternative formulation is **Crimen maiestatis.** *Compare with* **Perduellio.** *See also* **Laesa maiestas.**

Crimen maiestatis. krē´mān mayāsta´tēs. krī´men mâjesta´tis. *n.* "The crime of sovereignty." An alternative formulation of **Crimen laesae maiestatis.** *Compare with* **Perduellio.** *See also* **Laesa maiestas.**

Crimen trahit personam. krē´mān tra´hēt pārsō´nam. krī´men trā´hit pɜrsō´num. "The crime brings along the person." A maxim meaning that a state may assert personal jurisdiction over anyone of whatever nationality or domicile who has committed a crime within its territory. *See also* **Debet quis iuri subiacere ubi delinquit.**

Crimina iuris gentium. krē´mēna yū´rēs gān´tē-ūm. kri´minu jɜ´ris jen´tē-um. *n.* "Crime of the law of nations." A crime under international law. *Compare with* **Delictum iuris gentium.**

C

Cui bono? kū´ē bō´nō? kwē bō´nō? *int.* "For what good?" (1) An interrogative asking who will reap or has reaped the benefit or advantage of an act or condition. (2) An interrogative asking what benefit an act or condition could create.

Cuius. kū´yūs. kyū´jus. *adj.* (commonly used as a *n.*) "Whose." The person to which something belongs. *E.g.*, "The close connection between the personalities of the *cuius* and the heir is not a general principle of private law." Hersch Lauterpacht, Private Law Sources and Analogies of Public International Law 131 (1927).

Cuius est solum eius est usque ad coelum (et ad inferos). kū´yūs āst sō´lūm ā´yūs āst ūs´kwā ad kœ´lūm (āt ad ēn´fārōs). kyū´jus est sa´lum e´jus est yūs´kwē âd sē´lum (et âd in´fɜrōs). "To whomsoever it belongs, it is his all the way to the heavens (and all the way to hell)." A Roman private law maxim meaning that property or territory extends upward theoretically into the limits of the atmosphere and downward into the soil and substrate to the core of the Earth. This rule has sometimes been imported by analogy into international law. The Chicago Aviation Convention provides that every state has "complete and exclusive sovereignty" over the air space above its land territory and territorial waters and does not specify a vertical limit. *See* Convention on International Civil Aviation, Dec. 7, 1944, art. 1, 15 U.N.T.S. 295. The Outer Space Treaty forbids any party to claim sovereignty over any part of outer space. Treaty on Principles Governing the Activities of States in the Exploration and Use of Outer Space, Including the Moon and Other Celestial Bodies, Oct. 10, 1967, art. 2, G.A. Res. 2222 (XXI), G.A.O.R. Doc. A/6431, 21st Sess., Dec. 19, 1966. Whether state sovereignty ends where outer space begins, at the Kármán Line (altitude of 100 km), at the point of atmospheric drag on re-entry, or some other place has not been definitively resolved in international law. Downward sovereignty seems to be limited only by technology. *See also* **Ad coelum (et ad inferos).**

Cuius regio eius religio. kū´yūs rā´gēō ā´yūs rālē´gēō. kyū´jus re´jyō e´jus ruli´jēō. "Whosever territory, his religion." The principle, established by the Treaty of Westphalia of 1648, that the prince of any particular principality determines the religion of the inhabitants of that principality. The maxim has sometimes been applied as an expression of the concept of a state's sovereignty over its own territory.

Culpa. kūl´pa. k3l´pu. *n.* "Fault." (1) Moral responsibility for wrongdoing. (2) A breach of a binding legal obligation entailing liability. In Roman law, *culpa* referred to any illegal act of commission or omission. *E.g.*, "[T]he non-execution of a contractual obligation connotes, by itself, the existence of *culpa*, so that a debtor can only clear himself if he can prove the existence of an external cause; yet one may still consider that *culpa* itself is absent." *The Corfu Channel Case* (U.K. v. Alb.), 1949 I.C.J. Rep. 4, 84, ¶ 10 (Merits) (Judge Azevedo, dissenting). *See also* **dolus malus.** (3) Negligence; a failure to act with due diligence; a wrongful omission. *See* Justinian's *Digest* (50.16.213). *Contrast with* **Diligentia.**

C

Culpa in eligendo. kūl´pa ēn ālēgān´dō. k3l´pu in elijen´dō. *n.* "Fault in selecting." A poorly made decision. It has sometimes been hypothesized that the basis of a state's responsibility under international law for the acts of its officials is *culpa in eligendo*, or a failure to appoint officials who will comply with international law. Sometimes misspelled *culpa in elegiendo*. *See also* **Culpa in vigilando.**

Culpa in vigilando. kūl´pa ēn wēgēlan´dō. k3l´pu in vijilân´dō. *n.* "Fault in supervising." A failure to supervise properly or to exercise due diligence. It has sometimes been hypothesized that the basis of state liability under international law for the acts of its officials (or sometimes nationals or persons within its territory) is attributable to the state's failure to observe its duty to control these persons. *See also* **Culpa in eligendo.**

Culpae poena par esto. kūl´pī pœ´na par ās´tō. k3l´pā pē´nu par es´tō. "Let the punishment equal the crime." A maxim of Roman law meaning that the punishment prescribed for a crime should be proportional to the seriousness of the crime. *See* Marcus Tullius Cicero, De Legibus 3.4 (51 BCE).

Cum. kūm. kum. *adv.* "When; since; although." A term sometimes used in place of "when" or "insofar as."

Cum cura. kūm kū´ra. kum kyū´ru. *adv.* "With care." (1) Cautiously. (2) Carefully; not negligently.

Cum grano salis. kūm gra´nō sa´lēs. kum grâ´nō sâ´lis. *adv.* "With a grain of salt." (1) Skeptically; inferring or assuming that the speaker or writer is exaggerating or making an inaccurate assertion. *E.g.*, "Oppenheim, in the middle of the nineteenth century, contended that the analogy [of public international law] to private law should be rejected or taken *cum grano salis*, as against the assertions of Pufendorff, in the seventeenth century, that the analogy was reasonable." Carl W. Young, The International Legal Status of the

Kwantung Leased Territory 109 (1931). (2) With reservations to the general applicability of the assertion made.

Cum imperio. kūm ēmpā´rēō. kum impē´rēō. *adv.* "With sovereignty." Having the trait of sovereignty.

Cum laude. kūm lô´dā. kum lăd or -lă´dē. *adj.* or *adv. Neo.* "With praise." With distinction or honors. The term is commonly applied to a graduating student who has achieved academic distinction. *See also* **Magna cum laude** and **Summa cum laude.**

Cum onere. kūm ō´nārā. kum ō´nзrē. *adv.* "With burden." (1) With an existing charge, easement, restriction, or other burden. (2) Carrying or being responsible to carry the burden of proof.

Curator absentis. kūra´tōr absān´tēs. kyз´rātзr âb´sentis. *n.* "Caretaker of the absent." An alternative formulation of **Curator in absentia.**

Curator in absentia. kūra´tōr ēn absān´tē-a. kyз´rātзr in âbsen´ču. *n.* "Caretaker in the absence." The representative or counsel before a tribunal of a party not able or willing to appear before the tribunal. An alternative formulation is **Curator absentis.**

Curia novit (iura). kū´rē-a nō´wēt (yū´ra). kyз´rē-u na´vit (jз´ru). "The court knows (the laws)." An alternative formulation of **Iura novit curia.**

Curriculum vitae. kūrrē´kūlūm wē´tī. kзri´kyūlum vi´tī or -vē´tī. *n.* [*pl.* **Curricula vitae.** kūrrē´kūla wē´tī. kзri´kyūlu vi´tī or -vē´tī.] "The racecourse of life." A summary document explaining a person's qualifications for business, professional, or employment purposes; a summary biographical statement. Commonly abbreviated **C.V.**

Custodes treugarum. kūstō´dās trā-ūga´rūm. kustō´dēz trūga´rum. *n. Cel.* "Keepers of the truce." Hostages given voluntarily by one state or empire to another to guarantee the former state's performance of a treaty or other obligation. This practice was common in the ancient and medieval eras but is long obsolete.

Custodia legis. kūstō´dē-a lā´gēs. kustō´dē-u le´jis. *adv.* "In the law's custody." In the possession, or within the territorial jurisdiction, of an authoritative tribunal.

Custos. kūs´tōz. kus´tōz. *n.* "Guardian." Guardian; protector; warden.

D

Da mihi factum, dabo tibi ius. da mē´hē fak´tūm, da´bō tē´bē yūs. da mi´hē fâk´tum, dā´bō ti´bē jus. "Give me the facts, I will give you law." A maxim meaning that the parties to a dispute must present evidence to the tribunal, which will arrive at a legal decision based on the parties' evidence alone. *E.g.*, "In litigation, the parties are masters of the evidence: the court has a passive role. In the words of the traditional axiom of procedure, the court says to the party: *da mihi factum, dabo tibi jus*. The parties put forward facts and submit the evidence that they consider favourable to their claims, and the court takes them into consideration when making its decision (*secundum allegata et probata*)." *Advisory Opinion on the Western Sahara*, 1975 I.C.J. Rep. 12, 138 (separate opinion of Judge De Castro).

Damna. *See* **Damnum.**

Damni iniuria actio. dam´nē ēnyū´rē-a ak´tēō. dâm´nī injʒ´rē-u âk´tēō. *n.* "An action at law for wrongful damage." An alternative formulation of **Actio damni iniuria.**

Damnificatus. damnēfēka´tūs. dâmnifikā´tus. *n. Ecc.* "The injured." One who has suffered a compensable injury caused by another. *Contrast with* **Non damnificatus.**

Damnum. dam´nūm. dâm´num. *n.* [*pl.* **Damna.** dam´na. dâm´nu.] "Loss." An injury, harm, or loss that provides the basis for a legal claim for reparations.

Damnum absque iniuria. dam´nūm ab´skwā ēnyū´rē-a. dâm´num âb´skwē injū´rē-u. *n.* "Loss without wrong." Damage not caused by the wrong, negligence, fault, or injustice of any person or state (except possibly that of the injured party) and, therefore, usually giving rise to no liability. Such injury can arise, for example, from a legally permissible act, such as the normal use of water from a watercourse by an upstream state; the loss of water to the downstream state, if reasonable, gives rise to a *damnum absque iniuria*. Alternative formulations are **Absque iniuria damnum** and **Damnum sine iniuria.** *Contrast with* **Iniuria absque damno.** *See also* **Damnum sine iniuria esse potest, Non damnificatus,** and **Non omne damnum inducit iniuriam.**

D

Damnum emergens. dam´nūm āmār´gāns. dâm´num ēmɜr´jenz. *n.* "Direct loss." An injury arising directly from a wrong, without intervening causative events or factors. Speculative or prospective damages, such as lost profits, are not included in *damnum emergens*. *E.g.*, "In Indonesian law, like in all systems of civil law, damages are to compensate the whole prejudice, whose two classical components are the loss suffered (*damnum emergens*) and the expected profits which are lost (*lucrum cessans*)." *Amco Asia Corp. v. Indonesia*, ICSID Case No. ARB/81/1, Award of Nov. 20, 1984, ¶ 266. *Contrast with* **Lucrum cessans.**

Damnum fatale. dam´nūm fata´lā. dâm´num futâ´lē. *n.* "Damage ordained by fate." Damage caused by a *force majeure*, such as war, shipwreck, or natural catastrophe. In Roman law, a bailee was not held liable for damage to property held for the bailor caused by *damnum fatale*.

Damnum sine iniuria. dam´nūm sē´nā ēnyū´rē-a. dâm´num si´nē injɜ´rē-u. *n.* "Loss without wrong." An alternative formulation of **Damnum absque iniuria.**

Damnum sine iniuria esse potest. dam´nūm sē´nā ēnyū´rē-a ās´sā pō´tāst. dâm´num si´nē injɜ´rē-u e´sē pō´test. "There can be loss without wrong." A maxim meaning that an injury may occur without giving rise to any person's legal liability if no violation of law or a legal duty has occurred. *See also* **Damnum absque iniuria.**

Datio in solutum. da´tēō ēn sōlū´tūm. dā´šō in salū´tum. *n.* "A giving in payment." A payment made in order to discharge a duty.

De aequitate. dā īkwēta´tā. dā ekwitā´tē. *adv.* "In equity." (1) Equitably. (2) Under a system of equity. *See also* **Aequitas.**

De alto et basso. dā al´tō āt bas´sō. dā al´tō et bâ´sō. *adv. Neo.* "Of high and low." (1) Completely; entirely. (2) In reference to arbitration, a compromissory clause applies *de alto et basso* when it submits all disputes of any type whatsoever to the arbitral tribunal.

De ambitu. dā am´bētū. dā âm´bitū. *adv.* "Of moving about." By dishonest or fraudulent methods, as when one secures a position or advantage by bribery.

De caetero. dā kī´tārō. dā se´tɜrō. *adv.* "Of the remainder." In the future; from now on. An alternative spelling is **De cetero.**

De cetero. An alternative spelling of **De caetero.**

De Conflictu Legum. dā kōnflĕk´tū lā´gūm. dā kanflik´tū le´jum. *N.* "On the Conflict of Laws." The title to several works on the conflict of laws, including most notably Ulrich Huber's 1689 essay, *De Conflictu Legum Diversarum in Diversis Imperiis* ("On the Various Conflict of Laws in Various Empires").

D

De die in diem. dā dē´ā ēn dē´ām. dā dē in dē´um. *adv.* "From day to day." (1) Continually; ongoing. (2) Recurrently. (3) On a daily basis. An injury that occurs *de die in diem* is an ongoing injury that does not cease until a condition of illegality is terminated. Commonly abbreviated **In diem.**

De Dominio Maris. dā dōmē´nēō ma´rēs. dā dumi´nēō ma´ris. *N.* "On Dominion of the Ocean." The title to a 1703 work by Cornelius van Bynkershoek (1673–1743) on state jurisdiction over the oceans and acts occurring thereon.

De facto. dā fak´tō. dā fâk´tō. *adj.* "From the fact." (1) As a matter of fact or reality. *E.g.*, "States are not allowed on the one hand to act *de facto* through individuals and on the other to disassociate themselves from such conduct when these individuals breach international law." *Prosecutor v. Tadic*, I.C.T.Y. Case No. IT-94-a-A, ¶ 117, 38 I.L.M. 1518 (1999). *Contrast with* **In potentia.** (2) Existing in fact while lacking in legal or moral legitimacy. *Contrast with* **De lege.** *See also* **In actu.**

De Foro Legatorum. dā fō´rō lāgatō´rūm. dā fō´rō legutō´rum. *N.* "On the Forum of Legates." The title to a 1721 work by Cornelius van Bynkershoek (1673–1743) on state jurisdiction over diplomats in civil and criminal matters.

De futuro. dā fūtū´rō. dā fyū´čɜrō. *adv.* "Of the future." (1) With regard to the future. (2) Relating to that which will occur at a future time. *Compare with* **In futuro** and **Pro futuro.**

De gratia. dā gra´tē-a. dā grâ´šu. *adj.* or *adv.* "By favor." Gratuitous; gratuitously; not due to any legal duty.

De gustibus non est disputandum. dā gūs´tēbūs nōn āst dēspūtan´dūm. dā gus´tibus nan est dispyūtân´dum. "One should not argue over taste." The Latin version of the popular saying: "There's no accounting for taste."

De incremento. dā ēnkrāmān´tō. dā inkrumen´tō. *adj.* or *adv.* "Of increase." Additional; additionally. Damages awarded to a claimant *de incremento* are additional to amounts previously claimed or awarded. Note that this term does not mean "incremental" or "incrementally."

De industria. dā ēndūs´trē-a. dā indus´trē-u. *adv.* "Intentionally." Intentionally; purposely. An alternative formulation is **Ex industria.** *Compare with* **Ex proposito.**

De iniuria. dā ēnyū´rē-a. dā injз´rē-u. *adv.* "Of injury." Relating to a harm or injury.

De integro. dā ēntāg´rō. dā integ´rō. *adv.* "Of the whole." Again; another time.

De iure. dā yū´rā. dā jз´rē. *adj.* "From right." As a matter of right; by operation of law. *Compare with* **De lege.** *Contrast with* **De facto.**

De Iure Belli ac Pacis. dā yū´rā bāl´lē ak pa´kēs. dā jз´rē be´lī âk pâ´kis. *N.* "On the Laws of War and Peace." The title to a treatise on international law first published in 1625 by the Dutch philosopher Hugo Grotius, or Huig de Groot (1583–1645).

De Iure Belli Libri Tres. dā yū´rā bāl´lē lēb´rē trās. dā jз´rē be´lī lib´rī tres. *N.* "On the Laws of War in Three Volumes." The title to the treatise on the international law of war written in 1598 by the Italian scholar Alberico Gentili (1552–1608).

De iure condendo. dā yū´rā kōndān´dō. dā jз´rē kanden´dō. *adv.* "Of the law being established." With respect to law in a transitional stage or in the process of being established. *Contrast with* **De iure condito.** *See also* **Ius condendo.**

De iure condito. dā yū´rā kōn´dētō. dā jз´rē kan´ditō. *adv.* "Of the established law." Relating to the law presently in force. *Compare with* **De lege lata.** *Contrast with* **De iure condendo.**

De Iure Praedae Commentarius. dā yū´rā prī´dī kōmmānta´rē-ūs. dā jз´rē prā´dā kamente´rē-us. *N.* "Commentary on the Law of Prizes." The title to the posthumously published treatise on the international law relating to prizes written between 1604 and 1608 by the Dutch philosopher Hugo Grotius (1583–1645), but which Grotius himself entitled *De Rebus Indicis* ("On Indian Matters").

De iure gestionis. dā yū´rā gāstēō´nēs. dā jз´rē jestēō´nis. *adj.* "Of the law of behavior." *See* **Iure gestionis.**

De iure imperii. dā yū´rā ēmpā´rē-ē. dā jз´rē impē´rī. *adj.* "Of sovereign law." *See* **Iure imperii.**

De Iure Naturae et Gentium. dā yū´ra natū´rī āt gān´tē-ūm. dā jз´rē nā´čзrā et jen´tē-um. *N.* "On Natural and International Laws." The title to a treatise on international law written in 1672 by German scholar Samuel von Pufendorf (1632–94).

De lege. dā lā´gā. dā le´jā OR -le´jē. *adj.* "Of the written law." As a matter of law; according to law, regardless of whatever practices are in fact adopted. *Compare with* **De iure.** *Contrast with* **De facto.**

D

De lege ferenda. dā lā´gā fārān´da. dā le´jā- OR -le´jē f3ren´du. *adj.* "Of the law [that is] to be proposed." Relating to *lex ferenda. See* **Lex ferenda.** *E.g.*, "[I]t appears essential to this Tribunal to distinguish between those provisions stating the existence of a right on which the generality of the States has expressed agreement and those provisions introducing new principles which were rejected by certain representative groups of States and having nothing more than a *de lege ferenda* value only in the eyes of the States which have adopted them...." *The Caltex Arbitration* (Texaco v. Libya), 53 I.L.R. 87, ¶ 87 (1982). *Compare with* **Sub specie ferendae.** *Contrast with* **De lege lata.**

De lege lata. dā lā´gā la´ta. dā le´jā- OR -le´jē lâ´tu OR -la´tu. *adj.* "Of the existing law." Relating to *lex lata. See* **Lex lata.** *Contrast with* **De lege ferenda.**

De minimis. dā mē´nēmēs. dā mi´numis. *adj.* "Of minimal things." (1) In an insubstantial or trivial amount. (2) In or by the smallest possible amount. (3) Relating to a fact or matter so insignificant that the tribunal may disregard it as lacking in legal consequence. *See also* **De minimis non curat lex.**

De minimis non curat lex. dā mē´nēmēs nōn kū´rat lāks. dā mi´nimis nan kyū´rât leks. "The law is not concerned with trifles." A maxim meaning that an action at law based on an insignificant harm or injury will not be recognized by the competent tribunal or other legal authority. The maxim has also sometimes been used to convey the notion that the outcome of an important dispute should not turn on a highly trivial or technical point of law. An alternative formulation is **De minimis lex non curat.**

De minimis lex non curat. dā mē´nēmēs lāks nōn kū´rat. dā mi´nimis leks nan kyū´rât. "The law is not concerned with trifles." An alternative formulation of **De minimis non curat lex.**

De novo. dā nō´wō. dā nō´vō. *adv.* "Newly." (1) For the first time. *E.g.*, "Guyana distinguishes Suriname's approach, which it argues is aimed at the apportionment of maritime space *de novo*, from the delimitation of maritime areas that already appertain to the coast of a State." *Guyana v. Suriname*, Perm. Ct. Arb., Award of Sept. 17, 2007, ¶ 194, 47 I.L.M. 166 (2008). (2) Without deference to preceding authority or opinion, as when an appellate tribunal completely disregards a lower tribunal's opinions and decisions and considers the same case anew. An alternative term is **Ab novo.**

De plano. dā pla´nō. dā plā´nō. *adv.* "On ground level." (1) Summarily and automatically; as a matter of course. *E.g.*, "A rule of this kind adopted by the Powers in 1885 for the African continent does not apply *de plano* to other regions." *Island of Palmas Case* (U.S. v. Neth.), 2 R.I.A.A. 829 (1928).

Compare with **Ipso facto.** (2) Out of court; not before an authoritative tribunal. *Compare with* **Ex parte** and **Extra iudicium.**

De praesenti. dā prīsān´tē. dā prezen´tī. *adv.* "Of the present." (1) Relating to the present. (2) Currently. An alternative spelling is **De presenti.**

De presenti. An alternative spelling of **De praesenti.**

De quo. dā kwō. dā kwō. *adj. Med.* "Of which." Of which; relating to which. *E.g.*, "The Court cannot admit the objection that, the title to the bonds and shares in question *de quo* having been acquired by the enemy as war booty, they must be considered as definitely lost to the former owners." *Mazzoni v. Ministry of Finance*, Ct. of Venice, Judgment of Jan. 8, 1927, *in* ANNUAL DIGEST OF PUBLIC INTERNATIONAL LAW CASES, 1927–28, at 564 (Arnold D. McNair *et al.* eds., 1932).

De recenti. dā rākān´tē. dā resen´tī. *adv.* "Recently." Beginning or occurring in the very near past.

De rigore iuris. dā rēgō´rā yū´rēs. dā ri´gɜrē jɜ´ris. *adv.* "Of the law's strictness." According to the strict or literal requirements of law, without modification by creative interpretation or reference to equity or public policy. An alternative formulation is **In rigore iuris.** *Compare with* **Ex rigore iuris, Stricto iure,** and **Strictissimi iuris.**

De verbo in verbum. dā wār´bō ēn wār´būm. dā vɜr´bō in vɜr´bum. *adv.* "From word into word." Literally; exactly as previously spoken or written. *Compare with* **Ipsis verbis, Ipsissima verba, Totidem verbis,** and **Verbatim.**

Debellatio. dābālla´tēō. debulā´šō. *n. Neo.* "Conquest." Occupation and administration of a territory by a hostile power, usually following complete military conquest and subjugation of the territory's armed forces and deposal of its government for future replacement by a new government or system of governance. The term *debellatio* was formerly used in cases where the conquering power intended to annex or assume permanent sovereignty over the territory, but this usage is no longer current. *E.g.*, "But it appears to be a fair deduction from the principle, always admitted in theory, that conquest (unless by *debellatio*) requires to be completed by consent, even though the consent may be under duress." Th. Baty, *The Trend of International Law*, 33 AM. J. INT'L L. 653, 658 (1939).

Debet quis iuri subiacere ubi delinquit. dā´bāt kwēs yū´rē sūbya´kārā ū´bē dālēn´kwēt. de´bet kwis jɜ´rī subjā´sɜrē u´bē dulin´kwit. "Anyone ought to submit to the law where he violates the law." A maxim meaning that a state has jurisdiction to punish one who violates its law within its territory regardless of the violator's nationality or domicile. *See also* **Crimen trahit personam.**

Debile fundamentum fallit opus. dā´bēlā fūndamān´tūm fal´lēt ō´pūs. de´bilē fundumen´tum fâ´lit ō´pus. "Where the foundation is weak, the work collapses." A maxim meaning that a treaty, agreement, or other legal instrument that is defective in a critical aspect of formation cannot give rise to legal rights or obligations.

Decie(n)s. dā´kē-ā(n)s. de´sē(n)z. *adv.* "Tenthly." An adverbial number (the tenth) usually inserted into a consecutively numbered series by way of amendment. *See* the Appendix for a list of Latin adverbial numbers commonly used in international law. *See also* **Bis** and **Semel.**

Decrementum maris. dākrāmān´tūm ma´rēs. dekremen´tum ma´ris. *n.* "Decreasing of the sea." Reliction; the gradual recession of the sea, lake, or watercourse from the land, which exposes new land over which sovereignty may be claimed.

Decretum. dākrā´tūm. dekrē´tum. *n.* [*pl.* **Decreta.** dākrā´ta. dekrē´tu.] "Decree." A directive or decree issued by a sovereign authority. In Roman law, *decreta* indicated judgments and sentences of government officials, including frequently the emperor himself when sitting as a magistrate.

Deditio. dādē´tēō. dedi´šō. *n.* "Surrender." The surrender of a belligerent state, legally terminating that state's participation in an armed conflict.

Definitio. dāfēnē´tēō. defini´šō. *n.* [*pl.* **Definitiones.** dāfēnētēō´nās. definišō´nēz.] "Definition." (1) A definition or full description. (2) A defined territorial boundary.

Defunctus. dāfūnk´tūs. dēfunk´tus. *n.* "Deceased." A deceased person or, metaphorically, thing or idea.

Delegatus. dālāga´tūs. delegā´tus. *n.* [*pl.* **Delegati.** dālāga´tē. delegā´tī.] "Delegate." A diplomatic delegate, agent, or envoy.

Delegatus non potest delegare. dālāga´tūs nōn pō´tāst dālāga´rā. delegā´tus nan pō´test delega´rē. "A delegate cannot delegate." A maxim meaning that no sovereign or government, as the representative of a people, has the power to delegate the appointment of its diplomatic envoys to a foreign sovereign.

Deliberandum est diu quod statuendum est semel. dālēbāran´dūm āst dē´ū kwōd statūān´dūm āst sā´māl. dulibɜrân´dum est dī´ū kwad stačū-en´dum est se´mel. "What is once resolved is to be long deliberated upon." A maxim meaning that a tribunal should exercise care, consideration, and discretion in issuing a judgment of last resort.

Delictum. dālēk´tūm. dulik´tum. *n.* "Wrong." (1) An injurious or otherwise wrongful act. (2) An offense under law.

Delictum iuris gentium. dālēk´tūm yū´rēs gān´tē-ūm. dulik´tum j3´ris jen´tē-um. *n.* "Wrong against the law of nations." A breach of a duty under international law, especially one rising to the level of a criminal offense. *E.g.*, "As a *delictum juris gentium* the crime of genocide implies the cumulation of two elements—the material (the commission of the acts indicated a limine in Article II of the Convention) and the subjective (the intention (*dolus specialis*) to 'destroy, in whole or in part, a national, ethnical, racial or religious group, as such')." *Application of the Convention on the Prevention and Punishment of the Crime of Genocide* (Bosn. & Herz. v. Yugo.), 1993 I.C.J. Rep. 325, 460 (Judge *ad hoc* Kreća, dissenting). *Compare with* **Crimina iuris gentium.**

Denuntiatio belli. dānūntē-a´tēō bāl´lē. dēnuntē-ā´šō be´lī. *n.* "Declaration of war." A declaration of war, which was formerly considered a necessary formality prior to a state's armed attack on another state. With the advent of the United Nations Charter and its limits on the uses of armed force in international relations, the *denuntiatio belli* as such has become largely obsolete.

Derelictio. dārālēk´tēō. derelik´tēō. *n.* "Dereliction." The abandonment of occupation of a territory with the clear intent to renounce sovereignty over it. *E.g.*, "There is no reason to suppose that France has subsequently lost her right by *derelictio*, since she never had the *animus* of abandoning the island, and the fact that she has not exercised her authority there in a positive manner does not imply the forfeiture of an acquisition already definitively perfected." *Sovereignty over Clipperton Island Case* (Fr. v. Mex.), Award of Jan. 28, 1931, 26 AM. J. INT'L L. 390, 394 (1932). *See also* **Animus derelinquendi.**

Designatio unius (est) exclusio alterius. dāsēgna´tēō ūnē´ūs (āst) ākskl ū´sēō altārē´ūs. dezignā´šō ū´nē-us (est) eksklū´zēō alt3´rē-us. "The designation of one (is) the exclusion of the other." An alternative formulation of **Expressio unius (est) exclusio alterius.**

Dextras dare. dāks´tras da´rā. deks´trus da´rē. *v. inf.* "To give right hands." (1) To shake hands to show agreement, peaceful intentions, or friendship. (2) To surrender or submit to another.

Diatim. dē-a´tēm. dī´utim. *adv.* "Daily." On a daily basis.

Dicis causa. dē´kēs kô´sa. dī´sus kă´zu. *adv.* "For form's sake." For the sake of appearances; as a matter of legal form. This was a favorite phrase of Cicero.

Dictum. dēk´tūm. dik´tum. *n.* [*pl.* **Dicta.** dēk´ta. dik´tu.] "Saying." (1) A maxim. (2) A statement of opinion considered persuasive due to the authority of the commentator. *E.g.*, "The Permanent Court of International Justice [in the *S.S. Lotus* case]...started by saying that, as a matter of principle, jurisdiction is territorial and that a State cannot exercise jurisdiction outside its territory without a permission derived from international custom or from a convention. It however immediately added a qualification of this principle in a famous *dictum* that students of international law know very well: 'It does not, however, follow that international law prohibits a State from exercising jurisdiction in its own territory, in respect of any case which relates to acts which have taken place abroad, and in which it cannot rely on some permissive rule of international law." *Arrest Warrant of 11 April 2000* (Congo v. Belg.), 2002 I.C.J. Rep. 3, 167, ¶ 48 (Judge Van den Wyngaert, dissenting). (3) A common abbreviation for **Obiter dictum**.

Dies. dē´ās. dē´us. *n.* [*pl.* **Dies.** dē´ās. dē´us.] "Day." A day.

Dies a quo. dē´ās a kwō. dē´us a kwō. *n.* "The day from which...." The beginning moment of a stated period, especially when the specific commencement date of the period has legal consequences. *E.g.*, "[I]n international law parlance, there must be continuous national identity from the date of the events giving rise to the claim, which date is known as the *dies a quo*, through the date of the resolution of the claim, which is the date known as the *dies ad quem*." *Loewen Group v. United States*, ICSID Case No. ARB(AF)/98/3 (NAFTA ch. 11 Arb. Trib.), Award of June 26, 2003, 42 I.L.M. 811 (2003). *Compare with* **Terminus a quo**. *Contrast with* **Dies ad quem**.

Dies ad quem. dē´ās ad kwām. dē´us âd kwem. *n. pl.* "The day until which...." The final term or moment of a stated period, especially when the specific ending date of the period has legal consequences. *Compare with* **Terminus ad quem**. *Contrast with*, and *see* the example of usage in, **Dies a quo**.

Dies datus (partibus). dē´ās da´tūs (par´tēbūs). dē´us dā´tus (par´tibus). *n.* "A day given (to the parties)." A judicial continuance; a period of adjournment or respite given by a tribunal before a date of legal significance, such as a hearing date or deadline for written submissions.

Differentia specifica. dēffārān´tē-a spākē´fēka. difɜren´šu spesi´fiku. *n. pl.* "Specific difference." A basis for discriminating between two or more alternatives. *E.g.*, "The qualification 'as such' serves also as *differentia specifica* between discriminatory intent as suggestive of an element of the crime of persecution, which also may have, as its target for genocidal intent, a racial, excluding ethnic, group." *Application of the Convention on the Prevention and Punishment of the Crime of Genocide* (Bosn. & Herz. v. Yugo.), I.C.J. No. 91, Judgment of Feb. 26, 2007, at 48, ¶ 99 (separate opinion of Judge *ad hoc* Kreća).

Dilationes in lege sunt odiosae. dēlatēō´nās ēn lā´gā sūnt ōdēō´sī. dīlāšō´nez in le´jē sunt ōdēō´zā. "Delays in law are hateful." An alternative phrase for **Lex dilationes abhorret.**

Diligentia. dēlēgān´tē-a. dilijen´šu. *n.* "Diligence." (1) Observance or fulfillment of one's legal responsibilities. (2) Diligence; vigilance; due care. *Contrast with* **Culpa.**

D

Diligentia quam in suis (rebus). dēlēgān´tē-a kwam ēn sū´ēs (rā´būs). dilijen´šu kwam in sū´is (rē´bus). "Care in his own (matters)." In Roman law, a guardian's duty of care with respect to matters concerning the interests of his ward, which standard was the same as the guardian's duty of care in matters concerning himself. It has been applied by analogy in international law in service of the argument that states are obligated to provide ordinary rather than extraordinary protection (a kind of "national treatment") to foreign nationals found in their territory. *E.g.*, "The vigilance which, from the point of view of international law a State is obliged to exercise, may be characterised as a *diligentia quam in suis* applying Roman law by analogy…." Bin Cheng, General Principles of Law as Applied by International Courts and Tribunals 221 (1953).

Disiuncta. dēsyūnk´ta. disjunk´tu. *n. pl.* "Disjoined things." (1) Terms or concepts opposed to one another. (2) Separated things.

Disiunctim. dēsyūnk´tēm. disjunk´tim. *adv.* "Separately." Separately; independently; severally, as when liability attaches to multiple parties severally. An alternative term is **Divisim.**

Disputatio fori. dēspūta´tēō fō´rē. dispyūtā´šō fō´rī. *n.* "Argument of the forum." The practice of arguing a case before an authoritative tribunal.

Dissensus. dēssān´sūs. disen´sus. *n.* "Disagreement." (1) The voluntary mutual annulment of a contract clause or an entire contract. (2) Generally, a failure to agree; an absence of agreement.

Divisim. dēwē´sēm. divī´zim. *adv.* "Separately." An alternative term for **Disiunctim.**

Divisum imperium. dēwē´sūm ēmpā´rē-ūm. divī´zum impe´rē-um. *n.* "Divided empire." Divided jurisdiction, as when two or more authorities exercise concurrent jurisdiction over the same matter. In addition, under English law, the littoral coast between the high-tide mark and low-tide mark was formerly considered *divisum imperium* because it was high seas and subject to admiralty law during high tide and land territory subject to common law during low tide. *E.g.*, "The main or high seas are part of the realm of England, for thereon our courts of admiralty have jurisdiction, as will be shewn hereafter; but they are not subject to the common law. This main-sea begins at the low-water-mark. But between the high-water-mark, and the low-water-mark, where the sea ebbs and flows, the common law and the admiralty have *divisum imperium*, an alternate jurisdiction; one upon the water, when it is full sea; the other upon the land when it is an ebb." 1 William Blackstone, COMMENTARIES ON THE LAWS OF ENGLAND 109–10 (1860) (1765).

Divortium aquarum. dēwōr´tē-ūm akwa´rūm. divōr´šum ukwa´rum. *n.* "Division of waters." An imaginary line separating two submarine slopes or bordering fluvial river basins. The *divortium aquarum* is sometimes used in boundary delimitation as a convenient line to divide regions with complex or high-density fluvial channels and relatively few prominent geomorphological features. *E.g.*, "Chile's extreme claim at that time had been the continental *divortium aquarum*, which meant that the Atlantic basins would remain under Argentine jurisdiction and the Pacific basins under Chilean jurisdiction." *Boundary Dispute Concerning the Frontier Line Between Boundary Post 62 and Mount Fitzroy* (Arg. v. Chile), 22 R.I.A.A. 3, 26, ¶ 78 (1994).

Do ut des. dō ūt dās. dō ut des. "I give so that you may give." (1) In Roman law, an innominate contract in which one party's performance satisfies the condition for the other party's performance. (2) An adage conveying the sense of reciprocity inherent in early conceptions of international law.

Dolo facit qui petit quod statim redditurus est. dō´lō fa´kēt kwē pā´tēt sta´tēm rāddētū´rūs āst. dō´lō fā´sit kwē pe´tit kwad stā´tim redi´tɜrus est. "He who requests that which he will have to return acts by deceit." A maxim, originating in Justinian's *Digest* (44.4.2), meaning that one who owes something to another who possesses that very thing would only demand the thing from an intent to defraud the rightful possessor. *E.g.*, "The Trial Chamber held that even if a violation of State sovereignty had occurred [by the unlawful capture and rendition of the accused to the ICTY], the FRY would have been obliged, under Article 29 of the Statute, to immediately re-surrender the Accused after his return to the FRY. The Trial Chamber recalled the maxim '*dolo facit qui petit quod statim redditurus est*.'" *Prosecutor v. Nikolic*, ICTY Case No. IT-94-2-S, Judgment of Dec. 18, 2003, ¶ 26.

Dolus. dō´lūs. dō´lus. *n.* "Deceit." (1) Harm or injury, especially willfully caused. *Compare with* **Maleficium**. (2) Deceit, fraud, or bad faith; an alternative term for **Dolus malus**.

Dolus bonus. dō´lūs bō´nūs. dō´lus bō´nus. *n.* "Good deceit." (1) Shrewdness; any skillful contrivance not causing illegal consequences. (2) Morally or legally justifiable deceit, such as might be used to prevent an unlawful harm from occurring. *Contrast with* **Dolus malus**.

Dolus directus. dō´lūs dērāk´tūs. dō´lus direk´tus. *n.* "Direct deceit." The intention to perpetrate unlawful conduct or engage in a wrongful act. *Contrast with* **Dolus indirectus.**

Dolus indirectus. dō´lūs ēndērāk´tūs. dō´lus indirek´tus. *n.* "Indirect deceit." The intention to act in a manner that will foreseeably cause a wrongful harm to another without the specific intention to cause that harm. *Contrast with* **Dolus directus** and **Damnum emergens.**

Dolus malus. dō´lūs ma´lūs. dō´lus mâ´lus. *n.* "Evil deceit." (1) Evil intent; bad faith. In Roman law, the term could be used to designate any evil scheme or course of action to injure another illegally and was synonymous with **Dolus.** *Compare with* **Animus malus, Mens rea,** and **Scienter.** *See also* **Culpa.** (2) Morally or legally unjustifiable deceit; fraud. *Contrast with* **Dolus bonus.**

Dolus specialis. dō´lūs spākē-a´lēs. dō´lus spešâ´lus. *n.* "Special deceit." (1) A harm resulting from an act specifically intended to cause that harm. (2) The specific intent to cause a specific kind of harm. *E.g.*, "Genocide is distinct from other crimes inasmuch as it embodies a special intent or *dolus specialis.* Special intent of a crime is the specific intention, required as a constitutive element of the crime, which requires that the perpetrator clearly seek to produce the act charged." *Prosecutor v. Akayesu*, I.C.T.R. Case No. 96-4-T, Judgment of Sept. 2, 1998, ¶ 42, 37 I.L.M. 1399 (1998); "[T]here is no doubt that the conduct of an organ or a person furnishing aid or assistance to a perpetrator of the crime of genocide cannot be treated as complicity in genocide unless at the least that organ or person acted knowingly, that is to say, in particular, was aware of the specific intent (*dolus specialis*) of the principal perpetrator." *Application of the Convention on the Prevention and Punishment of the Crime of Genocide* (Bosn. & Herz. v. Serb. & Mont.), I.C.J. Case No. 91, Judgment of Feb. 26, 2007, at ¶ 421. *See also* **Actus non facit reum, nisi mens sit rea** and **Mens rea.**

Domicilium. dōmēkē´lē-ūm. dōmisi´lē-um. *n.* "Domicile." Domicile; one's fixed, true and foreseeably permanent home, as opposed to temporary residence. A person's *domicilium* is commonly used in private international law to establish jurisdiction over that person.

Domilicium ex proprio motu. dōmēkē´lē-ūm āks prōp´rēō mō´tū. dōmisi´lē-um eks prap´rēō mō´tū. *n.* "Domicile from one's own motion." In private international law, domicile established by the intent to remain in a place indefinitely. *See also* **Domicilium.**

Domicilium necessarium. dōmēkē´lē-ūm nākāssa´rē-ūm. dōmisi´lē-um nesesa´rē-um. *n.* "Necessary domicile." Domicile established by legal presumption, as when a child's domicile is determined automatically by the domicile of its parents.

Domicilium originis (vel nativitatis). dōmēkē´lē-ūm ōrē´gēnēs (wāl natēwēta´tēs). dōmisi´lē-um ōri´jinis (vel nātivitā´tus). *n.* "Domicile of origin (or nativity)." Domicile established by birth within the jurisdiction.

D

Domini terrae. dō´mēnē tār´rī. da´minī te´rā. *n. pl.* "Lords of the lands." Landlords; land owners. *E.g.*, "[T]he doctrine of international servitude...originated in the peculiar and now obsolete conditions prevailing in the Holy Roman Empire of which *domini terrae* were not fully sovereigns; they holding territory under the Roman Empire, subject at least theoretically, and in some respects also practically, to the courts of that Empire; their right being, moreover, rather of a civil than a public nature, partaking more of the character of *dominium* than of *imperium*, and therefore certainly not a complete sovereignty [*sic*]." *The North Atlantic Coast Fisheries Arbitration* (U.K. v. U.S.), 11 R.I.A.A. 167 (1910).

Dominium. dōmē´nē-ūm. dōmi´nē-um. *n.* "Title." Absolute public ownership of property or territory with the right to control all use thereof. *Dominium* is one of the two core characteristics of sovereignty. *See also* **Imperium** and **Maiestas.**

Dominium eminens. dōmē´nē-ūm ā´mēnāns. dōmi´nē-um e´minez. *n.* "Eminent domain." The state's right to exercise sovereignty and direct control over its territory, or any part thereof. *Compare with* **Ius praeminens.**

Dominus litis. dō´mēnūs lē´tēs. da´minus li´tis. *n.* "Lord of the lawsuit." (1) In civil law, the person in a lawsuit who makes the substantive decisions, which are executed by counsel. Usually, this person is the litigant, although a guardian, receiver, or other fiduciary may also act as *dominus litis.* (2) In maritime law, an agent acting in a lawsuit on behalf of a party unable to attend the proceedings.

Dominus navis. dō´mēnūs na´wēs. da´minus nâ´vis. *n.* "Lord of the ship." The ultimate owner of a seagoing vessel.

Dormiunt leges aliquando, nunquam moriuntur. dōr´mē-ūnt lā´gās alēkwan´dō, nūn´kwam mōrē-ūn´tūr. dōr´mē-unt le´jēz âlikwan´dō, nun´kwum mōrē-un´tɜr. "The laws sometimes sleep, but they never die." A maxim meaning that, although the operation of some laws may be suspended under special circumstances (such as certain human rights laws during time of war), the laws resume in full force upon the termination of these circumstances.

Dramatis personae. drama´tēs pārsō´nī. dramâ´tis pɜrsō´nā. *n. pl.* "Dramatic characters." Persons or characters directly involved in the relevant matter, usually as the key actors.

Dubii iuris. dū´bē-ē yū´rēs. dū´bī jɜ´ris. *adj.* "Of uncertain law." Relating to a point of law not clearly settled by precedent. *Compare with* **Non liquet.**

Dubio mitius. dū´bēō mē´tē-ūs. dū´bēō mišus. An abbreviated form of **In dubio mitius.**

Dubitante. dūbētan´tā. dūbitân´tē. *adj.* or *adv.* "While doubting." Skeptical(ly) or uncertain on a point of law.

Duodecie(n)s. dūōdā´kē-ā(n)s. dū´ōdesē(n)z. *adv.* "Twelfthly." An adverbial number (the twelfth) usually inserted into a consecutively numbered series by way of amendment. *See* the Appendix for a list of Latin adverbial numbers commonly used in international law. *See also* **Bis** and **Semel.**

Dum fervet opus. dūm fār´wāt ō´pūs. dum fɜr´vet ō´pus. "While the work glows." In the heat of the moment; while the iron is hot.

Dura lex sed lex. dū´ra lāks sād lāks. dɜ´ru leks sed leks. "The law is hard, but law." A maxim of Roman civil law meaning that, however regrettable the outcome of the legal decision may be, the law must be proclaimed and enforced. The maxim has been used both sincerely and disingenuously. *E.g.*, "I also understand perfectly that, once the goods are released, that is to say, once they are beyond the physical control of the customs agents, amendment [of a customs declaration] carries too great a risk of fraud to be allowed at that stage, and that a flexible approach, allowing amendments, subject to strict conditions, to matters unrelated to the physical characteristics of the goods could perhaps have been envisaged. However, no provision was made for such an approach. Must we then apply to [the petitioner/importer] the maxim *dura lex sed lex*, as the United Kingdom and the Commission do?" Opinion of Advocate General Mischo, *Overland Footwear Ltd. v. Commissioners of Customs & Excise*, E.C.J. Case C-379/00, ¶¶ 54–55, [2002] E.C.R. I-11133.

Durante. dūran´tā. dɜrân´tē. *prep.* "During." (1) Throughout a period of time. (2) At some point in a time span. Grammatically, *durante* is an ablative absolute participle and must precede a noun.

Durante bello. dūran´tā bāl´lō. dɜrân´tē be´lō. *adv.* "While the war lasts." (1) During an armed conflict. (2) Limited to the context of an armed conflict.

E

E contra. ā kōn´tra. ē kan´tru. *adv.* "From the contrary." On the contrary. *Compare with* **E converso.**

E converso. ā kōnwär´sō. ē kanv3r´sō. *adv.* "From the converse." (1) On the contrary. (2) On the other hand. *Compare with* **E contra.**

E.g. An abbreviation of **Exempli gratia.**

Ea intentione. ā-a ēntāntēō´nā. ē-u intenšō´nē. *adv.* "With that intention." Having that intention; with that goal in mind. *Compare with* **Eo intuitu.**

Eadem est ratio, eadem est lex. ā´adām āst ra´tēō, ā´adām āst lāks. ē´dem est rā´šō, ē´dem est leks. "The reason is the same, the law is the same." A maxim meaning that the law should be applied in the same way in cases with different facts where the rationale for the law applies equally under the diverse facts.

Efforcialiter. āffōrkē-a´lētār. efōrsē-ā´lit3r OR efōršā´lit3r. *adv.* "Forcibly." By means of force, especially armed force.

Eius est interpretare legem cuius condere. ā´yūs āst ēntārprāta´rā lā´gām kū´yūs kōn´dārā. ē´jus est int3rpreta´rē le´jum kū´jus kan´d3rē. "Whoever is authorized to establish the law is authorized to interpret it." A maxim meaning that the most authoritative interpreter of a legal instrument or of a judicial or arbitral decision is the body that drafted the law or issued the judgment or award. *E.g.*, "Without success it has been maintained…that the letter of November 13th, 1922, from the Conference of Ambassadors…is the most authoritative and most reliable interpretation of the intention expressed at that time, and that such an interpretation, being drawn from the most reliable source, must be respected by all, in accordance with the traditional principle: *ejus est interpretare legem cujus condere.*" *Advisory Opinion on the Delimitation of the Polish-Czechoslovakian Frontier (Question of Jaworzina)*, 1923 PCIJ (Ser. B) No. 8, at 37 (Dec. 6).

Eiusdem generis. āyūs´dām gā´nārēs. ājus´dem je´nɜris. *adv.* "Of the same kind." A principle according to which, where general words follow specific words (or *vice versa*) in an enumeration, the general words are construed to embrace only objects of similar nature to those enumerated by the specific words. *Compare with* **Noscitur a sociis is eiusdem generis.**

E

Electa una via (non datur recursus ad alteram). ālāk´ta ū´na wē´a (nōn da´tūr rākūr´sūs ad al´tāram). elek´tu ū´nu vī´u- OR -vē´u (nan dā´tɜr rekɜr´sus âd al´tɜrum). "One route having been chosen (no recourse to another is given)." A maxim meaning that a party wishing to bring a claim against another must choose a single forum even if multiple fora (*e.g.*, both a court and an arbitral tribunal) are available to it.

Electio fori. ālāk´tēō fō´rē. elek´tēō fō´rī. *n.* "Choice of forum." A choice of the forum to decide disputes arising from or relating to a legal relationship or the interpretation of a legal instrument. *E.g.*, "According to the jurisdiction of the Federal Tribunal in accordance with the international doctrine [of] jurisdiction, the conclusion from the *electio fori* to the *electio juris* is only admissible if the choice of the forum is accompanied by other clues." 3 REPERTORY OF INTERNATIONAL ARBITRAL JURISPRUDENCE 1499 (Vincent Coussirat-Coustère and Pierre Michel Eisemann eds., 1991). *See also* **Electio iuris.**

Electio iuris. ālāk´tēō yū´rēs. elek´tēō jɜ´ris. *n.* "Choice of law." A choice of the law of a specific jurisdiction to govern a legal relationship or the interpretation or enforcement of a legal instrument. *See also, and see example of usage under,* **Electio fori.**

Emptor. āmp´tōr. emp´tɜr. *n.* [*pl.* **Emptores.** āmptō´rās. emptō´rēz.]. "Buyer." Purchaser.

Ens et bonum est commune. āns āt bō´nūm āst kōmmū´nā. enz et bō´num est kamyū´nē. "Being and goodness is in common." A maxim meaning that the state of things as they currently exist (the *status quo*) is identical to how things should be normatively. *E.g.*, "But there is in this passage also a troubling equivocation of what actually happens (the Court's institutional behaviour) with what ought to happen (general law): *ens et bonum est commune.*" Jörg Kammerhofer and André de Hoogh, *All Things to All People? The International Court of Justice and Its Commentators*, 18 EUR. J. INT'L L. 971, 978 (2007).

Ens legis. āns lā´gēs. enz le´jis. *n.* "A being of the law." An entity created and existing by operation of law with independent legal personality, such as a corporation.

Enumeratio unius (est) exclusio alterius. ānūmāra´tēō ūnē´ūs (āst) ākksklū´sēō altār-ē´ūs. ēnūm3rā´šō ū´nyus (est) eksklū´zēō alt3´rē-us. "The enumeration of one (is) the exclusion of the other." An alternative phrase for **Expressio unius (est) exclusio alterius.**

E

Eo instante (tempore). ā´ō ēnstan´tā (tāmpō´rā). ē´ō instân´tē (tempō´rē). *adv.* "At the instant (of time)." At that same instant; at the very moment.

Eo instanti (tempore). A misspelling of **Eo instante (tempore).**

Eo intuitu. ā´ō ēntū´ētū. ē´ō intū´itū. *adv.* "In that respect." (1) With that perspective; in that belief. (2) With that intention; with that goal in mind. *Compare with* **Ea intentione.**

Eo ipso. ā´ō ēp´sō. ē´ō ip´sō. *adv.* "By that very same." By the same act or fact. *Compare with* **De plano** and **Ipso facto.**

Eo loci. ā´ō lō´kē. ē´ō lō´sī. *adv.* "In that condition." In that condition; in that state.

Eo loco. ā´ō lō´kō. ē´ō lō´kō. *adv.* "In that place." In that place.

Eo nomine. ā´ō nō´mēnā. ē´ō na´minē. "By name." By the specific name used; by the literal name. In customs law, an *eo nomine* entry on a tariff schedule means that the imported item is specifically listed by name on the schedule. *E.g.*, "[A]n *eo nomine* designation [on the tariff schedule], with no terms of limitation, will ordinarily include all forms of the named article. Stated otherwise, all forms, grades and qualities of the named article are embraced by such a designation." *Hayes-Sammons Chem. Co. v. United States*, 55 C.C.P.A. 69 (1968) (U.S.). *See also* **Nominatim.**

Equitas. An alternative spelling of **Aequitas.** For all entries using the term *equitas*, substitute *aequitas* instead.

Erga omnes. ār´ga ōm´nās. 3r´gu am´nēz. "Toward all." With respect to all states or persons in a relevant group. The phrase is usually applied to obligations owed by a state to all other states or the international community at large, such as the duty not to engage in genocide or piracy, or to claim sovereignty over the high seas. All states are considered to have a legal interest in deterring violations of *erga omnes* obligations. Note that, while *ius cogens* norms are often considered to arise from obligations *erga omnes*, the category of *erga omnes* obligations is broader than the scope of *ius cogens*. *E.g.*, "[O]bligations of a State towards the international community as a whole...[b]y their very nature...are the concern of all States. In view of the importance of the rights involved, all States can be held to have a legal interest in their protection; they are obligations *erga omnes.*" *Barcelona Traction, Light, and Power Company* (Belg. v. Spain), 1970 I.C.J. Rep. 3, ¶ 33. *See also* **Ius cogens.**

Ergo. ār´gō. 3r´gō. *adv.* "Therefore." Therefore; hence. Sometimes (though not always) used ironically to indicate a logically false conclusion. *E.g.*, "[I]t is quite clear that the only question at issue was whether in Article 12, in connection with Article 6, a concession for exclusive navigation was given or not—*ergo*, a question of doubt and controversy about the interpretation...." *The Orinoco Steamship Company Case* (U.S. v. Venez.), U.S.–Venez. Cl. Comm'n, Award of Feb. 22, 1904, H.C.R. (Series 1), at 265–66 (Scott, 1916). *Compare with* **Ideo** and **Per consequens.**

Errare humanum est, (sed) perseverare diabolicum. ārra´rā hūma´nūm āst, (sed) pārsāwāra´rā diabō´lēkūm. era´rē hyū´menum est, (sed) p3rsev3ra´rē dīuba´likum. "To err is human, (but) to persist is diabolical." A maxim meaning that to make mistakes is a common (and by implication forgivable) human attribute, but to persist in making the same mistake is a personal or moral flaw (and by implication less forgivable). The phrase may derive from Cicero (*Phil.* 12.5): "It is typical of any man to err, but the mark of no one but a fool to persist in error." *E.g.*, "I did not subscribe to that reasoning, and whilst I did vote with the majority in favor of finding that there had not been a violation that was because, in my view, the Articles of the [European Convention on Human Rights] relied on were not applicable...(but the Chamber did not agree with my reasoning on that point, and I will not go into it again here—*perseverare diabolicum*)." *E.B. v. France*, [2008] E.C.H.R. 43546/02 (Judge Türmen, dissenting).

Erratum. ārra´tūm. erâ´tum. *n.* [*pl.* **Errata.** ārra´ta. erâ´tu.] "Error." An error, usually typographical. *See also* **Corrigendum.**

Error calculi. ār´rōr kal´kūlē. e´r3r kâlkyūlī. *n.* "Error of calculation." An error in calculation, such as a mistake in computing damages or interest on an award.

Error in procedendo. ār´rōr ēn prōkādān´dō. e´r3r in prōsuden´dō. *n.* "Error in proceeding." An error in judicial or other formal procedure. *Contrast with* **Error iuris.**

Error in vacuo. ār´rōr ēn wa´kūō. e´r3r in vâ´kyūō. *n.* "Error in a void." Harmless error; error of insufficient consequence to affect a legal outcome.

Error iuris. ār´rōr yū´rēs. e´r3r j3´ris. *n.* "Error of law." An error in ascertaining, interpreting, or applying the law. *Contrast with* **Error in procendo.**

Error iuris nocet. ār´rōr yū´rēs nō´kāt. e´r3r j3´ris nō´set. "An error of law harms." A maxim meaning that an error in ascertaining, interpreting, or applying the law is harmful to the affected parties and to the consistency and coherence of the law itself. *See also* **Error iuris.**

Error lapsus. ār´rōr lap´sūs. e´r3r lâp´sus. *n.* "Error by inattention." An error caused by negligence or inattention.

Erronice. ārrō´nēkā. erō´nisē. *adv.* "Erroneously." Mistakenly; erroneously.

Et. āt. et. *conj.* "And." And.

Et al. (1) An abbreviation of **Et alii / Et aliae / Et alia.** (2) An abbreviation of **Et alibi.**

Et alia. *See* **Et alii / Et aliae / Et alia.**

Et aliae. *See* **Et alii / Et aliae / Et alia.**

Et alibi. āt a´lēbē. et â´libī. *conj.* + *adv.* "And elsewhere." And elsewhere; in other places as well. Sometimes abbreviated **Et al.**

Et alii / Et aliae / Et alia. āt a´lē-ē / āt a´lē-ī / āt a´lē-a. et â´lē / et â´lē-ā / et â´lē-u. "And others." Others of the kind listed are not mentioned. Commonly abbreviated **Et al.** The distinction between these three forms is that **Et alii** refers to masculine nouns, **Et aliae** to feminine nouns, and **Et alia** to neuter nouns.

Et cetera. āt kā´tāra. et se´t3ru. "And the rest." (1) And so forth. (2) And others of a similar kind. Commonly abbreviated **Etc.**

Et hoc genus omne. āt hōk gā´nūs ōm´nā. et hak jē´nus am´nē. "And all that kind of thing." A bombastic synonym of **Et cetera.**

Et seq. An abbreviation of **Et sequentes/sequentia.**

Et sequentes/sequentia. āt sākwān´tēs/sākwān´tē-a. et sekwen´tēz/sekwen´ču. *conj.* + *n. pl.* "And the following." Including whatever follows hereafter or thereafter. *Et sequentes* is the masculine form and *et sequentia* is the neuter form, but the difference is inconsequential in English. *Et sequentes* is a citation signal indicating that the reference material is to be found in the cited page and all materials following it up to their natural conclusion. *E.g.*, "It has been established, in any event, that from 1954 onwards officials from Dahomey exercised territorial authority over Lété Island, collecting taxes and intervening to restore order, as the Chamber itself notes (Judgment, paras. 90 *et seq.*)." *Frontier Dispute* (Benin v. Niger), 2005 I.C.J. Rep. 90, 161-62, ¶ 43 (Judge *ad hoc* Bennouna, dissenting). Commonly abbreviated **Et seq.**

Et sic ulterius. āt sēk ūltārē´ūs. et sik 3lte´rē-us. *conj.* + *adv.* "And so forth." And so forth; and so on.

Etc. An abbreviation of **Et cetera.**

Evidentia. āwēdān´tē-a. eviden´šu. *n. pl.* "Plainly visible things." Evidence.

Ex. āks. eks. *prep.* "Out of." (1) Originating from. (2) Out of. (3) Because of. (4) From.

Ex abundante cautela. āks abūndan´tā kôtā´la. eks âbundân´tē kăte´lu. An alternative spelling of **Ex abundanti cautela.**

Ex abundanti. āks abūndan´tē. eks âbundan´tī. *adv.* "From abundance." (1) Abundantly; profusely. (2) Superfluously; cloyingly.

Ex abundanti cautela. āks abūndan´tē kôtā´la. eks âbundân´tī kăte´lu. *adv.* "Out of an abundance of caution." Done solely or primarily to forestall some perceived risk. An alternative spelling is **Ex abundante cautela.** *Compare with* **Ob maiorem cautelam.** *See also* **Abundans cautela non nocet.**

Ex adverso. āks adwār´sō. eks âdv3r´sō. *adv.* "From the opposition." (1) Deriving from one in an adversarial position; deriving from one's opponent (as in a litigation). (2) On the contrary. (3) In contrast.

Ex aequitate. āks īkwēta´tā. eks ekwitā´tē. *adv.* "From equity." Arising or deriving from equity; based on equitable principles. An alternative spelling is **Ex equitate.**

Ex aequo et bono. āks ī´kwō āt bō´nō. eks e´kwō et bō´nō. *adv.* "From equity and goodness." A manner of deciding a case pending before a tribunal with reference to the principles of fairness and justice in preference to any principle of positive law. A decision *ex aequo et bono* may be sought especially when the law governing a dispute is unclear (*non liquet*) or might fail to resolve the dispute adequately for other reasons. *E.g.*, "This provision [relating to the sources of applicable law to be applied by the Court] shall not prejudice the power of the Court to decide a case *ex aequo et bono*, if the parties agree thereto." Statute of the International Court of Justice, art. 38(2). *See also* UN Convention on the Law of the Sea art. 293(2), Dec. 10, 1982, 21 I.L.M. 1245 (1982). Alternative formulations are **Secundum aequum et bonum** and **Secundum bonum et aequum.** *Compare with* **Ex arbitrio (boni) iudicis.**

Ex ante. āks an´tā. eks ân´tē. *adv.* or *adv.* "From before." (1) Based on prior surmise, assumption, foresight, or prediction; done without knowledge of subsequent events. (2) Prospective; prospectively. *Contrast with* **Ex post.** *See also* **Ab ante.**

Ex arbitrio (boni) iudicis. āks arbē´trēō (bō´nē) yū´dēkēs. eks arbit´rēō (bō´nī) jū´disis. *adv.* "From the (good) opinion of the judge." Made or done in a manner not strictly conforming to the law, but rather according to the judgment and discretion of the judge or tribunal. *See also* **Arbitrio boni iudicis.** *Compare with* **Ex aequo et bono.**

E

Ex bonis. āks bō´nēs. eks bō´nis. *adv.* "From goods." Relating to personal property.

Ex capite. āks ka´pētā. eks kâ´pitē. *adv.* "From the point." On the basis of; because or by reason of.

Ex cathedra. āks cat-hād´ra. eks cuθēd´ru. *adj.* or *adv.* "From the cathedral." Communicating in an official capacity; made with or by virtue of one's office or other authority; summarily and authoritatively. This term originates from the Catholic Church's claim that the Pope is infallible when speaking *ex cathedra*, and is accordingly sometimes used ironically. *E.g.*, "On this last point, however, the Judgment, *ex cathedra* and without giving much substantive reasoning, declares as follows...." *Certain Property* (Liecht. v. Ger.), 2005 I.C.J. Rep. 6, 61, ¶ 39 (Judge Owada, dissenting).

Ex causa mandati. āks kô´sa manda´tē. eks kă´zu mândā´tī. *adv.* "Because of the mandate." By reason of a mandate.

Ex causa potestatis. āks kô´sa pōtāsta´tēs. eks kă´zu pōtestā´tis. *adv.* "Because of the power." By reason of one's office or authority.

Ex colore. āks kōlō´rā. eks kulō´rē. *adv.* "From the color." (1) Under the pretense of. (2) Under the apparent authority of.

Ex comitate. eks kōmēta´tā. eks kamitā´tē. *adv.* "From courtesy." Under principles of comity.

Ex concessis. āks kōkās´sēs. eks kanse´sis. *adv.* "From concessions." From or according to what has been conceded, admitted, or permitted.

Ex consulto. āks kōnsūl´tō. eks kansɜl´tō. *adv.* "From consultation." Arising from group consultation or deliberation.

Ex contractu. āks kōntrak´tū. eks kantrâk´tū. *adv.* "Out of contract." Arising from an agreement or contractual right. *E.g.*, "While the United States have not expressly denied that such liens, rights and interests *ex contractu* [for the protection of the purchaser of a ship being built] must be considered as property in their law of eminent domain, they have contended that this property was an entity distinct from the material and other tangible things subjected to the property." *Norwegian Claims Case* (Nor. v. U.S.), Perm. Ct. Arb., Award of Oct. 13, 1922, H.C.R. (2d series), at 68 (Scott 1932). *Contrast with* **Ex delicto.**

Ex debito iustitiae. āks dā´bētō yūstē´tē-ī. eks de´bitō justi´šā. *adv.* "From the duty of justice." (1) Required by principles of justice or right. (2) Mandatorily or without discretion. Compensation to which the claimant is entitled as a matter of justice is a remedy *ex debito iustitiae.*

Ex delicto. āks dālēk´tō. eks dulik´tō. *adv.* "Out of injury." Arising from or caused by a wrongful act or crime. *Contrast with* **Ex contractu.**

Ex directo. āks dērāk´tō. eks durek´tō. *adv.* "Directly." (1) Directly (2) Immediately. (3) Next in order.

Ex diverso. āks dēwār´sō. eks divɜr´sō. *adv.* "Differently." (1) Conversely. (2) On the other hand; in contrast.

Ex dolo malo non oritur actio. āks dō´lō ma´lō nōn ōrē´tūr ak´tēō. eks dō´lō mâ´lō nan ō´ritɜr āk´tēō. "An action at law does not arise from evil deceit." An alternative phrase for **Nullus commodum capere (potest) de sua iniuria propria.**

Ex eo ob quod mittitur. āks ā´ō ōb kwōd mēt´tētūr. eks ē´ō ab kwad mi´titɜr. "From that with which he is being sent." Due to the character ascribed to the person. The refusal to receive a diplomat *ex eo ob quod mittitur* occurs because some aspect of the diplomat makes him or her unacceptable to the receiving state. *E.g.*, "A diplomatic agent may also be declined because of the character with which it is proposed to invest him, or, as it is tersely expressed in Latin, *ex eo ob quod mittitur*. If the Pope had announced his intention of sending a legate or *nuncio* to certain Protestant countries it is probable that such a representative would not have been received." Ernest Satow, A GUIDE TO DIPLOMATIC PRACTICE 134, § 225 (Neville Bland ed., 4th ed., 1957).

Ex equitate. An alternative spelling of **Ex aequitate.**

Ex eventu. āks āwān´tū. eks ēven´tū OR -ēven´čū. *adv.* "From the event." Following the occurrence.

Ex facie. āks fa´kē-ā. eks fā´šu. *adv.* "From the face." Superficially; evidently. A documentary defect that is noticeable *ex facie* is apparent from a superficial inspection of the document. *See also* **Prima facie.**

Ex facto. āks fak´tō. eks fâk´tō. *adv.* "From the fact." Arising from or attributable to the fact or event.

Ex facto ius oritur. āks fak´tō yūs ō´rētūr. eks fâk´tō jus ō´ritɜr. "The law arises from fact." A maxim meaning that, until the facts of a case are known, the applicable law cannot be ascertained. *Compare with* **Ex factis oritur ius.**

Ex factis oritur ius. āks fak´tēs ō´rētūr yūs. eks fâk´tis ō´ritɜr jus. "Law arises from actions." A maxim meaning that law arises from a long and consistent practice. *Compare with* **Ex facto oritur ius.**

E

Ex fictione iuris. āks fēktēō´nā yū´rēs. eks fikšō´nē jɜ´ris. *adv.* "From a legal fiction." Arising from a legal fiction (a fact presumed by law even in the face of contrary facts).

Ex gratia. āks gra´tē-a. eks grā´šu. *adj.* or *adv.* "From kindness." Done for reasons other than a sense of obligation; done voluntarily or altruistically. A compensation paid by a state to an injured party *ex gratia* is made in spite of the state's denial of legal responsibility for the injury. *E.g.*, "The Mexican Government desires that the claims shall be...decided [in accordance with principles of equity] because Mexico wishes that her responsibility shall not be fixed according to the generally accepted rules and principles of international law, but *ex gratia* feels morally bound to make full indemnification." Claims Convention of 10 Sept. 1923 (U.S.–Mex.), art. 2, 4 R.I.A.A. 780. An alternative formulation is **A gratia.**

Ex hypothesi. āks hüpō´t-hāsē. eks hīpo´θezī. *adv.* "From the hypothesis." (1) By hypothesis; hypothetically; by *a priori* assumption. *E.g.*, "Rights are *ex hypothesi* protected by law, otherwise they would not be rights." *Barcelona Traction, Light, and Power Company* (Belg. v. Spain), 1970 I.C.J. Rep. 3, ¶ 54. (2) For the sake of argument. An alternative formulation is **In hypothesi.** *See also* **Arguendo.**

Ex incommodo. āks ēnkōm´mōdō. eks inkumō´dō. *adj.* or *adv.* "From inconvenience." Due to or based on inconvenience. An argument *ex commodo* may be based on an appeal to apply a rule in a manner that avoids inconvenience to the person making the argument. *See also* **Argumentum ab inconvenienti.**

Ex incontinenti. āks ēnkōntēnān´tē. eks inkantinen´tī. *adv.* "From intemperance." (1) Immediately. (2) Summarily.

Ex industria. āks ēndūs´trē-a. eks indus´trē-u. *adv.* "From effort." An alternative formulation of **De industria.**

Ex iniuria ius non oritur. āks ēnyū´rē-a yūs nōn ō´rētūr. eks injɜ´rē-u jus nan ō´ritɜr. "A right does not arise from wrongdoing." A maxim meaning that one cannot generally rely on a violation of law to establish a new legal right or to confirm a claimed right. *E.g.*, "As Lauterpacht has indicated the maxim *ex injuria ius non oritur* is not so severe as to deny that any source of right whatever can accrue to third persons acting in good faith. Were it otherwise the general interest in the security of transactions would be too greatly invaded and the cause of minimizing needless hardship and friction would be hindered rather than helped." *Advisory Opinion on Legal Consequences For States Of The Continued Presence Of South Africa In Namibia (South West Africa) Notwithstanding Security Council Resolution 276 (1970)*, 1971 I.C.J. Rep. 16, 167 (separate opinion of Judge Dillard). An alternative formulation is **Ius ex iniuria non oritur**. *Compare with* **Nullus commodum capere (potest) de sua iniuria propria**.

Ex integro. āks ēntāg´rō. eks integ´rō. *adv.* "From the whole." Again from the beginning; repeated anew.

Ex iure. āks yū´rā. eks jɜ´rē. *adv.* "From the right." Arising from a legal right. *Compare with* **Ex lege**.

Ex iure naturae. āks yū´rā natū´rī. eks jɜ´rē nā´čɜrā. *adv.* "From right of nature." According to a right deriving from natural law.

Ex iusta causa. āks yūs´ta kô´sa. eks jus´tu kă´zu. *adv.* "From a just cause." Arising from a lawful or just right, title, or cause of action.

Ex iustitia. āks yūstē´tē-a. eks justi´šu. *adv.* "From justice." Justly; as a matter of justice.

Ex lege. āks lā´gā. eks le´jē. *adv.* "From the law." (1) By law or legal right. (2) Deriving from a legal right or obligation. *E.g.*, "Each State Party shall provide in its internal laws for its nationality to be acquired by children born on its territory who do not acquire at birth another nationality. Such nationality shall be granted at birth *ex lege*...." European Convention on Nationality art. 6.1, Nov. 6, 1997, 37 I.L.M. 44 (1998). *Compare with* **Ex iure**.

Ex legibus. āks lā´gēbūs. eks le´jibus. *adv.* "From the laws." Interpreted in a manner consistent with both the literal terms of the law and the intent or spirit of the law.

Ex maiore cautela. āks mayō´rā kôtā´la. eks mâjō´rē kă´telu. *adv.* "From greater caution." An alternative formulation of **Ob maiorem cautelam**.

Ex maleficio. āks malāfē´kēō. eks mâlufi´šō. *adj.* or *adv.* "By wrongful conduct." (1) Wrongful; wrongfully. (2) Tortious; tortiously.

Ex mandato. āks manda´tō. eks mândā´tō. *adv.* "By mandate." According to or deriving from an authoritative mandate.

Ex mero motu. āks mā´rō mō´tū. eks mē´rō mō´tū. *adv.* "From the pure motion." An alternative phrase for **Sua sponte**.

Ex mora. āks mō´ra. eks mō´ru. *adv.* "From delay." Arising from a delay. Interest from an unpaid debt or other obligation may be levied *ex mora* on a respondent to compensate the claimant for the delay in compensation. The term "moratory interest" derives from this Latin root. *See also* **Mora** and **Minus solvit qui tardius solvit.**

E

Ex more. āks mō´rā. eks mō´rē. *adv.* "From customs." Arising from or in accordance with customary practices.

Ex natura. āks natū´ra. eks nā´č3ru. *adv.* "From nature." According to nature; naturally.

Ex natura rei. āks natū´ra rā´ē. eks nā´č3ru rā. *adv.* "From the nature of the matter." According to the nature of the matter, thing, or transaction.

Ex naturali iure. āks natūra´lē yū´rā. eks nâč3râ´lī j3´rē. *adv.* "From natural right." According to natural law or natural justice.

Ex necessitate. āks nākāssēta´tē. eks nusesitā´tē. *adv.* "From necessity." (1) Necessarily. (2) Due to unavoidable exigencies.

Ex necessitate legis. āks nākāssēta´tā lā´gēs. eks nusesitā´tē le´jis. *adv.* "From the necessity of law." (1) Because of a legal requirement. (2) Because of the needs of the law.

Ex necessitate rei. āks nākāssēta´tā rā´ē. eks nusesitā´tē rā. *adv.* "From the necessity of the matter." Because of the necessity or urgency of the matter.

Ex nihilo. āks nē´hēlō. eks nī´hilō. *adv.* "Out of nothing." (1) Coming from no known or credible source; lacking any basis in law or fact. *E.g.*, "In the present case, in the absence of a power of revocation in the mandates system, neither the General Assembly nor even the Security Council can cause such a power to come to birth *ex nihilo.*" *Advisory Opinion on the Legal Consequences for States of the Continued Presence of South Africa in Namibia (South West Africa) Notwithstanding Security Council Resolution 276 (1970)*, 1971 I.C.J. Rep. 16, 339, ¶ 33 (Judge Gros, dissenting). (2) By surprise; without forewarning.

Ex nihilo nil fit. āks nē´hēlō nēl fēt. eks nī´hilō nil fit. "From nothing comes nothing." A maxim meaning that legal rights cannot arise from an invalid or illegitimate source. This maxim is not to be confused with the Billy Preston maxim "nothing from nothing leaves nothing," which means that you gotta have something if you wanna be with him.

Ex non scripto ius venit quod usus comprobavit. āks nōn skrēp´tō yūs wā´nēt kwōd ū´sūs kōmprōba´wēt. eks nan skrip´tō jus ve´nit kwad yū´zus kamprō´buvit. "Law that has been approved by custom comes from what is unwritten." A maxim, originating in Justinian's *Institutes* (1.2.3), meaning that custom originates in the longstanding practices of relevant parties leading to an expectation that the parties are legally bound to continue the practices.

Ex nudo pacto actio non oritur. āks nū´dō pak´tō ak´tēō nōn ōrē´tūr. eks nū´dō pâk´tō âk´tēō nan ō´ritɜr. "A cause of action does not arise from a naked agreement." A maxim meaning that an agreement lacking mutual consideration is unenforceable. The validity of this maxim in international law is called into question by the International Court of Justice's holding that a state's unilateral public pronouncement, made with intent to be bound, may be legally binding. *See Nuclear Tests* (Austl. v. Fr.), 1974 I.C.J. Rep. 252, ¶ 43 (Judgment). *Compare with* **Nuda pactio obligationem non parit.** *See also* **Nudum pactum.**

Ex nunc. āks nūnk. eks nunk. *adj.* or *adv.* "From now." (1) From this time. *E.g.*, "The Commission had mentioned that in Switzerland the courts recognise a change of sex and allow a corresponding entry in the birth register with effect *ex nunc*...." *Cossey v. United Kingdom*, 13 E.H.R.R. 622, 647 n.46 (1991). (2) Prospective(ly). *Contrast with* **Ex tunc.**

Ex officio. āks ōffē´kēō. eks ufi´šō. *adj.* or *adv.* "From office." (1) In an official capacity. (2) By virtue of the authority of an official position, without the need for additional authorization. *E.g.*, "[T]he Government noted that the applicant had rejected the Commission's invitation to consider her claims. In view of this, the Commission had proceeded to examine *ex officio* the applicant's claims." *Xenides-Arestis v. Turkey*, 44 E.H.R.R. SE13, ¶ 26 (2006).

Ex pari. eks pa´rē. eks pa´rī. *adv.* "Equally." Equally; equivalently. *Compare with* **A pari.**

Ex parte. āks par´tā. eks par´tā OR -par´tē. *adj.* "In part." Without all relevant parties are present; with only one party or side present before a tribunal. At a hearing or trial conducted *ex parte*, only one side is present during the proceedings. In an adversarial litigation, *ex parte* contact between an authoritative tribunal and one side in a litigation is generally considered to compromise justice because of the inability of the other side to represent its interests and to ensure that the contact does not involve any impropriety. *E.g.*, "On February 7, 1992 an interim injunction was applied for by the Attorney-General. It was obtained on an *ex parte* basis to restrain X from leaving the jurisdiction or from arranging or carrying out a termination of the pregnancy." *D. v. Ireland*, 43 E.H.R.R. SE16, ¶ 19 (2006). *Compare with* **Inaudita altera parte.** *Contrast with* **Inter partes.**

Ex post. āks pōst. eks pōst. *adj.* or *adv.* "From after." (1) Based on information known after the relevant time; done with knowledge of subsequent events. (2) Retrospective; retrospectively; with hindsight. *Contrast with* **Ex ante.**

E

Ex post facto. āks pōst fak´tō. eks pōst fâk´tō. *adj.* or *adv.* "From after the fact." (1) Occurring after the event under consideration. *E.g.*, "It is only when the general lines of the Judgment to be given become clear that the States 'affected' can be identified, if they exist at all. It is a curious situation: the finding as to whether there are third States parties to the multilateral treaties in question 'affected' by the decision, and which they are, can be established only *ex post facto*." *Military and Paramilitary Activities in and Against Nicaragua* (Nicar. v. U.S.), 1986 I.C.J. Rep. 14, 195 (separate opinion of Judge Sette-Camara). (2) Having retroactive effect. In general, states do not incur liability under international law for acts or omissions that breached no obligation at the time they occurred. *See* International Law Commission, *Draft Articles on State Responsibility* art. 13, UN GAOR 56th Sess., Supp. No. 10, at 155–68, UN Doc. A/56/10 (2001). An *ex post facto* law is one that takes effect retroactively to prohibit or punish conduct that was not illegal at the time it occurred. *Ex post facto* criminal laws are generally prohibited in international human rights law, except when the act "was criminal according to the general principles of law recognized by the community of nations." *See* International Covenant on Civil and Political Rights art. 15, Mar. 23, 1976, 999 U.N.T.S. 171; *see also* European Convention for the Protection of Human Rights and Fundamental Freedoms art. 7, Sept. 3, 1953, 213 U.N. T.S. 222. *Compare with* **Nunc pro tunc** and **Post hoc.** *Contrast with* **Ante factum** and **Ante hoc.** *See also* **Nulla poena sine lege** and **Nullum crimen sine lege.**

Ex praecedentibus et consequentibus optima fit interpretatio. āks prīkādān´tēbūs āt kōnsākwān´tēbūs ōp´tēma fēt ēntārprāta´tēō. eks prāsuden´tibus et kansekwen´tibus ap´timu fit intɜrpretā´šō. "The best interpretation is made from the preceding and following." A maxim meaning that treaties and other legal instruments should be interpreted according to the context in which the words appear, especially the language immediately preceding and following the relevant provisions. Sometimes misspelled **Ex procedentibus**.... *Compare with* **Ex tota materia emergat resolutio.**

Ex procedentibus. A misspelling of **Ex praecedentibus.**

Ex proposito. āks prōpō´sētō. eks prōpa´zitō. *adv.* "From intention." Intentionally; expressly. *Compare with* **Ex industria.**

Ex proprio (suo) motu. āks prōp´rēō (sū´ō) mō´tū. eks prap´rēō (sū´ō) mō´tū. *adv.* "From (its) own motion." An alternative phrase for **Sua sponte.** Alternative formulations are **Suo motu** and **Proprio (suo) motu.** *Compare with* **Ex proprio vigore.**

Ex proprio vigore. āks prōp´rēō wēgō´rā. eks prap´rēō vigō´rē. *adv.* "From its own force." (1) Begun or continued by its own impetus; self-impelled. (2) Without further authorization or authority necessity. *Compare with* **Ex proprio (suo) motu.**

Ex rel. An abbreviation of **Ex relatione.**

Ex relatione. āks rālatēō´nā. eks relāšō´nē. *adv.* "By relation." By the relation with. A claim made *ex relatione* is based on the relationship between the claimant and the real party in interest. A state may bring a claim for compensation against another state *ex relatione* on behalf of a national of that state. Commonly abbreviated **Ex rel.** *Compare with* **Parens patriae.**

Ex rigore iuris. āks rēgō´rā yū´rēs. eks rigō´rē jз´ris. *adv.* "From the strictness of right." (1) According to the rigor of the law or right. (2) By a strict reading and application of the letter of the law. *Compare with* **De rigore iuris.**

Ex situ. āks sē´tū. eks si´tū. *adv.* "Away from its place." Somewhere other than where the property was originally located. *E.g.*, "*Ex situ* techniques [of remedying ground oil contamination], especially sediment removal, are to be utilized only as a minor component of the overall remedial approach and generally limited to very specific areas where a discrete layer of asphalt pavement or heavily oil-contaminated sediment is present at or near the surface." UN Compensation Comm'n Governing Council, *Report and Recommendations Made by the Panel of Commissioners Concerning the Third Installment of "F4" Claims*, Dec. 18, 2003, Annex VI, ¶ 7, 43 I.L.M. 704, 742 (2004). *Contrast with* **In situ.**

Ex statuto. āks statū´tō. eks stâ´čūtō. *adv.* "From the statute." Deriving from or according to the statute.

Ex sua natura. āks sū´a natū´ra. eks sū´u nā´čзru. *adv.* "From its nature." By its own nature.

Ex tempore. āks tām´pōrā. eks tem´pōrē. *adv.* "From the time." (1) Due to considerations of or passage of time. (2) Unpremeditated and unprepared. *See also* **Ad libitum** and **Ratione temporis.**

Ex tota materia emergat resolutio. āks tō´ta matā´rē-a āmār´gat rāsōlū´tēō. eks tō´tu mutē´rē-u emзr´jut rezulū´šō. "From the whole matter the solution arises." (1) A maxim meaning that all relevant facts should be considered in arriving at a judgment. (2) A maxim meaning that a law should be interpreted in the context of related laws and of the law's purpose. *Compare with* **Ex praecedentibus et consequentibus optima fit interpretatio.**

E

Ex tunc. āks tūnk. eks tunk. *adj.* or *adv.* "From then." (1) From or at a former time. (2) Retroactively. *E.g.*, "[T]here is no doubt that genocide has been recognized as a crime under international law in the full legal meaning of this term, *ex tunc*; that is to say: The crimes of genocide committed against the Jewish People and other peoples were crimes under international law." *Attorney General v. Eichmann*, Dist. Ct. Jerusalem, Crim. Case No. 40/61, Judgment of Dec. 11, 1961, ¶ 19 (Isr.). *Contrast with* **Ex nunc.**

Ex turpi causa non oritur actio. āks tūr´pē kô´sa nōn ō´rētūr ak´tēō. eks tɜr´pī kă´zu nan ō´ritɜr âk´tēō. "An action does not arise from a loathsome cause." A maxim meaning that equity will not tolerate the use of the law to carry out a fraud. Based on this principle, a tribunal may refuse to enforce the positive law to aid one seeking to perpetrate a fraud under the aegis of legal technicalities. *See also* **Pacta quae turpem causam continent non sunt observanda.**

Ex una parte. āks ū´na par´tā. eks ū´nu par´tē OR -par´tā. *adv.* "From one part." On or from one side. *Contrast with* **Ex utraque parte.**

Ex utraque parte. āks ūtra´kwā par´tā. eks ūt´rukā par´tē OR -par´tā. *adv.* "From either side." On or from both sides. *Contrast with* **Ex una parte.**

Ex vi aut metu. āks wē ôt mā´tū. eks vī ăt me´tū. *adv.* "By either force or fear." Through force or threat of force.

Ex vi termini. āks wē tār´mēnē. eks vī tɜr´minī. *adv.* "By the force of the limit." From the meaning in the literal terms of the document. *E.g.*, "[E]xecutive powers *ex vi termini* do not include the rights of war & peace...." 1 RECORDS OF THE FEDERAL CONVENTION OF 1787, at 70 (Max Farrand ed., 1966) (statement of James Madison).

Ex visceribus. āks wēskā´rēbūs. eks visɜ´ribus. *adv.* "From the viscera." Relating to the essential or key part of a thing or matter.

Exacta diligentia. āksak´ta dēlēgān´tē-a. egzâk´tu dilijen´tē-u OR -dilijen´šu. *n.* "With precise diligence." With appropriate care or diligence.

Exceptio. āks-kāp´tēō. eksep´tēō. *n.* [*pl.* **Exceptiones.** āks-kāptēō´nās. eksepšō´nēz.]. "Exception." (1) A legal defense; an objection. (2) An exception; a rule or fact derogating from a more general, contrary rule or fact. (3) A defense to a claim on the basis that the claim, though admissible, names the wrong defendant. (4) In Roman law and some civil jurisdictions, a defense admitting the general allegations of the claim but denying its applicability in the case based on a fact or provision of law that excludes the defendant's liability.

Exceptio doli. äks-kāp´tēō dō´lē. eksep´tēō dō´lī. *n.* "Defense of fraud." A defense to the assertion of a legal obligation based on the claim that the defendant was the victim of another person's fraud.

Exceptio est strictissimae applicationis. äks-kāp´tēō äst strēktēs´sēmī applēkatēō´nēs. eksep´tēō est strikti´simā âplikāšō´nis. "An exception is of the strictest application." A maxim meaning that an exception to a general rule should be narrowly construed to avoid undermining the general rule.

Exceptio firmat regulam (in casibus non exceptis). äks-kāp´tēō fēr´mat rā´gūlam (ēn ka´sēbūs nōn aks-kāp´tēs). eksep´tēō fɜr´mât re´gyūlum (in kâ´zibus nan eksep´tis). "The exception affirms the rule (in cases not excepted)." An alternative phrase for **Exceptio probat regulam (de rebus non exceptis).**

Exceptio inadimplenti contractus. äks-kāp´tēō ēnadēmplān´tē kōntrak´tūs. eksep´tēō inâdimplen´tī kantrâk´tus. *n.* "Defense [in the case of] an unfulfilled contract." A defense to a claim of breach of an agreement based on the other party's prior breach of the agreement. *See also* **Inadimplenti non est adimplendum** and **Non adimplenti contractus.**

Exceptio probat regulam (de rebus non exceptis). äks-kāp´tēō prō´bat rā´gūlam (dā rā´būs nōn äks-kāp´tēs). eksep´tēō prō´bât re´gyūlum (dā rē´bus nan eksep´tis). "The exception proves the rule (regarding things not excepted)." A maxim meaning that the existence of an exception to a rule proves by its rarity the general validity of the rule. Alternative phrases are **Exceptio firmat regulam (in casibus non exceptis)** and **Exceptio quoque regulam declarat.**

Exceptio quoque regulam declarat. äks-kāp´tēō kwō´kwā rā´gūlam dākla´rat. eksep´tēō kwō´kwē re´gyūlum deklā´rut. "The exception also states the rule." An alternative phrase for **Exceptio probam regulam (de rebus non exceptis).**

Exceptio rei iudicatae. äks-kāp´tēō rā´ē yūdēka´tī. eksep´tēō rā jūdika´tā. *n.* "An objection to the adjudicated matter." An argument that a claim should be dismissed based on a previous binding judgment or award between the parties dealing with the same subject matter. *E.g.*, "The requirement of the identity of the parties for the application of the *exceptio rei judicatae* has the effect of preventing the right of third parties from being conclusively settled without being involved in litigation." Bin Cheng, General Principles of Law as Applied by International Courts and Tribunals 341 n.22 (1953).

Exceptis excipiendis. äks-kāp´tēs äks-kēpē-ān´dēs. eksep´tis eksipē-en´dis. *adv.* "With necessary exceptions." With all necessary exceptions.

Exeat. ā´ksā-at. e´gzē-ât. *v.* (commonly used as *n.*). "He may depart." A permission to depart from a state's territory or other place under its control. *See also* **Ne exeat (regno).**

E

Exempla illustrant, non restringant, legem. āksām´pla ēllūs´trant, nōn rāstrēn´gant, lā´gām. egzem´plu il´ustrânt, nan restriŋ´ent, le´jum. "Examples illustrate the law, they do not restrict it." A maxim meaning that, in interpreting a law containing examples, the examples should be read to clarify the purpose and scope of the law rather than to restrict the law's applicability only to those scenarios depicted by the examples. *Contrast with* **Expressio unius (est) exclusio alterius.**

Exempli gratia. āksām´plē gra´tē-a. egzemp´lī grā´šu. *adv.* "For the sake of an example." For example. Commonly abbreviated **E.g.**

Exequatur. āksākwa´tūr. eksekwa´tɜr. *imp. v.* (commonly used as a *n.*) "Let it be executed." A written, official recognition of a head of a consular post issued by the government to which the consular officer is accredited. *See* the Vienna Convention on Consular Relations art. 12, Apr. 24, 1963, 596 U.N.T.S. 261. Although the term is commonly written without an "s," the proper Latin spelling is **Exsequatur.**

Expedit rei publicae ut sit finis litium. ākspā´dēt rā´ē pūb´lēkī ūt sēt fē´nēs lē´tē-ūm. ekpē´dit rā pub´likā ut sit fī´nis lī´šum. "It is advantageous to the public that there be an end to lawsuits." A maxim meaning that protracted litigation puts a strain on the judicial system and undermines the law's role in dispute resolution, and so the public interest requires that disputes be resolved in some final form rather than continuing indefinitely to drain the resources of courts and the parties. This maxim has sometimes been used to justify or explain a tribunal's decision to encourage settlement or grant an early or time-delimited award. An alternative phrase is **Interest rei publicae ut sit finis litium.**

Expressio unius (est) exclusio alterius. āksprās´sēō ūnē´ūs (āst) āksklū´sēō altārē´ūs. ekspre´sēō ū´nē-us (est) eksklū´zēō altɜ´rē-us. "The express statement of one (is) the exclusion of the other." A canon of legal instrument construction according to which, when something is stated expressly in the instrument, any similar matter omitted from the instrument is presumed to have been omitted intentionally. The rationale underlying this doctrine is that the express inclusion of the subject matter indicates that the drafters were aware of similar matters and chose to exclude them by design. For example, a treaty providing for the right of innocent passage through a state's territorial waters "of civilian vessels without notice and of military vessels" would under this canon be presumed to require notice prior to a foreign warship entering a state party's territorial waters, because the "without notice" qualification was explicit for civilian vessels but not mentioned with respect to military vessels. *E.g.*, "[I]t is further contended by the United States...[t]hat, as the liberty to dry and cure on the treaty coasts and to enter bays and harbors on the non-treaty coasts are both subjected to conditions, and the latter to specific restrictions, it should therefore be held that the liberty to fish should be subjected to no restrictions, as none are provided for in the treaty. The tribunal is unable to apply the principle of *expressio unius exclusio alterius* to this case...[b]ecause these restrictions of the right to enter bays and harbors applying solely to American fishermen must have been expressed in the treaty, whereas regulations of the fishery, applying equally to American and British, are made by right of territorial sovereignty." *The North Atlantic Coast Fisheries Arbitration* (U.K. v. U.S.), 11 R.I.A.A. 167 (1910). Alternative formulations are **Affirmatio unius (est) exclusio alterius**, **Designatio unius (est) exclusio alterius**, and **Enumeratio unius (est) exclusio alterius.** *Compare with* **Expressum facit cessare tacitum.** *Contrast with* **Exempla illustrant, non restringant, legem.**

Expressis verbis. ākspräs´sēs wär´bēs. ekspre´sis vɜr´bis. *adv.* "In explicit terms." Explicitly; in clear words. *E.g.*, "[A] disagreement on a point of law or fact, a conflict of legal views or interests, or the positive opposition of the claim of one party by the other need not necessarily be stated *expressis verbis*. In the determination of the existence of a dispute, as in other matters, the position or the attitude of a party can be established by inference, whatever the professed view of that party." *Land and Maritime Boundary Between Cameroon and Nigeria* (Camer. v. Niger.), 1998 I.C.J. Rep. 275, 315, ¶ 89. *Compare with* **Claris verbis.**

Expressum facit cessare tacitum. ākspräs´sūm fa´kēt kässa´rā ta´kētūm. ekspre´sum fâ´sit sesa´rē tâ´situm. "What is expressly done causes the invalidation of what is silent." A doctrine according to which, when something is stated explicitly in a legal instrument, any matter omitted from the statement is presumed to have been omitted intentionally. *Compare with* **Expressio unius est exclusio alterius.**

Exsequatur. The proper Latin spelling of **Exequatur.**

Extense. ākstān´sā. eksten´sē. *adv.* "Extensively." (1) Comprehensively. (2) Extremely.

Extra. āks´tra. eks´tru. *prep.* "Beyond." (1) Beyond; outside. (2) Additional to. (3) Except; without.

Extra compromisum arbiter nihil facere potest. āks´tra kōmprōmē´sūm ar´bētār nē´hēl fa´kārā pō´täst. eks´tru kamprumī´zum ar´bitɜr nī´hil fâ´sɜrē pō´test. "The arbitrator cannot do anything outside the agreement." An alternative formulation of **Arbiter nihil extra compromisum facere potest.**

Extra iudicium. āks´tra yūdē´kē-ūm. eks´tru jūdi´šum. *adv.* "Outside the jurisdiction." (1) Out of the presence of the tribunal. *Compare with* **De plano.** (2) Beyond the jurisdiction of the tribunal or sovereign authority.

E

Extra ius. āks´tra yūs. eks´tru jus. *adv.* "Outside the right." More than what is required or granted by the law or as a matter of right.

Extra legem. āks´tra lā´gām. eks´tru le´jum. *adv.* "Outside the law." (1) Beyond the scope of the law. (2) Illegal. (3) Not within the subject matter regulated by the law.

Extra regnum. āks´tra rāg´nūm. eks´tru reg´num. *adj.* or *adv.* "Outside of the realm." Outside of the territory or jurisdiction of the state. *Compare with* **Extra territorium.**

Extra territorium. āks´tra tārrētō´rē-ūm. eks´tru teritō´rē-um. *adv.* "Outside the territory." Beyond the territorial boundary of a state or region. *Compare with* **Extra regnum.**

Extra territorium ius dicenti impune non paretur. āks´tra tārrētō´rē-ūm yūs dēkān´tē ēmpū´nā nōn parā´tūr. eks´tru teritō´rē-um jus disen´tī impyū´nē nan pa´retзr. "One who gives a judgment outside his territory may be disobeyed with impunity." A maxim, originating in Justinian's *Digest* (2.1.20), meaning that a court or other authority may not enforce its laws outside of its own territory. Modern state practice no longer fully conforms to this maxim, however; many states now regularly exercise prescriptive jurisdiction over extraterritorial acts and persons, and extraterritorial enforcement, sometimes unilateral but more commonly with the cooperation of the state on whose territory the accused is found, occurs with increasing frequency.

Extrema ratio. ākstrā´ma ra´tēō. ekstrē´mu rā´šō. *n.* "Extreme remedy." (1) A serious punishment. (2) A remedy or recourse having extreme consequences. *E.g.*, "[Safeguard measures] constitute an *extrema ratio*, applicable only when positive demonstration by the applying Member is given as to the unsuitability of the other tariff-based measures (tariff increases or tariff-rate quotas)." *United States—Definitive Safeguard Measures on Imports of Wheat Gluten from the European Communities*, Panel Report of July 31, 2000, WTO Doc. No. WT/DS166/R, at 155, ¶ 90.

Exuere patriam. āksū´ārā pat´trē-am. egzū´зrē pât´rē-um. *v.* "To renounce the country." The renunciation of one's citizenship. *Compare with* **Forisiurare provinciam.**

F

Facta concludentia. fak´ta kōnklūdān´tē-a. fâk´tu kanklūden´šu. *n. pl.* "Concluding deeds." Implicit or tacit consent. *E.g.*, "[I]f tacit abrogation [of a treaty] were recognized, it would be necessary to produce proof of the *facta concludentia* which would have to be relied on to demonstrate the *contrarius consensus* of the parties, and proof of sufficient force to relieve the parties of the obligation undertaken by them under the treaty." *Nuclear Tests* (Austl. v. Fr.), 1974 I.C.J. Rep. 253, 381 (Judge De Castro, dissenting). *See also* **Per facta concludentia.**

Facta praeterita. fak´ta prītā´rēta. fâk´tu pretɜ´ritu. *n. pl.* "Past events." Events or situations occurring or existing in the past. *E.g.*, "At the outset we shall have to examine…intertemporal law, which indicates what is the law to be applied to *facta praeterita.* To seek to establish what lies behind the use of a term in order to ascertain the intention of the party which made the declaration is one thing; to determine the effect which a new legal regime may have on an already existing situation is another." *Aegean Sea Continental Shelf* (Greece v. Turk.), 1978 I.C.J. Rep. 3, 67 (Jurisdiction).

Facto et animo. fak´tō āt a´nēmō. fâk´tō et â´nimō. *adv.* "In fact and intent." Factually and intentionally; done with the requisite intent.

Factum. fak´tūm. fâk´tum. *n.* [*pl.* **Facta.** fak´ta. fâk´tu.] "Deed." (1) An act or deed; a fact or event, or evidence thereof. *E.g.*, "El Salvador adds that '[t]he discovery of hitherto unknown documents is a typical example of the type of fact which lays open a case to revision…either because they themselves constitute the *factum* or because they are the source of knowledge of them.'" *Application for Revision of the Judgment of 11 September 1992 in the Case Concerning the Land, Island, and Maritime Frontier Dispute* (El Salv. v. Hond.), 2003 I.C.J. Rep. 392, ¶ 42 (Judgment). (2) A statement of facts for submission to a tribunal; a memorial.

Factum probandum. fak´tūm prōban´dūm. fâk´tum prōbân´dum. *n.* "Fact needing to be proved." A fact that, for some reason (usually to carry a burden of proof in a litigation), must be proved for a claim or defense to succeed.

Falsus. fal´sūs. fal´sus. *adj.* "False." (1) Untrue. (2) Deceptive. (3) Deceitful.

F

Falsus in uno, falsus in omnibus. fal´sūs ēn ū´nō fal´sūs ēn ōm´nēbūs. fal´sus in ū´nō, fal´sus in am´nibus. "Deceitful in one, deceitful in all." A maxim meaning that, when one has perjured himself once, his entire testimony and all of his or claims thereby are presumed false or at least fall under suspicion of deceit.

Fatuum iudicium. fa´tū-ūm yūdē´kē-ūm. fâ´čyū-um jūdi´šum. *n.* "Fatuous judgment." An erroneous judicial or arbitral decision.

Fauces terrae. fô´kās tār´rī. fă´cez te´rā. *n.* "The jaws of land." An ocean strait, inlet, or bay, partially enclosed by projecting headlands or promontories, in contradistinction to an open sea. In the practice of some states, such as England and the United States, such "arms" of the sea were considered state territory rather than open ocean when the land features were sufficiently narrow that a person can see one shore while standing on the opposite shore. *See also* **Inter fauces terrae.**

Favor negotii. fa´wōr nāgō´tē-ē. fā´vɜr negō´šī. *n.* "The encouragement of business." A principle of documentary interpretation whereby a treaty or other agreement is construed in a manner that sustains its validity under law whenever such a construction is reasonably possible to avoid undermining the dealings of the parties.

Favor solutionis. fa´wōr sōlūtēō´nēs. fā´vɜr salūšō´nis. *n.* "An inclination toward payment." A conflict of laws principle to the effect that a contract should be interpreted according to the law of the forum in which performance is to occur.

Favor validitatis. fa´wōr walēdēta´tēs. fā´vɜr vâliditā´tis. *n.* "An inclination toward certainty." A principle of legal instrument construction by which the instrument is interpreted in a manner calculated to uphold its validity. The term is commonly used in reference to contracts and treaties, which should generally be interpreted under *favor validitatis* to avoid frustrating the intentions of the parties by nullifying their legal relationship.

Felo de se. fā´lō dā sā. fe´lō dā sā. *n. Med.* "Felon of himself." A suicide. In medieval English law, a *felo de se* was given by law a punitive burial and forfeited all of his property to the Crown instead of his heirs.

Fera vagans est nullius in rebus. fā´ra wa´gans āst nūllē´ūs ēn rā´būs. fē´ra vā´genz est nɜ´lē-us in rē´bus OR -rā´bus. "A wandering beast belongs to no one." A maxim meaning that wild animals (such as migratory species) that cross man-made territorial boundaries do not become the exclusive property of the owner of the territory into which they cross.

Ferae bestiae. fā´rī bās´tē-ī. fe´rā bes´tē-ā. *n. pl.* "Wild animals." Feral animals. Traditionally, a state had complete sovereignty over *ferae bestiae* that lived within its territory, but new norms have developed with the recognition of the need for species conservation and the sharing of migratory species. An alternative term is **Ferae naturae** (*n.*).

F

Ferae naturae. fā´rī natū´rī. fe´rā nā´čɜrā. (1) *adj.* "Of wild nature." Wild; untamed; feral. (2) *n.* "Wild nature." An alternative term for **Ferae bestiae.**

Fetiales. fātē-a´lās. fetē-â´lēz. *n. pl.* In Roman law, priests belonging to the *Collegium fetialium*. Sometimes misspelled **Feciales.** *See also* **Collegium fetialium** and **Ius fetiale (divinum).**

Fiat iustitia, pereat mundus. fē´at yūstē´tē-a, pā´rā-at mūn´dūs. fē´ât justi´šu, pē´rē-ât mun´dus. "Let justice be done, though the world may perish." A maxim meaning that a just decision should be made at whatever cost in terms of practical consequences. An alternative phrase is **Fiat iustitia, ruat caelum.**

Fiat iustitia, ruat caelum. fē´at yūstē´tē-a, rū´at kī´lūm. fē´ât justi´šu, rū´ât sā´lum. "Let justice be done, though the heavens may fall." An alternative phrase for **Fiat iustitia, pereat mundus.**

Fictio. *See* **Fictio (iuris).**

Fictio cedit veritati; fictio iuris non est ubi veritas. fēk´tēō kā´dēt wārēta´tē; fēk´tēō yū´rēs nōn āst ū´bē wā´rētas. fik´šō sē´dit veritā´tī; fik´šō jɜ´ris nan est ū´bē ve´ritus. "Fiction yields to truths; there is no legal fiction where there is truth." A maxim meaning that tribunals rely on judicial fictions only in the absence of adequate evidence on the matter at issue. Sometimes abbreviated **Fictio iuris non est ubi veritas.** *See also* **Fictio legis inique operatur alicui damnum vel iniuriam.**

Fictio (iuris). fēk´tēō (yū´rēs). fik´šō (jɜ´ris). *n.* [*pl.* **Fictiones (iuris).** fēktēō´nās (yū´rēs). fikšō´nēz (jɜ´ris).] "(Legal) fiction." A presumption or assumption of law. Different judicial authorities treat *fictiones* differently. A *fictio* may apply despite contrary evidence, or it may be defeated by contrary evidence, depending on its purpose. A *fictio* intended to achieve a legal result otherwise not possible might apply despite proof of facts contrary to the presumption. A *fictio* that serves to render a decision more efficient by making evidence of the assumed fact unnecessary might be nullified by a showing that the legal fiction is inaccurate.

Fictio iuris non est ubi veritas. fēk´tēō yū´rēs nōn āst ū´bī wā´rētas. fik´šō jɜ´ris nan est ū´bē ve´ritus. "There is no legal fiction where there is truth." An abbreviated form of **Fictio cedit veritati; fictio iuris non est ubi veritas.**

F

Fictio legis inique operatur alicui damnum vel iniuriam. fēk´tēō lā´gēs ēnē´kwā ōpāra´tūr a´lēkwē dam´nūm wāl ēnyū´rē-am. fik´šō le´jis i´nikwē apɜrā´tɜr â´likwī dâm´num vel injɜ´rē-um. "A legal fiction works unfairly if it causes loss or injury to anyone." A maxim meaning that a legal fiction should be discarded if its use would create an injustice. *See also* **Fictio cedit veritati; fictio iuris non est ubi veritas.**

Fidelissimi magistri omnium iuris arcanorum conscii. fēdālēs´sēmē magēs´trē ōm´nē-ūm yū´rēs arkanō´rūm kōn´skē-ē. fideli´simī mâ´jistrī am´nē-um jɜ´ris arkânō´rum kōn´šī. *n. pl. Neo.* "Most faithful teachers, privy to the law of all mysteries." A bombastic term sometimes used to refer to the most learned jurists.

Fides servanda est. fē´dās sārwan´da āst. fi´dēz sɜrvân´du est. "Trust is preserved." A phrase meaning that, in the execution of treaty or contractual duties, each party must act in good faith toward the other.

Filum aquae. fē´lūm a´kwī. fi´lum a´kwā. *n.* "Thread of water." (1) A watercourse. (2) An abbreviation of **Medium filum acquae.**

Finalis concordia. fēna´lēs kōnkōr´dē-a. fi´nulis kankōr´dē-u. *n.* "Final agreement." A conclusive agreement, usually for the settlement of a dispute between the parties.

Firmior et potentior est operatio legis quam dispositio hominis. fēr´mēōr āt pōtān´tēōr āst ōpāra´tēō lā´gēs kwam dēspōsē´tēō hō´mēnēs. fɜr´mēōr et pōten´šɜr est apɜrā´šō le´jis kwam dispōzi´šō ha´minis. "The operation of law is more steadfast and capable than the management of man." (1) A maxim positing the superiority of the rule of law over the rule of man. (2) A maxim meaning that no person is above the law. (3) A maxim meaning that the rights of a third party cannot be limited or abrogated by an agreement between two other parties without the consent of the affected third party. An alternative formulation is **Fortior et potentior est dispositio legis quam hominis.**

Flagrans bellum. flag´rans bāl´lūm. flâg´runz be´lum. *n.* "Blazing war." An active armed conflict. *See also* **Flagrante bello.**

Flagrante bello. flagran´tā bāl´lō. flâgran´tē be´lō. *adv.* "With war blazing." During or in the middle of an active armed conflict. *See also* **Flagrans bellum.**

Flagrante delicto. flagran´tā dālēk´tō. flâgran´tē dulik´tō. *adv.* "In blazing wrong-doing." An abbreviation of **In flagrante delicto.**

Foedera. *n. pl. See* **Foedus.**

Foedus. fœ´dūs. fē´dus. *n.* [*pl.* **Foedera.** fœ´dāra. fē´dɜru.] "League." (1) A treaty of peace or alliance. In Roman law, *foedus* connoted a hierarchical relationship between the allies in which Rome was always superior. (2) A convention for the formation of an intergovernmental organization. *Compare with* **Pactum, Pactiones,** and **Sponsio.**

F

Fons et origo. fōns ăt ōrē´gō. fanz et ōri´gō. *n.* "Source and origin." (1) The conditions or events that give rise to or create (something); the source and origin (of something). *E.g.*, "[I]t is clear that the *fons et origo* of the dispute was the atmospheric nuclear tests conducted by France in the South Pacific region, and that the original and ultimate objective of the Applicant was and has remained to obtain a termination of those tests." *Nuclear Tests Cases* (N.Z. v. Fr.), 1974 I.C.J. Rep. 457, 467, ¶ 31. (2) The creator (of something). (3) The geographical source (of something).

Fons et origo mali. fōns ăt ōrē´gō ma´lē. fanz et ōri´gō mâ´lī. *n.* "Source and origin of evil." The origin of an unfortunate or regrettable problem or event.

Fons iuris. fōns yū´rēs. fanz jɜ´ris. *n.* "Fount of law." The source of legal authority.

Forisiurare provinciam. fōrēsyūra´rā prōwēn´kē-am. fōrisjɜra´rē pruvin´sē-um. *v.* + *n.* "To forswear allegiance." To renounce one's citizenship under oath. This act may be required to obtain citizenship in another state that does not accept the concept of dual nationality. *Compare with* **Exuere patriam.**

Forma legalis forma essentialis. fōr´ma lāga´lēs fōr´ma ăssāntē-a´lēs. fō´rmu lēgâ´lis fōr´mu esenšâ´lis. "Legal form is essential form." A maxim (of limited application in international law) meaning that acts not complying with legal formalities are considered void or illegal.

Fortior et potentior est dispositio legis quam hominis. fōr´tēōr ăt pōtān´tēōr ăst dēspōsē´tēō lā´gēs kwam hō´mēnēs. fōr´tyɜr et pōten´šɜr est dispōzi´šō le´jis kwam ha´minis. "The management of law is stronger and more capable than the management of man." An alternative phrase for **Firmior et potentior est operatio legis quam dispositio hominis.**

Fortior obligatio ratio vincit. fōr´tēōr ōblēga´tēō ra´tēō wēn´kēt. fōr´šōr abligā´šō rā´šō vin´sit. "The stronger basis for an obligation prevails." A principle according to which, when two or more obligations conflict, the obligation with a weaker basis yields to the obligation with a stronger one. *Compare with* **Fortior obligatio vincit.**

Fortior obligatio vincit. fŏr´tēōr ōblēga´tēō wēn´kēt. fŏr´šōr abligā´šō vin´sit. "The stronger obligation prevails." A principle according to which, when two or more obligations conflict, the less important obligation yields to the more important one. *Compare with* **Fortior obligatio ratio vincit.**

F

Forum actoris. fō´rūm aktō´rēs. fō´rum âk´tɜris. *n.* "Forum of the actor." The forum in which the claimant or plaintiff resides or has domicile. *E.g.*, "Unlike under the Brussels Convention, where a company based outside the EU, say the U.S., is sued on the basis of Dutch internal jurisdiction law, the possibility of suing before the court of the plaintiff's domicile exists: the so-called *forum actoris*, as opposed to the court of the place of domicile of the defendant. (In other words: the mirror view of the main jurisdictional rule of the place of domicile of the defendant)." Gerrit Betlem, *Transnational Litigation against Multinational Corporations before Dutch Civil Courts*, *in* LIABILITY OF MULTINATIONAL CORPORATIONS UNDER INTERNATIONAL LAW 283 (M. Kamminga and S. Zia-Zarifi eds., 2000).

Forum actus. fō´rūm ak´tūs. fō´rum âk´tus. *n.* "Forum of the act." The jurisdiction in which the legally relevant act was performed.

Forum arresti. fō´rūm arrās´tē. fō´rum ures´tī. *n. Neo.* "Forum of the arrest." The forum or jurisdiction in which an arrest or seizure, usually of personal property, took place. *E.g.*, "In the United States the *forum arresti* was introduced when the American colonies adopted the process of foreign attachment from England, where its origin was said to be the 'custom of London, under which a creditor might attach money or goods of the defendant either in plaintiff's own hands or in the custody of a third person." Lawrence Collins, 1992-III RECEUIL DES COURS 32.

Forum celebrationis. fō´rūm kālābratēō´nēs. fō´rum selubrāšō´nis. *n.* "Forum of the concourse." An abbreviation of **Forum loci celebrationis.**

Forum competens. fō´rūm kōm´pātāns. fō´rum kam´putenz. *n.* "Competent forum." The forum or court having jurisdiction over the relevant dispute. *Contrast with* **Forum non competens.**

Forum connexitatis. fō´rūm kōnnāksēta´tēs. fō´rum kōneksitā´tis. *n. Faux* "Forum of connection." A forum or jurisdiction having a connection to a party or matter sufficient to justify an assertion of personal jurisdiction. This term is false Latin—the word *connexitatis* being recently invented—and should be avoided. It is sometimes used erroneously to designate a tribunal seised of a claim in which some parties to a dispute are outside of the tribunal's territorial jurisdiction but are considered to be sufficiently necessary to the resolution of the dispute to justify an assertion of judicial jurisdiction nonetheless.

F

Forum contractus. fō´rūm kōntrak´tūs. fō´rum kantrâk´tus. *n.* "Forum of the contract." An abbreviation of **Forum loci contractus.**

Forum conveniens. fō´rūm kōnwā´nē-āns. fō´rum kanvē´nē-enz. *n.* "Convenient forum." A court or jurisdiction convenient to the resolution of the dispute. A *forum conveniens* need not be the most convenient forum, so long as it is sufficiently accessible to the relevant parties and witnesses, and no serious obstacles to the resolution of the dispute or inefficiencies will result from the use of that forum. *Contrast with* **Forum non conveniens.**

Forum delicti. fō´rūm dālēk´tē. fō´rum dulik´tī. *n.* "Forum of the wrongdoing." An abbreviation of **Forum loci delicti.**

Forum domicilii. fō´rūm dōmēkē´lē-ē. fō´rum damisi´lī. *n.* "Forum of domicile." The jurisdiction in which a relevant party (usually the defendant or respondent) has his domicile. *See also* **Domicilium.**

Forum ligeantiae rei. fō´rūm lēgā-an´tē-ī rā´ē. fō´rum lijē-ân´tē-ā rā. *n.* "Forum of the defendant's allegiance." An alternative formulation of **Forum rei ligeantiae.**

Forum loci celebrationis. fō´rūm lō´kē kālābratēō´nēs. fō´rum lō´sī selebrāšō´nis. *n.* "Forum of the place of concourse." The jurisdiction in which an agreement was formally concluded. *Compare with* **Forum loci contractus.** *See also* **Forum loci solutionis.**

Forum loci contractus. fō´rūm lō´kē kōntrak´tūs. fō´rum lō´sī kantrâk´tus. *n.* "Forum of the place of the contract." The jurisdiction in which an agreement was executed. *Compare with* **Forum loci celebrationis.** *See also* **Forum loci solutionis.**

Forum loci delicti. fō´rūm lō´kē dālēk´tē. fō´rum lō´sī dulik´tī. *n.* "Forum of the place of the wrongdoing." The jurisdiction in which an injurious act or crime took place.

Forum loci patrimonii. fō´rūm lō´kē patrēmō´nē-ē. fō´rum lō´sī pâtrimō´nī. *n.* "Forum of the patrimonial place." The jurisdiction in which the defendant's or respondent's property is located, despite the absence of the defendant or respondent from the territory of the jurisdiction itself. *Compare with* **Forum situs.** *See also* **Quasi in personam.**

Forum loci solutionis. fō´rūm lō´kē sōlūtēō´nēs. fō´rum lō´sī sōlūšō´nis. *n.* "Forum of the place of resolution." The jurisdiction in which contractual obligations are or were to be performed. *See also* **Forum loci celebrationis** and **Forum loci contractus.**

Forum non competens. fō´rūm nōn kōm´pātāns. fō´rum nan kam´putenz. *n.* "Forum lacking competence." A forum or court lacking jurisdiction over the relevant dispute. *Contrast with* **Forum competens.**

F

Forum non conveniens. fō´rūm nōn kōnwā´nē-āns. fō´rum nan kanvē´nē-enz. *n.* "An inconvenient forum." A common law doctrine under which a tribunal may decline in its discretion to exercise jurisdiction if it determines that it is a seriously inconvenient forum for the litigation, as long as a more appropriate forum is available to the claimant. *E.g.*, "The principle of *forum non conveniens* is simply that a court may resist imposition upon its jurisdiction even when jurisdiction is authorized by the letter of a general venue statute." *Gulf Oil Corp. v. Gilbert*, 330 U.S. 501, 506 (1947). *See* Restatement (Second) of Conflict of Laws § 84 (1971). *Contrast with* **Forum conveniens.**

Forum patrimonii. fō´rūm patrēmō´nē-ē. fō´rum pâtrimō´nī. *n.* "Forum of the patrimony." An abbreviation of **Forum loci patromonii.**

Forum prorogatum. fō´rūm prōrōga´tūm. fō´rum prōrōgā´tum. *n.* "The deferred forum." The jurisdiction to whose authority the parties have acquiesced through an *ad hoc* agreement. In the absence of such agreement, the parties are deemed to have selected the default forum as the *forum prorogatum. E.g.*, "[T]he rule requiring the consent of the parties is quite compatible with a certain degree of flexibility in the ascertainment of that fact, in virtue of the principle of the *forum prorogatum.*" *Advisory Opinion Concerning the Interpretation of Peace Treaties with Bulgaria, Hungary, and Romania*, 1950 I.C.J. Rep. 65, 81, ¶ 5 (separate opinion of Judge Azevedo).

Forum rei ligeantiae. fō´rūm rā´ē lēgā-an´tē-ī. fō´rum rā lijē-ân´tē-ā. *n.* "Forum of the defendant's allegiance." A forum or court in the state of the defendant's nationality. An alternative formulation is **Forum ligeantiae rei.**

Forum rei sitae. fō´rūm rā´ē sē´tī. fō´rum rā si´tā. *n.* "Forum in which the thing (is situated)." The venue or territorial jurisdiction in which property that is the subject of a dispute is physically located. In the case of patents or trademarks, this is the jurisdiction in which the patent or trademark was granted. *Compare with* **Forum loci patrimonis** and **Forum situs.** *See also* **In rem.**

Forum situs. fō´rūm sē´tūs. fō´rum sī´tus. *n.* "Forum of the site." The jurisdiction in which property under dispute is located. *Compare with* **Forum loci patrimonii** and **Forum rei sitae.** *See also* **In rem.**

Forum solutionis. fō´rūm sōlūtēō´nēs. fō´rum sōlūšō´nis. *n.* "Forum of the resolution." An abbreviation of **Forum loci solutionis.**

Fraus est celare fraudem. frôs āst kāla´rā frô´dām. frăs est sela´rē fră´dum. "To conceal a fraud is fraud." A maxim meaning that, by concealing a fraud, one thereby participates in the fraud or commits an additional fraud.

F

Fraus et ius nunquam cohabitant. frôs āt yūs nūn´kwam kōha´bitant. frăs et jus nun´kwam kōhâ´bitânt. "Fraud and justice never cohabitate." A maxim meaning that fraud corrupts justice regardless of the good faith or just intentions of the participants.

Fraus legis facta. frôs lā´gēs fak´ta. frăs le´jis fâk´tu. *n.* "A legal fraud done." An attempt to fraudulently avoid the application of the law of one jurisdiction (where an act would be illegal) by resort to another jurisdiction (where the act would be legal). In general, *legi fraudem facere* means to circumvent or evade the law, as opposed *contra legem facere*, which means to do what is prohibited by the law.

Fraus meretur fraudem. frôs mārā´tūr frô´dām. frăs me´retɜr fră´dum. *Neo.* "Fraud obtains fraud." A maxim meaning that one fraud tends to breed other frauds necessary to conceal the original fraud.

Fraus omnia corrumpit. frôs ōm´nē-a kōrrūm´pēt. frăs am´nē-u kɜrum´pit. "Fraud corrupts all." A principle according to which the discovery of fraud invalidates all aspects of a judicial decision or arbitral award.

Frusca terra. frūs´ka tār´ra. frus´ku te´ru. *n.* "Barren land." A desert or wasteland.

Fumus boni iuris. fū´mūs bō´nē yū´rēs. fyū´mus bō´nī jɜ´ris. *n.* "The smoke of good law." The evident or superficial merit of a petition, argument, or plea. According to the principle of *fumus boni iuris*, a valid claim should generally be heard by the petitioned tribunal. *E.g.*, "The criterion of *fumus boni juris* as a condition to the order of provisional measures having an obligatory character is well known in certain international jurisdictions (for example, the European Court of Justice…) as well as numerous national judicial systems. It applies, indeed, by a kind of logical necessity." *Pulp Mills on the River Uruguay* (Arg. v. Uru.), I.C.J. Case No. 135, Order of July 13, 2006, Annex, ¶ 9 (Provisional Measures) (separate opinion of Judge Abraham) (our translation from the French). An alternative formulation is **Bonus fumus iuris.**

Functus officio. fūnk´tūs ōffē´kēō. funk´tus ufi´šō. *adv.* "Having performed in its office." Lacking in jurisdiction or authority because one's duties or functions have been fulfilled. A tribunal, law, regulation, or edict becomes *functus* *officio* after it has played out its official role and no longer has any basis for exercising authority.

Fungibiles res. fūngē´bēlās rās. funji´bilēz res. *n. pl.* "Fungible things." Personal property having the character of being functionally identical with, and therefore freely substitutable for, other personal property of like kind.

F

G

Gabella emigrationis. gabāl´la āmēgratēō´nēs. gâ´belu emigrāšō´nis. *n. Neo.* "Emigration tax." A tax on the act of emigration itself or on personal property taken out of the country while emigrating.

Generale dictum generaliter est interpretandum. gānāra´lā dēk´tūm gānāra´lētār āst ēntārprātan´dūm. jen3râ´lē dik´tum jen3râ´lit3r est int3rpretân´dum. "A general saying is interpreted generally." A maxim meaning that a generally worded provision of a legal instrument should be construed to apply broadly and by default, with the understanding that some exceptions may be justified. *Compare with* **Generalis regula generaliter est intelligenda.**

Generalia specialibus non derogant. gānāra´lē-a spākē-a´lēbūs nōn dā´rōgant. jen3rā´lē-u spešyâ´libus nan de´rōgânt. "General things do not derogate from specific things." A maxim meaning that specific or detailed provisions of a legal instrument should prevail over more general, conflicting provisions. *Compare with* **Generalis clausula non porrigitur ad ea quae antea specialiter sunt comprehensa** and **Specialia generalibus derogant.**

Generalis clausula non porrigitur ad ea quae antea specialiter sunt comprehensa. gānāra´lēs klô´sūla nōn pōrrē´gētūr ad ā´a kwī an´tā-a spākē-a´lētūr sūnt kōmprāhān´sa. jen3râ´lis klă´zyūlu nan pōri´jit3r âd ē´u kwā ân´tē-u spešâ´lit3r sunt kamprēhen´su. "A general clause does not extend to those things that previously have been comprehended in a special way." A maxim meaning that a general clause in a legal instrument is presumed not to apply to situations specifically provided for elsewhere in the same instrument. *Compare with* **Generalia specialibus non derogant.**

Generalis regula generaliter est intelligenda. gānāra´lēs rā´gūla gānāra´lētār āst ēntāllēgān´da. jen3râ´lis re´gyūlu jen3râ´lit3r est intelijen´du. "A general rule is to be interpreted generally." A maxim meaning that a rule of general application should be applied broadly, with the understanding that some exceptions may be justified. *Compare with* **Generale dictum generaliter est interpretandum.**

Gentes. gān´tās. jen´tēz. *n. pl.* "Peoples." The peoples or nations of the world as a collectivity. The term *gentes* was used in both Roman and medieval law primarily to indicate those peoples or nations with which formal international relations were conducted.

G

Gestio. gās´tēō. jes´tēō. *n.* "Action." (1) Behavior; course of action. (2) The conduct of business.

Gleboe adscripti. glā´bœ adskrēp´tē. glē´bē âdskrip´tī. *n. pl.* "Joined to the land." Things permanently a part of the land. *E.g.*, "In civilized nations the greater part of mankind are *gleboe adscripti*, fixtures to the soil on which they are born." Jeremy Bentham, *The Principles of International Law: Essay II*, *in* 2 THE WORKS OF JEREMY BENTHAM 542 (John Bowring ed. 1843).

Gradatim. grada´tēm. grudā´tim. *adv.* "By degrees." Incrementally; by steps; gradually.

Gratis. gra´tēs. grâ´tis. *adj.* or *adv.* "From kindness." Free; freely; not requiring any remuneration.

Gratis dictum. gra´tēs dēk´tūm. grâ´tis dik´tum. *n.* "A statement given willingly." (1) An unnecessary statement. (2) An unproven assertion.

Gravitas. gra´wētas. grâ´vitas. *n.* "Seriousness." (1) Importance. (2) Gravity. (3) A dignified demeanor.

H

Haec est conventio. hīk āst kōnwān´tēō. hāk est kanven´šō. "This is the custom." (1) A statement declaring the putative customary practices of relevant parties. (2) A statement declaring the explicit terms of an agreement.

Haec verba. hīk wār´ba. hāk vɜr´bu. *n. pl.* "(In) those words." An alternative formulation of **In haec verba.**

Hereditas. hārā´dētas. hɜre´ditus. *n.* "Heritage." (1) Heritage. (2) Inheritance.

Holus bolus. hō´lūs bō´lūs. hō´lus bō´lus. *adv. Faux* "Hocus pocus." As if by magic; instantly, completely, and mysteriously. *E.g.*, "[T]he scope of the jurisdiction of this Chamber, or of any other chamber composed by the Court under the present Rules, is neither definitive nor final, so that one cannot regard jurisdiction as being transferable *holus bolus* from the International Court of Justice itself to its affiliate envisaged in Article 26 of the Statute, or by any other text." *Land, Island, and Maritime Frontier Dispute* (El Sal. v. Hond.), 1990 I.C.J. Rep. 3, 9 (Application to Intervene) (Judge Elias, dissenting).

Hominum causa (omne) ius constitutum est. hō´mēnūm kô´sa (ōm´nā) yūs kōnstētū´tūm āst. ha´minum kă´zu (am´nē) jus kanstitū´tum est. "(Every) law has been created for the sake of men." A maxim of Roman law meaning that every law is ultimately designed to serve the good of persons. The maxim implies that the law is a means rather than an end and should aspire to improve the lives of real persons rather to achieve doctrinal purity or to perfect abstract principles.

Homo. hō´mō. hō´mō. *n.* "Man." (1) A person. (2) A man.

Homo civitatis. hō´mō kēwēta´tēs. hō´mō sivitā´tis. *n.* "Man of the city." A person in his or her role or capacity as a citizen. *E.g.*, "Since the *Martinez Sala* case, European citizenship has received a unique boost, taking an innovative precedence in the Court's jurisprudence that…has interpreted legislative intent to attribute to the citizen moving between countries a more privileged status than that of the economic actor. Put more simply, the Court has transformed the model of the *homo economicus* into that of the *homo civitatis*." Opinion of Advocat General Damaso Ruiz-Jarabo Colomer, *Petersen v. Arbeitsmarktservice Niederosterreich*, E.C.J. Case C-228/07, ¶ 15 (2008).

H

Homo economicus. hō´mō ākōnō´mēkūs. hō´mō ekuna´mikus. *n.* "Economic man." A person in his or her role or capacity as an economic actor; a person seeking to maximize his or her wealth. *E.g.*, "As most people spend most of their time on the production of goods and services (such as education) as a means to acquire other goods and services (such as medical and cultural services, transport, telecommunication and tourism) inside and outside their home country, the frequent double standard cultivated by many lawyers and courts—i.e. their preference for and higher level of scrutiny accorded to civil and political rights, rather than to economic and social rights, let alone to their increasingly transnational exercise in the modern global economy—reflects a strange legal anachronism and disregard of the global development problems and actual needs of the modern *homo economicus*." Ernst-Ulrich Petersmann, THE GATT/WTO DISPUTE SETTLEMENT SYSTEM 3 (1997).

Homo politicus. hō´mō pōlē´tēkūs. hō´mō pōli´tikus. *n.* "Political man." A person in his or her role or capacity as a political actor; a person seeking to maximize his or her political power. *E.g.*, "[T]he *homo politicus* who pursues nothing but power is as unreal a myth as the *homo economicus* who pursues nothing but gain. Political action must be based on a co-ordination of morality and power." Christian Reus-Smit, *The Politics of International Law*, *in* THE POLITICS OF INTERNATIONAL LAW 14, 25 (Christian Reus-Smit ed., 2004).

Homo sociologicus. hō´mō sōkēōlō´gēkūs. hō´mō sōsēōla´jikus. *n.* "Sociological man." A person in his or her capacity or role as a social being and member of a society.

Hostis humani generis. hōs´tēs hūma´nē gā´nārēs. has´tis hyu´mânī jen´ɜris. *n.* [*pl.* **Hostes humani generis.** hōs´tās hūma´nē gā´nārēs. has´tēz hyu´mânī jen´ɜris.] "Enemy of humankind." A common enemy of all peoples, such as a pirate, slave trader, or terrorist, whose acts are repugnant or threatening to the international community generally. A person accused of being *hostis humani generis* may be subject to universal jurisdiction. *See also* **Pirata est hostis humani generis.**

I(J)

Note: In classical Latin, the letter "j" was not commonly used; the letter "i" represented two separate sounds, one like the "ee" in "see" (represented here with the phoneme "ē"), and another pronounced more like the English "y" in "yes" (the so-called palatal approximant, represented here with the phoneme "y"). To distinguish the two sounds, it eventually became common to represent the "i" used in consonant form with the letter "j". Except for abbreviations, which almost always use "j" instead of "i" in modern usage, whenever you see a "j" in a Latin phrase and wish to find it in this guidebook, look up the equivalent with "i" substituted for the "j". For example, if you are looking for *jus cogens*, locate *ius cogens*.

J.D. An abbreviation of **Iuris doctor**.

I.e. An abbreviation of **Id est**.

J.S.D. An abbreviation of **Iuris scientiae doctor**.

J.U.D. An abbreviation of **Iuris utriusque doctor**.

Ibid. ē´bēd. i´bid OR ī´bid. An abbreviation of **Ibidem**.

Ibidem. ēbē´dām. ibi´dem. "In that same place." In the same source just cited. This term is used as citation signal interchangeably with **Idem**. Commonly abbreviated as **Ibid.** *See also* **Opera citato**.

Ictu oculi. ēk´tū ō´kūlē. ik´tū a´kyūlī. *adv.* "At the glance of the eye." (1) At first glance; superficially. (2) Evidently. *E.g.*, "The latter contention of Thailand is *ictu oculi* unfounded for the following reasons…" *Temple of Preah Vihear* (Camb. v. Thail.), 1961 I.C.J. Rep. 17, 44, ¶ 3 (separate opinion of Judge Morelli). *Compare with* **Prima facie** and **Primo fronte**.

Id. An abbreviation of **Idem**.

I(J)

Id est. ēd äst. id est. "It is." An expression that signals that the author or speaker will explain a previous phrase or word in alternative terms or elaborate on the previous phrase or word. Commonly abbreviated **I.e.** *E.g.*, "International law—and consequently the principle of *uti possidetis*—applies to the new State (as a State) not with retroactive effect, but immediately and from that moment onwards. It applies to the State as it is, *i.e.*, to the 'photograph' of the territorial situation then existing." *Frontier Dispute* (Burk. Faso v. Mali), 1986 I.C.J. Rep. 554, 568, ¶ 30.

Idem. ē´dām. ī´dem. "That same." The same source just cited. *Idem* or, more commonly, its abbreviation (**Id.**), is used as a citation signal to indicate that support for the assertion may be found in the same source cited immediately previously, usually on the same page unless otherwise specified. The term is used interchangeably with **Ibidem**. *Compare with* **Ante.**

Idem est facere et nolle prohibere cum possis. ē´dām äst fa´kārā āt nōl´lā prōhē´bārā kūm pōs´sēs. ī´dem est fâ´sɜrē et nɜ´lē prōhi´bɜrē kum pa´sis. "It is the same thing to act and to refuse to prohibit when you can." A maxim meaning that a person in a position of authority who tolerates a wrongful act assumes equal responsibility for the act, as if he had performed it himself. *See also* **Respondeat superior.**

Identidem. ēdān´tēdām. īden´tidem. "Repeatedly." (1) Repeatedly; recurrently. (2) Continually.

Ideo. ē´dāō. i´dēō. *adv.* "Therefore." Consequently; for this reason. *Compare with* **Ergo** and **Per consequens.**

Ignorantia elenchi. ēgnōran´tē-a ālān´kē. ignōrân´šu elen´čī. "Ignorance of the argument to which a refutation pertains." The situation in which it is unclear what claims a specific counterargument is intended to refute.

Ignorantia excusatur non iuris sed facti. ēgnōran´tē-a āks-kūsa´tūr nōn yū´rēs sād fak´tē. ignōrân´šu eks-kyū´zutɜr nan jɜ´ris sed fâk´tī. "Ignorance of fact but not of the law is excused." An alternative phrase for **Ignorantia legis neminem excusat.** This phrasing originates in Justinian's *Digest* (22.6.9).

Ignorantia facti excusat, ignorantia iuris non excusat. ēgnōran´tē-a fak´tē āks-kū´sat, ēgnōran´tē-a yū´rēs nōn aks-kū´sat. ignōrân´šu fâk´tī eks-kyū´zât, ignōrân´šu jɜ´ris nan eks-kyū´zât. "Ignorance of facts excuses; ignorance of the law does not excuse." An alternative phrase for **Ignorantia legis neminem excusat.**

Ignorantia iuris neminem excusat. ēgnōran´tē-a yū´rēs nā´mēnām āks-kū´sat. ignōrân´šu jɜ´ris ne´minem eks-kyū´zât. "Ignorance of the law excuses no one." An alternative phrase for **Ignorantia legis neminem excusat.**

Ignorantia iuris non excusat. ēgnōran´tē-a yū´rēs nōn āks-kū´sat. ignōrân´šu jɜ´ris nan eks-kyū´zât. "Ignorance of the law does not excuse." An phrase for **Ignorantia legis neminem excusat.**

Ignorantia legis neminem excusat. ēgnōran´tē-a lā´gēs nā´mēnām āks-kū´sat. ignōrân´šu le´jis ne´minem eks-kyū´zât. "Ignorance of the law excuses no one." A doctrine requiring all persons to know their legal duties, such that actual ignorance of these duties will not prevent a finding of liability for their violation. *Bone fide* ignorance of relevant facts, in contrast, may excuse a failure to fulfill a legal duty that should have been fulfilled had those facts been known. Alternative phrases are **Ignorantia excusatur non iuris sed facti; Ignorantia facti excusat, ignorantia iuris non excusat; Ignorantia iuris neminem excusat; Ignorantia iuris non excusat**; and **Ignorantia legis non excusat.**

Ignorantia legis non excusat. ēgnōran´tē-a lā´gēs nōn āks-kū´sat. ignōrân´šu le´jis nan eks-kyū´zât. "Ignorance of the law does not excuse." An alternative phrase for **Ignorantia legis neminem excusat.**

Illegitimati non carborundum. ēllāgētēma´tē nōn karbōrūn´dūm. ileji´timatī nan karbōrun´dum. *Neo.* "The bastards should not grind [you down]." This motto of encouragement, loosely translated as "don't let the bastards grind you down," is popularly attributed to Second World War U.S. General Joseph Stilwell.

Immobilia situm sequuntur. ēmmōbē´lē-a sē´tūm sākwūn´tūr. imōbi´lē-u sī´tum se´kwuntɜr. "Immovables follow the locality." A maxim meaning that the law of the jurisdiction in which real property is found governs the disposition of and rights in the property.

Imperium. ēmpā´rē-ūm. impē´rē-um. *n.* "Authority." The general power of government and administration—one of the two core characteristics of sovereignty. In Republican Rome, the power of superior magistrates was termed *imperium*; in Imperial Rome, the emperor's much expanded power was known by the same name. In modern usage, it refers to the power of the government to legislate and execute laws. *See also* **Dominium** and **Maiestas.**

Imperium in imperio. ēmpā´rē-ūm ēn ēmpā´rēō. impē´rē-um in impē´rēō. *n.* "A sovereignty within a sovereignty." A term describing multiple or hierarchical sovereigns within a single territory, as where municipal, provincial, or federal authorities all govern different aspects or territorial subdivisions of the same greater territory.

Impossibilium nulla obligatio est. ēmpōssēbē´lē-ūm nūl´la ōblēga´tēō āst. impasibi´lē-um nɜ´lu abligā´šō est. "The impossible is no legal obligation." A maxim meaning that a legal obligation that is impossible to perform must be excused. An alternative phrase is **Ad impossibilia nemo tenetur.** *Compare with* **Impotentia excusat legem, Lex neminem cogit ad vana seu impossibilia, Lex non cogit impossibilia,** and **Ultra posse nemo tenetur.**

Impotentia excusat legem. ēmpōtān´tē-a āks-kū´sat lā´gām. impōten´šu eks-kyū´zât le´jem. "Inability excuses the law." A maxim meaning that impossibility of performing a legal obligation due to a reasonably unforeseeable or unpreventable event excuses a failure to perform the legal obligation. *Compare with* **Impossibilium nulla obligatio est, Lex neminem cogit ad vana seu impossibilia,** and **Lex non cogit impossibilia.**

Imprimatur. ēmprēma´tūr. impri´mutɜr. *v.* (used as a *n.*) "May it be stamped." A mark of approval. *E.g.*, "Even with the assumptions and presumptions of the consent by the Rulers of Bahrain and Qatar, the Court did not necessarily have to lend its *imprimatur* to the British decision without looking into its substantive grounding in law." *Maritime Delimitation and Territorial Questions* (Qatar v. Bahr.), 2001 I.C.J. Rep. 40, 220, ¶ 10 (declaration of Judge Vereshchetin).

Imprimis. ēmprē´mēs. impri´mis. *adv.* "Among the first; principally; especially." An alternative formulation of **In primis.**

In absentia. ēn absān´tē-a. in âbsen´šu. *adv.* "In the absence." In the absence of a person during proceedings such as a hearing or criminal trial in which the absent person is the accused. *E.g.*, "Some jurisdictions provide for trial *in absentia*; others do not.... If, as we believe to be the case, a State may choose to exercise a universal criminal jurisdiction *in absentia*, it must also ensure that certain safeguards are in place." *Arrest Warrant of 11 April 2000* (Congo v. Belg.), 2002 I.C.J. Rep. 3, 79–80, ¶¶ 56, 59 (separate opinion of Judge Higgins).

In abstracto. ēn abstrak´tō. in âbstrâk´tō. *adv.* "In the abstract." Abstractly or theoretically speaking; without reference to specific or real facts. *E.g.*, "It does not enter into the adjudicatory functions of the Court to deal with issues *in abstracto*, once it has reached the conclusion that the merits of the case no longer fall to be determined." *Nuclear Tests* (Austl. v. Fr.), 1974 I.C.J. Rep. 252, ¶ 43 (Judgment). *Compare with* **In vacuo.** *Contrast with* **In concreto.**

In actu. ēn ak´tū. in âk´tū. *adj.* "In action." In practice; in action. *E.g.*, "As regards the *pactum de compromittendo*, international law has made certain progress in developing the formulas regulating passage from arbitration *in potentia* to arbitration *in actu*, particularly in respect of the appointment of arbitrators by the act of a third party." *Advisory Opinion on Interpretation of Peace Treaties with Bulgaria, Hungary, and Romania*, 1950 I.C.J. Rep. 221, 248 (Judge Azevedo, dissenting). *Contrast with* **In potentia.** *See also* **de facto.**

In adimplenti non est adimplendum. ēn adēmplān´tē nōn āst adēmplān´dūm. in âdimplen´tī nan est âdimplen´tum. "It is not necessary to fulfill [one's obligation] to a person who fails to fulfill his own." A principle providing that a party in breach of a contractual or treaty obligation usually sacrifices its right to demand performance by the other party unless the breach is *de minimis* and not material.

In aequali iure. ēn īkwa´lē yū´rā. in ekwa´lī jɜ´rē. *adj.* or *adv.* "In equal right." Having equal or equivalent rights.

In aequo. ēn ī´kwō. in e´kwō. *adj.* or *adv.* "In equity." According to principles of equity.

In aeternum. ēn ītār´nūm. in etɜr´num. *adv.* "For eternity." (1) Permanently. (2) Continuously and indefinitely. (3) In perpetuity. *Compare with* **In perpetuum.**

In ambiguis orationibus maxime sententia spectanda est eius qui eas protulisset. ēn ambē´gū-ēs ōratēō´nēbūs ma´ksēmā sāntān´tē-a spāktan´da āst ā´yūs kwē ā´as prōtūlēs´sāt. in âmbi´gyūis ōrāšō´nibus mâ´ksimē senten´šu spektân´du est ē´jus kwē ē´us prōtuli´set. "In ambiguous statements, the greatest regard is for the views of the person who made them." A maxim, originating in Justinian's *Digest* (50.17.96), meaning that, in interpreting an ambiguous statement, provision, or rule, the opinion of the original speaker or drafter on its interpretation should carry the greatest weight. *Contrast with* **Contra proferentem.**

In ambiguo. ēn ambē´gūō. in âmbi´gwō. *adj.* or *adv.* "In doubt." In doubt or uncertainty.

In camera. ēn ka´māra. in kâ´mɜru. *adj.* or *adv.* "In the room." (1) In the judge's or arbitrator's private chambers. (2) In the room. *Contrast with* **In curia.**

In casu. ēn ka´sū. in kā´sū. *adj.* "In the case." In, during, or throughout the judicial action. *E.g.*, "If, for more than a decade, it was so clear to the Court that the Respondent was not a Member of the United Nations, and the quality of being a Member of the United Nations is the only basis on which the Respondent could have been considered a party to the Statute of the

Court, it follows that the Court deliberately avoided recognizing the jurisdictional fact affecting the very legality of the totality of its actions *in casu*." *Application of the Convention on the Prevention and Punishment of the Crime of Genocide* (Bosn. & Herz. v. Yugo.), I.C.J. No. 91, Judgment of Feb. 26, 2007, at 30, ¶ 60 (separate opinion of Judge *ad hoc* Kreća).

In casu consimili. ēn ka´sū kōnsē´mēlē. in kā´sū kansi´milī. *adv.* "In a similar case." An alternative formulation of **In consimili casu.**

In communi. ēn kōmmū´nē. in ka´myūnī. *adj.* "In common." Communal; in common.

In concreto. ēn kōnkrā´tō. in kankrē´tō. *adv.* "In the concrete." (1) Concretely or palpably thinking or speaking. (2) With reference to actual, verifiable facts, rather than theoretically. *E.g.*, "[T]he 'peaceful and continuous exercise of State authority' is not in itself a principle of international law, but a manifestation of a given unilateral conduct of the State concerned, whose eventual legal effects ought to be defined *in concreto* in the light of the various circumstances and, first of all, of the operating norm of international law relevant in final analysis to the said unilateral conduct." *Land, Island, and Maritime Frontier Dispute* (El Salv. v. Nicar.), 1992 I.C.J. Rep. 351, 677. *Contrast with* **In abstracto.**

In coniunctivis oportet utramque partem esse veram. ēn kōnyūnktē´wēs ōpōr´tāt ūtram´kwā par´tām ās´sā wā´ram. in kanjunctī´vis upōr´tet ūt´ramkwā par´tum ve´rum. "In conjunctive phrases, it is proper for each part to be true." A maxim meaning that in phrases containing two or more conditions connected by the word "and" or its equivalent, the phrase must be interpreted as requiring all conditions to be true. In other words, under this maxim, a treaty providing that a state party must do *A*, *B*, and *C* means that the state party will not have satisfied its obligations by doing any one or two of *A*, *B*, or *C*, but must instead perform all three conditions. *See also* **In disiunctivis sufficit alteram partem esse veram.**

In consequentiam. ēn kōnsākwān´tē-am. in kansekwen´tē-um. *adj.* "In consequence." As a consequence.

In consimili casu. ēn kōnsē´mēlē ka´sū. in kansi´milī kā´sū. *adv.* "In a similar case." In an analogous or similar position, situation, or constellation of facts. Sometimes abbreviated **Consimili casu.** An alternative formulation is **In casu consimili.** *Compare with* **Ad consimili casu.** *See also* **In consimili casu consimile debet esse remedium.**

In consimili casu consimile debet esse remedium. ēn kōnsē´mēlē ka´sū kōnsē´mēlā dā´bāt ās´sā rāmā´dē-ūm. in kansi´milī kā´sū kansi´milē de´bet e´sē remē´dē-um. "In a similar case, the remedy should be similar." A maxim meaning that, in order for the law to be applied uniformly, claims based on similar facts should give rise to comparable remedies.

In contractibus tacite insunt quae sunt moris et consuetudinis. ēn kōntrak´tēbūs ta´kētā ēn´sūnt kwī sūnt mō´rēs āt kōnswātū´dēnēs. in kantrâk´ibus tâ´sitē in´sunt kwā sunt mō´ris et kanswātū´dinis. "In contracts, matters of custom and course of dealing are tacitly present." A maxim meaning that contracts should be read in light of trade customs and past dealings between the parties.

In corpore. ēn kōr´pōrā. in kōrpō´rē. *adv.* "In the body." (1) In person. (2) In the flesh; specifically present. (3) In substance.

In conventionibus, contrahentium voluntas potius quam verba spectari placuit. ēn kōnwāntēō´nēbūs, kōtrahān´tē-ūm wōlūn´tas pō´tē-ūs kwam wār´ba spākta´rē pla´kū-ēt. in kanvenšō´nibus, kantruhen´šum va´luntas pō´tē-ūs kwam v3r´bu spekta´rī plâ´swit. "In agreements, the intentions of the contracting parties are to be regarded more than their words." A maxim, originating in Justinian's *Digest* (50.16.219), meaning that the language of an agreement that seems to disserve the intentions of the parties should be read to conform to those intentions. *But see* the Vienna Convention on the Law of Treaties arts. 31–32, May 23, 1969, 1155 U.N.T.S. 331. *Contrast with* **In dubio, haec legis contructio quam verba ostendunt.**

In curia. ēn kū´rē-a. in ky3´rē-u. *adv.* "In court." In open court; before a formally constituted tribunal. *Compare with* **In facie curiae.** *Contrast with* **In camera.**

In diem. ēn dē´ām. in dē´um. *adj.* "To the day." An abbreviation of **De die in diem.**

In disiunctivis sufficit alteram partem esse veram. ēn dēsyūnktē´wēs sūf´fēkēt al´tāram par´tām ās´sā wā´ram. in disjunktī´vis sufī´sit al´terum par´tum e´sē ve´rum. "In disjunctive phrases, it suffices if either part is true." A maxim meaning that in phrases containing two or more conditions connected by "or," the phrase must be interpreted as requiring only one of the conditions to be true. For example, a treaty providing that state parties may take annually no more than 9 megagrams or 5000 specimens of adult salmon from a specific river would be read under this maxim as exhausting its rights after taking either 9 megagrams or 5000 specimens of salmon, whichever occurs first. *See also* **In coniunctivis oportet utramque partem esse veram.**

In dubio. ēn dū´bēō. in dū´bēō. *adj.* or *adv.* "In doubt." (1) Having doubts. (2) Of doubtful or uncertain character.

In dubio haec legis constructio quam verba ostendunt. ēn dū´bēō hīk lā´gēs kōnstrūk´tēō kwam wār´ba ōstān´dūnt. in dū´bēō hek le´jis kanstruk´šō kwam v3r´bu asten´dunt. "When in doubt, the construction of the law is the one that the words indicate." A maxim meaning that when the meaning or intent of a law, agreement, or treaty is uncertain, the words should be read according to their plain meaning. *See* the Vienna Convention on the Law of Treaties art. 31, May 23, 1969, 1155 U.N.T.S. 331. *Contrast with* **In conventionibus, contrahentium voluntas potius quam verba spectari placuit** and **In verbis non verba sed res et ratio quaerenda est.**

In dubio mitius. ēn dū´bēō mē´tē-ūs. in dū´bēō mi´šus OR –mi´tē-us. "More leniently in case of doubt." (1) The principle that, where the evidence in a criminal case is ambiguous or uncertain, the defendant should be found not guilty. (2) The principle that an award or sentence should be reduced where the evidence of liability or damages does not fully support the claim or prosecution. (3) The principle that, where there is doubt about the existence of an obligation under international law, no obligation will be found in order to avoid limiting state sovereignty.

In dubio pro lege fori. ēn dū´bēō prō lā´gā fō´rē. in dū´bēō prō le´jē fō´rī. "When in doubt, in favor of the law of the forum." A maxim meaning that, when the law applicable to a dispute is uncertain, the law of the forum should be applied.

In dubio pro natura. ēn dū´bēō prō natū´ra. in dū´bēō prō nā´čзru. "When in doubt, in favor of nature." A maxim meaning that, when in doubt as to whether an activity harmful to the environment should proceed, the doubt should be resolved in favor of protecting the environment. This statement reflects to a degree the "precautionary principle" commonly adopted in international environmental law instruments. *E.g.*, "However, the interests of Czechoslovakia were of a financial nature, theoretically easy to compensate, whereas those of Hungary related to the safeguarding of its ecological balance and the difficult and uncertain struggle against damage to its environment. *In dubio pro natura.*" *Gabcikovo-Nagymaros Project* (Hung. v. Slovk), 1997 I.C.J. Rep. 7, 187 (Judge Herczegh, dissenting).

In dubio pro reo. ēn dū´bēō prō rā´ō. in dū´bēō prō rā´ō. "When in doubt, in favor of the defendant." A maxim meaning that, when the applicable laws or the relevant facts are unclear or ambiguous, all doubt should be resolved in a manner favorable to the defendant. This maxim is applied most commonly in criminal cases, but may also apply in civil cases.

In eadem causa. ēn ā-a´dām kô´sa. in ē´udem kă´zu. *adv.* "In the same case." (1) In the same case or legal action. (2) In identical states or conditions.

In eo quod plus sit semper inest et minus. ēn ā´ō kwōd plūs sēt sām´pār ē´nāst āt mē´nūs. in ē´ō kwad plus sit sem´pɜr i´nest et mī´nus. "In the greater is always included the lesser." A maxim, originating in Justinian's *Digest* (50.17.110), meaning that a reference to a composite or more general thing always encompasses a reference to its subdivisions or components. *E.g.*, "The parties to the main proceedings consider that the German authorities were entitled to exclude commercial transport from the Regulation. Referring to the principle '*in eo quod plus sit, semper inest et minus*,' they contend that if the second subparagraph of Article 1 (1) permits the application of the Regulation to be excluded for a complete category of transport (namely, urban, suburban and regional services), it must, *a fortiori*, permit a limited part of those services to be excluded." Opinion of Advocate General Leger, *Altmark Trans GmbH v. Nahverkehrsgesellschaft Altmark GmbH*, [2003] E.C.R. I-7747, ¶ 39. Alternative formulations are **In maiori stat minus, In toto et pars continetur, Maior continet (in se) minus**, and **Omne maior continet in se minus.**

I(J)

In eodem negotio. ēn āō´dām nāgō´tēō. in ē´ōdem negō´šō. *adv.* "In the same activity." (1) In the same transaction. (2) In the same course of business conduct.

In esse. ēn ās´sā. in e´sē. *adv.* "In being." Currently in effect; currently existing. *E.g.*, "Yet even if a company is no more than a means for its shareholders to achieve their economic purpose, so long as it is *in esse* it enjoys an independent existence." *Barcelona Traction, Light, and Power Company* (Belg. v. Spain), 1970 I.C.J. Rep. 3, ¶ 45. *Contrast with* **In posse.**

In exitu. ēn ā´ksētū. in e´gzitū. *adj.* or *adv.* "At the end." At issue; at hand.

In extenso. ēn ākstān´sō. in eksten´sō. *adv.* "With extension." Extensively. This ungrammatical term should be avoided. The correct Latin for "extensively" is **Extense.**

In extremis. ēn ākstrā´mēs. in ekstrē´mis OR -ekstre´mis. *adv.* "In the extreme." (1) In extreme circumstances. (2) In the final portion; at the end.

In facie curiae. ēn fa´kē-ā kū´rē-ī. in fā´šu kyū´rē-ā. *adj.* or *adv.* "In the presence of the court." Before a constituted and sitting tribunal. *Compare with* **In curia.**

In faciendo. ēn fakē-ān´dō. in fāsē-en´dō. *adj.* or *adv.* "In doing." During or through the performance of an act. An alternative phrase is **In facto praestando.**

In facto. ēn fak´tō. in fāk´tō. *adv.* "In fact." Factually; as a matter of fact.

In facto praestando. ēn fak´tō prīstan´dō. in fāk´tō prestan´dō. *adv.* "In the furnishing of fact." An alternative phrase for **In faciendo.**

In favorem debitoris. ēn fawō´rām dābētō´rēs. in fâvō´rem debitō´ris. *adv.* "In favor of the debtor." A principle of interpretation of legal instruments of credit whereby ambiguous terms should be construed in the manner most favorable to the interests or position of the debtor. *Compare with* **Contra proferentem**.

In favorem vitae, libertatis, et innocentiae omnia praesumuntur. ēn fawō´rām wē´tī, lēbārta´tēs, āt ēnnōkān´tē-ī ōm´nē-a prīsūmūn´tūr. in fâvō´rem vi´tā, libɜrtā´tis, et inōsen´šā am´nē-u prēzūm´untɜr. "All things are to be presumed to be in favor of life, liberty, and innocence." A maxim meaning that, in a criminal prosecution, the defendant should be presumed innocent and at liberty in the absence of sufficient proof to the contrary.

In fine. ēn fē´nā. in fīn. *adv.* "At the end." (1) Ultimately. (2) In the final analysis. (3) In summary. (4) At the conclusion. This term is also sometimes used as a citation signal to indicate that the relevant material is found at the end of the cited source. *E.g.*, "[S]ee *Vilvarajah* (1992) 14 E.H.R.R. 249, at § 108 *in fine*." *Nnyanzi v. United Kingdom*, 47 E.H.R.R. 18, n.19 (2008),

In flagrante delicto. ēn flagran´tā dālēk´tō. in flâgrân´tā dulik´tō. *adv.* "In evident crime." Red-handed; during the actual commission of an illegal act. *E.g.*, "There were reports that in May/June 2000, during the war with Ethiopia, deserters who were caught *in flagrante delicto* were executed." *Said v. Netherlands*, 43 E.H.R.R. 14, ¶ 23 (2006). Sometimes abbreviated **Flagrante delicto**.

In foro. ēn fō´rō. in fō´rō. *adj.* "In the forum." In the forum; before the tribunal.

In foro conscientiae. ēn fō´rō kōnskē-ān´tē-ī. in fō´rō kanšen´šā. *adv.* "In the forum of the conscience." In one's conscience; according to moral, as opposed to legal, considerations. *E.g.*, "Nothing is more common than confusion between a rule of law, the penalties of which are to be enforced upon external evidence, and a rule of morals, which is to have its application settled, as it is aptly said, *in foro conscientiae*." 1635 ATHENAEUM 281, 282 (1859).

In foro externo. ēn fō´rō ākstār´nō. in fō´rō ekstɜr´nō. *adj.* or *adv.* "In the external forum." In a different or foreign forum or jurisdiction. *E.g.*, "It seems obvious that the issue of an act by a single state cannot by itself qualify as a unilateral act capable of producing legal effects *in foro externo*." *Application of the Convention on the Prevention and Punishment of the Crime of Genocide* (Bosn. & Herz. v. Yugo.), I.C.J. No. 91, Judgment of Feb. 26, 2007, at 31, ¶ 63 (separate opinion of Judge *ad hoc* Kreća).

In futuro. ēn fūtū´rō. in fyū´čɜrō. *adv.* "In the future." (1) At a future time. (2) During the future. *Compare with* **De futuro** and **Pro futuro**. *Contrast with* **In praesenti**.

In genere. ēn gā´nārā. in je´nɜrē OR -je´nɜrā. *adv.* "In kind." (1) Of a general kind. *E.g.*, "Article 25 of Decree 2591 of 1991 enables *tutela* judges, under certain conditions, to impose *in genere* or "abstract" penalties upon violators of fundamental rights. The quantification of these penalties is left to ordinary judges, in front of whom plaintiffs must reappear in order to obtain a specific indemnity." Manuel José Cepeda-Espinosa, *Judicial Activism in a Violent Context: The Origin, Role, and Impact of the Colombian Constitutional Court*, 3 WASH. U. GLOBAL STUD. L. REV. 529, 593 n.154 (2004). *Contrast with* **In specie.** (2) In the same kind or class; in similar property, as opposed to in cash, as when substitute restitution is made. *See also* **Restitutio in genere.**

In gremio. ēn grā´mēō. in gre´mēō. *adj.* or *adv.* "In the bosom/lap." In the heart or center.

In gremio legis. ēn grā´mēō lā´gēs. in gre´mēō le´jis. *adj.* or *adv.* "In the lap of the law." Under the protection and control of the law. For example, property held by a court pending a valid claim of ownership is *in gremio legis.*

In haec verba. ēn hīk wār´ba. in hāk vɜr´bu. *prep.* + *n. pl.* "In those words." In the identical words used previously. *E.g.*, "Turning to the issue of agreement *vel non*, Ghana points out that the parties nowhere have referred to, let alone recited *in haec verba*, the second clause of Article 25(2)(b)." *Vacuum Salt Products, Ltd. v. Ghana*, ICSID Case No. ARB/92/1, Award of Feb. 16, 1994, ¶ 31. An alternative formulation is **Haec verba.** *Compare with* **De verbo in verbum, Ipsis verbis, Ipsissima verba, Totidem verbis,** and **Verbatim.**

In hypothesi. ēn hüpōt´hāsē. in hīpa´θezī. *adv.* "In hypothesis." An alternative formulation of **Ex hypothesi.**

In infinitum. ēn ēnfēnē´tūm. in infinī´tum. *adj.* or *adv.* "Into infinity." An alternative formulation of **Ad infinitum.**

In initio. ēn ēnē´tēō. in ini´šō. *adj.* or *adv.* "In the beginning." At or during the beginning. *Compare with* **A limine, Ab initio,** and **In principio.** *Contrast with* **In ipso termino.**

In integrum. ēn ēntāg´rūm. in integ´rum. *adj.* "In the whole." (1) Entire; in the entirety. (2) Perfect or complete.

In ipso termino. ēn ēp´sō tār´mēnō. in ip´sō tɜr´minō. *adv.* "At the end itself." At the termination; during or at the end. *Contrast with* **In initio.**

In iure. ēn yū´rā. in jɜ´rē. *adj.* or *adv.* "In right." (1) In or according to a legal decision or rule of law. (2) Within the scope of a legal right.

I(J)

In limine. ēn lē´mēnā. in li´minē. *adv.* "At the threshold." (1) From the beginning. (2) At the outset; preliminarily. In a judicial or arbitral setting, a submission made *in limine* is presented prior to the commencement of main proceedings. *Compare with* **Ab initio, In initio,** and **In principio.**

In limine litis. ēn lē´mēnā lē´tēs. in li´minē li´tis. *adj.* or *adv.* "At the threshold of litigation." Immediately before the commencement of a legal case.

In linea recta. ēn lē´nā-a rāk´ta. in li´nē-u rek´tu. *adv.* "In a straight line." In the direct line or path; in a direct line of descendance.

In litem. ēn lē´tām. in li´tem OR -lī´tem. *adv.* "To a lawsuit." (1) During the dispute or litigation. (2) Involved in a dispute or litigation. (3) Before a court or other authoritative tribunal.

In litem vocare. ēn lē´tām wōka´rā. in li´tem- OR -lī´tem vō´karē. *v. inf.* "To call to court." (1) To hale before a court. (2) To instigate litigation.

In loco. ēn lō´kō. in lō´kō. *adj.* "In the place." In the specific place. *E.g.*, "This divergence of fundamental standpoints between the Parties is reflected in their attitudes as to what extent their contentions depend on the evidence. Contrary to the Applicants' attitude in denying the necessity of calling witnesses and experts and of an inspection *in loco*, the Respondent abundantly utilized numerous witnesses and experts and requested the Court to visit South West Africa, South Africa and other parts of Africa to make an inspection *in loco*." *South West Africa Cases* (Eth. v. S. Afr.; Liber. v. S. Afr.), 1966 I.C.J. Rep. 6, 302 (Judge Tanaka, dissenting).

In loco parentis. ēn lō´kō parān´tēs. in lō´kō puren´tis. "In the place of the parent." In the capacity of a guardian or protector. When a state acts on behalf of one or more of its citizens, and not on its own behalf, in a foreign or international tribunal or other legal or political forum, it is often said to act *in loco parentis*. *Compare with* **Parens patriae.**

In maiori stat minus. ēn mayō´rē stat mē´nūs. in mujō´rī stât mī´nus. "In the greater is the lesser." An alternative phrase for **In eo quod plus sit semper inest et minus.** *E.g.*, "Italy established several zones of ecological protection, where only some of the powers set out for the EEZ are to be exerted in accordance with the *in maiore stat minus* principle." Angela del Vecchio Capotosti, In Maiori Stat Minus: *A Note on the EEZ and the Zones of Ecological Protection in the Mediterranean Sea*, 39 OCEAN DEV. & INT'L L. 257, 293 (2008).

In malam partem. ēn ma´lam par´tām. in mâ´lum par´tem. *adj.* "In an evil sense." Having an ill will or intention. *Compare with* **Mala fide.**

In medias res. ēn mā´dē-as rās. in mē´dē-us res. *adv.* "Into the middle of the thing." (1) In the middle of a proceeding, without formal introduction or preparation. (2) Abruptly.

In memoriam. ēn māmō´rē-am. in memō´rē-um. *adv.* "In the memory." In dedication to the memory of a deceased or departed person or thing.

In mercibus illicitis non sit commercium. ēn mār´kēbūs ēllē´kētēs nōn sēt kōmmār´kē-ūm. in mɜr´sibus ili´situs nan sit kumɜr´šum. "Let there be no trade in illicit merchandise." A maxim meaning that a contract relating to or for the sale of contraband should be considered void.

In mitiori sensu. ēn mētēō´rē sān´sū. in mišō´rī sen´sū. *adv.* "In the milder sense." In an inoffensive or more favorable sense or meaning. An alternative formulation is **Mitiori sensu.**

In mora (esse). ēn mō´ra (ās´sā). in mō´ru (e´sē). *adj.* "(To be) in delay." (1) Delayed. (2) In default by failure to act in a timely manner.

In omnibus. ēn ōm´nēbūs. in am´nibus. *adv.* "In all things." Entirely; completely; in every manner.

In pari causa. ēn pa´rē kô´sa. in pa´rī kă´zu. *adv.* "In a balanced case." In a case in which the opposing parties have or present equally persuasive facts or arguments.

In pari causa possessor potior haberi debet. ēn pa´rē kô´sa pōssās´sōr pō´tēōr habā´rē dā´bāt. in pa´rē kă´zu pōze´sɜr pō´tēōr hâ´bɜrī de´bet. "In a balanced case, the possessor should be regarded as the stronger." A maxim, originating in Justinian's *Digest* (50.17.128), meaning that, when two parties have equal claim to property, the claims of the one currently in possession should be preferred. Alternative phrases are **In pari causa potior est condicio possidentis, In pari delicto potior est condicio possidentis, Melior est causa possidentis**, and **Melior est condicio possidentis.**

In pari causa potior est condicio possidentis. ēn pa´rē kô´sa pō´tēōr āst kōndē´kēō pōssēdān´tēs. in pa´rī kă´zu pō´tē-ɜr est kundi´šō pōsiden´tis. "When the parties have equal claims, the possessor's position is more compelling." An alternative phrase for **In pari causa possessor potior haberi debet.**

In pari delicto. ēn pa´rē dālēk´tō. in pa´rī dulik´tō. *adj.* "Equally at fault." Having equal liability; having acted with equal wrongfulness; having equally contributing to an injury. This phrase is sometimes used as an abbreviation of **In pari delicto potior est condicio defendentis.** *Compare with* **Par delictum.**

In pari delicto potior est condicio defendentis. ēn pa´rē dālēk´tō pō´tēōr āst kōndē´kēō dāfāndān´tēs. in pa´rī dulik´tō pō´šōr est kundi´šō dufendân´tis." When the parties are equally at fault, the defendant's position is more compelling." An alternative phrase for **In pari causa possessor potior haberi debet.** *See also* **In pari delicto potior est condicio possidentis.**

In pari materia. ēn pa´rē matā´rē-a. in pa´rī matē´rē-u. *adv.* "On equal subject matter." (1) A canon of legal document interpretation by which two or more relevant instruments should be interpreted as consistent with each other whenever reasonably possible. (2) Having jurisdiction with respect to the same subject matter; having concurrent jurisdiction. *See also* **Optimus interpretandi modus est sic leges interpretari ut legibus concordant.**

In pari passu. ēn pa´rē pas´sū. in pa´rī pâ´sū. *adv.* "At equal pace." (1) Simultaneously. (2) Proceeding together in synchronicity. An alternative formulation is **A pari passu.**

In perpetuum. ēn pārpā´tū-ūm. in pɜrpe´čū-um. *adj.* or *adv.* "In perpetuity." (1) Permanently. (2) Continuously and indefinitely. (3) In perpetuity. *Compare with* **In aeternum.**

In personam. ēn pārsōn´am. in pɜrsō´num. *adj.* or *adv.* "Upon the person." Relating to a person or a person's rights or obligations. Jurisdiction *in personam* relates to jurisdiction by reason of the tribunal's power over the respondent himself. *Contrast with* **In rem** and **Quasi in rem.**

In pleno. ēn plā´nō. in ple´nō. *adv.* "In fullness." In plenary session, as when the entire membership of a court divided into chambers sits together (*en banc*) to hear the same case. *E.g.*, "Lord Phillimore succeeded in convincing the members that the Court should always sit *in pleno* so as to 'make use of all of its resources.'" W. Michael Reisman, Nullity and Revision 456 (1971).

In poenalibus causis benignius interpretandum est. ēn pœna´lēbūs kô´sēs bānēg´nē-ūs ēntārprātan´dūm āst. in pēnâ´libus kă´zis bunig´nē-us intērpretân´dum est. "In penal cases, the more forgiving interpretation should be made." A maxim meaning that in criminal cases the prosecution must present compelling evidence in favor of guilt, as the defendant benefits from a strong presumption of innocence.

In posse. ēn pōs´sā. in pa´sē. *adv.* "In capability." (1) Potentially existing or coming into effect. (2) Not yet existing or having effect but containing the possibility of doing so. *Compare with* **In potentia.** *Contrast with* **In esse.**

In potentia. ēn pōtān´tē-a. in pōten´šu. *adj.* or *adv.* "In potentiality." (1) Potential; potentially. *E.g.*, "As regards the *pactum de compromittendo*, international law has made certain progress in developing the formulas regulating passage from arbitration *in potentia* to arbitration *in actu*, particularly in respect of the appointment of arbitrators by the act of a third party." *Advisory Opinion on Interpretation of Peace Treaties with Bulgaria, Hungary, and Romania*, 1950 I.C.J. Rep. 221, 248 (Judge Azevedo, dissenting). *Contrast with* **In actu.** (2) Theoretical; theoretically. *Compare with* **In posse.** *Contrast with* **De facto.**

I(J)

In praesenti. ēn prīsān´tē. in prēzen´tī. *adv.* "In the present time." (1) In the present era. (2) Currently. *Contrast with* **In futuro.**

In primis. ēn prē´mēs. in pri´mis. *adv.* "Principally; especially." (1) Mainly; primarily. (2) Most importantly; especially. (3) First; among the first. An alternative term is **Imprimis.**

In principio. ēn prēnkē´pēō. in prinsi´pēō. *adv.* "In the beginning." At the beginning. *Compare with* **Ab initio, In initio,** and **In limine.**

In quantum meruit. ēn kwan´tūm mā´rūēt. in kwan´tum mār´ū-it. *adv.* "In the amount deserved." In an amount equal to that which the claimant is owed, usually for the value of an uncompensated benefit conferred on the respondent. *E.g.*, "Princz sought compensatory and punitive damages, as well as the value *in quantum meruit* of his [forced] labor at the I.G. Farben and Messerschmidt plants." *Princz v. Federal Republic of Germany*, 26 F.3d 1166, 1177 (D.C. Cir.), *cert. denied*, 513 U.S. 1121 (1994). *Compare with* **In quantum valeat.** *See also* **Quantum meruit.**

In quantum valeat. ēn kwan´tūm wa´lā-at. in kwan´tum vâ´lē-ât. *adj.* "In the amount it is worth." To the extent of its value; for what it is worth. *Compare with* **In quantum meruit.**

In re. ēn rā. in rā. *adv.* "In the matter." With reference to or concerning a matter (to be named or described). *Compare with* **In rebus.**

In re ipsa. ēn rā ēp´sa. in rā ip´su. *adj.* or *adv.* "In the very same thing." (1) Inherent (ly); by itself and without intermediation. (2) In the very same matter.

In re minime dubio. ēn rā mē´nēmā dū´bēō. in rā mi´nimē dū´bēō. *adv.* "In a matter of the least doubt." Whenever the evidence is so exceptionally strong as to leave little or no doubt of the facts. *E.g.*, "[A reprisal for an unlawful taking of prize is justified only in] case of violent injuries, directed or supported by the State, and justice absolutely denied, *in re minime dubio* by all the Tribunals and afterwards by the prince." *Report of the British Law Officers, on the Rules of Admiralty Jurisdiction, &c. in Time of War*, 20 Brit. & Foreign State Papers 889, 892–93 (1832–33).

In rebus. ēn rā´būs. in rē´bus. *adv.* "In the thing." In the matter; in the case at hand or under discussion. *Compare with* **In re.**

In rem. ēn rām. in rem. *adj.* or *adv.* "Upon the thing." Relating to a thing, as opposed to a person. A tribunal may exercise *in rem* authority to adjudicate matters relating to property situated within the tribunal's territorial jurisdiction. *E.g.*, "Thus the court of the owner's domicil or of his actual *situs* will not assume jurisdiction, in a proceeding *in rem*, over chattels actually situated in another jurisdiction." Raleigh C. Minor, Conflict of Laws; or, Private International Law 274, § 120 (1901). *Contrast with* **In personam** and **Quasi in rem.**

In republica maxime conservanda sunt iura belli. ēn rāpū´blēka ma´ksēmā kōnsārwan´da sūnt yū´ra bāl´lē. in repub´liku mâ´ksimē kansɜrvân´du sunt jɜ´ru be´lī. "In the state the laws of war are especially preserved." A maxim meaning that states should take special care to enforce the international law of war (*ius in bello*) with its domestic civil or military legal system. The maxim especially reaffirms the subjection of persons accused of violating the laws of war to military justice.

In rigore iuris. ēn rēgō´rā yū´rēs. in ri´gɜrē jɜ´ris. *adv.* "In the law's strictness." An alternative formulation of **De rigore iuris.**

In situ. ēn sē´tū. in si´tū. *adj.* "In (its) place." In the place where a thing belongs or an event normally occurs. *E.g.*, "The [1992 Biodiversity] Convention notes further that one of the fundamental requirements for the conservation of biological diversity is *in situ* conservation, defined as 'the conservation of ecosystems and natural habitats and the maintenance…of viable populations of species in their natural surroundings.'" *Kasikili/Sedudu Island* (Bots. v. Namib.), 1999 I.C.J. Rep. 1045, 1182, ¶ 87 (Vice President Weeramantry, dissenting). *Contrast with* **Ex situ.**

In specie. ēn spā´kē-ā. in spē´šē. *adv.* "In the specific kind." In a specific kind or class. *Contrast with* **In genere.**

In statu libertatis. ēn sta´tū lēbārta´tēs. in stâ´čū libɜrtā´tis. *adj.* "In a state of freedom." Having no obligations or constraints. *See also* **Status libertatis.**

In statu nascendi. ēn sta´tū naskān´dē. in stâ´čū nusen´dī. *adj.* "In the state of being born." In the middle of the process of coming into existence, as when a treaty is being negotiated and has not yet been finalized or an organization is in the process of being formed. *E.g.*, "The Joint Session of the SFRY Assembly, the National Assembly of the Republic of Serbia and the Assembly of the Republic of Montenegro was not constituted as the Parliament of the Federal

Republic of Yugoslavia; rather it was a body of representatives *in statu nascendi.*" *Application of the Convention on the Prevention and Punishment of the Crime of Genocide* (Bosn. & Herz. v. Yugo.), I.C.J. No. 91, Judgment of Feb. 26, 2007, at 31 ¶ 64 (separate opinion of Judge *ad hoc* Kreća).

In statu quo. ēn sta´tū kwō. in stâ´čū kwō. *adj.* or *adv.* "In that status." In the current condition or status. *Contrast with* **In statu quo ante.** *See also* **Status quo.**

In statu quo ante. ēn sta´tū kwō an´tā. in stâ´čū kwō ân´tē. *adj.* or *adv.* "In that former status." In the same condition or status that previously existed. *Contrast with* **In statu quo.** *See also* **Status quo ante.**

In tantum. ēn tan´tūm. in tân´tum. *adv.* "In so much." An alternative formulation of **Pro tanto.**

In terminis. ēn tār´mēnēs. in tɜr´minis. *adv.* "In terms." Using express language; explicitly rather that implicitly. *E.g.*, "[I]t is scarcely admissible that the Umpire should have misunderstood the text [of the agreement between the parties to review a prior arbitral award]...by failing to appreciate the connection between the concession in question and the exterior navigation, the Umpire having decided *in terminis* that 'the permission to navigate these channels was only annexed to the permission to call at Trinidad'..." *Orinoco Steamship Company Case* (U.S. v. Venez.), 11 R.I.A.A. 237, 239 (1910) (Award).

In terrorem. ēn tārrō´rām. in terō´rem. *adv.* "Toward fear." Creating fear, especially to deter violations of the law or other undesirable acts. *E.g.*, "[T]he US makes the rather extravagant claim that if section 45 patents are excluded from the Agreement then all forms of intellectual property that existed prior to the application date would receive 'absolutely no protection under TRIPS' and then advances '*in terrorem*' arguments that Members could revoke, for no reason at all, patents issued before January 1996 and still remain in compliance with TRIPS." *Canada—Term of Patent Protection*, Panel Report of May 5, 2000, WTO Doc. No. WT/DS170/R, at 112.

In toto. ēn tō´tō. in tō´tō. *adv.* "In all." (1) In totality; completely. (2) Generally; on the whole.

In toto et pars continetur. ēn tō´tō āt pars kōntēnā´tūr. in tō´tō et parz kanti´netɜr. "The part is also included in the whole." An alternative phrase for **In eo quod plus sit semper inest et minus.** This formulation originates in Justinian's *Digest* (50.17.113).

In traiectu. ēn trayāk´tū. in trujek´tū. *adj.* or *adv.* "In the passage." An alternative formulation is **Intra traiectum.**

In transitu. ēn tran´sētū. in trân´zitū. *adj.* "In transit." In the process of being transported from one place to another. *E.g.*, "A somewhat similar question has arisen with respect to property acquired by either consort, while the married pair are actually *in transitu* from one State to another, having abandoned one domicil and not yet reached the other." Raleigh C. Minor, Conflict of Laws; or, Private International Law 178, § 81 (1901).

In vacuo. ēn wa´kūō. in vâ´kyūō. *adv.* "In a vacuum." Without consideration of context. *E.g.*, "The Court is entitled to presume…that [the respondent's] statements were not made *in vacuo*, but in relation to the tests which constitute the very object of the present proceedings." *Nuclear Tests* (Austl. v. Fr.), 1974 I.C.J. Rep. 252, ¶ 50 (Judgment). *Compare with* **In abstracto**.

In verbis non verba sed res et ratio quaerenda est. ēn wār´bēs nōn wār´ba sād rās āt ra´tēō kwīrān´da āst. in vɜr´bis nan vɜr´bu sed res et rā´šō kwāren´du est. "In phrasing, the substance and rationale, not the words, is sought." A maxim meaning that, in construing a legal instrument, undue attention should not be paid to the precise phrasing at the expense of the meaning and intent. *But see* the Vienna Convention on the Law of Treaties arts. 31–32, May 23, 1969, 1155 U.N.T.S. 331. *Contrast with* **In dubio, haec legis constructio quam verba ostendunt**. *See also* **In conventionibus, contrahentium voluntas potius quam verba spectari placuit**.

In vinculis. ēn wēn´kūlēs. in vin´kyūlis. *adj.* "In chains." In the custody of authorities, most commonly said of one awaiting criminal trial.

Inadimplenti non est adimplendum. ēnadēmplān´tē nōn āst adēmplān´dūm. inâdimplen´tī nan est âdimplen´dum. "There is no need to perform for one who has not performed." A maxim meaning that one who reneges on a legal obligation cannot invoke the law to force other parties to fulfill their own, reciprocal obligations. *See also* **Exceptio inadimplenti contractus** and **Non adimplenti contractus**.

Inaudita altera parte. ēnôdē´ta al´tāra par´tā. inā´ditu al´tɜru par´tē. "The other part not having been heard." Not in the presence of the other or opposing party. This phrase is often used as a procedural expression, as when a prosecution brings proceedings *inaudita altera parte* against an unavailable criminal defendant. *E.g.*, "The judicial authorities shall have the authority to adopt provisional measures *inaudita altera parte* where appropriate, in particular where any delay [in the enforcement of intellectual property rights] is likely to cause irreparable harm to the right holder, or where there is a demonstrable risk of evidence being destroyed." Agreement on Trade-Related Aspects of Intellectual Property Rights art. 50(2), Apr. 15, 1994, 33 I.L.M. 81. An alternative phrase is **Parte inaudita.** *Compare with* **Ex parte.**

Incidenter tantum. ēnkēdān´tar tau´tūm. insiden´tɜr tân´tum. "So much incidentally." Purely incidentally. *E.g.*, "Gariboldi...contended that..., should the Court of Justice find that the defendant is in any way liable under the contract *de quo*, [then the Court should] declare that henceforth (*incidenter tantum*) Orzya Srl is neither concerned nor liable in that it was not the defendant's sole shareholder during the period in which the obligation in question arose." Opinion of Advocate General Saggio, *Commission of the European Communities v. Cascina Laura Sas de Arch Aldo Delbo & C.*, [1999] E.C.R. I-1017, ¶ 15.

I(J)

Incivile. ēnkēwē´lā. insi´vilē. *adj.* "Irregular." Not following or having followed proper legal procedures.

Incorporalia bello non adquiruntur. ēnkōrpōra´lē-a bāl´lō nōn adkwērūn´tūr. inkōrpɜrā´lē-u be´lō nan adkwir´untɜr. "Incorporeal things are not acquired by war." A maxim meaning that the advent of war cannot nullify peacetime rights and obligations, but only suspend them until the restoration of peace.

Inde datae leges ne fortior omnia posset. ēn´dā da´tī lā´gās nā fōr´tēōr om´nē-a pōs´sāt. in´dē dâ´tā le´jēz nē fōr´tē-ɜr am´nē-u pō´set. "So he gave them laws, lest the stronger be all-powerful." A quotation from Ovid's *Fasti* referring to the decision of an early Roman king (Numa) to restrain the Romans with law because they were overly prone to war. The quotation is sometimes used to convey the notion that it is the purpose of laws to limit political power, military power, or physical force.

Indicium. ēndē´kē-ūm. indi´šum. "Mark." A mark; an indicator; a sign. *E.g.*, "The circumstance, then, which is taken for the *indicium* of sovereignty on the one part, and the subjection on the other, should not be a *situation*, which at any time may change, but an *event*." Jeremy Bentham, *The Principles of International Law: Essay II*, *in* 2 THE WORKS OF JEREMY BENTHAM 543 (John Bowring ed. 1843).

Indutiae. ēndū´tē-ī. indū´tē-ā. *n.* "Truce." (1) An armistice. (2) A cessation of hostilities; a truce.

Infra. ēn´fra. in´fru. *adj.* or *adv.* "Below." Below; subsequent(ly). The term *infra* is commonly misused to mean "within." The proper term for "within" is **Intra.** For the use of the term *infra* as a citation signal, *see* **Infra (citatum).**

Infra (citatum). ēn´fra (kēta´tūm). in´fru (sītā´tum). *adj.* "(Cited) below." A citation signal used to refer the reader to a statement made at a point later or below in the text in which the signal appears. *E.g.*, "This difficulty in identifying reliable base points is compounded by the differences, addressed more fully, *infra*, that apparently still remain between the Parties...." *Territorial and Maritime Dispute in the Caribbean Sea* (Nicar. v. Hond.), I.C.J. Case No. 120, Judgment of Oct. 8, 2007, ¶ 279, 46 I.L.M. 1053. *Compare with* **Post**. *Contrast with* **Supra (citatum)**.

Infra civitatem. A misspelling of **Intra civitatem**.

Infra iurisdictionem. A misspelling of **Intra iurisdictionem**.

Infra legem. ēn´fra lā´gām. in´fru le´jem. *adj.* or *adv.* "Under the law." (1) In a manner consistent with accepted law; legally permissible. (2) Subject to limited discretion within the bounds of the law; as in the phrase **Aequitas infra legem**. *E.g.*, "The fewer the points (or points of reference) involved in [the] definition [of a frontier line], the greater the court's 'degrees of freedom' (in the statistical sense). And it is here that considerations of equity *infra legem*...come into play, to guide the court in the exercise of this freedom when interpreting and applying the law and the legal titles involved." *Frontier Dispute* (Burk. Faso v. Mali), 1986 I.C.J. Rep. 554, ¶ 15 (separate opinion of Judge Abi-Saab). *Contrast with* **Contra legem** and **Praeter legem**.

Infra petita. ēn´fra pātē´ta. in´fru petē´tu. *adj.* "Less than what was requested." An award in an amount or otherwise of a nature less than what was sought by the claimant. *E.g.*, "Barbados stated clearly that its submissions in respect of its claim to a right to fish within the EEZ of Trinidad and Tobago were made on the basis that such a right could be awarded by the Tribunal as a remedy *infra petita* in the dispute concerning the course of the maritime boundary." *Barbados v. Trinidad & Tobago*, Perm. Ct. Arb., Award of Apr. 11, 2006, ¶ 277, 45 I.L.M. 800, 846. An alternative phrase is **Minus petita**.

Infra praesidia. ēn´fra prīsē´dē-a. in´fru prāzi´dē-u. *adj.* "Under the fortifications." An alternative term for **Intra praesidia**.

Iniquissima pax est anteponenda iustissimo bello. ēnēkwēs´sēma paks āst antāpōnān´da yūstēs´sēmō bā´lō. inukwi´simu pâks est ântēpunen´du justi´simō be´lō. "The most unfair peace is preferable to the most just war." A rhetorical maxim meaning that a state should resort to armed force only when no other option is available, even if this creates an ongoing injustice.

Iniuria. ēnyū´rē-a. inj3´rē-u. *n.* [*pl.* **Iniuriae.** ēnyū´rē-ī. inj3´rē-ā.] "Injury." A wrongful or injurious act.

Iniuria absque damno. ēnyū´rē-a ab´skwā dam´nō. inj3´rē-u âbskwē dâm´nō. *n.* "Injury without wrong." (1) A wrongful act that causes no actual damages, and therefore will give rise to at most a symbolic remedy such as apology. (2) A wrongful act, the definition of which does not include damage as an essential element. An alternative phrase is **Iniuria sine damno.** *Contrast with* **Damnum absque iniuria.**

Iniuria non excusat iniuriam. ēnyū´rē-a nōn āks-kū´sat ēnyū´rē-am. injз´rē-u nan eks-kyū´zât injз´rē-um. "A wrong does not excuse a wrong." A maxim of dubious general application meaning that an illegal act by one state cannot justify an illegal act in retaliation by the other. This maxim is obviously not accepted as reflecting law in the matter of belligerent reprisals except for those reprisals forbidden by the 1949 Geneva Conventions and the 1977 Additional Protocols. Even today, the maxim runs contrary to the custom of using countermeasures to enforce international legal rights in some situations, especially when authorized by treaty.

Iniuria non fit volenti. ēnyū´rē-a nōn fēt wōlān´tē. injз´rē-u nan fit vulen´tī. "One consenting is not injured." A principle according to which a party that consents to receive a harm or to risk receiving a harm cannot claim to be the victim of an offense after the expected harm results.

Iniuria propria non cadet in beneficium facientis. ēnyū´rē-a prōp´rē-a nōn ka´dāt ēn bānāfē´kē-ūm fakē-ān´tēs. injз´rē-u prap´rē-u nan kâ´det in benufi´šum fâšen´tis. "One's own wrong does not fall to the advantage of the wrongdoer." An alternative phrase for **Nullus commodum capere (potest) de sua iniuria propria.**

Iniuria servi dominum pertingit. ēnyū´rē-a sār´wē dō´mēnūm pārtēn´gēt. injз´rē-u sзr´vī da´minum pзrtiŋ´it. "A servant's wrong extends to his master." A maxim meaning that a principal may be held liable for his or her agent's violation of law, even though the principal may not have authorized the wrongful act. *See also* **Qui facit per alium, facit per se** and **Respondeat superior.**

Iniuria sine damno. ēnyū´rē-a sē´nā dam´nō. injз´rē-u si´nē dâm´nō. *n.* "Wrong without injury." An alternative phrase for **Iniuria absque damno.**

Instanter. ēnstan´tār. instân´tзr. *adv.* "Pressingly; vehemently." Without delay; as a matter of urgency. *E.g.*, "This motion was accompanied by a separate motion filed the same day, in which the Defence sought leave to file the former motion *instanter*." *Prosecutor v. Furundzija*, ICTY Case No. IT-95-17/1-T, Judgment of Dec. 10, 1998, ¶ 9, 38 I.L.M. 317, 322.

Instrumentum. ēnstrūmān´tūm. instrūmen´tum. *n.* "Instrument." (1) Generically, an instrument; a means or tool for achieving something. (2) A legal document, such as a treaty, statute, or contract.

I(J)

Inter absentes. ēn´tār absān´tās. in´tɜr âbsen´tēs. *adj.* "Between those absent." Relating to persons or entities not present at an event or not involved in a matter at issue.

Inter alia. ēn´tār a´lē-a. in´tɜr â´lē-u. *adv.* "Among others." Among other things. The use of *inter alia* indicates that things other than those named may also exist or be material. By implication, the subset named is either more relevant to the issue under discussion or merely serves as an example of the larger set not fully listed. *E.g.*, "Trinidad and Tobago refers to scholarly commentary for support of its view, as well as to the text of UNCLOS itself, where it points out, *inter alia*, that sedentary species, unlike other living marine natural resources, are deemed part of the continental shelf under Article 77, as they had been prior to the adoption of the Convention." *Barbados v. Republic of Trinidad & Tobago*, Permanent Ct. of Arb., Award of Apr. 11, 2006, ¶ 175, 45 I.L.M. 800, 828 (2006). *Compare with* **Inter alios.**

Inter alios. ēn´tār a´lēōs. in´tɜr â´lēōs. *adj.* "Among other persons." Among other persons. *Compare with* **Inter alia.**

Inter apices iuris. ēn´tār a´pēkās yū´rēs. in´tɜr ā´pisez jɜ´ris. *adv.* "Between the extremes of law." (1) Relating to an extreme interpretation of law or an interpretation of law that causes great hardship to one or more parties. *E.g.*, "Be this case as it may, it is the only exception to the general doctrine; and *inter apices juris*; a case so unjust as that which robbed an unfortunate woman not only of the moiety which vested in her by survivorship from her husband, but of the other moiety absolutely vested in her by grant, I am glad to find is a judicial anomaly." *United States v. 1,960 Bags of Coffee*, 12 U.S. (8 Cranch) 398, 412 (1814). (2) Relating to an unusually subtle point of law.

Inter arma silent leges. ēn´tār ar´ma sē´lānt lā´gās. in´tɜr ar´mu sī´lent le´jēz. "Among arms, laws are silent." A maxim meaning that, during a military emergency, civil laws may be suspended in deference to the national interest in self-defense. Although this aphorism might seem to suggest that, during armed conflicts, the rule of law is seldom or never observed, the phrase self-evidently does not originate in international law but rather in municipal law. An alternative formulation is **Silent leges inter arma.**

Inter Caetera Divinae. ēn´tār kī´tāra dēwē´nī. in´tɜr se´tɜru divī´nā. *N.* "Among other…to the Divine…" The title to a papal bull from 1493 issued by Pope Alexander VI purporting to divide hegemony over the New World between Catholic Spain and Portugal. The title consists of the first three words of the bull's opening phrase: *Inter caetera Divinae Majestati beneplacita opera….*" ("Among other works well pleasing to the Divine Majesty….").

Inter fauces terrae. ēn´tăr fô´kās tăr´rī. in´tɜr fă´sez te´rā. *adv.* "Between the jaws of the land." An alternative formulation of **Inter fauces terrarum.**

Inter fauces terrarum. ēn´tăr fô´kās tărra´rūm. in´tɜr fă´sez tera´rum. *adv.* "Between the jaws of the lands." Nearly enclosed or surrounded by dry land, as when the mouth of a bay is very small relative to the size of the bay because the littoral lands almost meet where the bay adjoins the open ocean. *E.g.*, "[T]here is no valid reason to draw [straight baselines] only across bays...and not also to draw them between islands, islets and rocks, across the sea areas separating them, even when such areas do not fall within the conception of a bay. It is sufficient that they should be situated between the island formations of the [rocky coastal outcroppings], *inter fauces terrarum.*" *Norwegian Fisheries Case* (U.K. v. Nor.), 1951 I.C.J. Rep. 116. An alternative formulation is **Inter fauces terrae.** *See also* **Fauces terrae.**

Inter gentes. ēn´tăr găn´tās. in´tɜr jen´tēz. "Between nations." A Latin term for the concept of "international." Thus, international law, or the law of nations as it was until recently called, was translated as *ius inter gentes.*

Inter instrumenta regni. ēn´tăr ēnstrūmăn´ta răg´nē. in´tɜr instrūmen´tu reg´nī. *adv.* "Among the ruler's instruments." Among other means that a state or sovereign may use or typically uses in the exercise of its power. *E.g.*, "It is not necessary to repeat that at the time, and especially in the countries treated of here, the preaching and propagation of faith was *inter instrumenta regni*... and which refers to that kind of solidarity between Church and State which existed in Mexico under the Colonial Government, and a long time after that country became independent." *The Pious Funds Case* (Mex. v. U.S.), Perm. Ct. Arb. Award of Oct. 14, 1902, H.C.R. (Series 1), at 29 (Scott 1916).

Inter pacem et bellum nihil medium. ēn´tăr pa´kăm ăt băl´lūm nē´hĕl mā´dē-ūm. in´tɜr pâ´sem et be´lum nī´hil mē´dē-um. "There is no middle course between peace and war." A maxim from Cicero's *Phillipics* meaning that states can be either in a state or war or of peace, but not in between. This observation was made arguably before the concept of armed conflict short of war between states was widely recognized as giving rise to specific legal consequences.

Inter pares. ēn´tăr pa´rās. in´tɜr pā´rēz. *adv.* "Among equals." Among persons or entities having equal stature or position.

Inter partes. ēn´tăr par´tās. in´tɜr par´tēz. *adj.* or *adv.* "Between parties." Between parties relevant to or involved in the matter at hand, as opposed to between either party (or both) and a third party, or between either party (or both) and the community at large. *E.g.*, "[The 1648 Treaty of Münster between the United Netherlands and Spain] cannot be invoked as having transformed a state of possession into a conventional title *inter partes*, for the reason that Dutch possession of the island Palmas (or Miangas) is not proved to have existed at the critical date." *The Island of Palmas Case* (U.S. v. Nether.), Perm. Ct. Arb., Award of Apr. 4, 1928, H.C.R. (2d series), at 122 (Scott 1932). *Contrast with* **Ex parte.**

I(J)

Inter se. ēn´tār sā. in´tɜr sā. *adj.* or *adv.* "Between themselves." (1) Between the relevant parties. *E.g.*, "[A] reservation [to a treaty by one party with respect to a specific other party] does not modify the provisions of the treaty for the other parties to the treaty *inter se.*" Vienna Convention on the Law of Treaties art. 21(2), May 23, 1969, 1155 U.N.T.S. 331. (2) A doctrine formerly recognized that denoted the position of the British Empire refusing to recognize that international law applied in relations among members of the British Commonwealth. This doctrine was ultimately abandoned when members of the Commonwealth gained most of the attributes of independent sovereignty. *Compare with* **Inter sese.**

Inter sese. ēn´tār sā´sā. in´tɜr sā´sā. *adj.* or *adv.* "Between themselves." Relating to the relevant parties. *Inter sese* differs from *inter se* stylistically, not in meaning. *Inter sese* emphasizes the identities of parties more than *inter se. Compare with* **Inter se.**

Interest rei publicae ut sit finis litium. ēn´tārāst rā´ē pūb´lēkī ūt sēt fē´nēs lē´tē-ūm. in´tɜrest rā pub´likā ūt sit fi´nis li´šum. "The public interest of a matter so that a litigation should end." An alternative phrase for **Expedit rei publicae ut sit finis litium.**

Interpretare et concordare leges legibus est optimus interpretandi modus. ēntārprāta´rā āt kōnkōrda´rā lā´gās lā´gēbūs āst ōp´tēmūs ēntārprātan´dē mō´dūs. intɜrpreta´rē et kankōrda´rē le´jēz le´jibus est ap´timus intɜrpretân´dī mō´dus. "To interpret and harmonize laws is the best method of interpretation." A maxim meaning that, whenever possible, laws of equal authority should be read in a manner that will not bring them into conflict with each other.

Intra. ēn´tra. in´tru. *adv.* or *prep.* "Within." Within; in; inside. *See also* **Infra.**

Intra civitatem. ēn´tra kēwēta´tām. in´tru sivitā´tem. *adj.* or *adv.* "Within the state." Inside the territory (of the state). *See also* **Intra iuridictionem.**

Intra iurisdictionem. ēn´tra yūrēsdēktēō´nām. in´tru jɜrisdikšō´num. *adj.* or *adv.* "Within the jurisdiction." Within the jurisdiction (of). *See also* **Intra civitatem.**

Intra praesidia. ēn´tra prīsē´dē-a. in´tru prāzi´dē-u. *adj.* "Within the fortifications." A term descriptive of maritime prizes that have been brought completely in the control of the capturing power's port, vessels, or fleet and that, by such capture, become the property of the captor. The term derives from the Roman law concept referring to capture of soldiers by an enemy. A soldier *intra praesidium* was considered in a sense "dead" under Roman law, and his civil and property rights were suspended until his return from captivity. *See also* **Postliminium** and **Spes recuperandi**. An alternative term is **Infra praesidia**.

Intra traiectum. ēn´tra trayāk´tūm. in´tru trujek´tum. *adj.* or *adv.* "Within the passage." During or on the voyage. An alternative formulation is **In traiectu**.

Intra vires. ēn´tra wē´rās. in´tru vī´rēz. *adj.* or *adv.* "Within the powers." (1) Within the scope of the legal authority. An agent's promise *intra vires* may impose a binding obligation on the principal if it is within the apparent scope of the agent's authority, and an agent's wrongful act *intra vires* may give rise to liability on the part of the principal under the same conditions. (2) Not illegal or extralegal. *E.g.*, "[A]s a simple textual matter, an amendment to the Statutes [of the defendant bank] accomplished according to the procedures required by [the Statutes] would be *intra vires* and valid so long as it were not inconsistent with one of the enumerated reserved provisions." *Bank for International Settlements Arbitration*, Perm. Ct. of Arb., Partial Award of Nov. 22, 2002, at 66, ¶ 144. *Compare with* **Colore officii**. *Contrast with* **Ultra vires**.

Ipse. ēp´sā. ip´sē. *n.* "The same." (1) The same. (2) The very person or the very thing.

Ipse dixit. ēp´sā dē´ksēt. ip´sē di´ksit. *v.* (commonly used as a *n.*) "He himself said." (1) A tautological statement. (2) An assertion made or written without evidence or proof, relying on no other authority than the speaker or author's own opinion.

Ipsis verbis. ēp´sēs wār´bēs. ip´sis v3r´bis. *adv.* "In the same words." In the precise words used in the relevant source. *E.g.*, "[T]he Community legislature… prohibited, *ipsis verbis*, the use of weapons with a magazine capable of containing more than two rounds of ammunition." Opinion of Advocate General Vilaça, *Commission v. Italy*, E.C.J. Case No. 262/85, [1987] E.C.R. 3073. *Compare with* **De verbo in verbum**, **In haec verba**, **Ipsissima verba**, **Totidem verbis**, and **Verbatim**.

Ipsissima verba. ēpsēs´sēma wār´ba. ipsi´simu v3r´bu. *n. pl.* (sometimes used as an *adv.*) "The very same words." (1) The exact words used by a quoted source. *E.g.*, "Hence, if Article 3 is interpreted literally, any infliction of pain severe enough in degree to amount to torture would involve a breach of that provision whatever the circumstances in which it had occurred—for instance, the case of an army surgeon who amputates a leg on the battlefield under emergency conditions and without an anaesthetic. In all such cases (and others can easily be thought of), the 'victim' is, according to the *ipsissima verba* of Article 3, 'subjected to torture' which the Article states that 'No one may be.'" *Tyrer v. United Kingdom*, 2 E.H.R.R. 1, 17 (1979–80) (separate opinion of Judge Fitzmaurice). (2) A literal translation. *Compare with* **De verbo in verbum**, **In haec verba**, **Ipsis verbis**, **Totidem verbis**, and **Verbatim**.

Ipso facto. ēp´sō fak´tō. ip´sō fâk´tō. *adv.* "By the fact itself." By virtue of the fact alone and without other, intervening, facts; by the very nature of the facts. *E.g.*, "A State Party may, upon depositing its instrument of ratification or adherence to this Convention, or at any subsequent time, declare that it recognizes as binding, *ipso facto*, and not requiring special agreement, the jurisdiction of the Court on all matters relating to the interpretation or application of this Convention." American Convention on Human Rights art. 62(1), July 18, 1978, 1144 U.N.T.S. 123. *Compare with* **De plano** and **Eo ipso**.

Ipso iure. ēp´sō yū´rā. ip´sō jɜ´rē. *adv.* "By the right itself." By straightforward application of a right, without the need to apply any additional interpretation or supplemental law. *E.g.*, "[I]t is solely by virtue of the coastal State's sovereignty over the land that rights of exploration and exploitation in the continental shelf can attach to it, *ipso jure*, under international law." *Aegean Sea Continental Shelf* (Greece v. Turk.), 1978 I.C.J. Rep. 3, 36, ¶ 86.

Irredenta. ērrādān´ta. iruden´tu. *n. Ital.* "Unredeemed place." A region related historically, ethnically, or linguistically to a state other than the one exercising sovereignty over the region. For example, Germany used alleged abuses of the *irredenta* in Poland as an excuse for invading and occupying Poland—the act that instigated the Second World War.

Ita lex scripta est. ē´ta lāks skrēp´ta āst. i´tu leks skrip´tu est. "Thus is the law written." A phrase, originating in Justinian's *Digest* (40.1.12.1), indicating that the foregoing words recited are the literal expression of a written or codified law. In their original context, the phrase follows an acknowledgment that the consequences of strictly applying the law may be very harsh, "*sed ita lex scripta est*" ("but thus is the law written").

Item quae ex hostibus capiuntur, iure gentium statim capientium fiunt. ē´tām kwī āks hōs´tēbūs kapē-ūn´tūr, yū´rā gān´tē-ūm sta´tēm kapē-ān´tē-ūm fē´ūnt. ī´tum kwā hōs´tibus kâ´pē-untɜr, jɜ´rē jen´tē-um stā´tim kâpē-en´tē-um fī´unt. "Likewise, property that is captured from the enemy immediately becomes the property of the captor under the law of nations." A maxim, originating in Justinian's

Digest (40.1.5.7), meaning that, under the laws of war, any property of one belligerent captured by the other becomes the captor's own lawful property. This maxim is considered invalid under the modern laws of war, which forbid pillage and aggressive war for territorial conquest. An alternative formulation is **Quae ab hostibus capiuntur, statim capientium fiunt.**

Iudex. yū´dāks. jū´deks. *n.* [*pl.* **Iudices.** yū´dēkās. jū´disēz.] "Judge." (1) Arbitrator. (2) Judge. In Roman practice, a *iudex* was a private person appointed by a magistrate to hear and decide a case on the magistrate's authority.

Iudex a quo. yū´dāks a kwō. jū´deks a kwō. *n.* "Judge from which." The judge or court from whom an appeal is taken. *Compare with* **Iudex ad quem.**

Iudex ad quem. yū´dāks ad kwām. jū´deks âd kwem. *n.* "Judge to which." The judge or court to whom an appeal is or should be directed. *Compare with* **Iudex a quo.**

Iudex aequitatem semper spectare debet. yū´dāks īkwēta´tām sām´pār spākta´rā dā´bāt. jū´deks ekwita´tem sem´pɜr spekta´rē de´bet. "A judge should always look to equity." A maxim meaning that a tribunal should always consider equity in its judgments or decisions rather than relying exclusively on the positive law.

Iudex corruptus. yū´dāks kōrrūp´tūs. jū´deks kōrup´tus. *n.* "Corrupt judge." A judge or arbitrator who has received bribes, committed fraud, or engaged in corruption. Any decision of a *iudex corruptus* is invalid. *Compare with* **Iudex suspectus.**

Iudex decidere debet. yū´dāks dākē´dārā dā´bāt. jū´deks desī´dʒrē de´bet. "The judge should decide." A maxim meaning that the judicial or arbitral tribunal charged with resolving a dispute should decide all questions raised in the claim that are within its jurisdiction. *E.g.*, "A judge does not fulfil his judicial duty (*judex decidere debet*) if he fails to give a decision on one of the *causae petendi* of the application (*non est judex minus petita partium*)." *Advisory Opinion on the Application for Review of Judgement No. 158 of the United Nations Administrative Tribunal*, 1973 I.C.J. Rep. 166, 291, ¶ 41 (Judge De Castro, dissenting). *Compare with* **Non est iudex minus petita partium.** *But see* **Non liquet.**

Iudex est lex loquens. yū´dāks āst lāks lō´kwāns. jū´deks est leks lō´kwenz. "The judge is the law speaking." A maxim meaning that a judge's role is authoritatively to declare what the law is and how it applies to facts presented to him or her in a case. *See also* **Ius dicere** and **Ius dicere, non ius dare.**

Iudex non reddit plus quam quod petens ipse requirit. yū´dāks nōn rād´dēt plūs kwam kwōd pā´tāns ēp´sā rākwē´rēt. jū´deks nan re´dit plus kwam kwad pe´tenz ip´sē rekwī´rit. "A judge does not award more than the plaintiff himself requests." A maxim, originating in civil law, meaning that a judge or arbitrator may not award more than the plaintiff or claimant has demanded, regardless of magnitude of the actual injury sustained. This maxim, when applied, derogates from the general rule of **Iura novit curia**.

Iudex suspectus. yū´dāks sūspāk´tūs. jū´deks suspek´tus. *n.* "Suspected judge." (1) A judge or arbitrator suspected of having received bribes, committed fraud, or otherwise corruptly submitted to bias. (2) A judge or arbitrator having some direct or indirect interest in the outcome of a dispute of which he or she is seised, creating an appearance of bias. *Compare with* **Iudex corruptus**.

Iudicia posteriora sunt in lege fortiora. yūdē´kē-a pōstārēō´ra sūnt ēn lā´gā fōrtēō´ra. jūdi´šu pōstērēō´ru sunt in le´jē fōrtēō´ru. "Later judgments are stronger in law." A maxim meaning that more recent legal precedents should be given greater weight than, if they do not supersede, older precedents.

Iudicis est ius dicere, non dare. yū´dēkēs āst yūs dē´kārā, nōn da´rā. jū´disis est jus di´sɜrē, nan da´rē. "It is the judge's role to state the law, not to give it." A civil law maxim of judicial restraint meaning that the role of a judicial authority is to declare what the law is rather than to create new law. An alternative phrase is **Ius dicere, non ius dare**. *See also* **Iudex est lex loquens**.

Iudicium finium regundorum. yūdē´kē-ūm fē´nē-ūm rāgūndō´rūm. judi´šum fi´nē-um regundō´rum. *n.* "Judgment of drawing the boundaries." A judicial or arbitral award settling a difficult boundary dispute.

Iudicium illusorum. yūdē´kē-ūm ēllūsō´rūm. jūdi´šum ilūžō´rum. *n.* "Illusory judgment." A legal decision of more apparent than real authority. To label a decision *iudicium illusorum* is something of a tautology, as the precedential authority of a legal decision is determined by its influence on later cases. If later cases depart from decision on the basis of its putative lack of authority, this very departure will contribute to sapping the decision of authority. *E.g.*, "The [Court majority's] reasoning...*nolens volens* leads to the creation of the Court's own, judicial reality in contrast to the objective legal one, producing a proper *judicium illusorum*." *Application of the Convention on the Prevention and Punishment of the Crime of Genocide* (Bosn. & Herz. v. Yugo.), I.C.J. No. 91, Judgment of Feb. 26, 2007, at 30, ¶ 59 (separate opinion of Judge *ad hoc* Kreća).

Iura. yū´ra. jɜ´ru. *n. pl.* "Rights; laws." *See* **Ius**.

Iura communis. yū´ra kōmmū´nēs. jɜ´ru kamyū´nis. *n. pl.* "Rights of the community." Rights held in common by the entire community. *Compare with* **Iura universalia.** *See also* **Publici iuris.**

Iura in re. yū´ra ēn rā. jɜ´ru in rā. *n. pl.* "Rights in the thing." Property rights.

I(J)

Iura in re aliena. yū´ra ēn rā alē-ā´na. jɜ´ru in rā ālē-e´nu. *n. pl.* "Rights in the foreign thing." Rights in property belonging to a foreign national or situated in foreign territory.

Iura maiestatis. yū´ra mayāsta´tēs. jɜ´ru mâjestā´tis. *n. pl.* "Rights of the sovereign." Rights belonging to the sovereign or state.

Iura naturae sunt immutabilia. yū´ra natū´rī sūnt ēmmūtabē´lē-a. jɜ´ru nā´čɜrā sunt imyūtubi´lē-u. "The laws of nature are immutable." A maxim meaning that natural law, being universal and eternal, does not evolve with changing social, political, or other conditions.

Iura novit curia. yū´ra nō´wēt kū´rē-a. jɜ´ru nō´vit kyɜ´rē-u. "The court knows the laws." A doctrine providing that, because a tribunal is presumed to know and apply the law, the parties to a dispute are not required to invoke all applicable legal rules explicitly or to convince the tribunal of the law's content. A major implication of this doctrine is that a judicial or arbitral tribunal is not bound by the construction of the law or a legal instrument proposed by any of the parties to the dispute. *E.g.*, "The precept contained [in Article 1(1) of the American Convention on Human Rights] constitutes the generic basis of the protection of the rights recognized by the Convention and would be applicable, in any case, by virtue of a general principle of law, *iura novit curia*, on which international jurisprudence has repeatedly relied and under which a court has the power and the duty to apply the juridical provisions relevant to a proceeding, even when the parties do not expressly invoke them." *Velasquez Rodriguez Case*, Inter-Am. Ct. Hum. Rts., Judgment of July 29, 1988, ¶ 163, 28 I.L.M. 291. An alternative formulation is **Curia novit (iura).**

Iura privata. yū´ra prēwa´ta. jɜ´ru privâ´tu. *n. pl.* "Private rights." Rights applicable or belonging to private individuals. *Contrast with* **Iura publica.** *See also* **Iura publica anteferenda privatis.**

Iura publica. yū´ra pūb´lēka. jɜ´ru pub´liku. *n. pl.* "Public rights." Rights applicable or belonging to the government or state. *Contrast with* **Iura privata.** *See also* **Iura publica anteferenda privatis.**

Iura publica anteferenda privatis. yū´ra pūb´lēka antāfārān´da prēwa´tēs. jɜ´ru pub´liku ântēfɜren´du prīvâ´tis. "Public rights should take precedence over private." A maxim meaning that, when a state and private rights conflict, state rights should prevail. *Compare with* **Necessitas publica maior est quam privata.** *See also* **Iura privata** and **Iura publica.**

Iura universalia. yū´ra ūnēwārsa´lē-a. jз´ru yūnivзrsā´lē-u. *n. pl.* "Universal rights." Rights or laws belonging to or applicable to everyone; universal rights. *Compare with* **Iura communis.**

I(J)

Iurat. yū´rat. jз´rât. *v.* (commonly used as a *n.*). "He or she swears." A statement in an affidavit indicating the time and place of affirmation before a qualified witness, usually followed by the signature of the witness.

Iure gentium. yū´rā gān´tē-ūm. jз´rē jen´tē-um. *prep.* + *n.* "By the law of peoples." According to or pursuant to international law. *E.g.*, "[A] distinction must be drawn between piracy under any municipal Act of a particular country and piracy *jure gentium*." *R. v. Jones*, [2006] W.L.R. 772, 784, ¶ 21 (U.K).

Iure belli. yū´rā bāl´lē. jз´rē be´lī. *adv.* "By the law of war." According to or pursuant to the international law of war. *E.g.*, "The principle [of distinction between occupation and title] also excludes reliance on principles concerning acquisition of *territorium nullius* or titles *jure belli*." *Land, Island, and Maritime Frontier Dispute* (El Salv. v. Hond.; Nicar. intervening), 1992 I.C.J. Rep. 351, 635, ¶ 11 (separate opinion of Judge Torres Bernárdez).

Iure gestionis. yū´rā gāstēō´nēs. jз´rē jestēō´nis. *adv.* "By the right of behavior." By an act of private nature (i.e., performable by private citizens), which according to a restrictive theory of sovereign immunity may confer jurisdiction on a court even if the act was undertaken by a foreign sovereign. *Compare with* **Tanquam quilibet.** *Contrast with* **Iure imperii.** *See also* **Acta iure gestionis** and **De iure gestionis.**

Iure imperii. yū´rā ēmpā´rē-ē. jз´rē impз´rī. *adv.* "By the right of the sovereign." By an act of the kind that only a sovereign may undertake, which generally cannot confer jurisdiction on a court over a foreign sovereign even under a restrictive theory of sovereign immunity. *Contrast with* **Iure gestionis.** *See also* **Acta iure imperii** and **De iure imperii.** *Compare with* **Acta imperii.**

Iure pacis. yū´rā pa´kēs. jз´rē pâ´kis. *adv.* "By the law of peace." Arising from or related to the international law governing peacetime activities. *Contrast with* **Iure belli.**

Iure repraesentationis. yū´rā rāprīsāntatēō´nēs. jз´rē reprēzentāšō´nis. *adv.* "By the right of representation." By the legal right of an agent to represent his or her principal.

Iuris doctor. yū´rēs dōk´tōr. jɜ´ris dak´tɜr. *n.* "Doctor of law." A basic professional graduate degree in law awarded in the United States, usually after successful completion of a three-year program of study by persons holding a bachelor's degree. Commonly abbreviated **J.D.** *Compare with* **Legum baccalaureus**. *See also* **Legum magister** and **Magister iuris.**

Iuris et Iudicii Fecialis, Sive Iuris Inter Gentes et Quaestionum de Eodem Explicatio. yū´rēs āt yūdē´kē-ē fākē-a´lēs, sē´wā yū´rēs ēn´tār gān´tās āt kwīstēō´nūm dā āō´dām āksplēka´tēō. jɜ´ris et jūdi´šī fešâ´lis, si´vē jɜ´ris in´tɜr jen´tēz et kwestēō´num dā ē´ōdem eksplikā´šō. *N.* "On the Law and Procedure of the Fetiales, Be It of the Law of Nations and Questions Concerning the Same. . . ." The beginning of the title of the treatise on international law written in 1650 by English scholar Richard Zouche (1590–1661).

Iuris scientiae doctor. yū´rēs skē-ān´tē-ī dōk´tōr. jɜ´ris sī-en´tē-ā dak´tɜr. *n.* "Doctor of the science of law." An advanced graduate degree in law awarded in the United States and a few other countries, usually after successful completion of a *juris doctor* or bachelor of laws degree. This degree is often offered in preparation for a career in academia rather than practice. Abbreviated **J.S.D.** An alternative formulation is **Scientiae iuris doctor.**

Iuris tantum. yū´rēs tan´tūm. jɜ´ris tân´tum. *adv.* (commonly used as a *n.*). "Of law and nothing more." A rebuttable legal presumption made in the absence of any contradictory evidence.

Iuris utriusque doctor. yū´rēs ūtrē-ūs´kwā dōk´tōr. jɜ´ris ūtrē-us´kwā dak´tɜr. *n.* "Doctor of both laws." A law degree available at some European law schools for expertise in both civil and canonical law. Abbreviated **J.U.D.**

Iurisdictio inhaeret, cohaeret, adhaeret imperio; par in parem non habet iudicium. yūrēsdēk´tēō ēnhī´rāt, kōhī´rāt, adhī´rāt ēmpā´rēō; par ēn pa´rām nōn ha´bāt yūdē´kē-ūm. jɜrisdik´šō in´heret, cō´heret, âd´heret impē´rēō; par in pa´rem nan hâ´bet jūdi´šum. "Legal authority clings to sovereignty, belongs to it, and remains inherent to it; no one passes judgment upon an equal." A maxim meaning that the courts of one sovereign have no power to sit in judgment over the actions of another sovereign because such an exercise of jurisdiction implicitly subordinates the defendant to the adjudicating sovereign. *See also* **Par in parem non habet imperium.**

Ius. yūs. jus. *n.* [*pl.* **Iura.** yū´ra. jɜ´ru.] "Right; law." (1) A legal right; an entitlement. (2) The entire body of applicable laws relating to public and private rights and obligations. *E.g.*, "It should be recalled that when the principle of the *uti possidetis juris* is involved, the *jus* referred to is not international law but the constitutional or administrative law of the pre-independence sovereign...." *Land, Island, and Maritime Frontier Dispute* (El Salv. v. Hond.), 1992 I.C.J. Rep. 351, 558–59, ¶ 333. (3) Customary law specifically as a body of principles. (4) Justice in the abstract. *Compare with* **Lex**.

Ius abutendi. yūs abūtān´dē. jus abyūten´dī. *n.* "Right to consume entirely." The right to exercise complete dominion over certain property, including the right to let it lie fallow, to let it go unused, or to damage or destroy it.

Ius ad bellum. yūs ad bāl´lūm. jus âd be´lum. *n.* "Law/right relating to war." (1) The international law governing when and how military action may lawfully be commenced by one state against another, as set forth in the United Nations Charter (*see especially* Article 2(4) and Chapters VI and VII) and customary international practice. *See* Eritrea-Ethiopia Claims Comm'n, *Decision No. 7: Guidance Regarding* Jus Ad Bellum *Liability*, July 27, 2007, 46 I.L.M. 1121 (2007). Although today the cases in which the use of armed force are considered legal are limited primarily to individual and collective self-defense, this was not always the case. Throughout most of history, wars could legally (if not morally) be commenced for almost any reason so long as the required formalities of the *ius ad bellum* were observed. These included rules regarding the treatment of neutral powers and the necessity of a formal declaration of war prior to the commencement of hostilities. (2) The right of a state to deploy armed force against another state consistent with international law or natural law concepts of justice. *Contrast with* **Ius in bello**. *See also* **Casus belli**.

Ius ad rem. yūs ad rām. jus âd rem. *n.* "Right concerning the thing." An imperfect right in property. *E.g.*, "If the view most favorable to the American arguments is adopted—with every reservation as to the soundness of such view—that is to say, if we consider as positive law at the period in question the rule that discovery as such, i.e. the mere fact of seeing land, without any act, even symbolical, of taking possession, involved *ipso jure* territorial sovereignty and not merely an 'inchoate title,' a *jus ad rem*, to be completed eventually by an actual and durable taking of possession within a reasonable time, the question arises whether sovereignty yet existed at the critical date." *The Island of Palmas Case* (U.S. v. Nether.), Perm. Ct. Arb., Award of Apr. 4, 1928, H.C.R. (2d series), at 100 (Scott 1932).

Ius advenae. yūs adwā´nī. jus âdve´nā. *n.* "Foreign law." Law of a foreign jurisdiction.

Ius aequum. yūs ī´kū-ūm. jus e´kwum. *n.* "Equitable law." A legal system in which rights are modified or controlled by equitable concepts, such that they must be exercised fairly and in good faith. International tribunals in some cases exercise their discretion to resort to *ius aequum* to avoid an unjust result, although the validity of this practice has been the subject of debate. *Contrast with* **Ius iniquum**. *See also* **Ius strictum**.

Ius albinagii. yūs albēna´gē-ē. jus âlbina´jī. *n.* "Law of the Albinagi." The sovereign right, no longer recognized in international law, to confiscate all of the property that an alien domiciled in the sovereign's territory possessed at death. Also known in French as *droit d'aubaine*. *Contrast with* **Ius detractus**.

Ius angariae. yūs anga´rē-ī. jus ânga´rē-ā. *n.* "Right of angary." A state's right during national emergency or armed conflict to requisition neutral merchant vessels, aircraft, or property in its territory, territorial waters, ports, or inland waters for a public purpose and subject to the duty eventually to compensate for the seizure.

Ius antiquum. yūs antē´kū-ūm. jus ânti´kwum. *n.* "Antique law." (1) Law formerly applicable and no longer valid. (2) Law of ancient origin. (3) In Roman law, the body of law developed during the Republican period (prior to the fourth century CE), as opposed to laws originating in Imperial Rome. An alternative term is **Ius vetus**. *Contrast with* **Ius novum**.

Ius armorum. yūs armō´rūm. jus armō´rum. *n.* "Law of arms." (1) Medieval chivalric law. (2) The law governing the conduct of war by individual combatants.

Ius asyli. yūs asülē. jus âsī´lī. *n.* "The law (or right) of asylum." (1) The law relating to the granting of asylum or political refugee status. (2) The right to asylum based on refugee status.

Ius belli. yūs bāl´lē. jus be´lī. *n.* [*pl.* **Iura belli.** yū´ra bāl´lē. jɜ´ru be´lī] "Law of war." The totality of international law relating to war, comprising both *ius ad bellum* (the law relating to when armed action may be taken against another state or group) and *ius in bello* (the law relating to the conduct of hostilities against combatants and civilians). *See* **Ius ad bellum** and **Ius in bello**.

Ius bellum dicendi. yūs bāl´lūm dēkān´dē. jus be´lum disen´dī. *n.* "The right to declare war." The right under the law of war (*ius ad bellum*) to declare war for some legitimate cause (*casus belli*).

Ius civile. yūs kēwē´lā. jus si´vilē. *n.* "Civil law." (1) Civil law. (2) Law relating to relationships between private citizens; private law. *Ius civile* derives from the Roman law relating to the rights and duties of Roman citizens.

Ius cogens (superveniens). yūs kō´gāns (sūpārwā´nē-āns). jus kō´jenz- OR -ka´jenz (sūpɜrvē´nyenz). *n.* "(Supervening) coercive law." The set of peremptory norms of international law owed by all states *erga omnes*; law of a mandatory nature that the international community generally recognizes and accepts as not admitting of any objection or derogation by treaty. *Ius cogens* finds its historical basis in natural law, but is considered by some to be a creature of a general state consent or other sources. Commonly cited examples of violations of *ius cogens* include state-sponsored torture, slavery, and genocide. Violations of *ius cogens*, unlike most violations of international law, are thought by some to give rise to universal jurisdiction. *E.g.*, "Norms of *jus cogens* do not tolerate derogation, so any concurrent regime or situation, whether it be established by way of a bilateral or unilateral act, cannot acquire legal force due to the peremptoriness of *jus cogens*—more specifically, this act or acts remains in the sphere of simple facts." *Application of the Convention on Prevention and Punishment of Genocide* (Bosn. & Herz. v. Yugo.), 1996 I.C.J. Rep. 595, 754, ¶ 90 (Judge *ad hoc* Kreća, dissenting). *See* the Vienna Convention on the Law of Treaties arts. 53 and 64, May 23, 1969, 1155 U.N.T.S. 331. *Compare with* **Ius erga omnes**. *Contrast with* **Ius dispositivum**. *See also* **Erga omnes** and **Ius naturale**.

Ius commercii. yūs kōmmär´kē-ē. jus kamɜr´šī. *n.* "Right of commerce." The right to engage in business transactions, including the right to negotiate and conclude contracts and to transport goods to friendly states for sale or purchase.

Ius commune. yūs kōmmū´nā. jus kamyū´nē. *n.* "Common law." (1) The body of law, developed from the fusion of the Roman civil law with canon law in twelfth century Italy, which eventually spread throughout medieval Europe to provide a basis for a general law common to most of Christendom. (2) A public law or right of general application. (3) Law developed by the decisions of tribunals in pursuit of a deontological or political principle of decision-making; common law.

Ius commune gentium. yūs kōmmū´nā gān´tē-ūm. jus kamyū´nē jen´tē-um. *n.* "Common law of the people." An alternative term for **Ius gentium**.

Ius commune humanitatis. yūs kōmmū´nā hūmanēta´tēs. jus kamyū´nē hyūmânita´tis. *n.* "Common law of humanity." Law relating to or governing all humanity, such as universal human rights law.

Ius condendum. yūs kōndān´dūm. jus kanden´dum. *n.* "Law needing to be made." A gap in the law that seems to require completion. *Contrast with* **Ius conditum**.

Ius conditum. yūs kōn´dētūm. jus kan´ditum. *n.* "Established law." Law fully established on a subject or in a field. *Compare with* **Lex lata**. *Contrast with* **Ius condendum**.

Ius consuetudinarium. yūs kōnsūātūdēna´rē-ūm. jus kanswetūdina´rē-um. *n.* "Customary law." Customary international law; the international law formed by the longstanding and consistent customary practices of states in the belief that such practices are legally mandated. *See also* **Opinio iuris (sive necessitatis).**

Ius cudendae monetae. yūs kūdān´dī mōnā´tī. jus kyūden´dā ma´netā. *n.* "Right to coin money." The right of the state to stamp, print, issue, and circulate money for use in its territory.

Ius dare. yūs da´rā. jus da´rē. *v. inf.* + *n.* "To give law." To create law; to legislate. *Contrast with* **Ius dicere.** *See also* **Ius dicere, non ius dare.**

Ius denegare. yūs dānāga´rā. jus denega´rē. *n.* "Right to refuse." The right to decline or refuse a request or offer.

Ius detractus. yūs dātrak´tūs. jus dētrâk´tus. *n.* "Right of taking away." The right of a state to tax the estate of a deceased alien upon the estate's removal from the state's territory. *Contrast with* **Ius albinagii.**

Ius dicere. yūs dē´kārā. jus dī´s3rē. *v. inf.* + *n.* "To speak the law." To practice a judicial authority to declare what is lawful. *Contrast with* **Ius dare.** *See also* **Ius dicere, non ius dare.**

Ius dicere, non ius dare. yūs dē´kārā, nōn yūs da´rā. jus dī´s3rē, nan jus da´rē. "To speak the law, not to give law." An alternative phrase for **Iudicis est ius dicere, non dare.**

Ius dispositivum. yūs dēspōsētē´wūm. jus dispazitī´vum. *n.* "Law not settled by agreement." (1) Positive law. (2) Law capable of creation or modification by the consent or agreement of relevant parties. *E.g.*, "If we can introduce in the international field a category of law, namely *jus cogens*...a kind of imperative law which constitutes the contrast to the *jus dispositivum*, capable of being changed by way of agreement between States, surely the law concerning the protection of human rights may be considered to belong to the *jus cogens*." *South West Africa Cases* (Eth. v. S. Afr.; Liber. v. S. Afr.), 1966 I.C.J. Rep. 6, 250, 298 (Judge Tanaka, dissenting). (3) Law developed by a legal authority for reasons of public policy not necessarily based on principles of morality or justice. *Contrast with* **Ius cogens** and **Ius naturale.**

Ius erga omnes. yūs ār´ga ōm´nās. jus 3r´gu am´nēz. *n.* "Right before all." An absolute right owed to all states by all states, such as the obligation not to deplete stocks of living pelagic resources or to use the moon or other celestial bodies for warlike purposes. *See also* **Erga omnes** and **Ius cogens.**

Ius est ars aequi et boni. yūs āst ars ī´kwē āt bō´nē. jus est arz e´kwī et bō´nī. "The law is the art of equity and goodness." An alternative formulation of **Ius est ars boni et aequi.**

Ius est ars boni et aequi. yūs āst ars bō´nē āt ī´kwē. jus est arz bō´nī et e´kwī. "The law is the art of goodness and equity." A maxim meaning that in general the purpose of the law is to determine what is equitable and fair. The phrase is found in the preamble to Justinian's *Digest* (1.1.pr). *E.g.*, "The just and equitable solution, in the sense given by Ulpian's definition of law: *jus est ars boni et aequi*, is not to be confused with the faculty possessed by the Court by virtue of Article 38 *in fine* to decide a case, with the agreement of the parties, *ex aequo et bono*, in the sense which modern law gives to that expression." *North Sea Continental Shelf* (F.R.G. v. Den./F.R.G. v. Nether.), 1969 I.C.J. 3, 138, ¶ 37 (separate opinion of Judge Fouad Ammoun). An alternative formulation is **Ius est ars aequi et boni.**

Ius europaeum. yūs āūrōpī´ūm. jus yūrōpē´um. *n. Neo.* "European law." (1) European Community law. (2) The regional law historically or presently regulating intercourse between the states of Europe.

Ius ex iniuria non oritur. yūs āks ēnyū´rē-a nōn ō´rētūr. jus eks injɜr´ē-u nan ō´ritɜr. "A right does not arise from wrongdoing." An alternative formulation of **Ex iniuria ius non oritur.**

Ius excludendi. yūs āks-klūdān´dē. jus eks-klūden´dī. *n.* "Right of exclusion." A right to exclude others from use of property. *E.g.*, "Though in most instances intellectual property rights confer a *ius excluendi*, this is far from being an absolute rule." Carlos Maria Correa, *Unfair Competition under the TRIPS Agreement: Protection of Data Submitted for the Registration of Pharmaceuticals*, 3 Chi. J. Int'l L. 69, 72 (2002).

Ius feciale. A misspelling of **Ius fetiale (divinum).**

Ius fetiale (divinum). yūs fātē-a´lā (dēwē´nūm). jus fetē-â´lē (divī´num). *n.* "(Divine) law relating to the *fetiales*." (1) Roman law relating to the Roman college of priests (*fetiales*) who presided over treaties and conducted rituals prior to the declaration of war against an enemy to ensure that the war would be considered as just by the gods. Before commencing a war, the representative of the Roman people would swear an oath that the god Iupiter had a right of retribution if the war was unjust. The *ius fetiale* is a species of **Ius sacrum.** (2) More modernly, the term has occasionally been applied in a very loose sense to the international law relating to diplomacy, which is more properly called *ius legationis*. *See also* **Collegium fetialium** and **Fetiales.**

Ius gentium. yūs gän´tē-ūm. jus jen´tē-um. *n.* "Law of peoples." (1) In Roman law, *ius gentium* was originally the law applicable to persons lacking Roman citizenship, but, in Imperial Rome, its scope expanded to denote natural law rules supposedly applicable to all persons of any nationality, including Roman citizens. *Ius gentium* thus engulfed the *ius civile* applicable to Roman citizens in Justinian's *Code*. (2) In more modern usage, a body of law that is universally accepted by the international community as a whole (usually, though not always, based on a theory of natural law). The term is not synonymous with "international law." An alternative formulation is **Ius commune gentium.** *Contrast with* **Ius inter gentes.** *See also* **Ius naturale.**

Ius gentium inter se. yūs gän´tē-ūm ēn´tär sā. jus jen´tē-um in´tɜr sā. *n.* "Law of peoples between themselves." An archaic term for international law. *Compare with* **Ius inter gentes.** *Contrast with* **Ius gentium intra se.**

Ius gentium intra se. yūs gän´tē-ūm ēn´tra sā. jus jen´tē-um in´tru sā. *n.* "Law of peoples within themselves." An archaic term for the domestic law of states. *Compare with* **Ius gentium.** *Contrast with* **Ius gentium inter se.**

Ius Gentium Methodo Scientifica Perpetractatum. yūs gän´tē-ūm māt´hōdō skē-äntē´fēka pärpātrakta´tūm. jus jen´tē-um me´θudō sī-enti´fiku pɜrpetrâktā´tum. *N.* "The Law of Peoples Fully Treated by Scientific Method." The title of a 1749 treatise by German philosopher Christian Wolff (1679–1754) on international law.

Ius gentium privatum. yūs gän´tē-ūm prēwa´tūm. jus jen´tē-um prīvā´tum. *n.* "Private law of peoples." Private international law; international conflict of laws rules. The *ius gentium privatum* is specifically the law governing which state has jurisdiction over which persons, relationships, contracts, rights, duties, acts, and property (personal or real) when it is possible for more than one state to exercise jurisdiction over such subjects. *E.g.*, "The common law of both [England and the United States] has been expanded to meet the exigencies of the times as they have arisen; and so far as the practice of nations, or the *jus gentium privatum*, has been supposed to furnish any general principle, it has been followed out." Joseph Story, COMMENTARIES ON THE CONFLICT OF LAWS §§ 23–24 (1834).

Ius habendi. yūs habän´dē. jus hâben´dī. *n.* "Right to have." A right to possess certain property.

Ius in bello. yūs ēn bäl´lō. jus in be´lō. *n.* "Law in war." The international law governing the conduct of parties during wartime. Its primary components include international humanitarian law; the international law of neutrality; and the law of wartime espionage, propaganda, and *ruses de guerre* ("deceptions of war"). *Compare with* **Ius armorum.** *Contrast with* **Ius ad bellum.**

Ius in personam. yūs ēn pārsō´nam. jus in pɜrsō´num. *n.* [*pl.* **Iura in personam.** yū´ra ēn pārsō´nam. jɜ´ru in pɜrsō´num.] "Right in the person." A right vesting in the individual, such as a right to some government-granted benefit or the right to seek to vindicate an interest in court.

I(J)

Ius in re. yūs ēn rā. jus in rā. *n.* "Right in the matter." A complete right to specific property enforceable *erga omnes* (against all others in the community). *E.g.*, "[T]here should be applied to territorial questions the principle that, failing any specific provision of law to the contrary, a *jus in re* once lawfully acquired shall prevail over *de facto* possession however well established." *Island of Palmas Case* (U.S. v. Nether.), Perm. Ct. Arb., Award of Apr. 4, 1928, H.C.R. (2d series), at 94 (Scott 1932). *Compare with* **Ius in rem.** *See also* **Erga omnes.**

Ius in rem. yūs ēn rām. jus in rem. *n.* [*pl.* **Iura in rem.** yū´ra ēn rām. jɜ´ru in rem.] "Right in the thing." A property right. *E.g.*, "When such provisions [for a ship purchaser's lien on the ship being built and construction materials] are inserted [into the purchase agreement], it is obvious that the contract is *prima facie* evidence of a *jus in rem*, arising out of the contract, while the contractor or his sub-contractor might otherwise deny the existence of this superior 'interest' equivalent to ownership." *Norwegian Claims Case* (Nor. v. U.S.), Perm. Ct. Arb., Award of Oct. 13, 1922, H.C.R. (2d series), at 68 (Scott 1932). *Compare with* **Ius in re.**

Ius incognitum. yūs ēnkōg´nētūm. jus inkagnī´tum. *n.* "Unknown law." (1) An obscure or rarely referenced law. (2) An obsolete law.

Ius iniquum. yūs ēnē´kū-ūm. jus ini´kwum. *n.* "Inequitable law." (1) A law whose application in a specific case would be unjust or inequitable. (2) A law that is in general unjust or inequitable. *Contrast with* **Ius aequum.**

Ius inter gentes. yūs ēn´tār gān´tās. jus in´tɜr jen´tēz. *n.* "Law between peoples." An archaic term for international law, formerly translated as "the law of nations." *Contrast with* **Ius gentium.**

Ius legationis. yūs lāgatēō´nēs. jus legašō´nis. *n.* "Law of legation." The international law relating to the appointment, recognition, and treatment of foreign ambassadors, consuls, envoys, and other diplomats.

Ius naturae. yūs natū´rī. jus nā´čɜrā. *n.* "Law of nature." An alternative term for **Ius naturale.**

Ius naturale. yūs natūra´lā. jus nâčɜrâ´lē. *n.* "Natural law." Natural law; a body of law developed to dictate principles of human conduct demanded either by a metaphysical vision of the universe's natural order or by the alleged pronouncements of a deity. An alternative term is **Ius naturae.** *Compare with* **Lex naturale.** *Contrast with* **Ius dispositivum.** *See also* **Ius cogens.**

Ius naturale est quod apud omnes homines eandem habet potentiam. yūs natūra´lā āst kwōd a´pūd ōm´nās hō´mēnās ā-an´dām ha´bāt pōtān´tē-am. jus nâčзrâ´lē est kwad ā´pud am´nēz ha´minēz ēn´dem hâ´bet pōten´šum. "Natural law is that which has the same force among all men." A maxim meaning that some laws, by their moral force, apply universally to all persons (the obvious example being human rights). This maxim is an ancient expression of Natural Law Theory challenged by proponents of Legal Positivism and later theories of jurisprudence. *See also* **Ius naturale**.

Ius navigandi. yūs nawēgan´dē. jus nâvigân´dī. *n.* "The right of navigation." The right under customary international law to engage in exploration and international trade though the use of vessels on the high seas.

Ius necessarium. yūs nākāssa´rē-ūm. jus nesese´rē-um. *n. Neo.* "Necessary law." A term used to denote rules of customary international law necessarily inherent in the world public order for its continued functioning. *Contrast with* **Ius voluntarium**.

Ius necessitatis. yūs nākāssēta´tēs. jus nesesitā´tis. *n.* "Right of necessity." A purported right to disregard the law in order to do something fundamentally necessary in the protection of one's interest. The existence of such rights is highly contested, especially with respect to rights that would in their exercise violate *ius cogens*. *See also* **Necessitas non habet legem**.

Ius non scriptum. yūs nōn skrēp´tūm. jus nan skrip´tum. *n.* "Unwritten law." An alternative term for **Lex non scripta**.

Ius novum. yūs nō´wūm. jus nō´vum. *n.* "New law." (1) Law of recent origin. (2) In Roman law, the collection of laws developed during the Imperial period (from the fourth century CE and later), as opposed to the law originating in the Republican period. *Contrast with* **Ius antiquum**.

Ius paciarri. yūs pakē-ar´rē. jus pâča´rī. *n. Neo.* "Law of the peaceful." A neologism sometimes used to refer to the international law governing the activities of UN forces deployed by authorization of the Security Council to make or keep peace in unstable or warring states.

Ius post bellum. yūs pōst bāl´lūm. jus pōst be´lum. *n. Neo.* "Law after war." The international law relating to the situation following an international armed conflict, especially when one belligerent occupies and administers territory of another. *See also* **Ius in bello**.

Ius posteriori derogat priori. yūs pōstārēō´rē dā´rōgat prēō´rē. jus pōstērī´ōrī de´rōgât prīō´rī. "The right of those who follow repeals the right of those who preceded." A maxim meaning that rights arising later in time applying to specific parties supersede earlier, conflicting rights with respect to the same parties. *Compare with* **Leges posteriores priores contrarias abrogant.**

Ius postliminii. yūs pōstlēmē´nē-ē. jus pōstlimi´nī. *n.* "The right of *postliminium.*" (1) The right of a slave in Roman law to freedom upon returning to his or her native land. (2) The law relating to, or the right of, **Postliminium.**

Ius praeminens. yūs prī´mēnāns. jus prē-em´inenz. *n. Neo.* "Preeminent right." (1) A right of highest precedence. (2) The state's right to exercise sovereignty in its own territory. *Compare with* **Dominium eminens.**

Ius primi occupatis. yūs prē´mē ōkkūpa´tēs. jus prī´mī akyūpā´tis. *n.* "Right of the first over the occupied." The right of the first state settling a territory to claim sovereignty over that territory. *See also* **Res nullius naturaliter fit primi occupantis.**

Ius privatum. yūs prēwa´tūm. jus prīvâ´tum. *n.* "Private law." (1) The law regulating the conduct of private persons (as opposed to governments or government officials). (2) A right held by a private individual. *Contrast with* **Ius publicum.**

Ius protectionis. yūs prōtektēō´nēs. jus prōtekšō´nis. *n.* "Right of protection." The right to protection that every citizen may claim from his or her state of nationality.

Ius publicum. yūs pūb´lēkūm. jus pub´likum. *n.* "Public law; public right." (1) The law regulating relations between or with governmental actors. (2) The law maintained by the state. (3) A right of the state or sovereign. *Contrast with* **Ius privatum.**

Ius puniendi. yūs pūnē-ān´dē. jus pyūnē-en´dī. *n.* "Right to punish." The state's right to punish criminal offenses pursuant to its laws within the limits of the international law respecting jurisdiction and human rights.

Ius quarteriorum. yūs kwartārēō´rūm. jus kwartɜrēō´rum. *n.* "Law of quarter parts." The now antiquated international law limiting a state's extraterritorial jurisdiction over foreign diplomatic residences within its territory. Because these were often grouped together into neighborhoods with high concentrations of diplomatic residences, the *ius quarteriorum* effectively created a municipal region subject to the extraterritorial application of foreign law. This term is also known by its French name, *franchise du quartier.*

Ius representationis (omnimodae). yūs rāprāsāntatēō´nēs (ōmnēmō´dī). jus reprēzentāšō´nis (amnēmō´dā). *n.* "Right of representation (of all kinds)." The right to represent another person with respect to all matters, usually in the capacity of a plenipotentiary agent.

Ius resistendi. yūs rāsēstān´dē. jus rezisten´dī. *n.* "Right to resist." (1) The right to resist (*e.g.*, occupation by force of arms). (2) The right to offer opposition (*e.g.*, against an opposing party before a tribunal).

Ius sacrum. yūs sak´rūm. jus sâk´rum. *n.* "Sacred law." (1) Divine law. (2) Natural law. (3) The Roman law relating to religious matters, known specifically as **Ius fetiale (divinum).**

Ius sanguinis. yūs san´gwēnēs. jus sâŋ´winis. *n.* "Right of blood." The right to claim citizenship based on race or nationality, as when a person acquires the nationality of a state because one or both parents have the nationality of the state. *See also* **Ius soli.**

Ius scriptum. yūs skrēp´tūm. jus skrip´tum. *n.* "Written law." An alternative term for **Lex scripta.**

Ius singulare. yūs sēngūla´rā. jus singyūle´rē. *n.* "Singular right." (1) A law or right applicable in a unique situation. (2) A law or right applicable within a single jurisdiction.

Ius soli. yūs sō´lē. jus sō´lī. *n.* "Right of the soil." A right to acquire the nationality of a state by virtue of having been born within its territory. *See also* **Ius sanguinis.**

Ius standi. yūs stan´dē. jus stân´dī. *n.* "Right of standing." (1) The customary international law establishing who has rights to appear before a tribunal or to make representations to another under international law, and what is the content of these rights. (2) The right to appear before a tribunal based on the tribunal's jurisdiction over the party appearing, and the party's right to represent itself or another in the case in dispute. *E.g.*, "[T]he Belgian Government has advanced the proposition that it is inadmissible to deny the shareholders' national State a right of diplomatic protection merely on the ground that another State possesses a corresponding right in respect of the company itself. In strict logic and law this formulation of the Belgian claim to *jus standi* assumes the existence of the very right that requires demonstration." *Barcelona Traction, Light, and Power Company* (Belg. v. Spain), 1970 I.C.J. Rep. 3, ¶ 51.

Ius strictum. yūs strēk´tūm. jus strik´tum. *n.* "Exact law." (1) A system of positive customary law conferring rights or obligations interpreted literally and with no modification by or resort to principles of equity or public policy. (2) An alternative formulation of **Strictum ius.** *See also* **Actio stricti iuris, De rigore iuris, Ius aequum, Stricto iure,** and **Strictissimi iuris.**

Ius talionis. yūs talēō´nēs. jus tâlēō´nis. *n.* "Right of retaliation." The right, postulated in Natural Law Theory, that certain kinds of violations of the law or of moral obligations give the right or duty to punish the transgressor precisely in kind or proportionally. *Compare with* **Lex talionis.**

I(J)

Ius tertii. yūs tär´tē-ē. jus tɜr´šī. *n.* "Right of a third party." The right of nonparty to an agreement or treaty. In the common law, *ius tertii* is the right of a third party to property being held by a possessor, which right the possessor uses to defend the property against claims by persons other than the third-party owner. In international law, it is generally recognized that treaties do not create enforceable rights for nonparty (*tertius*) states. *See also* **Pacta in favorem tertii** and **Pacta tertiis (nec nocent nec prosunt).**

Ius transitus innoxii. yūs tran´sētūs ēnnō´ksē-ē. jus trân´zitus ina´ksī. *n.* "Right of safe passage." The right of a person, vessel, or aircraft to traverse foreign land or territorial seas for peaceful and legal purposes without being exposed to arrest, unnecessary obstruction, or threat of harm.

Ius utendi. yūs ūtān´dē. jus yūten´dī. *n.* "Right of use." The right to use property in the absence of an accompanying right of ownership.

Ius vetus. yūs wā´tūs. jus vē´tus. *n.* "Old law." An alternative term for **Ius antiquum.**

Ius voluntarium. yūs wōlūnta´rē-ūm. jus valunte´rē-um. *n. Neo.* "Volitional law." (1) A term for customary international law that emphasizes its voluntary character. (2) A term used by German philosopher Christian Wolff (1679-1754) in his *Ius Gentium Methodo Scientifica Perpetratum* (1749) to denote rules of international law undertaken for the mutual benefit of states as opposed to those that are inherent in the world public order. *Contrast with* **Ius necessarium.**

Iusta causa. yūs´ta kô´sa. jus´tu kă´zu. *n.* "Just cause." Just or lawful grounds (*e.g.*, for declaring war). *See also* **Casus belli.**

Iustitia. yūstē´tē-a. justi´šu. *n.* "Justice." Justice; fairness; The allocation of rewards or penalties in strict conformity with each person's merits or failings.

Iustitia nemini neganda est. yūstē´tē-a nā´mēnē nāgan´da āst. justi´šu ne´minī negân´du est. "Justice is to be denied to no one." A maxim meaning that all persons must be afforded their legal rights without discrimination. *See also* **Iustitia non est neganda, non differenda.**

Iustitia non est neganda, non differenda. yūstē´tē-a nōn āst nāgan´da, nōn dēffārān´da. justi´šu nan est negan´du, nan difɜren´du. "Justice is not to be denied, not to be delayed." A maxim meaning that all persons must be afforded their legal rights promptly. *See also* **Iustitia nemini neganda est.**

Iusto tempore. yūs´tō tām´pōrā. jus´tō tem´pōrē. *adv.* "At the proper time." In a timely manner.

Iustum bellum. yūs´tūm bāl´lūm. jus´tum be´lum. *n.* "Just war." (1) An armed conflict considered permissible under the international law relating to the use of armed force (*ius ad bellum*). (2) A war, the initiation and conduct of which are morally, if not legally, justifiable.

Iustus titulus. yūs´tūs tē´tūlūs. jus´tus ti´tyūlus. *n.* "Just title." A just or valid basis for a claim of ownership.

L

L.L.B. *n.* An abbreviation of **Legum baccalaureus.**

L.L.M. *n.* An abbreviation of **Legum magister.**

Laesa maiestas. lī´sa mī-ā´stas. lā´zu mâjes´tus. *n.* "Injured sovereignty." (1) The act (as opposed to the legally defined crime) of treason; *lèse-majesté.* (2) An injury to the sovereign dignity of the state. *See also* **Crimen laesa maiestatis** and **Perduellio.**

Laesio. lī´sēō. lē´šō. *n.* "Injury." Loss caused by the failure of a counterparty to an agreement or treaty to perform its duties.

Latens. la´tāns. lā´tenz. *adj.* "Hidden." (1) Hidden; secret. (2) Latent.

Latine dictum. latē´nā dēk´tūm. lâ´tinē dik´tum. *adj.* "Spoken in Latin." Spoken or said in the Latin language. *See also* **Latine scriptum.**

Latine scriptum. latē´nā skrēp´tūm. lâ´tinē skrip´tum. *adj.* "Written in Latin." Written or printed in the Latin language. *See also* **Latine dictum.**

Lato sensu. la´tō sān´sū. lâ´tō sen´sū. *adv.* "In the broad sense." Speaking or writing approximately, broadly, or generally. *Contrast with* **Stricto sensu.**

Ledo. lā´dō. lē´dō. *n.* "Neap tide." Neap tide; a tide having the minimum variation between high tide and low tide that occurs in the first and third quarters of the moon.

Legatos violare contra ius gentium est. lāga´tōs wēōla´rā kōn´tra yūs gān´tē-ūm āst. legā´tus vīōla´rē kan´tru jus jen´tē-um est. "It is against international law to harm diplomats." A maxim meaning that any harm to or forcible arrest or detention of an accredited diplomats violates customary international law. *See* the Vienna Convention on Diplomatic Relations arts. 29–31, Apr. 18, 1961, 500 U.N.T.S. 95.

L

Legatus. lāga´tūs. legā´tus. *n.* [*pl.* **Legati.** lāga´tē. legā´tī.] "Diplomat." (1) Generally, a diplomat of any rank. (2) An ambassador or head of mission.

Legatus a latere. lāga´tūs a la´tārā. legā´tus a lâ´tɜrē. *n.* [*pl.* **Legati a latere.** lāga´tē a la´tārā. legā´tī a lâ´tɜrē.] "Diplomat from the side [of the Catholic Pope]." A high diplomatic representative of the Holy See having the status of cardinal. The Holy See was in the past and sometimes still is treated as its own state with corresponding diplomatic privileges. The *legatus a latere* falls within the more general category of **Legatus missus.** *Contrast with* **Legatus natus** and **Nuncio.**

Legatus datus. lāga´tūs da´tūs. legā´tus dā´tus. *n.* "Given diplomat." An alternative term for **Legatus missus.**

Legatus missus. lāga´tūs mēs´sūs. legā´tus mi´sus. *n.* "Sent diplomat." A diplomat charged with a special, limited mission. An alternative term is **Legatus datus.** *See also* **Legatus a latere.**

Legatus natus. lāga´tūs na´tūs. legā´tus nā´tus. *n.* "A born diplomat." A representative of the Holy See who lacks official diplomatic status. The claim of a *legatus natus* to diplomatic status was based on the rank of the claimant—usually a bishop or archbishop representing an important diocese. *Contrast with* **Legatus a latere** and **Nuncio.**

Legatus regis vice fungitur a quo destinatur. lāga´tūs rā´gēs wē´kā fūn´gētūr a kwō dāstēna´tūr. legā´tus rē´jis vī´su fun´jitɜr a kwō desti´nutɜr. "A diplomat substitutes for the king by whom he is appointed." A maxim meaning that a diplomat represents the state on behalf of whom he or she is accredited and should be treated with the same respect to which the foreign head of state is entitled. *See* the Vienna Convention on Diplomatic Relations arts. 3(1), 22–37, Apr. 18, 1961, 500 U.N.T.S. 95.

Lege artis. lā´gā ar´tēs. le´jē ar´tis. *prep.* + *n.* (commonly used as an *adv.*) "By the rule of the art." (1) In accordance with the approved rules of the profession or art, as opposed to novel or improvised methods. (2) Done successfully in the manner consistent with the most up-to-date professional or artistic standards. *E.g.*, "It appears, however, that the procedure of inference has not been followed *lege artis*, by respecting inherent requirements which inference as such necessarily implies. The substratum from which special intent may be inferred must satisfy with respect to its components the relevant standards, both quantitative and qualitative." *Application of the Convention on the Prevention and Punishment of the Crime of Genocide* (Bosn. & Herz. v. Yugo.), I.C.J. No. 91, Judgment of Feb. 26, 2007, at 87, ¶ 150 (separate opinion of Judge *ad hoc* Kreća).

Leges. lā´gās. le´jēz. *n. pl.* "Laws." Laws; legislation. *See* **Lex.**

L

Leges barbarorum. lā´gās barbarō´rūm. le´jēz barburō´rum. *n. pl.* "Barbarian laws." The customary laws of early medieval German and Frankish tribes, mostly codified between the fifth and ninth centuries. These codes were heavily influenced by Roman law and included the Visigothic Code of Euric, **Lex Alamannorum**, **Lex Baiuvariorum**, **Lex Burgundionum**, **Lex Frisionum**, **Lex Langobardorum**, **Lex Ripuari**, **Lex Saxonum**, **Lex Salica**, and **Lex Visigothorum**. Some separate codes were also written to govern relations between Roman subjects rather than relations between Germanic peoples or between Romans and Germanic peoples. These latter codes included the **Lex Romana Burgundionum**, the **Lex Romana Curiensis**, and the **Lex Romana Visigothorum**.

Leges enim contractus dat. lā´gās ā´nēm kōntrak´tūs dat. le´jēz e´nim kantrâk´tus dât. "Indeed, the contract gives the laws." A maxim meaning that an agreement creates legally binding obligations between the contracting parties.

Leges imperfecti. lā´gās ēmpārfāk´tē. le´jēz imp3rfek´tī. *n. pl.* "Unfinished laws." Laws without well defined rights or duties, generally used as norms for guidance. Such laws are usually difficult to interpret and to enforce. *Contrast with* **Leges perfectae.**

Leges perfectae. lā´gās pārfāk´tī. le´jēz p3rfek´tā. *n. pl.* "Finished laws." Laws with well-defined rights or duties that are, consequently, not unduly difficult to interpret and to enforce. *Contrast with* **Leges imperfecti.**

Leges posteriores priores contrarias abrogant. lā´gās pōstārēō´rās prēō´rās kōntra´rē-as abrō´gant. le´jēz pōstērēō´rēz prīō´rez kantra´rē-us âb´rōgânt. "Later laws abrogate earlier, contrary ones." A maxim meaning that, where two laws or legal instruments conflict, the one adopted later in time, rather than the one adopted earlier, is considered binding on the relevant parties. In treaty law, this rule applies only to states that are parties to both the earlier and later treaty. *Compare with* **Ius posteriori derogat priori.**

Leges vigilantibus non dormientibus subserviunt. lā´gās wēgēlan´tēbūs nōn dōrmē-ān´tēbūs sūbsār´wē-ūnt. le´jēz vijilân´tibus nan dōrmē-en´tibus subs3r´vē-unt. "The laws serve those who are vigilant, not those who are sleeping." A maxim expressing the concept of laches, meaning that a claimant who has slept on his rights may be denied enforcement when the resulting delay would cause an unfair prejudice to the respondent.

Legibus solutus. lā´gēbūs sōlū´tūs. le´jibus salū´tus. *adj.* "Released from the laws." (1) Not subject to laws. (2) Above the law, as a tyrannical dictator might claim to be. *Contrast with* **Nemo est supra leges.**

L

Legitima persona standi in iudicio. lāgē´tēma pārsō´na stan´dē ēn yūdē´kēō. leji´timu pɜrsō´nu stân´dī in jūdi´šō. *n. Neo.* "A legitimate person of standing in a court of justice." A person having standing to assert rights or seek enforcement of obligations, usually before a court or other tribunal.

Legum baccalaureus. lā´gūm bakkalô´rā-ūs. le´jum bâkulō´rē-us. *n.* "Bachelor of laws." A basic professional degree in law awarded in common law countries. This degree was formerly awarded in the United States until the degree requirements were changed toward the end of the nineteenth century. In 1902, the University of Chicago awarded the first *juris doctor* (J.D.) degree and the *legum baccalaureus* gradually fell into desuetude in the United States until 1971, when the last major school, the Yale Law School, abandoned the *legum baccalaureus*. Commonly abbreviated **LL.B.** *Compare with* **Iuris doctor.** *See also* **Legum magister** and **Magister iuris.**

Legum magister. lā´gūm magēs´tār. le´gum mâjis´tɜr. *n.* "Master of laws." An advanced professional degree in law awarded after the *juris doctor* or *legum baccalaureus*, usually following one or two years of additional study. Commonly abbreviated **L.L.M.** *Compare with* **Magister iuris.**

Levandae navis causa. lāwan´dī na´wēs kô´sa. levân´dā nâ´vis kă´zu. *adv.* (commonly used as a *n.*) "For the sake of lightening the ship." The jettison of some goods on a seagoing vessel overboard to avoid the sinking of the vessel and the consequent loss of all cargo. In maritime law, *levandae navis causa* typically entitles the owner of the jettisoned goods to *pro rata* compensation by the other owners of goods onboard the vessel whose property was thereby saved. *See also* **Adventurae maris.**

Levato velo. lāwa´tō wā´lō. levā´tō ve´lō. *adv.* (commonly used as a *n.*) "With the curtain raised." The principle of Roman law, expressed in Justinian's *Code* (11.6.5), that maritime cases should be heard in public. Originally, the principle applied only to cases involving wreck and salvage, but was later extended to maritime disputes generally.

Lex. lāks. leks. *n.* [*pl.* **Leges.** lā´gās. le´jēz.] "Law." (1) A law or statute. (2) A code or collection of statutes dealing with a specific domain of activity or class of persons. (3) A collection of all statutes applicable in a specific jurisdiction; a code of laws. (4) Positive law; law promulgated by a competent authority. (5) A provision or clause of a binding agreement. (6) An established body of customary or codified law. *Compare with* **Ius.**

Lex abrogata. lāks abrōga´ta. leks âbrōgā´tu. *n.* "Abrogated law." A law that has expired or been repealed, or is otherwise no longer in force.

Lex actus. lāks ak´tūs. leks âk´tus. *n.* "Law of the act." An abbreviation of **Lex loci actus.**

Lex Alamannorum. lāks alamannō´rūm. leks âlumânō´rum. *N.* "Alamannic Law." The early medieval codification of the customary laws of the Alamanni (a Germanic tribe inhabiting the duchies between the Rhine and Lech rivers), dating from the early eighth century. The code appears to be based on the *Pactus Alamannorum* completed by the Frankish king Dagobert I in the early seventh century. This is one of the **Leges barbarorum.**

Lex anterior. lāks antār´ēōr. leks ântē´rēōr. *n.* "Prior law." (1) A law adopted or effective before another, later law. (2) The law effective prior to a specific event. *Contrast with* **Lex posterior.** *See also* **Lex posterior derogat (legi) priori.**

Lex arbitri. lāks arbēt´rē. leks ar´bitrī. *n.* "Law of the arbitration." The law applicable to the relationship between an arbitral tribunal and the courts of the jurisdiction in which the tribunal sits. The *lex arbitri* governs such largely procedural matters as the steps that the tribunal must follow to ensure that its award is valid and enforceable (such as service of notice of the arbitration on the parties) and the extent to which the parties may resort to national courts to review or appeal an award. The *lex arbitri* is not the substantive law applied by the tribunal to resolve the dispute before it.

Lex Baiuvariorum. lāks bayūwarēō´rūm. leks bujūverēō´rum. *N.* "Bavarian Law." The early medieval codification of the customary laws of the Bavarians (a Germanic tribe inhabiting the duchy east of the Lech river), completed between 744 and 748 CE. These laws were heavily influenced by the law of the Franks, whose suzerainty the Bavarians recognized. This is one of the **Leges barbarorum.**

Lex barbara. lāks bar´bara. leks bar´bɜru. *n.* "Barbaric law." The laws of tribes beyond the suzerainty of the Roman Empire.

Lex Burgundionum. lāks būrgūndēō´nūm. leks bɜrgundēō´num. *N.* "Burgundian Law." The early medieval codification of the customary laws of the Burgundians (an eastern Germanic tribe that later colonized the area of Gaul now known as Burgundy), completed by the Burgundian king Gundobad sometime between 500 and 516 CE. This is one of the **Leges barbarorum.**

Lex causae. lāks kô´sī. leks kă´zā. *n.* "Law of connection." (1) The law properly applicable to a dispute (or agreement in dispute) by default. (2) The law under which a contractual or other legal relationship was formed.

Lex celebrationis. lāks kālābratēō´nēs. leks selebrāšō´nis. *n.* "The law of concourse." An abbreviation of **Lex loci celebrationis.**

Lex considerationis. lāks kōnsēdāratēō´nēs. leks kunsiderāšō´nis. *n.* "The law of consideration." An abbreviation of **Lex loci considerationis.**

Lex commercii. lāks kōmmār´kē-ē. leks kumɜr´šī. *n.* "Law of commerce." Commercial law; law relating to commerce or business. *See also* **Lex mercatoria.**

Lex contractus. lāks kōntrak´tūs. leks kantrâk´tus. *n.* "Law of the contract." (1) The choice of law designated in an agreement. (2) An abbreviation of **Lex loci contractus.**

Lex Cornelia. lāks kōrnā´lē-a. leks kōrnē´lē-u. *N.* "Cornelian Law." A collection of statutes enacted by Lucius Cornelius Sulla (138 to 78 BCE), Roman consul and later dictator, in 82 to 81 BCE, and continuing in force until the time of Gaius Iulius Caesar in 49 BCE. *See also* **Lex Cornelia de sicariis (et veneficis).**

Lex Cornelia de sicariis (et veneficis). lāks kōrnā´lē-a dā sēka´rē-ēs (āt wānāfē´kēs). leks kōrnē´lē-u dā sike´ris (et venefi´šis). *N.* "The Cornelian Law of Assassins (and Poisoners)." A Roman statute passed circa 81 BCE for the punishment of various kinds of murder, including group murder, poisoning, and corrupt acts leading to death. *See also* **Lex Cornelia.**

Lex dabit remedium. lāks da´bēt rāmā´dē-ūm. leks dā´bit remē´dē-um. "The law provides a remedy." A maxim meaning that the infringement of a legal right necessarily entails a remedy appropriate to the violation. *Compare with* **Ubi ius ibi remedium (est)** and **Ubicunque est iniuria, ibi damnum sequitur.**

Lex delicti (commissi). lāks dālēk´tē (kōmmēs´sē). leks dulik´tī (kumi´sī). *n.* "Law of the (committed) delict." An alternative term for **Lex loci delicti.**

Lex dilationes abhorret. lāks dēlatēō´nās abhōr´rāt. leks dīlāšō´nēz âbhō´ret. "The law abhors delay." A maxim meaning that unnecessary delays in the administration of justice dilute the quality of that justice. The maxim is a Latin equivalent to "justice delayed is justice denied" and may justify an award of moratory damages or, in extreme cases, a default judgment, to the injured party. Alternative phrases are **Dilationes in lege sunt odiosae, Lex dilationes exhorret, Lex dilationes semper abhorret,** and **Lex dilationes semper exhorret.**

Lex dilationes exhorret. lāks dēlatēō´nās āks-hōr´rāt. leks dīlāšō´nēz eks-hō´ret. "The law shudders at delay." An alternative phrase for **Lex dilationes abhorret.**

Lex dilationes semper abhorret. lāks dēlatēō´nās sām´pār abhōr´rāt. leks dīlāšō´nēz sem´pɜr âbhō´ret. "The law always abhors delay." An alternative phrase for **Lex dilationes abhorret.**

Lex dilationes semper exhorret. lāks dēlatēō´nās sām´pār āks-hōr´rāt. leks dīlāšō´nēz sem´pɜr eks-hō´ret. "The law always shudders at delay." An alternative phrase for **Lex dilationes abhorret.**

Lex domicilii. lāks dōmēkē´lē-ē. leks damisi´lī. *n.* "Law of the domicile." An abbreviation of **Lex loci domicilii.**

Lex est dictamen rationis. lāks āst dēk´tamān ratēō´nēs. leks est dik´tumen râšō´nis. "Law is the word of reason." A maxim meaning that the law should always be interpreted rationally and as intended to achieve a rational result.

Lex ferenda. lāks fārān´da. leks fɜren´du. *n.* "Law to be proposed." The law considered to be normatively preferable when the existing rule of law causes an unclear or undesirable result. *Lex ferenda* is thus a proposed law or proposed interpretation of law rather than a statement of law in force as reflected by positive sources of authority. *Contrast with* **Lex lata.**

Lex fori. lāks fō´rē. leks fō´rī. *n.* [*pl.* **Lege fori.** lā´gā fō´rē. le´jē fō´rī.] "Law of the forum." The law of the jurisdiction in which a case is pending before a tribunal. By default and in the absence of a contrary choice of law by the litigants, national courts usually apply the law of their own state as the *lex fori.* An alternative term is **Lex ordinandi.** *See also* **Lex fori et situs.**

Lex fori et situs. lāks fō´rē āt sē´tūs. leks fō´rī et sī´tus. *n.* "Law of the forum and position." The law of the jurisdiction in which a dispute relating to property, which is located within the jurisdiction, is pending before a tribunal. *See also* **Lex fori** and **Lex situs.**

Lex Frisionum. lāks frēsēō´nūm. leks frizēō´num. *N.* "Frisian Law." The early medieval codification of the customary law of the Frisians (a Germanic tribe inhabiting coastal Denmark and the Netherlands), completed in the early ninth century. The law had a significant pagan component despite the Frisian ties to the Catholic Frankish Empire. This is one of the **Leges barbarorum.**

Lex generalis. lāks gānāra´lēs. leks jenɜrâ´lis. *n.* "General law." Law as it applies generally to all subjects or with respect to all subject matters as opposed to a specialized legal regime applying only to specific subject matter, such as international trade law disciplines, or to specific persons, such as parties to an applicable treaty. *Contrast with* **Lex specialis.** *See also* **Lex specialist derogat legi generali** and **Lex posterior generalis non derogat priori specialis.**

Lex imperfecta. lāks ēmpārfāk´ta. leks impɜrfek´tu. *n. Neo.* "Unfinished law." (1) A law not typically enforced, often designed to disguise a discrepancy between unofficially authorized behavior and publicly expected behavior. (2) Sources of law that appear superficially to be authoritatively binding but that are in fact merely indicative of an incipient intent to create binding norms. *Compare with* **Lex simulata.**

Lex incorporationis. lāks ēnkōrpōrateō´nēs. leks inkōrpзrāšō´nis. *n. Neo.* "Law of incorporation." The law of the jurisdiction in which an organization is formed or incorporated. In private international law, the *lex incorporationis* may govern a wide range of the organization's affairs.

L

Lex inferior. lāks ēnfā´rēōr. leks infē´rēōr. *n.* "Lower law." (1) A body of law of lesser legitimacy than another body of law. (2) A body of law that is superseded by another, conflicting body of law. *Contrast with* **Lex superior.**

Lex lata. lāks la´ta. leks lâ´tu. *n.* "Ratified law." The positive law currently in force, without modification to account for any rules subjectively preferred by the interpreter. *Compare with* **Ius conditum.** *Contrast with* **Lex ferenda.**

Lex loci actus. lāks lō´kē ak´tūs. leks lō´sī âk´tus. *n.* "Law of the place of the act." The law of the jurisdiction in which performance of a contract or other a relevant act (such as the commission of a wrong) took place. Sometimes abbreviated **Lex actus.**

Lex loci celebrationis. lāks lō´kē kālābrateō´nēs. leks lō´sī selubrāšō´nis. *n.* "The law of the place of concourse." The law of the jurisdiction in which the relevant contract (most commonly, a contract of marriage) came into force. Commonly abbreviated **Lex celebrationis.** *E.g.*, "If parties are domiciled in one State by whose law they are prohibited to marry, but the marriage occurs in another State where such marriages are permitted, and the validity of the marriage is impugned in the *latter* or any *third* State, the general rule is that the *lex celebrationis*, not the *lex domicilii*, will govern." Raleigh C. Minor, CONFLICT OF LAWS; OR, PRIVATE INTERNATIONAL LAW 150, § 73 (1901). *Compare with* **Lex loci contractus.**

Lex loci considerationis. lāks lō´kē kōnsēdārateō´nēs. leks lō´sī kunsiderāšō´nis. *n.* "The law of the place of consideration." The law of the jurisdiction in which consideration that gives rise to a contract either is located or will be transferred to the other contracting party. Commonly abbreviated **Lex considerationis.**

Lex loci contractus. lāks lō´kē kōntrak´tūs. leks lō´sī kantrâk´tus. *n.* "Law of the place of the contract." The law of the jurisdiction in which a contract was concluded. The *lex loci contractus* should not be confused with the law of the place in which the contract came into force (*see* **Lex loci celebrationis**), is performed (see **Lex loci actus** and **Lex loci solutionis**), or where the consideration is exchanged (*see* **Lex loci considerationis**). Sometimes abbreviated **Lex contractus**.

Lex loci delicti. lāks lō´kē dālēk´tē. leks lō´sī dulik´tī. *n.* "Law of the place of the wrong." The law of the jurisdiction in which a wrongful act was committed. An alternative formulation is **Lex delicti (commissi)**.

L

Lex loci delictus. An incorrect spelling of **Lex loci delicti**.

Lex loci domicilii. lāks lō´kē dōmēkē´lē-ē. leks lō´sī dōmusi´lī. *n.* "Law of the place of domicile." (1) The law of the jurisdiction in which the respondent is domiciled. *E.g.*, "[T]he application of the legislation of another Member State, in particular the State of residence, is not always precluded under Regulation No 1408/71, since the rule laid down in Article 13 of that regulation—that an employed person is subject to the legislation of the Member State of employment—does not rule out certain benefits governed by the more specific rules of that regulation. Thus, the application of the provisions against overlapping...may lead to a reversal of priorities in favour of the competence of the Member State of residence (*lex loci domicilii*), with the result that there may be entitlement to allowances in that State, and the benefits payable by the Member State of employment may be suspended." Opinion of Advocate General Mazak, *Bosmann v. Bundesagentur fur Arbeit*, E.C.J. Case No. C-352/06, ¶¶ 48–49. (2) The principle of private international law that a person's rights or obligations may be determined by the law of the person's domicile. Commonly abbreviated **Lex domicilii**.

Lex loci protectionis. lāks lō´kē prōtāktēō´nēs. leks lō´sī prōtekšō´nis. *n. Neo.* "The law of the place of protection." The law of the jurisdiction in which property (especially intellectual property) is legally registered or protected. *See also* **Lex originis**.

Lex loci rei (sitae). lāks lō´kē rā´ē (sē´tī). leks lō´sī rā (si´tā). *n.* "Law of the place where the thing (is situated)." The law of the jurisdiction in which the property at issue is located. Commonly abbreviated **Lex rei (sitae)**. *Compare with* **Lex situs**.

Lex loci solutionis. lāks lō´kē sōlūtēō´nēs. leks lō´sī salūšō´nis. *n.* "The law of the place of performance." The law of the jurisdiction in which a contract will be performed or payment on a contract will be made.

Lex locus. A grammatically incorrect version of *lex loci*. For example, **Lex loci actus** is sometimes erroneously written: **Lex locus actus**.

Lex Langobardorum. lāks langōbardō´rūm. leks lâɲōbardō´rum. *N.* "Lombardian Law." The early medieval codification of the customary law of the Lombards (a northern Germanic tribe that established a kingdom in northern Italy from the sixth century until 774 CE), first promulgated in 643 CE. The early chapters of this law, known as the *Edictus Langobardorum*, represents Germanic law with minimal Roman or Frankish influence. This is one of the **Leges barbarorum.**

L

Lex ligeantiae. lāks lēgā-an´tē-ī. leks ligē-ân´tē-ā. *n. Neo.* "Law of allegiance." The law of the state to which a person owes his or her allegiance. Some commentators have argued that, in private international law, the *lex ligeantiae* should carry more weight than the *lex loci domicilii*, on the theory that an individual's state of domicile is less important than the state to which he owes his loyalty.

Lex maioris partis. lāks mayō´rēs par´tēs. leks mujō´ris par´tis. *n.* "The law of the majority." A rule to the effect that, when a deliberative body (such as a council, commission, court, or arbitral tribunal) must decide a question, the simple majority decision binds the body. This rule usually applies by default when the body's constitution, statute, or rules of procedure do not specify by what procedure decisions are to be made.

Lex maritima. lāks marē´tēma. leks maritī´mu. *n. Neo.* "Maritime law." The law and customs developed in seventeenth-century Europe to govern international commercial shipping. The *lex maritima* formed part of the **Lex mercatoria.**

Lex mercatoria. lāks mārkatō´rē-a. leks mзrkutō´rē-u. *n.* "The law merchant." The law merchant; the customary international law governing transnational commercial transactions. The *lex mercatoria* dates back to the seventeenth century in Europe and continues to be used as an interpretive aid even today by some tribunals in international commercial disputes. It includes rules and customs governing both transnational commercial relations and shipping. Alternative terms are **Consuetudo mercatoria** and **Consuetudo mercatorum.** *See also* **Lex commercii** and **Lex maritima.**

Lex monetae. lāks mōnā´tī. leks ma´netā. *n.* "The law of money." The law governing the printing, use, and disposal of currency in the issuing state.

Lex mitior. lāks me´tēōr. leks mi´šōr. *n.* "Milder law." A principle providing that, if a law relating to an offense is enacted or amended after the offense was committed, the more lenient law applies.

Lex mitius. lāks mē´tē-ūs. leks mi´šus. *n.* "The law of leniency." The law of the jurisdiction with relatively more lenient rules or penalties. The principle that retrospective application of new criminal laws violates the right of the accused to a fair trial may be qualified by applying the *lex mitius* to afford the accused the benefit of a law more lenient than the one in force at the time the crime was allegedly committed. *See also* **In dubio mitius.**

Lex naturale. lāks natūra´lā. leks nâčɜrâ´lē. *n.* "Natural law." A law that codifies a principle of human conduct demanded by a divine power or consistent with a posited natural moral order. *Compare with* **Ius naturale.**

Lex neminem cogit ad vana seu impossibilia. lāks nā´mēnām kō´gēt ad wa´na sā´ū ēmpōssēbē´lē-a. leks ne´minum ka´jit âd vâ´nu sē´yū impasibi´lē-u. "The law compels no one toward vain or impossible things." A maxim meaning that a legal obligation, whether arising by treaty, statute, contract, or otherwise, that is impossible to perform must be excused. Alternative phrases are **Lex non cogit ad impossibilia; Lex non intendit aliquid impossibile;** and **Quod vanum et inutile est, lex non requirit.** *Compare with* **Impossibilium nulla obligatio est** and **Impotentia excusat legem.** *See also* **Lex nil frustra facit** and **Lex non cogit ad inutilia.**

Lex nil facit frustra. lāks nēl fa´kēt frūs´tra. leks nil fâ´sit frus´tru. "The law does nothing in vain." A maxim meaning that the law will not compel an act that would with great probability be frustrated, ineffectual, or pointless. Alternative phrases are **Lex nil frustra facit** and **Lex non cogit ad inutilia.** *See also* **Impossibilium nulla obligatio est, Impotentia excusat legem, Lex neminem cogit ad vana seu impossibilia,** and **Lex non cogit ad impossibilia.**

Lex nil frustra facit. lāks nēl frūs´tra fa´kēt. leks nil frus´tru fâ´sit. "The law does nothing in vain." An alternative formulation of **Lex nil facit frustra.**

Lex non cogit ad impossibilia. lāks nōn kō´gēt ad ēmpōssēbē´lē-a. leks nan ka´jit âd impasibi´lē-u. "The law does not compel one to impossible things." An alternative phrase for **Lex neminem cogit ad vana seu impossibilia.**

Lex non cogit ad inutilia. lāks nōn kō´gēt ad ēnūtē´lē-a. leks nan ka´jit âd inyūti´lē-u. "The law does not compel one to useless things." An alternative phrase for **Lex nil frustra facit.**

Lex non intendit aliquid impossibile. lāks nōn ēntān´dēt a´lēkwd ēmpōssē´bēlā. leks nan inten´dit â´likwid impasi´bulē. "The law does not intend anything impossible." An alternative phrase for **Lex neminem cogit ad vana seu impossibilia.**

Lex non oritur ex iniuria. lāks nōn ō´rētūr āks ēnyū´rē-a. leks nan ō´ritɜr eks injɜ´rē-u. "The law does not arise from wrongdoing." A maxim meaning that one cannot change the law merely by violating it. Generally, customary international law only changes with long, consistent, and widespread change in state practice.

Lex non scripta. lāks nōn skrēp´ta. leks nan skrip´tu. *n.* "Unwritten law." A term denoting customary law that has not been codified in any treaty or convention. An alternative term is **Ius non scriptum.**

Lex ordinandi. lāks ōrdēnan´dē. leks ōrdinân´dī. *n.* "Law of ordering." (1) Law relating to the procedures used before a tribunal (as opposed to the substantive law governing the dispute being litigated or arbitrated). (2) An alternative term for **Lex fori.** The procedural law of the forum usually governs a trial or arbitration regardless of the substantive law applied by the tribunal.

Lex originis. lāks ōrē´gēnēs. leks ōri´jinis. *n.* "The law of origination." The law of the jurisdiction in which property originated. For example, if intellectual property was first invented or fixed on a tangible medium in State A, and the alleged infringement occurred in State B, it is permissible for a court of State B seised of an infringement claim to apply its own law (*lex fori*) instead of the law of State A (*lex originis*). *See also* **Lex loci protectionis.**

Lex pacificatoria. lāks pakēfēkatō´rē-a. leks pâsifikutō´rē-u. *n. Neo.* "Pacific law." The law relating to agreements or treaties terminating a state of war or establishing a permanent peace between states or between states and private armed groups. *See* Christine Bell, On the Law of Peace: Peace Agreements and The *Lex Pacificatoria* (2008).

Lex patriae. lāks pat´rē-ī. leks pāt´rē-ā. *n.* "Law of the nation." The national law of a state.

Lex patrimonii. lāks patrēmō´nē-ē. leks pâtrimō´nī. *n.* "Law of paternal estate." The law of the jurisdiction having the greatest sovereign authority over the subject matter in question.

Lex posterior. lāks pōstā´rēōr. leks pōstē´rē-ɜr. *n.* "Later law." (1) A law or agreement adopted or effective later than another law or agreement. In general, a later law is presumed to supersede a prior, conflicting law on the same subject. *E.g.*, "Colombia points out that, in the present case, the argument that the Pact of Bogotá takes precedence is even stronger since the optional clause declarations of Nicaragua and Colombia [accepting the jurisdiction of the PCIJ] were made before the entry into force of the Pact of Bogotá. Therefore, the Pact of Bogotá is not only *lex specialis* but also *lex posterior.*" *Territorial and Maritime Dispute* (Nicar. v. Colom.), I.C.J. Case No. 124, Judgment of Dec. 13, 2007, ¶ 125, 47 I.L.M. 5. *Compare with* **Vetus ius.** (2) The law effective after a specific event, especially the act to which the law is being applied. For example, based on human rights principles of due process of law, a defendant in a criminal case cannot generally be convicted of violating a *lex posterior*. *See also* **Lex prospicit, non respicit** and **Nullum**

crimen sine lege. (3) An abbreviation of **Lex posterior derogat (legi) priori.** *Contrast with* **Lex anterior.**

Lex posterior derogat (legi) priori. lāks pōstā´rēōr dā´rōgat (lā´gē) prēō´rē. leks pōstē´rē-ɜr de´rōgât (le´jī) prīō´rī. "A later law repeals an earlier (law)." A maxim meaning that a legal rule arising after a conflicting legal rule prevails over the earlier rule to the extent of the conflict. The principle may apply both to customary rules of law and to provisions of conflicting treaties between the same parties. It is sometimes referred to by way of abbreviation as the **Lex posterior** principle. *But see* **Lex posterior generalis non derogat priori specialis.** *See also* **Lex specialis derogat legi generali.**

Lex posterior generalis non derogat priori specialis. lāks pōstā´rēōr gānāra´lēs nōn dā´rōgat prēō´rē spākē-a´lēs. leks pōstē´rē-ɜr jenɜrâ´lis nan de´rōgât prīō´rī spešâ´lis. "A later, general law does not repeal an earlier, specialized law." A principle according to which a rule of *lex specialis* that conflicts with a later general treaty provision or rule of customary law is not usually considered to be repealed or amended. The rationale for this rule is that, in adopting general rules, the international community should not be assumed to intend to expunge preexisting nuances of the law. *But see* **Lex posterior derogat legi priori.** *See also* **Lex specialis derogat legi generali.**

Lex praevia(, stricta, scripta, et certa). lāks prī´wē-a(, strēk´ta, skrēp´ta, āt kār´ta). leks prē´vē-u(, strik´tu, skrip´tu, et sɜr´tu). *n.* "Prior(, strict, written, and settled) law." Law that fulfills the legality requirement in being antecedent, published, clear, and authoritative on the legality or illegality of an act. These criteria are often considered preconditions for finding a defendant liable for a criminal act under human rights principles of due process of law. An alternative spelling is **Lex previa.** *See also* **Nulla poena sine lege** and **Nullum crimen sine lege.**

Lex previa(, stricta, scripta, et certa). An alternative spelling of **Lex praevia(, stricta, scripta et certa).**

Lex privata. lāks prēwa´ta. leks prīvā´tu. *n.* "Private law." In Roman law, a contract rule binding only on parties to the agreement in which the rule appears. This term should not be confused with the concept of "private international law."

Lex prospicit non respicit. lāks prōs´pēkēt nōn rās´pēkēt. leks prōspi´sit nan respi´sit. "The law looks forward, not backward." A maxim meaning that laws are generally deemed or presumed not to have retroactive effect. In the case of international criminal law, this rule is generally considered mandatory under the doctrine *nullum crimen sine lege. See also* **Ex post facto, Lex posterior,** and **Nullum crimen sine lege.**

L

Lex publica. lāks pūb´lēka. leks pub´liku. *n.* "Public law." In Roman law, published legislation binding on the populace at large.

Lex rei (sitae). An abbreviation of **Lex loci rei (sitae).**

Lex respicit aequitatem. lāks rāspē´kēt īkwēta´tām. leks respi´sit ekwitā´tum. "The law considers equity." A maxim meaning that, in applying law, a tribunal should consider and incorporate principles of equity to avoid injustice. *Compare with* **Aequitas nunquam contra venit legem.**

Lex Ripuaria. lāks rēpūa´rē-a. leks ripyū-e´rē-u. *N.* "Law of the Ripuarians." The early medieval codification of the customary law of the Ripuarian Franks (a tribe of Franks inhabiting the mid-Rhine river area), completed in the seventh century. The *Lex Ripuaria* is based on the **Lex Salica** and strongly influenced later codes, such as the **Lex Saxonum.** This is one of the **Leges barbarorum.**

Lex Romana Burgundionum. lāks rōma´na būrgūndēō´nūm. leks rōmâ´nu bɜrgundēō´num. *N.* "Roman Law of the Burgundians." The early medieval codification of the law of the Burgundians (*see* **Lex Burgundionum**) governing relations between Roman subjects living in Burgundian territory. The code was strongly influenced by Roman law and dates to the seventh century at the latest. This is one of the **Leges barbarorum.**

Lex Romana Curiensis. lāks rōma´na kūrē-ān´sēs. leks rōmâ´nu kɜrē-en´zis. *N.* "Roman Law of the Chur." The early medieval codification of the law of the Germanic peoples inhabiting eastern Switzerland governing relations between Roman subjects living in the duchy of Chur, completed between the eighth and mid-ninth centuries. The code was strongly influenced by Roman law and the **Lex Romana Visigothorum.** This is one of the **Leges barbarorum.**

Lex Romana Visigothorum. lāks rōma´na wēsēgōt-hō´rūm. leks rōmâ´nu vizigaθō´rum. *N.* "Roman Law of the Visigoths." The early medieval codification of the law of the Visigoths (*see* **Lex Visigothorum**), completed by Alaric II in 506 CE. This code governed relations between Roman subjects rather than Visigoths or between Romans and Visigoths. Also known as the Breviary of Alaric. This is one of the **Leges barbarorum.**

Lex Salica. lāks sa´lēka. leks sâ´liku. *N.* "Salic Law." The early medieval codification of the customary law of the Salian Franks (a Frankish tribe inhabiting the northern Netherlands), completed by Clovis I in the sixth century. The *Lex Salica* strongly influenced the laws later issued by the Frankish king Charlemagne (Carolus Magnus). This is one of the **Leges barbarorum.**

Lex Saxonum. lāks saksō´nūm. leks sâksō´num. *N.* "Saxon Law." The early medieval codification of the customary law of the Saxons (a confederation of Germanic tribes inhabiting Netherlands and Britain), issued by the Frankish king Charlemagne (Carolus Magnus) in 785 CE. The law was issued to help subdue the Saxons by blending Frankish law with Saxon pagan customs. This law was heavily influenced by the **Lex Ripuaria** and is one of the **Leges barbarorum**.

Lex scripta. lāks skrēp´ta. leks skrip´tu. *n.* [*pl.* **Leges scriptae.** lā´gās skrēp´tī. le´jēz skrip´tā.] "Written law." A written or codified law or treaty, as opposed to unwritten customary law. An alternative formulation is **Ius scriptum**. *Contrast with* **Lex non scripta**.

Lex semper dabit remedium. lāks sām´pār da´bēt rāmā´dē-ūm. leks sem´pɜr dā´bit rumē´dē-um. "The law will always give a remedy." A maxim meaning that every violation of a legal right should give rise to some form of remedy to the aggrieved party. *See, e.g.*, International Covenant on Civil and Political Rights art. 2(3), Dec. 9, 1966, 999 U.N.T.S. 171.

Lex simulata. lāks sēmūla´ta. leks simyūla´tu. *n. Neo.* "Simulated law." Documents, statements, or practices that appear superficially to be legally binding but in fact merely appear or are intended to appear to create binding norms. *Compare with* **Lex imperfecta**.

Lex situs. lāks sē´tūs. leks sī´tus OR -si´tus. *n.* "The law of position." The law of the jurisdiction in which the property that is the subject of litigation is located. *Compare with* **Lex (loci) rei (sitae)**. *See also* **Lex fori et situs**.

Lex societatis. lāks sōkē-āta´tēs. leks sōsī-etā´tis. *n.* "The law of the society." The law governing a defined group, such as a group of state members of an intergovernmental organization. With some exceptions, such law does not generally bind nonmembers of the organization.

Lex specialis. lāks spākē-a´lēs. leks spešâ´lis. *n.* "Special law." Law unique to a particular regime or applicable in specific scenarios, such as international trade law disciplines or international humanitarian law, as opposed to law generally applicable in a variety of international relations, such as general rules of treaty interpretation or state liability for wrongful acts. *E.g.*, "The test of what is an arbitrary deprivation of life [during armed conflict]...fails to be determined by the applicable *lex specialis*, namely, the law applicable in armed conflict which is designed to regulate the conduct of hostilities." *Advisory Opinion Concerning the Legality of the Threat or Use of Nuclear Weapons*, 1996 I.C.J. Rep. 226, ¶ 25. *Contrast with* **Lex generalis**. *See also* **Lex specialis derogat legi generali** and **Lex posterior generalis non derogat priori specialis**.

Lex specialis derogat legi generali. lāks spākē-a´lēs dā´rōgat lā´gē gānāra´lē. leks spešâ´lis de´rōgât le´jī jenɜrâ´lī. "Special law repeals general laws." A principle according to which a rule of *lex specialis* is deemed to apply notwithstanding contrary general principles of international law. The priority given to *lex specialis* is considered justified by the fact that the *lex specialis* is intended to apply in specific circumstances regardless of the rules applicable more generally where those circumstances may be absent. *See also* **Lex posterior generalis non derogat priori specialis, Lex posterior derogat legi priori**, and **Lex specialis.**

Lex sportiva (internationalis). lāks spōrtē´wa (ēntārnatēōna´lēs). leks spōrti´vu (intɜrnâšunâ´lis). *n. Neo.* "The (international) law of sports." (1) The international laws and regulations relating to athletic contests, such as the Olympic Games or World Cup. (2) The jurisprudence of international tribunals on matters relating to sports, especially that of the Court of Arbitration for Sport. *See* Gérald Simon, PUISSANCE SPORTIVE ET ORDRE JURIDIQUE ÉTATIQUE (Paris: Librairie générale de droit et de jurisprudence ed., 1990).

Lex superior. lāks sūpā´rēōr. leks sūpē´rēōr. *n.* "Higher law." (1) A body of law of greater legitimacy than another body of law. (2) A body of law that supersedes another, conflicting body of law. *Contrast with* **Lex inferior.**

Lex talionis. lāks talēō´nēs. leks tâlēō´nis. *n.* "The law of retaliation." A law requiring punishment of a crime no greater than, or that mirrors or is proportional to, the crime itself. The term derives from a Roman law in which a false accusation that caused the accused to be unjustly tortured would, upon discovery, subject the accuser to torture himself or herself. Earlier examples of similar laws may be found in the Torah's Exodus 21:23–25, the Code of Hammurabi, and elsewhere. *Compare with* **Ius talionis.**

Lex uno ore omnes alloquitur. lāks ū´nō ō´rā ōm´nās allō´kwētūr. leks ū´nō ō´rē am´nēz ulō´kwitɜr. "The law speaks to all with one mouth." A maxim meaning that all persons are treated equally under the law regardless of power, wealth, or connections. The equality of all persons before the law has been adopted as a foundational principle in most major international human rights instruments. *See, e.g.*, Universal Declaration of Human Rights art. 1, G.A. Res. 217 A(III), UN Doc. A/810 (Dec. 10, 1948); International Covenant on Civil and Political Rights arts. 2(1), 3, Dec. 9, 1966, 999 U.N.T.S. 171.

Lex validitatis. lāks walēda´tēs. leks vuliditā´tis. *n.* "Law of validity." The principle that contracts entered into in one state are presumptively valid and enforceable in other states absent a conflicting public policy in the state in which recognition or enforcement is sought.

L

Lex Visigothorum. lāks wēsēgōt-hō´rūm. leks vizigaθō´rum. *N.* "Visigothic Law." The early medieval codification of the customary law of the Visigoths (a Germanic tribe inhabiting Spain and France south of the Loire River), originally compiled by King Chindasuinth in 642 or 643 CE. Later versions of this code abolished the distinction between Visigoths and Romans that gave rise to the **Lex Romana Visigothorum**. This is one of the **Leges barbarorum**.

Liber amicorum. lē´bār amēkō´rūm. lī´bɜr- OR li´bɜr âmikō´rum. *n.* "Book of the friends." A volume containing essays in honor of a celebrated person, or sometimes organization or subject. The topics treated in the essays may be unrelated or may relate to the work of the celebrated person or subject. A *liber amicorum* is sometimes referred to by its German name, *Festschrift*.

Libertas. lēbār´tas. li´bɜrtas. *n.* "Liberty." Freedom; liberty.

Liberum veto. lē´bārūm wā´tō. li´bɜrum vē´tō. *n.* "Free veto." A legally uninhibited right to veto a decision or law. The use of a *liberum veto* rule is not common in international law, but it is sometimes used when majoritarian decision-making threatens the perceived vital interests of some members of the organization—a notable example being the *liberum veto* of the permanent members of the UN Security Council on nonprocedural matters. *See* UN CHARTER art. 27(3). The term appears to originate in seventeenth-century Poland, where the *sejm* (parliament) adopted a *liberum veto* procedure giving each member a right to veto a bill under consideration as well as any other legislative act during the session. *See* J.B. Bury, 8 CAMBRIDGE MEDIEVAL HISTORY 566–67 (C.W. Previté-Orton and Z.N. Brooke eds., 1936).

Licentia. lēkān´tē-a. līsen´šu. *n.* "License." Permission; authorization.

Liga. lē´ga. li´gu. *n.* "A tying together." A confederation or league; an alliance.

Ligius. lē´gē-ūs. li´jus. *n.* "Liege." A person owing a duty of loyalty to another (usually, to a sovereign).

Lingua franca. lēn´gūa fran´ka. liŋ´wu frân´ku. *n.* "Frankish language." A language widely used as a common means of communication among peoples of diverse speech. Examples include Latin in ancient and medieval Europe, Arabic in the medieval Islamic Empire, and French from the seventeenth century in Europe until modern times. *E.g.*, "[T]here is no modern *lingua franca* in international commercial and legal relations, despite the dominance of English." Opinion of Advocate General Trstenjak, *Ingenieurburo Michael Weiss & Partner GbR v. Industrie- & Handelskammer Berlin*, E.C.J. Case No. C-14/07, ¶ 58.

Lis. lēs. lis. *n.* "Lawsuit." A dispute; a lawsuit.

Lis alibi pendens. lēs a´lēbē pān´dāns. lis â´libī pen´denz. *n.* "Lawsuit pending elsewhere." A lawsuit or dispute currently under consideration by a tribunal in another jurisdiction. In some circumstances, *lis alibi pendens* functions as a defense to duplicative litigation in a forum other than the one originally seised of the dispute. The term is sometimes, though rarely, abbreviated **Lis pendens.**

Lis pendens. lēs pān´dāns. lis pen´denz. *n.* "Pending lawsuit." (1) A lawsuit currently under consideration by a tribunal. *Compare with* **Lis sub iudice.** *See also* **Pendente lite.** (2) In common law jurisdictions, an encumbrance on property filed for the duration of a trial to secure the defendant's assets against an eventual judgment. (3) An abbreviation of **Lis alibi pendens.**

Lis sub iudice. lēs sŭb yū´dēkā. lis sub jū´disē OR -jū´dīs. *n.* "Lawsuit before the judge." A case currently under consideration by a tribunal. *Compare with* **Lis pendens.** *See also* **Sub iudice.**

Literae mortuae. lē´tārī mōr´tū-ī. li´tɜrā mōr´čū-ā. *n. pl.* "Dead letters." Words in a legal instrument having no meaning or purpose; filler language. In international treaty interpretation practice, there is a strong presumption against interpreting treaty provisions as *literae mortuae* except in preambular language. *See South West Africa Cases* (Eth. v. S. Afr.; Liber. v. S. Afr.), 1966 I.C.J. Rep. 6, 125, ¶ 38 (Second Phase) (separate opinion of Judge Van Wyk).

Litus est quousque maximus fluctus a mari pervenit. lē´tūs āst kwō-ūs´kwā ma´ksēmūs flūk´tūs a ma´rē pārwā´nēt. li´tus est kwōs´kwē mâ´ksimus fluk´tus ā ma´rī pɜrve´nit. "The coast is the point up to which the highest tide from the sea reaches." An archaic maxim, originating in Justinian's *Digest* (50.16.96), meaning that, for the purpose of measuring the breadth of the territorial sea for determining jurisdiction under the law of the sea, measurement begins at the high-water line along the coast. The *Digest* attributes the maxim to one of Cicero's pronouncements as an arbitrator. *But see* the UN Convention on the Law of the Sea art. 5, Dec. 10, 1982, 21 I.L.M. 1245 (1982).

Litus maris. lē´tūs ma´rēs. li´tus me´ris. *n.* "Shore of the sea." (1) The shore of the sea between the neap high tide and low tide. (2) The coastal area of the sea generally.

Loc. cit. An abbreviation of **Loco citato.**

Loco citato. lō´kō kēta´tō. lō´kō sitā´tō. *adj.* "In the place cited." A citation signal referring to a reference previously cited in the same work of authorship. Commonly abbreviated **Loc. cit.**

L

Loco parentis. lō´kō parān´tēs. lō´kō paren´tis. An abbreviation of **In loco parentis.**

Locus. lō´kūs. lō´kus. *n.* "Place." (1) Venue. (2) Place. (3) Location.

Locus actum regit. lō´kūs ak´tūm rā´gēt. lō´kus âk´tum re´jit. "The place rules the act." A maxim of conflict of laws jurisprudence meaning that the law of the jurisdiction in which a wrongful act occurred, or where a contract was concluded, normally determines the legal consequences of the act or validity of the contract. An alternative formulation is **Locus regit actum.** *See also* **Lex loci actus.**

Locus actus. lō´kūs ak´tūs. lō´kus âk´tus. *n.* "Place of the act." The place where an act occurred; the place where a contract was performed. *See also* **Lex loci actus.**

Locus classicus. lō´kūs klas´sēkūs. lō´kus klâ´sikus. *n.* "Classic place." The paradigm or original of a thing or idea. *E.g.*, "The obligation to negotiate has been well defined by the Court in a passage of an Advisory Opinion which has become a *locus classicus.*" *Continental Shelf Case* (Tunis.-Libya), 1982 I.C.J. Rep. 18, 144 (Judge Gros, dissenting).

Locus contractus. lō´kūs kōntrak´tūs. lō´kus kantrâk´tus. *n.* "Place of the contract." The place was a contract was concluded. *See also* **Lex loci contractus.**

Locus criminis. lō´kūs krē´mēnēs. lō´kus kri´minis. *n.* "Place of the crime." The place where the crime was committed.

Locus damni. lō´kūs dam´nē. lō´kus dâm´nī. *n.* "The place of injury." The jurisdiction in which a wrongful injury occurred.

Locus delicti (commissi). lō´kūs dālēk´tē (kōmmēs´sē). lō´kus dulik´tī (kami´sī). *n.* "Place of the (committed) wrongdoing." The place where a wrongful or injurious act took place.

Locus in quo. lō´kūs ēn kwō. lō´kus in kwō. *n.* "Place in which." The place where the relevant event occurred.

Locus publicus. lō´kūs pūb´lēkūs. lō´kus pub´likus. *n.* "Public place." A place owned by the state or the community in common.

Locus regit actum. lō´kūs rā´gēt ak´tūm. lō´kus re´jit âk´tum. An alternative formulation of **Locus actum regit.**

Locus solutionis. lō´kūs sōlūtēō´nēs. lō´kus salūšō´nis. *n.* "Place of the solution." The place of performance of an obligation.

Locus standi. lō´kūs stan´dē. lō´kus stân´dī. *n.* "Place of standing." The place or tribunal where a party has standing to appear or bring an action.

L

Longa patientia trahitur ad consensum. lōn´ga patē-ān´tē-a tra´hētūr ad kōnsān´sūm. la´ɲu pāšen´šu trā´hitɜr âd kunsen´sum. "Long forbearance is interpreted as consent." A maxim meaning that longstanding toleration of a practice, arguably including a violation of a state's recognized right under international law, is construed as consent or agreement in the legality or acceptability of the practice in the absence of coercion or duress.

Longa possessio ius parit. lōn´ga pōssās´sēō yūs pa´rēt. la´ɲu puze´sēō jus pa´rit. "Long possession begets a right." A maxim meaning that a claim to territory or property is strengthened by the longstanding, peaceful, and uncontested possession of the property. *See also* **Uti possidetis.**

Lucrum cessans. lūk´rūm kās´sans. lūk´rum se´senz. *n. pl.* "Ceased profits." Lost profits resulting from the destruction of, damage to, or deprivation of an income-producing asset or nonperformance of an obligation. *E.g.*, "In Indonesian law, like in all systems of civil law, damages are to compensate the whole prejudice, whose two classical components are the loss suffered (*damnum emergens*) and the expected profits which are lost (*lucrum cessans*)." *Amco Asia Corp. v. Indonesia*, ICSID Case No. ARB/81/1, Award of Nov. 20, 1984, ¶ 266. *Contrast with* **Damnum emergens.**

Lux. lūks. luks. *n.* "Light." (1) Light. (2) Enlightenment. (3) Metaphorically, the source of knowledge or understanding.

M

M.Jur. An abbreviation of **Magister iuris.**

M.O. An abbreviation of **Modus operandi.**

Magister iuris. magēs´tär yū´rēs. mâ´jistɜr jɜ´ris. *n.* "Master of law." A postgraduate professional law degree first introduced by Oxford University and usually awarded after one year of study. Commonly abbreviated **M.Jur.**

Magister navis. magēs´tär na´wēs. mâ´jistɜr nâ´vis. *n.* "Master of the ship." A ship's master; the captain of a seagoing merchant vessel.

Magna Carta (Libertatum). mag´na kar´ta (lēbārta´tūm). mâg´nu kar´tu (libɜrtā´tum). *N.* "Great Charter (of Freedoms)." A charter executed in 1215 to resolve disagreements among Pope Innocent III and King John and his English barons about the scope of the English king's powers and the rights of the barons and freemen. The Magna Carta was renewed repeatedly during the medieval period and thereafter. Only a few provisions remain in force in England today, but the document exerted a substantial influence on the early constitutions of common law countries and on the foundational concepts of international human rights law.

Magna cum laude. mag´na kūm lô´dā. mâg´nu kum lăd OR -lă´dē. *adj.* or *adv. Neo.* "With great praise." With great distinction or honors. The term is commonly applied to a graduating student who has achieved notable academic distinction, more than a student who simply graduates *cum laude* but less than one who graduates *summa cum laude*. *See also* **Cum laude** and **Summa cum laude.**

Magnum opus. mag´nūm ō´pūs. mâg´num ō´pus. *n.* "Great work." An alternative formulation of **Opus magnum.**

Maiestas. mī-ās´tas. mâ´jestus. *n.* "Sovereign power." The sovereign power, comprised of **Dominium** and **Imperium**, to legislate or act publicly on behalf of a political entity.

Maior continet (in se) minus. ma´yōr kōntē´nāt (ēn sā) mē´nūs). mā´jur kan´tinet (in sā) mī´nus. "The greater includes (in itself) the lesser." An alternative phrase for **In eo quod plus sit semper inest et minus.**

Maius ius. ma´yūs yūs. mâ´jus jus. *n.* "Greater right." A right that is considered superior to another right.

Mala fide. ma´la fē´dā. mâ´lu fid OR -fī´dē. *adv.* "In bad faith." Done with injurious, immoral, or unlawful intent. *Compare with* **In malam partem** and **Malo animo.**

Mala fides. ma´la fē´dās. mâ´lu fī´dēz. *n.* "Bad faith." Injurious, immoral, or unlawful intent. *Contrast with* **Bona fides.**

Male captus bene detentus. ma´lā kap´tūs bā´nā dātān´tūs. mâ´lē kâp´tus be´nē dēten´tus. "Wrongly captured, well kept." A doctrine according to which the wrongfulness of an arrest or abduction does not negate the validity of detention or imprisonment. Under this doctrine, although jurisdiction over a defendant may have been acquired by the forum state through a violation of international law, such as an excess of enforcement jurisdiction, the forum state may nonetheless exercise its jurisdiction lawfully over the defendant once he is within its judicial jurisdiction. For example, if a person accused of violating the law of the forum state is illegally apprehended on the high seas or forcibly abducted from a different, nonconsenting country, the doctrine of *male captus bene detentus* could be invoked with the intention of defeating challenges to the legality of his subsequent trial. The doctrine is contested, however, and has not been consistently applied by national or international tribunals.

Mala in se. *See* **Malum in se.**

Mala prohibita. *See* **Malum prohibitum.**

Maleficium. malāfē´kē-ūm. mâlefi´šum. *n.* "Harm." An injury or harm. *Compare with* **Dolus.**

Malo animo. ma´lō a´nēmō. mâ´lō â´nimō. *adv.* "With evil intent." Done with the intent to cause harm or to violate the law. *Compare with* **Mala fide.**

Malum in se. ma´lūm ēn sā. mâ´lum in sā. *n.* [*pl.* **Mala in se.** ma´la ēn sā. mâ´lu in sā.] "An evil in itself." An act that is considered ethically wrong or wrong under a theory of natural law. *Contrast with* **Malum prohibitum.**

M

Malum necessarium. ma´lūm nākāssa´rē-ūm. mâ´lum nesese´rē-um. *n.* "A necessary evil." A condition or situation thought to be unfortunate but unavoidable.

Malum prohibitum. ma´lūm prōhē´bētūm. mâ´lum prōhi´bitum. *n.* [*pl.* **Mala prohibita.** ma´la prōhē´bēta. mâ´lu prōhi´bitu.] "An evil by prohibition." An act that is illegal because of a specific law forbidding it, but that does not violate any tenet of ethics or theory of natural law. *Contrast with* **Malum in se.**

Mandamus. manda´mūs. mândā´mus. *v.* (commonly used as a *n.*) "We command." An order from a tribunal, usually from an appellate tribunal ordering a lower tribunal to perform a ministerial function.

Mandatum. manda´tūm. mândā´tum. *n.* "Command; contract." (1) In maritime law, a contract by which the owner of property authorizes an agent to sell or otherwise dispose of the property without fee or reward. (2) A command given from a superior to an inferior, such as a governor might issue to his officials. (3) In Roman law, a contract. An *actio mandati* at Roman law was a lawsuit premised on the nonperformance of a contract. *See also* **Accomenda.**

Manifesta probatione non indigent. manēfās´ta prōbatēō´nā nōn ēndē´gānt. mânifes´tu prōbāšō´nē nan in´dijent. "Obvious facts need no proof." A maxim meaning that, in a litigation, there is no need to produce evidence to prove what is self-evident or well known to everyone.

Manu militari. ma´nū mēlēta´rē. mâ´nū milite´rī. *adv.* "By the hand of the military." By armed force; by military action.

Manu propria. ma´nū prōp´rē-a. mâ´nū prap´rē-u. *adv.* "By one's own hand." By one's own act.

Mare. ma´rā. ma´rē. *n.* "Sea." (1) A sea. (2) The high seas; an alternative term for **Altum mare.**

Mare adiacens. ma´rā ad´yakāns. ma´rē âdjā´senz. *n.* "Adjacent sea." The area of sea adjacent to the littoral coast of a state. *E.g.*, "[T]he delimitation of sea areas is considered from a legal point of view when it concerns the question of *mare adjacens.*" *Fisheries Jurisdiction* (U.K. v. Ice.), 1974 I.C.J. Rep. 3, 80 (separate opinion of Judge De Castro).

Mare altum. ma´rā al´tūm. ma´rē âl´tum. *n.* "High sea." An alternative formulation of **Altum mare.**

Mare apertum. ma´rā apār´tūm. ma´rē âpɜr´tum. *n.* "Open sea." An alternative term for **Mare liberum.**

Mare clausum. ma´rā klô´sūm. ma´rē klă´zum. *n.* "Closed sea." (1) A sea the access to which by seagoing vessels is restricted. (2) An expression denoting the idea that the seas or waterways may not be traversed without the consent of states with powerful navies that have staked a claim to the traversed area. *Contrast with* **Mare apertum** and **Mare liberum.**

Mare Clausum Sive de Dominio Maris. ma´rā klô´sūm sē´wā dā dōmē´nēō ma´rēs. ma´rē klă´zum si´vē dā dōmi´nēō ma´ris. *N.* "A Closed Sea Follows from Maritime Sovereignty." The title of the treatise on international law of the sea written in 1635 by English jurist John Selden (1584–1654).

Mare liberum. ma´rā lē´bārūm. ma´rē li´bɜrum. *n.* "Free sea." (1) The high seas; a sea open to unimpeded navigation by vessels of all states. *Compare with* **Altum mare.** (2) An expression denoting the idea that the high seas and oceans may be traversed by all without interference or territorial claim by any state. An alternative term is **Mare apertum.** *Contrast with* **Mare clausum.**

Mare nostrum. ma´rā nōs´trūm. ma´rē nas´trum. *n.* "Our sea." The high seas conceived as the common heritage of humankind. *See* Philip Allott and John Boroughs, Mare Nostrum*: A New International Law of the Sea*, 86 Am. J. Int'l L. 764 (1992).

Maritima incrementa. marē´tēma ēnkrāmān´ta. meritī´mu inkrumen´tu. *n.* "Marine increase." Land gained from the sea over time by gradual alluvial accretion.

Maxime paci sunt contraria vis et iniuria. ma´ksēmā pa´kē sūnt kōntra´rē-a wēs āt ēnyū´rē-a. mâ´ksimē pâ´sī sunt kantre´rē-u vis et injɜ´rē-u. "The greatest opponents of peace are force and wrongdoing." An alternative formulation of **Paci sunt maxime contraria vis et iniuria.**

Mea culpa. mā´a kūl´pa. mā´u kɜl´pu. *n.* "My fault." (1) An admission that an act or omission was the fault of the speaker or author. (2) By extension, an apology.

Media concludendi. mā´dē-a kōnklūdān´dē. mē´dē-u kanklūden´dī. *n.* "Means of concluding." The means of argumentation; the links in a chain of reasoning.

Media sententia. mā´dē-a sāntān´tē-a. mē´dē-u senten´šu. *n.* "Middle thought." A moderate view; a view between two extremes.

Medio tempore. mā´dēō tām´pōrā. mē´dēō tempō´rē. *adv.* "In middle time." Meanwhile; in the meantime.

Medium filum acquae. mā´dē-ūm fē´lūm ak´kwī. mē´dē-um fī´lum a´kwā. *n.* "The middle thread of water." The geographical middle of a watercourse (such as a river or stream) as measured by a line equidistant from the river banks that divides the watercourse into two halves of equal width. The *medium filum* *aquae* is sometimes used for delimiting a boundary between two owners of territory on opposite sides of the watercourse. In international practice, the *filum aquae* and the thalweg (the middle of the navigable fluvial channel) are alternative means of delimiting a boundary using a watercourse, with the latter usually preferred because of its navigational importance. *E.g.*, "A line midway between the banks of a river, known as the *medium filum acquae*,...is easily established, for every point of the midline is equidistant from the nearest points on the opposite shores." *Georgia v. South Carolina*, 497 U.S. 376, 400–01 (1990). Sometimes abbreviated **Filum acquae**. *See also* **Usque ad filum acquae**.

Melior est causa possidentis. mā´lēōr āst kô´sa pōssēdān´tēs. me´lē-ɜr est kă´zu pōsiden´tis. "The possessor's case is better." An alternative phrase for **In pari causa possessor potior haberi debet**.

Melior est condicio defendentis. mā´lēōr āst kōndē´kēō dāfāndān´tēs. me´lē-ɜr est kundi´šō defenden´tis. "The defendant's condition is better." An alternative phrase for **In pari delicto potior est condicio defendantis**.

Melior est condicio possidentis. mā´lēōr āst kōndē´kēō pōssēdān´tēs. me´lē-ɜr est kundi´šō pōsiden´tis. "The possessor's condition is better." An alternative phrase for **In pari causa possessor potior haberi debet**.

Mens legis. māns lā´gēs. menz le´jis. *n.* "Intent of the law." The intent or spirit of the law.

Mens rea. māns rā´a. menz rā´u. *n.* "A guilty thought." The element of mental guilt necessary for a finding of criminality, except in strict or absolute liability offenses. Most crimes require not only the performance of a prohibited physical act (*actus reus*), but wrongful intent (*mens rea*) as well. *E.g.*, "The coordinated fashion and number of crimes is an indication of the existence of an organized scheme. Kordic had the necessary *mens rea* since he intended the crimes or accepted the risk that they would be committed." *Prosecutor v. Kordic*, I.C.T.Y. Case No. IT-95-14, Judgment of Feb. 26, 2001, ¶ 832. *Compare with* **Animus malus**, **Dolus malus**, and **Scienter**. *See also* **Actus reus**.

Mercenarius. mārkāna´rē-ūs. mɜrsene´rē-us. *n.* "Mercenary." (1) A mercenary; a professional soldier working for a government other than that of his own state of nationality. (2) An employee; hired labor.

Merces. mār´kās. mɜr´sēz. *n.* "Wealth." (1) Wealth; money. (2) In Roman law, payment made for goods or services either pursuant to a contract or gratuitously as a gift or honorarium.

Mero motu. mā´rō mō´tū. mē´rō mō´tū. *adv.* "By mere motion." An alternative term for **Sua sponte.**

Merx. mārks. mɜɪks. *n. pl.* "Merchandise." Merchandise; commercial goods.

Meum. mā´ūm. mā´um OR mē´um. *adj.* (often used as a *n.*) "My." That which is mine, as opposed to that which does not belong to me. The expression "*meum* and *tuum*," or "*meum versus tuum*," generally refers to the concept of individual private property ownership. *E.g.*, "By means of a newly conceived law of the sea made within the social processes of a newly conceived international society, humanity can participate in and with the sea space of the world with unlimited sophistication and sensitivity, not stifled by the artificial bonds of *meum* and *tuum*, not condemned to the rule of the past over the future, but free to create a social future of material and moral progress." Philip Allott and John Boroughs, Mare Nostrum*: A New International Law of the Sea*, 86 AM. J. INT'L L. 764, 779 (1992). *Contrast with* **Tuum.**

Miles. mē´lās. mī´lēz. *n.* [*pl.* **Milites.** mē´lētās. mi´litēz.] "Soldier." (1) A soldier. (2) A soldier of noble rank; a knight.

Minus petita. mē´nūs pātē´ta. mī´nus peti´tu. *adv.* "Less than requested." An alternative term for **Infra petita.**

Minus solvit qui tardius solvit. mē´nūs sōl´wēt kwē tar´dē-ūs sōl´wēt. mī´nus sal´vit kwī- OR –kwī tar´dē-us sal´vit. "He who pays later pays less." A maxim, originating in Justinian's *Digest* (50.15.12.1), meaning that a debtor who pays its creditor later in time pays less than the amount owed, in the sense that the debtor deprives the creditor of the interest on the debt (in economic terms, the time value of the money) that would have accrued to the creditor had payment been made when originally due. An alternative formulation is **Qui tardius solvit minus solvit.** *See also* **Ex mora** and **Mora.**

Mirabile dictu. mēra´bēlā dēk´tū. mirâ´bilē dik´tū. *adj.* "Wonderful to relate." Wonderful to tell. In modern usage, the phrase is sometimes, though not always, used ironically. *E.g.*, "Then of course, you turn it round the other way because you go on to say, '*Mirabile dictu* both [Pakistan and Malaysia, which provided 93.4% of the initial funding for the International Criminal Tribunal for the Former Yugoslavia,] have been given the right to appoint judges to the panel,' so the suggestion there is because they gave the money, they got the judges." Transcript of Mar. 18, 2003, at 13802, *Prosecutor v. Stakic*, ICTY Case No. IT-97-24-T.

Mitiori sensu. mētēō´rē sān´sū. mišō´rī sen´sū. *adv.* "In the milder sense." An abbreviation of **In mitiori sensu.**

M

Mobilia sequuntur personam. mōbē´lē-a sākū-ūn´tūr pārsō´nam. mōbi´lē-u sekwun´tɜr pɜrsō´num. "Movable things follow the person." A maxim meaning that, when the owner of personal property (and not real property) changes his domicile, the law of the new domicile governs the property even if the property is physically located in a different jurisdiction. This maxim expresses an exception applicable to certain specific matters (such as succession) rather than the rule, which is that a state may exercise jurisdiction over, and apply its law to, any personal property within its borders. *E.g.*, "If *A* dies domiciled in the United States of America, leaving movable property locally situate in England, the latter country has complete jurisdiction over the property, but the law of England, in order to decide on whom the property devolves on the death of *A* will not apply the English law of succession, but will ascertain and apply the American law. In other words, it is the law of England—not the law of America—that applies the principle of *mobilia sequuntur personam* in exercising its jurisdiction over the movable property in England, the locus of the latter remaining unchanged; in no sense could the property be described as 'within America.'" *Alberta (Provincial Treasurer) v. Kerr*, [1933] A.C. 710, ¶ 18 (Can.).

Modus et conventio vincunt legem. mō´dūs āt kōnwān´tēō wēn´kūnt lā´gām. mō´dus et kanven´šō vin´kunt le´jem. "A course of dealing and agreement conquer law." A maxim meaning that parties to an agreement or custom may establish practices (*e.g.*, by treaty) that trump contrary rules of law as between themselves. This maxim applies not only to private contracts, but to treaties that may derogate from customary international law without affecting the rights of third parties. The usual exception applies to rules of *ius cogens*.

Modus operandi. mō´dūs ōpāran´dē. mō´dus apɜrân´dī. *n.* "Manner of operating." The habitual or traditional means or procedure by which one pursues or achieves one's goals. Sometimes abbreviated **M.O.**

Modus procedendi. mō´dūs prōkādān´dē. mō´dus prōsuden´dī. *n.* "Manner of proceeding." The order in which contracting or treaty parties are to perform their respective obligations.

Modus transferrendi. mō´dūs transfārrān´dē. mō´dus trânsfɜren´dī. *n.* "Manner of transfer." The means by which an instrument or property is transferred.

Modus vacandi. mō´dūs vakan´dē. mō´dus vukân´dī. *n.* "Manner of vacating." The method one uses for renouncing one's own claims to or legal rights in something.

Modus vivendi. mō´dūs wēwān´dē. mō´dus viven´dī. *n.* "Manner of living." A provisional agreement intended to be temporary but binding for its duration. In international practice, a *modus vivendi* is usually adopted by states with the intent of preserving a *status quo* until a more detailed or permanent treaty can be concluded. The *modus vivendi* may or may not state its provisional character explicitly and may take the form of an exchange of notes or of an executed agreement or treaty. *E.g.*, "Suriname asserts that based on the oil concession practice of the Parties, Guyana's actions were in breach of the 1989 *modus vivendi* and signalled an aggressive posture by Guyana." *Guyana v. Suriname*, Perm. Ct. Arb., Award of Sept. 17, 2007, ¶ 183, 47 I.L.M. 166 (2008).

Mora. mō´ra. mō´ru. *n.* "Delay." A delay. In Roman law, *mora* signified a willful delay in fulfilling a contractual obligation that could give rise to an obligation to compensate for the delay, such as the payment of moratory interest on a mature debt. *See also* **Ex mora** and **Minus solvit qui tardius solvit.**

More uxorio. mō´rā ūksō´rēō. mō´rē ugzō´rēō. *adv.* "In the manner of a married woman." In a relationship not formalized as a marriage but sufficiently comparable to impose duties on and create at least some rights similar to a marriage between the partners, as when romantically involved persons have cohabited over a long period. Such relationships may have consequences under conflict of laws principles.

Motu proprio. mō´tū prōp´rēō. mō´tū prap´rēō. *adv.* "By its own motion." An alternative formulation of **Proprio (suo) motu.**

Mutatio libelli. mūta´tēō lēbāl´lē. myūtā´šō lī´belī. *n.* "Modification of the complaint." An amendment to or revised version of a complaint or petition.

Mutatis mutandis. mūta´tēs mūtan´dēs. myūtā´tis myūtân´dis. *adv.* "With the necessary changes." A phrase denoting that a statement applies to matters or things other than those mentioned, with appropriate alterations or adjustments as to the particularities or details. *E.g.*, "[I]t shall be recorded in an exchange of notes between the undersigned that the convention between Great Britain and Venezuela of October 29, 1834, which adopted and confirmed, *mutatis mutandis*, the treaty of April 18, 1825, between Great Britain and the State of Colombia, shall be deemed to be renewed and confirmed." Protocol Between Great Britain and the United States of Venezuela Relating to the Settlement of British Claims and Other Matters, signed at Washington, D.C., Feb. 13, 1903, *in The Venezuelan Preferential Case* (Ger., Gr. Brit., & Italy v. Venez.), Perm. Ct. Arb. Award of Feb. 22, 1904, H.C.R. (Series 1), at 69 (Scott 1916).

Mutuus dissensus. mū´tū-ūs dēssān´sūs. myū´čū-us disen´sus. *n.* "Mutual disagreement." (1) A difference of opinion. (2) A dispute or the basis therefor.

N

N.B. An abbreviation of **Nota bene.**

n.l. An abbreviation of **Non liquet.**

Nasciturus pro iam nato habetur quotiens de commodis eius agitur. naskētū´rūs prō ē´am na´tō habā´tūr kwō´tē-āns dā kōm´mōdēs ā´yūs a´gētūr. nâšitɜ´rus prō jâm nā´tō hâ´betɜr kwō´tē-enz dā ka´mōdis e´jus â´jitɜr. "An unborn child is considered born when his interests are taken into account." A maxim, originating in Justinian's *Digest* (1.5.7), meaning that a person's interests define his or her relevance to the law and no interest can be disregarded once some interests are taken into account. It follows from this maxim that a person is defined from the law's point of view by the whole of his or her rights (and, correspondingly, duties).

Naulum. nô´lūm. nă´lum. *n. Gr.* "Fare." Passenger or freight fare; a shipper's fee for the maritime transportation of goods or persons.

Nauta. nô´ta. nă´tu. *n.* "Seaman." A seaman; a sailor.

Navicularius. nawēkūla´rē-ūs. nâvikyūle´rē-us. *n.* "Small ship; shipowner." The owner of a seagoing merchant vessel or freighter.

Navis. na´wēs. nâ´vis. *n.* "Ship." A seagoing vessel; a ship.

Ne bis in idem. nā bēs ēn ē´dām. nā bis in īd´um. "Not twice for the same thing." A principle of civil law dictating that no person should be tried twice for the same illegal act. The principle, sometimes called the "double jeopardy rule" in common law countries, has been incorporated into international criminal law. *See* Rome Statute of the International Criminal Court art. 20. An alternative formulation is **Non bis in idem.** An alternative phrase is **Nemo bis vexari pro (una et) eadem causa.** *Compare with* **Nemo bis punitur pro eodem delicto.**

N

Ne exeat (regno). nā āks´ā-at (rāg´nō). nā e´gzē-ât (reg´nō). *v.* "May he not depart (from the state)." (1) Any prohibition on departure from a territory. (2) An equitable writ or an order restraining a person from leaving a territory, usually issued against a defendant pending a criminal trial or against a person having temporary custody of a child pending a final custody decision. Also sometimes written in modern times as **Ne exeat republica**. *Contrast with* **Exeat**.

Ne exeat republica. nā āks´ā-at rāpūb´lēka. nā e´gzē-ât rēpub´liku. *imp. v.* "Do not let him depart from the republic." A modern alternative phrase for **Ne exeat (regno)**.

Ne impediatur legatio. nā ēmpādē-a´tūr lāga´tēō. nā impe´dē-ut3r legā´šō. "May the legation not be impeded." A maxim expressing the immunity of diplomatic persons and their papers to detention, civil suit, or arrest. This term may also apply to the premises of an embassy or, to a lesser extent, consulate. *See* Vienna Convention on Diplomatic Relations arts. 22, 27, 29–31, Apr. 18, 1961, 500 U.N.T.S. 95; Vienna Convention on Consular Relations arts. 31–35, 41, 43, 49–50, Apr. 24, 1963, 596 U.N.T.S. 261.

Ne iudex ultra petita partium. nā yū´dāks ūl´tra pātē´ta par´tē-ūm. nā jū´deks 3l´tru peti´tu par´tē-um. "May the judge not award beyond the demands of the parties." An alternative phrase for **Ne ultra petita (partium)**.

Ne plus ultra. nā plūs ūl´tra. nā plus 3l´tru. *n.* "No further." (1) The highest point capable of being reached or attained. (2) The pinnacle of achievement. (3) The point beyond which one cannot proceed.

Ne varietur. nā warē-ā´tūr. nā ve´rē-ut3r. *v. imp.* "May there be no variation." A form of initialing on a document by treaty negotiators to indicate that the document is authentic. The *ne varietur* initialing is not considered to convert the document from a nonbinding draft to binding treaty, but merely to indicate provisional agreement on the accuracy and authenticity of the negotiated text. *E.g.*, "[A]n *acte authentique* is an instrument certified by a third authority who is competent for the purpose. It has a public and permanent character. It is perfect in itself, without ratification. It is inserted in the minutes of the notaries, *ne varietur*." Ernest Satow, A Guide to Diplomatic Practice 110, § 176 (Neville Bland ed., 4th ed., 1957)

Nec vi nec clam nec precario. nāk wē nāk klam nāk prāka´rēō. nek vī nek klâm nek preka´rēō. *adv.* "Neither by force, nor secretly, nor by entreaty." An abbreviated form of **Possessio nec vi nec clam nec precario**.

Necessitas culpabilis. nākās´sētas kūlpa´bēlēs. nuse´sitas k3lpâ´bilis. *n.* "Culpable necessity." A harmful act that was factually necessary or unavoidable but that nonetheless reflects blame on the actor, such as when the actor's own prior negligence created the necessity of the act.

N

Necessitas facit lictum quod alias non est lictum. nākās´sētas fa´kēt lēk´tūm kwōd a´lē-as nōn āst lēk´tūm. nuse´sitas fâ´sit lik´tum kwad ā´lē-us nan est lik´tum. "Necessity makes lawful what is otherwise unlawful." An alternative phrase for **Necessitas non habet legem.**

Necessitas non habet legem. nākās´sētas nōn ha´bāt lā´gām. nuse´sitas nan hâ´bet le´jum. "Necessity has no law." A maxim meaning that the violation of a law may be excused by necessity. This is not a rule of general application in international law, but it may be applied in some exceptional cases for reasons of equity. Alternatively, it may be invoked for no better reason than as a cynical excuse for departing from one's legal obligations. Alternative phrases are **Necessitas facit lictum quod alias non est lictum**, **Necessitas non habet leges**, and **Quod necessitas cogit, defendit.** *See also* **Ius necessitatis.**

Necessitas non habet leges. nākās´sētas nōn ha´bāt lā´gās. nuse´sitas nan hâ´bet le´jēz. "Necessity has no laws." An alternative phrase for **Necessitas non habet legem.**

Necessitas publica maior est quam privata. nākās´sētas pūb´lēka ma´yōr āst kwam prēwa´ta. nuse´sitas pub´liku mā´jɜr est kwam prīvâ´tu. "Public necessity is more important than private (necessity)." A maxim meaning that what is necessary to the safety or prosperity of private persons must yield to what is necessary to the safety or prosperity of the state. This principle is generally limited by international human rights law and, most especially, *ius cogens*. *Compare with* **Iura publica anteferenda privatis.**

Negotiorum gestio. nāgōtēō´rūm gās´tēō. negōšō´rum jes´tēō. *n.* "Performance of business." (1) The management of business generally. (2) The unauthorized management of or interference with the business or affairs of another. (3) At civil law, a claim by an unauthorized agent for *quantum meruit* when the agent acted on behalf of a principal to protect the principal's business interests during an inability of the principal. To recover *quantum meruit*, the agent could not have acted in his self-interest. *E.g.*, "As regards the civil law action based on *negotiorum gestio*, the applicant claims that to found such an action according to the principles of law common to the Member States the following five conditions must be satisfied: the management of the principal's affairs, whether legal or material, must benefit the principal; at the relevant time the principal was unable to manage his own affairs, but there was a need for his affairs to be managed; the manager had no intention to act gratuitously—there was no *animus donandi*; the manager was under no contractual obligation to manage the affairs of the principal; the principal could reasonably have been expected to take the action undertaken by the manager had the principal been aware of the need for action." *Masdar (UK) Ltd. v. Commission of the European Communities*, [2006] E.C.R. II-4377, ¶ 76.

N

Negotium. nāgō´tē-ūm. negō´šum. *n.* "Business." (1) The conduct of business; a business transaction. (2) A matter or case. (3) The intention behind, or policy goal of, a legal instrument.

Nemine contra dicente. nā´mēnā kōn´tra dēkān´tā. ne´minē kan´tru disen´tē. *adv.* "With no one speaking in opposition." (1) Unanimously. (2) Without dissent, as when a decision is made or legislation passed without opposition. *Compare with* **Nemine contra dicente** and **Una voce**.

Nemo ad factum praecise cogi potest. nā´mō ad fak´tūm prīkē´sā kō´gē pō´tāst. nē´mō âd fâk´tum prēsī´zē kō´jī pō´test. "Nobody can be forced to a specific act." An alternative formulation of **Nemo potest praecise cogi ad factum.** *E.g.*, "Once the respect of the human person has been reserved—*nemo ad factum proecise cogi potest*—the execution of the obligations to 'perform' is therefore pursued until a remedy is found for a mere declaration of will which the debtor persists in refusing to make without reason." *Advisory Opinion on Interpretation of Peace Treaties with Bulgaria, Hungary, and Romania*, 1950 I.C.J. Rep. 221, 248 (Judge Azevedo, dissenting).

Nemo auditur propriam turpitudinem allegans. nā´mō ô´dētūr prō´prē-am tūrpētū´dēnām allā´gans. nē´mō ă´ditɜr prōp´rē-um tɜrpitū´dinem âle´genz. "Nobody is heard recounting his own turpitude." A principle to the effect that indirect proof of one's guilt or liability usually suffices for a conviction because of the rarity of a confession of one's own guilt or liability.

Nemo bis punitur pro eodem delicto. nā´mō bēs pūnē´tūr prō ā-ō´dām dālēk´tō. nē´mō bis pyū´nitɜr prō ēō´dem dulik´tō. "May no one be punished twice for the same offense." A maxim meaning that multiple punishments for a single violation of law are impermissible. *Compare with* **Ne bis in idem.**

Nemo bis vexari pro (una et) eadem causa. nā´mō bēs wāksa´rē prō (ū´na āt) ā-a´dām kô´sa. nē´mō bis veksa´rī prō (ū´nu et) ē´dem kă´zu. "May no one be troubled twice for (one and) the same reason." An alternative phrase for **Ne bis in idem.**

Nemo cogitationis poenam patitur. nā´mō kōgētatēō´nēs pœ´nam pa´tētūr. nē´mō kajitāšō´nis pē´num pâ´titɜr. "No one suffers punishment for his thoughts." An alternative formulation of **Cogitationis poenam nemo patitur.**

Nemo commodum capere potest de iniuria sua propria. nā´mō kōm´mōdūm ka´pārā pō´tāst dā ēnyū´rē-a sū´a prōp´rē-a. nē´mō kumō´dum kâ´pɜrē pō´test dā injɜ´rē-u sū´u prap´rē-u. "No one may gain profit from his own wrongdoing." An alternative phrase for **Nullus commodum capere (potest) de sua iniuria propria.**

N

Nemo dat non quod habet. nā´mō dat nōn kwōd ha´bāt. nē´mō dât nan kwad hâ´bet. "No one gives that which he does not have." An alternative phrase for **Nemo plus iuris transfere potest quam ipse habet.**

Nemo debet esse iudex in (propria) sua causa. nā´mō dā´bāt ās´sā yū´dāks ēn (prō´prē-a) sū´a kô´sa. nē´mō de´bet e´sē jū´deks in (prap´rē-u) sū´u kâ´zu. "Nobody should be the judge in his (own) case." A doctrine according to which the decision of a person vitally interested in the outcome of an authoritative decision, including a pronouncement about the legality of his own act or conduct, lacks prescriptive value and cannot bind others. In a judicial context, the doctrine precludes a judge from adjudicating a case in which the judge has a direct interest in the outcome. Alternative phrases are **Nemo iudex in causa sua** and **Nemo iudex in re sua.**

Nemo est supra leges. nā´mō āst sūp´ra lā´gās. nē´mō est sūp´ru le´jēz. "No one is above the laws." A maxim meaning that no person is exempt from the binding force of the law. *Contrast with* **Legibus solutus.**

Nemo iudex in causa sua. nā´mō yū´dāks ēn kô´sa sū´a. nē´mō jū´deks in kâ´zu sū´u. "Nobody is the judge in his own case." An alternative formulation of **Nemo debet esse iudex in (propria) sua causa.**

Nemo iudex in re sua. nā´mō yū´dāks ēn rā sū´a. nē´mō jū´deks in rā sū´u. "Nobody is the judge in his own matter." An alternative phrase for **Nemo debet esse iudex in (propria) sua causa.**

Nemo locupletari potest cum alterius iactura. nā´mō lōkūplāta´rē pō´tāst kūm altārē´ūs yaktū´ra. nē´mō lakyūplete´rī pō´test kum altɜ´rē-us jâktɜ´ru. "Nobody can be made rich at the expense of another." A maxim meaning that a claimant seeking relief may not be awarded damages greater than his or her loss.

Nemo patriam (in qua natus est) exuere potest (nec ligeantiae debitum eiurare possit). nā´mō pa´trē-am (ēn kwa na´tūs āst) āksū´ārā pō´tāst (nāk lēgā-an´tē-ī dā´bētūm āyūra´rā pōs´sēt). nē´mō pât´rē-um (in kwā nâ´tus est) egzyū´ɜrē pō´test (nek lijē-ân´tē-ā de´bitum ejɜra´rē pa´sit). "Nobody can renounce the country (in which he was born) (nor refuse the obligation of allegiance to it)." A civil law maxim meaning that no person can change nationalities without the consent of one's state of citizenship, nor may one renounce the obligation of loyalty to one's state by refusing to serve it when called upon. The continued validity of this maxim is called into question by the widespread adoption by states of municipal laws allowing the renunciation of citizenship. An alternative phrase is **Nemo potest exuere patriam.** *Compare with* **Semel civis semper civis.**

N

Nemo plus iuris transfere (ad alium) potest quam ipse habet. nā´mō plūs yū´rēs transfä´rā (ad a´lē-ūm) pō´tāst kwam ēp´sā ha´bāt. nē´mō plus jɜ´ris trâns´fɜrē (âd â´lē-um) pō´test kwam ip´sē hâ´bet. "No one can transfer more rights (to another) than he himself has." A maxim meaning that one cannot transfer legal rights greater than those that one lawfully possesses. One consequence of this principle is that a principal cannot empower his agent to exercise more rights than the principal himself possesses. It further follows that no one can transfer more rights in property than he possesses in the property. Alternative phrases are **Nemo dat qod non habet** and **Nemo potiorem potest transfere quam ipse habet.** *Compare with* **Res transit cum suo onere.**

Nemo potest exuere patriam. nā´mō pō´tāst āksū´ārā pat´rē-am. nē´mō pō´test egzū´erē pât´rē-um. "No one can cast off his country." An alternative phrase for **Nemo patriam (in qua natus est) exuere potest (nec ligeantiae debitum eiurare possit).**

Nemo potest mutare consilium suum in alterius iniuriam. nā´mō pō´tāst mūta´rā kōnsē´lē-ūm sū´ūm ēn altārē´ūs ēnyū´rē-am. nē´mō pō´test myūta´rē kansi´lē-um sū´um in altɜ´rē-us injɜ´rē-um. "Nobody can change his argument to the detriment of another." An alternative phrase for **Nullus commodum capere (potest) de sua iniuria propria.** *E.g.*, "Whatever term or terms be employed to designate this principle such as it has been applied in the international sphere, its substance is always the same: inconsistency between claims or allegations put forward by a State, and its previous conduct in connection therewith, is not admissible (*allegans contraria non audiendus est*). Its purpose is always the same: a State must not be permitted to benefit by its own inconsistency to the prejudice of another State (*nemo potest mutare consilium suum in alterius injuriam*)." *Temple of Preah Vihear* (Camb. v. Thail.), 1962 I.C.J. Rep. 6, 41 (separate opinion of Vice President Alfaro).

Nemo potest praecise cogi ad factum. nā´mō pō´tāst prīkē´sā kō´gē ad fak´tūm. nē´mō pō´test prēsī´zē kō´jī âd fâk´tum. "Nobody can be forced to a specific act." A maxim of civil law meaning that, while a respondent may be required to pay damages for injuries caused by him, he may not be forced to perform a specific obligation. While the doctrine has sometimes been invoked in an international legal context, it is not generally applicable except with respect to the performance of personal services. *E.g.*, "Where specific relief is not possible, because the person responsible cannot or will not provide it (*nemo potest praecise cogi ad factum*), there is to be equivalent compensation."

Advisory Opinion on the Application for Review of Judgment No. 158 of the United Nations Administrative Tribunal, 1973 I.C.J. Rep. 166, 289 (Judge De Castro, dissenting). An alternative formulation is **Nemo ad factum praecise cogi potest.**

N

Nemo potiorem potest transfere (ad alium) quam ipse habet. nā´mō pōtēō´rām pō´tāst trans´fārā (ad a´lē-ūm) kwam ēp´sā ha´bāt. nē´mō pōšō´rem pō´test trâns´f3rē (âd â´lē-um) kwam ip´sē hâ´bet. "No one can transfer a better title (to another) than he himself possesses." An alternative phrase for **Nemo plus iuris transfere potest quam ipse habet.**

Nemo punitur pro alieno delicto. nā´mō pūnē´tūr prō alē-ā´nē dālēk´tō. nē´mō pyū´nit3r prō ālē-e´nō dulik´tō. "No one is punished for the crime of another." A maxim prohibiting collective punishments under international human rights law and international humanitarian law.

Nihil. nē´hēl. nī´hil. *n.* "Nothing." (1) Nothing; a void. (2) A legal or factual nullity.

Nihil ad rem. nē´hēl ad rām. nī´hil âd rem. *adj.* "Nothing to the matter." Irrelevant; off point. *E.g.*, "Mrs. Roberts contends, to use the words of the Court of Appeal, that the fact she receives a payment from a third party (in this case the State) which a male comparator does not receive is *nihil ad rem* and cannot affect the obligation of the employer under Article 119 to pay her and her male comparator equally." Opinion of Advocate General Van Gerven, *Birds Eye Walls Ltd. v. Roberts*, [1993] 3 C.M.L.R. 822, 830, ¶ 9 (E.C.J.). *See also* **Ad rem.**

Nisi. nē´sē. ni´zē. *conj.* (commonly used as an *adj.*) "Unless." *Nisi* is typically used as an adjective to denote that the rule or order (*e.g.*, an "order *nisi*") to which it is attached will take effect at a given time unless before that time some stipulated condition is (or is not) fulfilled.

Nolens volens. nō´lāns wō´lāns. nō´lenz vō´lenz. *adv.* "Unwillingly or willingly." Whether willingly or unwillingly. *E.g.*, "The [Court majority's] reasoning… *nolens volens* leads to the creation of the Court's own, judicial reality in contrast to the objective legal one, producing a proper *judicium illusorum.*" *Application of the Convention on the Prevention and Punishment of the Crime of Genocide* (Bosn. & Herz. v. Yugo.), I.C.J. No. 91, Judgment of Feb. 26, 2007, at 30, ¶ 59 (separate opinion of Judge *ad hoc* Kreća).

Nolle prosequi. nōl´lā prōsā´kwē. nō´lē pra´sekwī. *v. inf.* "To not wish to pursue." (1) A formal decision not to proceed in pressing a claim against another, usually because of insufficient evidence or a settlement of the claim. (2) The loss of a right to bring a claim based on earlier neglect to prosecute the claim.

Nolo contendere. nō´lō kōntān´dārā. nō´lō kanten´dʒrē. "I do not wish to contest." A plea in which the pleader declines to admit or deny the validity or truth of the claims or charges brought against him or her. A plea of *nolo contendere* is often treated as a tacit admission of willingness to accept liability or punishment for the claims or charges. An alternative term is **Non contendere.**

Nolumus. nō´lūmūs. na´lyūmus. *v.* "We do not wish." *See* **Non volumus.**

Nominatim. nōmēna´tēm. naminā´tim. *adv.* "By name." (1) One by one, in sequence. (2) Each one by its individual name. *See also* **Eo nomine.**

Non adimplenti contractus. nōn adēmplān´tē kōntrak´tūs. nan âdimplen´tī kantrâk´tus. *n.* "An unfulfilled contract." A contract, the obligations of which have not been performed by at least one party. *See also* **Exceptio inadimplenti contractus** and **Inadimplenti non est adimplendum.**

Non bis in idem. nōn bēs ēn ē´dām. nan bis in ī´dum. "Not twice for the same thing." An alternative phrase for **Ne bis in idem.**

Non compos (mentis). nōn kōm´pōs (mān´tēs). nan kam´pus (men´tis). *adj.* "Not having mastery (over the mind)." (1) Mentally incompetent due to youth, advanced age, handicap, *etc.* (2) Insane. *Contrast with* **Compos mentis.**

Non contendere. nōn kōntān´dārā. nan kanten´dʒrē. *v. inf.* "Not to contest." An alternative term for **Nolo contendere.**

Non damnificatus. nōn damnēfēka´tūs. nan dâmnifikā´tus. *n. Ecc.* "The uninjured." One who has suffered a harm not attributable to the legal liability of another. *Contrast with* **Damnificatus.** *See also* **Damnum absque iniuria.**

Non est iudex minus petita partium. nōn āst yū´dāks mē´nūs pātē´ta par´tē-ūm. nan est jū´deks mī´nus peti´tu par´tē-um. "He is not a judge [who decides] less than what is requested from the parties." A maxim meaning that a judicial or arbitral tribunal should not decide less than all questions presented that are within its jurisdiction and presented in the claim. *E.g.*, "A judge does not fulfil his judicial duty (*judex decidere debet*) if he fails to give a decision on one of the *causae petendi* of the application (*non est judex minus petita partium*)." *Advisory Opinion on the Application for Review of Judgement No. 158 of the United Nations Administrative Tribunal*, 1973 I.C.J. Rep. 166, 291, ¶ 41 (Judge De Castro, dissenting). *Compare with* **Iudex decidere debet.** *But see* **Non liquet.**

Non grata. nōn gra´ta. nan gra´tu. *adj.* "Unwelcome." (1) A term used to designate a person (usually a diplomat or member of a mission staff) whose request to enter a state or continued presence in a state is rejected, and who, if present in the state, is required to leave. *E.g.*, "A person may be declared *non grata* or not acceptable before arriving in the territory of the receiving State." Vienna Convention on Diplomatic Relations art. 9(1), Apr. 18, 1961, 500 U.N.T.S. 95; *see* Vienna Convention on Consular Relations art. 23, Apr. 24, 1963, 596 U.N.T.S. 261. (2) In a general sense, unwelcome or unwanted. *See also* **Persona non grata.**

Non licet. nōn lē´kāt. nan li´set. *v.* "It is impermissible." A judgment denoting that the tribunal lacks jurisdiction to issue a binding judgment, decision, or award on the parties or subject matter before it.

Non liquet. nōn lē´kūāt. nan li´kwet. *v.* "It is unclear." A judgment denoting that the tribunal refuses to render an award or judgment in the belief that the law supplies no rule applicable to the case before it. This term was widely used by Roman jurisprudes such as Cicero and Quintilian, but has become less common in modern times when tribunals are commonly expected to fill gaps in the law by the application of legal reasoning. In some legal systems, judges may explicitly be forbidden to enter a declaration of *non liquet*. *E.g.*, "[I]t is the evident will of the Parties that the arbitral award shall not conclude by a '*non liquet*,' but shall in any event decide that the island forms a part of the territory of one or the other of two litigant Powers." *Island of Palmas Case* (U.S. v. Neth.), 2 R.I.A.A. 829 (1928). Sometimes abbreviated **n.l.** *Compare with* **Dubii iuris** and **Vacuum iuris.** *See also* **Non possumus** and **Non volumus.** *But see* **Iudex decidere debet.**

Non omne damnum inducit iniuriam. nōn ōm´nā dam´nūm ēndū´kēt ēnyū´rē-am. nan am´nē dâm´num indū´sit injз´rē-um. "Not every loss brings injury." A maxim of the civil law, incorporated into the common law according to William Blackstone, John Bouvier, and others, meaning that some harms or losses, such as those resulting from faultless accidents or acts of nature, may occur without giving rise to any person's legal liability. *See also* **Damnum absque iniuria** and **Non damnificatus.**

Non possumus. nōn pōs´sūmūs. nan pa´syūmus. *v.* (commonly used as a *n.*) "We cannot." A declaration that the speaker or author cannot engage in some behavior. *E.g.*, "A *non possumus* must, whenever the circumstances require the Court to indicate provisional measures, be very solidly grounded. Legal reasons that are compelling and incontrovertible are necessary if the dictates of prudence are to be justifiably set aside." *Case Concerning the Arbitral*

Award of 31 July 1989, 1990 I.C.J. Rep. 64, 81 (Judge Thierry, dissenting). *Contrast with* **Non volumus.** *See also* **Non liquet.**

Non quieta movere. nōn kwē-ā´ta mōwā´rā. nan kwī-e´tu mō´v3rē. "Not to disturb what is settled." An alternative phrase for **Stare decisis.**

N

Non scire quod scire debemus et possumus culpa est. nōn skē´rā kwōd skē´rā dābā´mūs āt pōs´sūmūs cūl´pa āst. nan ski´rē kwad ski´rē de´bemus et pa´syūmus k3l´pu est. "Not to know what one ought to know is a fault." A maxim meaning that one who fails to gain the knowledge of law that would prevent a violation of the law is liable for any resulting violation. The maxim may also be applied to those cases in which a person failed to fulfill an obligation to investigate facts that would have prevented a harm from occurring to another. *Compare with* **Ignorantia legis neminem excusat.**

Non sequitur. nōn sē´kwētūr. nan se´kwit3r. *v.* (commonly used as a *n.*) "It does not follow." A fallacy in logic arising from a case in which the arguer draws a nonsensical inference, or arrives at an unproven conclusion, from his or her premises. *E.g.*, "It does not follow from the facts that the decisions of the Security Council must be in accordance with the Charter, and that the International Court of Justice is the principal judicial organ of the United Nations, that the Court is empowered to ensure that the Council's decisions do accord with the Charter. To hold that it does so follow is a monumental *non sequitur*, which overlooks the truth that, in many legal systems, national and international, the subjection of the acts of an organ to law by no means entails subjection of the legality of its actions to judicial review." *Questions of Interpretation and Application of the 1971 Montreal Convention Arising from the Aerial Incident at Lockerbie* (Libya v. U.S.), 1998 I.C.J. Rep. 115, 167 (President Schwebel, dissenting).

Non solent quae abundant vitiare scripturas. nōn sō´lānt kwī abūn´dant wētē-a´rā skrēptū´ras. nan sō´lent kwā ubun´dent viša´rē skrip´č3rus. "Superfluous expressions do not usually impair writings." A maxim of civil law, originating in Justinian's *Digest*, meaning that oral statements of parties to an agreement do not normally derogate from the written expression of the agreement (called in common law the "parol evidence rule"). Such statements can, however, serve as sources for the interpretation of vague or ambiguous terms. *See* the Vienna Convention on the Law of Treaties arts. 31–32, May 23, 1969, 1155 U.N.T.S. 331.

Non totidem verbis. nōn tō´tēdām wār´bēs. nan tō´tidem v3r´bis. "Not in so many words." Phrased differently from what was previously said or written, but having essentially the same meaning. *Contrast with* **Totidem verbis.**

Non ultra petita (partium). nōn ŭl´tra pātē´ta (par´tē-ūm). nan ɜl´tru putē´tu (par´tē-um). *adj.* "Not beyond the pleadings (of the party)." A doctrine providing that a tribunal should not unnecessarily decide questions of law or fact not raised by the parties to a dispute, on the theory that the tribunal's jurisdiction is limited to deciding matters raised by the parties. *E.g.*, "The Court would recall the well-established principle that 'it is the duty of the Court not only to reply to the questions as stated in the final submissions of the parties, but also to abstain from deciding points not included in those submissions.' While the Court is thus not entitled to decide upon questions not asked of it, the *non ultra petita* rule nonetheless cannot preclude the Court from addressing certain legal points in its reasoning." *Arrest Warrant of 11 April 2000* (Congo v. Belg.), 2002 I.C.J. Rep. 3, 18–19, ¶ 43 (citation omitted). An alternative phrase is **Ne iudex ultra petita partium.** *See also* **Ultra petita.**

Non volumus. nōn vō´lūmūs. nan va´lyūmus. *v. Neo.* "We do not wish." A declaration that the speaker or authority declines voluntarily to engage in some behavior. *E.g.*, "The direct consequence of the doctrine which India advances before us is to confer on member States the possibility of freeing themselves at will from their obligations as members of the Organization *vis-à-vis* another member State. It affords a convenient cover for a *non volumus.*" *Jurisdiction of the ICAO Council* (India v. Pak.), 1972 I.C.J. Rep. 46, 133 (separate opinion of Judge De Castro). *Contrast with* **Non possumus.** The phrase is a relative neologism; the classic Latin form is *Nolumus.*

Noscitur a sociis (eiusdem generis). nōs´kētūr a sō´kē-ēs (āyūs´dām gā´nārēs). nas´kitɜr- OR nōs´kitɜr a sō´šis (ējus´dem je´nɜris). "It is known by its companions (of the same kind)." A doctrine of legal instrument interpretation providing that, in an enumeration of specific items that contains a general term, the general term will be construed to include only things similar to the specific items proximate to the general term. This doctrine is based on the assumption that the words surrounding a general term are exemplary of the kinds of things that term was intended to encompass. *Compare with* **Eiusdem generis.**

Nota. nō´ta. nō´tu. *n.* [*pl.* **Notae.** nō´tī. nō´tā.] "Note." A promissory note.

Nota bene. nō´ta bā´nā. nō´tu be´nā *or* -be´nē. *v. imp.* "Note well." A phrased use to draw one's attention to an item of particular interest. Commonly abbreviated **N.B.**

Novie(n)s. nō´wē-ā(n)s. nō´vē(n)z. *adv.* "Ninthly." An adverbial number (the ninth) usually inserted into a consecutively numbered series by way of amendment. *See* the Appendix for a list of Latin adverbial numbers commonly used in international law. *See also* **Bis** and **Semel.**

N

Novus actus interveniens. nō´wūs ak´tūs ēntārwā´nē-āns. nō´vus âk´tus intзrvē´nē-enz. *n.* "A new intervening act." A doctrine according to which an injury caused by a combination of an original act and an intervening act of a third party does not engage the liability of the original actor if, in the absence of the intervening act, no wrongful harm would have resulted. *See Certain Property* (Liecht. v. Ger.), 2005 I.C.J. Rep. 6, 70 *et seq.* (Preliminary Objections) (Judge *ad hoc* Berman, dissenting).

Nuda pactio obligationem non parit. nū´da pak´tēō ōblēgatēō´nām nōn pa´rēt. nū´du pâk´tēō abligāšō´nem nan pa´rit. "A naked agreement does not give rise to obligations." A maxim, originating in Justinian's *Digest* (2.14.7.4), meaning that an agreement lacking mutual consideration is void. The purpose of this rule is the prevention of fraud on or coercion of a party to the agreement and the separation of purely moral obligations from legally binding ones. The International Court of Justice has implicitly rejected the maxim, however, in holding that a state's unilateral public pronouncement, made with intent to be bound, may be binding. *See Nuclear Tests* (Austl. v. Fr.), 1974 I.C.J. Rep. 252, ¶ 43 (Judgment). *Compare with* **Ex nudo pacto actio non oritur**. *See also* **Nudum pactum.**

Nuda possessio. nū´da pōssās´sēō. nū´du puze´sēō. *n.* "Naked possession." Mere possession of property, not necessarily accompanied by legal title or right.

Nudum ius. nū´dūm yūs. nū´dum jus. "Naked right." A right or norm of undefined limits, such that it may be invoked to sustain widely divergent claims in the discretion of the invoker.

Nudum ius domini. nū´dūm yūs dō´mēnē. nū´dum jus da´minī. *n.* "An unexecuted right of the lord." A right not yet exercised.

Nudum pactum. nū´dūm pak´tūm. nū´dum pâk´tum. *n.* "A bare agreement." (1) In Roman law, an agreement that is not legally binding because it fails to comply with all required formalities. (2) In modern municipal practice, an agreement that is invalid for lack of mutual consideration. *See also* **Ex nudo pacto actio non oritur** and **Nuda pactio obligationem non parit.**

Nulla crimen sine lege. A common but incorrect spelling of **Nullum crimen sine lege.**

Nulla lex nulla iniuria. nūl´la lāks nūl´la ēnyū´rē-a. nз´lu leks nз´lu injз´rē-u. "No law no wrong." A maxim meaning that, unless an act violated a preexisting legal obligation, it cannot give rise to any liability; a law may not impose retroactive civil liability. This maxim, though expressing a basic principle of due process of law, is not uniformly followed in state practice. *Compare with* **Nullum crimen sine lege.**

Nulla poena sine lege. nūl´la pœ´na sē´nā lā´gā. n3´lu pē´nu si´nē le´jē. "No punishment without law." A doctrine holding that no punishment is permissible for an act that was not defined as a crime in the applicable law at the time of commission. The doctrine is the corollary to the prohibition on *ex post facto* criminal laws and is a basic principle of international criminal law. *See* ROME STATUTE OF THE INTERNATIONAL CRIMINAL COURT art. 23. *Compare with* **Nullum crimen sine lege.** *See also* **Ex post facto** and **Lex previa(, stricta, scripta et certa).**

Nullius. nūllē´ūs. n3´lē-us. *adj.* "Of none; of nobody." Relating to territory or property lacking any sovereign authority and, therefore, open to future claims of sovereignty. *E.g.*, "Mexico maintains...that the French occupation was not valid, and consequently her own right to occupy the island which must still be considered as *nullius* in 1897." *Sovereignty over Clipperton Island Case* (Fr. v. Mex.), Award of Jan. 28, 1931, 26 AM. J. INT'L L. 390, 393 (1932).

Nullius iuris. nūllē´ūs yū´rēs. n3´lē-us j3´ris. *adv.* "Of no legal value." (1) Lacking legal effect or validity. (2) Having no standing under the law.

Nullum arbitrium. nūl´lūm arbēt´rē-ūm. n3´lum arbit´rē-um. *n.* "No arbitration." A defense to an action to recognize or enforce an arbitral award denying that the arbitral tribunal ever rendered a binding award. *Compare with* **Nullum fecerunt arbitrium.**

Nullum crimen nulla poena sine lege. A combination of **Nulla poena sine lege** and **Nullum crimen sine lege.** *See* each separate entry.

Nullum crimen sine lege. nūl´lūm krē´mān sē´nā lā´gā. n3´lum krī´men si´nē le´jē. "No crime without law." A doctrine of criminal law holding that no person may be convicted of a crime for an act that was not forbidden by law at the time of commission. In many countries, this rule has been incorporated into the national constitution. It is also an integral part of the right to due process of law under both international human rights law and international criminal law. *See* ROME STATUTE of the INTERNATIONAL CRIMINAL COURT art. 22; International Covenant on Civil and Political Rights art. 15, Mar. 23, 1976, 999 U.N.T.S. 171. *E.g.*, "The Trial Chamber is aware that it must interpret the Convention [on the Prevention and Punishment of the Crime of Genocide] with due regard for the principle of *nullum crimen sine lege*. It therefore recognizes that, despite recent developments, customary international law limits the definition of genocide to those acts seeking the physical or biological destruction of all or part of the group." *Prosecutor v. Krstic*,

I.C.T.Y. Case No. IT-98-33-T, Judgment of Aug. 2, 2001, ¶ 580. *Compare with* **Nulla lex nulla iniuria** and **Nulla poena sine lege**. *See also* **Ex post facto**; **Lex previa(, stricta, scripta et certa)**; and **Lex prospicit, non respicit.**

Nullum fecerunt arbitrium. nūl´lūm fākā´rūnt arbēt´rē-ūm. nɜ´lum fe´sɜrunt arbit´rē-um. "They did not submit to arbitration." A defense to an action to recognize or enforce an arbitral award denying that the party seeking to resist enforcement of the award had contractually agreed to submit to the arbitration. *Compare with* **Nullum arbitrium.**

Nullum tempus occurrit regi. nūl´lūm tām´pūs ōkkūr´rēt rā´gē. nɜ´lum tem´pus ōkɜ´rit re´jī. "No time runs against the king." A maxim of medieval common law meaning that a sovereign is not bound by any temporal limitations in seeking damages, such as a statute of limitations. *See* Henry de Bracton, De Legibus et Consuetudinis Angliae (ca. 1253).

Nullus commodum capere (potest) de sua iniuria propria. nūl´lūs kōm´mōdūm ka´pārā (pō´tāst) dā sū´a ēnyū´rē-a prōp´rē-a. nɜ´lus ka´mōdum kâ´pɜrē (pō´test) dā sū´u injɜ´rē-u prap´rē-u. "No advantage (may be) gained from one's own wrong." A maxim meaning that the law will not recognize or validate any profit a person derives from his own wrongdoing. For example, one may not destroy evidence of the extent of damages caused by one's illegal act, then counter a claim for damages based on that act by pointing to the lack of evidence. *E.g.*, "[T]he State must not be allowed to benefit by its inconsistency when it is through its own wrong or illegal act that the other party has been deprived of its right or prevented from exercising it. (*Nullus commodum capere de sua injuria propria.*)" *Temple of Preah Vihear* (Camb. v. Thail.), 1962 I.C.J. Rep. 6, 41 (Merits) (separate opinion of Vice President Alfaro). This maxim has numerous alternative phrasings, including **Commodum ex iniuria non oritur, Commodum ex iniuria sua nemo habere debet, Commodum ex iniuria sua non habere debet, Ex dolo malo actio non oritur, Iniuria propria non cadet in beneficium facientis**, and **Nemo commodum capere potest de iniuria sua propria.** *See also* **Ius ex iniuria non oritur** and **Nemo potest mutare consilium suum in alterius iniuriam.**

Nunc pro tunc. nūnk prō tūnk. nunk prō tunk. *adj.* or *adv.* "Now in place of then." (1) Having retroactive effect. *E.g.*, "[B]y tacking back the effects of the [claimant's] conduct *nunc pro tunc*, the Tribunal has conflated the ideas of a formal jurisdictional defect in the [claimant's] waiver [of court jurisdiction required for submission of a claim to a NAFTA arbitral tribunal] in September 1998 with a subsequent disqualification of the waiver in 1998 or 1999." *Waste Management, Inc. v. Mexico*, ICSID Case No. ARB(AF)/98/2, Award of June 2, 2000, ¶ 53 (K. Highet, dissenting). *Compare with* **Ex post facto**

and **Post hoc.** (2) Deemed by legal fiction to occur in the past or in a timely manner, though done belatedly, as when a motion is granted after the deadline to file the motion has passed. *E.g.*, "On April 20, 2000, the Malaysian government moved to amend its answer *nunc pro tunc* to assert sovereign immunity and to dismiss the complaint under Rule 12(b)(1) of the Federal Rules of Civil Procedure for lack of subject matter jurisdiction." *Robinson v. Government of Malaysia*, 269 F.3d 133, 137 (2d Cir. 2001).

Nuncio. nūn´kēō. nun´sēō. *v.* (commonly used as a *n.*) "I announce." A high diplomatic representative of the Holy See lacking the status of cardinal. The Holy See was in the past and sometimes still is treated as its own state with corresponding diplomatic privileges. *E.g.*, "Under Article 4 of the Vienna *Règlement* of 1815, the *nuncio* was regarded as the *doyen* of the resident diplomatic body. This might apparently be construed as making a *nuncio* the *doyen* in every country to which he may be accredited, or only in such countries as those to which a *nuncio* was in 1815 accredited, and to whom a privileged position was by the *Règlement* accorded." Ernest Satow, A GUIDE TO DIPLOMATIC PRACTICE 169, § 290 (Neville Bland ed., 4th ed., 1957). An alternative spelling is **Nuntio.** *Contrast with* **Legatus a latere** and **Legatus natus.**

Nunquam crescit ex post facto praeteriti delicti aestimatio. nūn´kwam krās´kēt āks pōst fak´tō prītā´rētē dālēk´tē īstēma´tēō. nun´kwum kre´šit eks pōst fâk´tō pretз´ritī delik´tī estimā´šō. "The assessment of damages for a past offense never increases by what happens subsequently." A maxim, originating in Justinian's *Digest* (50.17.139), meaning that an unforeseeable event occurring subsequent to a wrongful act giving rise to liability cannot thereby increase the damages that may be claimed for the original act.

Nunquam decurritur ad extraordinarum sed ubi deficit ordinarium. nūn´kwam dākūr´rētūr ad ākstraōrdēna´rūm sād ū´bē dā´fēkēt ōrdēna´rē-ūm. nun´kwum dēkз´ritзr âd ekstru-ōrdine´rē-um sed ū´bē de´fisit ōrdine´rē-um. "Never resort to the extraordinary until the ordinary fails." A maxim of civil law meaning that the language of a legal instrument should be read according to its normal meaning unless a reasonable reading of the instrument implies that the drafters intended a more specific or technical meaning.

Nuntio. nun´sēō. An alternative spelling of **Nuncio.**

O

Ob maiorem cautelam. ōb mayō´rām kôtā´lam. ab mujō´rum kă´telum. *adv.* "For greater security." Done for the purpose of preventing accidents or other undesirable results. This term is sometimes used to explain a provision of an agreement having as its purpose additional security for one or both parties. Alternative phrases are **Ex maiore cautela** and **Pro maiori cautela.** *Compare with* **Ad abundantiorem cautelam.**

Obiter dictum. ō´bētār dēk´tūm. ō´bit3r dik´tum. *n.* [*pl.* **Obiter dicta.** ō´bētār dēk´ta. ō´bit3r dik´tu.] "Thing said in passing." A statement made, in the course of a judgment, that is not binding as legal precedent because the matter upon which the statement bears is not necessary to the conclusions drawn in the judgment. *E.g.*, "Argentine law is irrelevant in this respect, as recognized in the Award and in many other ICSID decisions. The observations which were made in passing by the Tribunal on the piercing of the corporate veil in Argentine law are thus *obiter dicta.*" *CMS Gas Transmission Co. v. Argentine Rep.*, ICSID Case No. ARB/01/8, Decision on the Application for Annulment, Sept. 25, 2007, ¶ 68, 46 I.L.M. 1136, 1144 (2007). Commonly abbreviated as **Dictum** *(s.)* or **Dicta** *(pl.).*

Obligatio. ōblēga´tēō. abligā´šō. *n.* [*pl.* **Obligationes.** ōblēgatēō´nās. abligāšō´nēz.] "Obligation." A legally binding obligation or duty.

Obligatio civilis. ōblēga´tēō kēwē´lēs. abligā´šō si´vilis. *n.* "Civil law obligation." A legally enforceable obligation arising in law or by binding contract.

Obligatio ex contractu. ōblēga´tēō āks kōntrak´tū. abligā´šō eks kantrâk´tū. *n.* "Obligation from contract." A legal liability arising from a contractual undertaking or the breach thereof. This is a kind of **Obligatio civilis.**

Obligatio ex delicto. ōblēga´tēō āks dālēk´tō. abligā´šō eks dulik´tō. *n.* "Obligation from an offense." A legal liability arising from a violation of law, such as a duty to compensate the victim of the violation.

Obligatio ex pacto. ōblēga´tēō āks pak´tō. abligā´šō eks pâk´tō. *n.* "Obligation from a treaty." A legal liability arising from a treaty obligation or the breach thereof.

O

Obses. ōb´sās. ab´sēz. *n.* [*pl.* **Obsides.** ōb´sēdās. ab´sidēz.] "Hostage." A person held hostage in an armed conflict. The use of hostages has long been prohibited by international humanitarian law. *See* Convention (IV) Relative to the Protection of Civilian Persons in Time of War art. 34, Aug. 12, 1949, 75 U.N.T.S. 287.

Occultatio thesauri inventi. ōkkūlta´tēō t-hāsô´rē ēnwān´tē. akɜltā´šō θesă´rī inven´tī. *n.* "Concealment of found treasure." The concealment of a treasure trove, which in medieval English and Roman law in some periods belonged to the sovereign. Therefore, *occultatio thesauri inventi* was at certain times and countries defined as a crime against the sovereign if the person concealing could not show that the treasure rightfully belonged to him. *See also* **Thesaurus inventus.**

Occupatio. ōkkūpa´tēō. akyūpā´šō. *n.* "Seizure." Seizure or occupation, usually in the context of acquiring title to territory or appurtenances previously unclaimed by anyone else.

Occupatio bellica. ōkkūpa´tēō bāl´lēka. akyūpā´šō be´liku. *n.* "Military seizure." The temporary occupation and administration of the territory of a sovereign by a power hostile to that sovereign, usually following a conquest in battle. *Contrast with* **Occupatio pacifica.**

Occupatio non praecedit nisi in re terminata. ōkkūpa´tēō nōn prīkā´dēt nē´sē ēn rā tārmēna´ta. akyūpā´šō nan prēsē´dit ni´zē in rā tɜrmina´tu. "Seizure does not lead the way except in a resolved situation." A maxim meaning that occupation does not create legal rights in the absence of an ascertainable boundary to define the territory occupied. For this reason, neither the high seas nor the seabed can be "occupied" in a legal sense. The maxim is attributable to Hugo Grotius, 2 De Iure Belli ac Pacis Libri Tres, ch. 2, para. 3(2) (1625).

Occupatio pacifica. ōkkūpa´tēō pakē´fēka. akyūpā´šō pusi´fiku. *n.* "Peaceful seizure." A nonhostile or consensual occupation, as when a government is unable to maintain order in its own territory and, therefore, requests the assistance of the armed forces of a friendly foreign state. The occupying power does not exercise governmental functions other than those delegated by the occupied power and makes no claim to sovereignty over the occupied territory. *Contrast with* **Occupatio bellica.**

Octie(n)s. ōk´tē-ā(n)s. ak´tē(n)z. *adv.* "Eighthly." An adverbial number (the eighth) usually inserted into a consecutively numbered series by way of amendment. *See* the Appendix for a list of Latin adverbial numbers commonly used in international law. *See also* **Bis** and **Semel**.

Odium ideologicum. ō´dē-ūm ēdāōlō´gēkūm. ō´dē-um īdēōla´jikum. *n.* "Ideological hatred." Hatred or enmity based on ideological reasons. *E.g.*, "[I]t was also in many places a civil conflict, technically beyond the scope of [the international] law [of war] and with its ordinary horrors magnified by *odium ideologicum.*" Geoffrey Best, WAR AND LAW SINCE 1945, at 61 (1997).

Officiis belli. ōffē´kē-ēs bāl´lē. ōfi´šis be´lī. *adj.* "By the duties of war." Required by the international law of war.

Omne maior continet in se minus. ōm´nā ma´yōr kōntē´nāt ēn sā mē´nūs. am´nē mā´jɜr kanti´net in sā mī´nus. "Every larger thing contains in itself a lesser." An alternative phrase for **In eo quod plus sit semper inest et minus.**

Omni exceptione maiores. ōm´nē āks-kāptēō´nā mayō´rās. am´nē eksepšō´nē mujō´rēz. "All exceptions are important." A maxim meaning that exceptions to a general rule should not be made (or disregarded) lightly, because the rationale for the exception must be sufficiently cogent to justify departing from an established rule.

Omnia rex imperio possidet, singuli dominio. ōm´nē-a rāks ēmpā´rēō pōs´sēdāt, sēn´gūlē dōmē´nēō. am´nē-u reks impe´rēō pō´sidet, siŋ´yūlī dumi´nēō. "The king possesses all by right of his sovereignty, while each individual [possesses] by his own property right." A maxim meaning that the state's sovereign rights encompass power over the entirety of its territory, and individuals within the territory may have property rights over parts of the territory subject to the state's law and overarching sovereignty.

Omnis exceptio est ipsa quoque regula. ōm´nēs āks-kāp´tēō āst ēp´sa kwō´kwā rā´gūla. am´nis eksep´tēō est ip´su kwō´kwē re´gyūlu. "Every exception is itself a rule as well." A maxim meaning that the exception to a general rule is itself effectively a legal rule relating to the specific matter covered and does not necessarily represent a disintegration or contradiction of the rule excepted.

Omnis indemnatus pro innoxio legibus habetur. ōm´nēs ēndāmna´tūs prō ēnnō´ksēō lā´gēbūs habā´tūr. am´nis indemnā´tus prō ina´ksēō le´jibus hâ´betɜr. "Everyone who has not been found guilty is deemed innocent by the laws." A maxim meaning that the law presumes that persons charged with a crime are deemed innocent until proven guilty in a fair trial. The presumption of innocence has been incorporated into both international human rights law and international criminal law as a fundamental due process right. *See* ROME STATUTE OF THE INTERNATIONAL CRIMINAL COURT art. 66; International

Covenant on Civil and Political Rights art. 14(2), Mar. 23, 1976, 999 U.N.T.S. 171.

Omnis ratihabitio retrotrahitur et mandato aequiparatur. ōm´nēs ratēhabē´tēō rātrōtra´hētūr āt manda´tō īkwēpara´tūr. am´nis râtihabi´šō retrōtrā´hitɜr et mândā´tō ekwipa´rutɜr. "Every ratification is drawn back and placed on equal footing with what has been commanded." A maxim meaning that an authority may ratify retroactively an act that was, at the time done, *ultra vires* or illegal due to lack of authoritative mandate.

Onus probandi. ō´nūs prōban´dē. ō´nus- OR a´nus prōbân´dī. *n.* "Burden of proof." The duty to produce evidence of a certain character and persuasiveness determined by the law in order to proceed or prevail on a claim or motion before an authoritative tribunal.

Op. cit. An abbreviation of **Opera citato.**

Opera citato. ō´pāra kēta´tō. a´pɜru sīta´tō. *adj.* "In the work cited." A citation signal indicating that the support for the proposition cited in a work appears in a reference cited previously in the same work. Commonly abbreviated **Op. cit.** *Compare with* **Ante** and **Supra (citatum).** *See also* **Ibidem.**

Opinio iuris communis. ōpē´nēō yū´rēs kōmmū´nēs. upin´ēō jɜ´ris kumyū´nis. *n.* "Communal legal opinion." An alternative phrase for **Opinio iuris gentium.** *E.g.*, "On the basis of the circumstances of adoption…and by expressing an *opinio juris communis*, [UN General Assembly] Resolution 1803 (XVII) seems to this Tribunal to reflect the state of customary law existing in this field." *The Caltex Arbitration* (Texaco v. Libya), 53 I.L.R. 87, ¶ 87 (1982).

Opinio iuris gentium. ōpē´nēō yū´rēs gān´tē-ūm. upi´nēō jɜ´ris jen´tē-um. *n.* "Legal opinion of the people." The opinion of the international community as a whole regarding the content of international law. An alternative phrase is **Opinio iuris communis.** This term has a more general meaning than **Opinio iuris (sive necessitatis).**

Opinio iuris (sive necessitatis). ōpē´nēō yū´rēs (sē´wā nākāssēta´tēs). upi´nēō jɜ´ris (si´vē nusesitā´tis). *n.* "Legal opinion (or else, necessity)." The belief by the international community as a whole that a norm is legally binding, either because it is an established custom or because the norm is a necessary condition to the maintenance of a stable world public order. When accompanied by long, widespread, and consistent state practice, *opinio iuris sive necessitatis* is considered a precondition to the formation of customary international law. *E.g.*, "[F]or a new customary rule to be formed, not only must the acts concerned 'amount to settled practice,' but they must be accompanied by the *opinio juris sive necessitatis*. Either the States taking such action or other States in a position to react to it, must have behaved so that their conduct is 'evidence of a belief that this practice is rendered obligatory by the existence of a rule of law requiring it. The need for such a belief, i.e. the existence of a subject element, is implicit in the very notion of the *opinio juris sive necessitatis*.'" *Military and Paramilitary Activities in and Against Nicaragua* (Nicar. v. U.S.), 1986 I.C.J. Rep. 14, 108–09, ¶ 207 (quoting *North Sea Continental Shelf Case* (F.R.G. v. Den./F.R.G. v. Nether.), 1969 I.C.J. Rep. 3, 44, ¶ 77). *Opinio iuris sive necessitatis* is one kind of **Opinio iuris gentium**. An alternative phrase is **Convictio iuris (sive necessitatis)**. *Compare with* **Communis opinio**.

Optima est legis interpres consuetudo. ōp´tēma āst lā´gēs ēntār´prās kōnswātū´dō. ap´timu est le´jis intɜr´pres kanswātū´dō. "Custom is the best interpreter of law." A maxim, originating in Justinian's *Digest*, meaning that a vague, ambiguous, or incomplete law should be interpreted in light of customary practices. *See* the Vienna Convention on the Law of Treaties art. 31(3)(b), May 23, 1969, 1155 U.N.T.S. 331. Alternative formulations are **Consuetudo est optima interpres legum**, **Optima legum interpres est consuetudo**, and **Optimus interpres rerum usus**.

Optima fide. ōp´tēma fē´dā. ap´timu fī´dē OR -fīd. *adv.* "In the best faith." Having the highest standard of integrity or good will. *Compare with* **Bona fide**.

Optimus interpres rerum usus. ōp´tēmūs ēntār´prās rā´rūm ū´sūs. ap´timus intɜr´pres rē´rum yū´zus. "The best interpretation comes from usage." An alternative phrase for **Optima est legis interpres consuetudo**, originating in Justinian's *Institutes*.

Optimus interpretandi modus est sic leges interpretare ut leges legibus accordant. ōp´tēmūs ēntārprātan´dē mō´dūs āst sēk lā´gās ēntārprāta´rā ūt lā´gās lā´gēbūs akkōr´dant. ap´timus intɜrpretân´dī mō´dus est sik le´jēz intɜrpreta´rē ūt le´jēz le´jibus ukōr´dunt. "The best manner of interpretation is to interpret laws in such a way that laws agree with each other." A maxim of common law, attributable to Edward Coke, meaning that, whenever two laws can reasonably be read in a manner that avoids conflict between them, they should be so read, because the drafters should not be presumed to have intended to contradict themselves.

Optimus legum interpres est consuetudo. ōp´tēmūs lā´gūm ēntār´prās āst kōnswātū´dō. ap´timus le´jum intɜr´pres est kanswetū´dō. "Custom is the best interpreter of the law." An alternative formulation of **Optima est legis interpres consuetudo**, originating in Justinian's *Institutes*.

Opus magnum. ō´pūs mag´nūm. ō´pus mâg´num. *n.* "Great work." An author's or artist's masterpiece. An alternative formulation is **Magnum opus.**

Ordinandi lex. ōrdēnan´dē lāks. ōrdinân´dī leks. *n.* "Law of ordering." An alternative formulation of **Lex ordinandi.**

Ore tenus. ō´rā tā´nūs. ō´rē te´nus. *adj.* or *adv.* "By word of mouth." An alternative phrase for **Viva voce.**

P

Pacem in maribus. pa´kām ēn ma´rēbūs. pā´sum in ma´ribus. *n. acc.* "Peace on the seas." The accusative declension of **Pax in maribus**, which would be used in Latin when the term occupies the place of the direct object of a verb.

Pacem in terris. pa´kām ēn tār´rēs. pā´sum in te´ris. *n. acc.* "Peace on the lands." The accusative declension of **Pax in terris**, which would be used in Latin when the term occupies the place of the direct object of a verb.

Paci sunt maxime contraria vis et iniuria. pa´kē sūnt ma´ksēmā kōntra´rē-a wēs āt ēnyū´rē-a. pâ´sī sunt mâ´ksimē kantra´rē-u vis et injɜ´rē-u. "Force and wrong are greatly contrary to peace." A maxim, attributable to Edward Coke, meaning that the use of force to harm another, even backed by a legal right, tends to undermine public order. An alternative formulation is **Maxime paci sunt contraria vis et iniuria.**

Pacta. *See* **Pactum.**

Pacta in favorem tertii. pak´ta ēn fawō´rām tār´tē-ē. pâk´tu in fâvō´rem tɜr´šī. *n.* "Agreement in favor of a third party." A treaty benefitting a nonparty to the treaty. A general rule of treaty interpretation provides that treaties will not normally be construed to confer rights on a nonparty unless the treaty clearly indicates that such was the intent of the parties, and the third party consents. *See* the Vienna Convention on the Law of Treaties arts. 34, 36, May 23, 1969, 1155 U.N.T.S. 331. *See also* **Pacta tertiis (nec nocent nec prosunt).**

Pacta non obligant nisi gentes inter quas inita. pak´ta nōn ōb´lēgant nē´sē gān´tās ēn´tār kwas ēnē´ta. pâk´tu nan ab´ligant ni´zē jen´tēz kwas ini´tu. "Agreements bind only those who sign them." A maxim meaning that a treaty cannot create binding obligations on nonparties. *See* the Vienna Convention on the Law of Treaties arts. 34–36, May 23, 1969, 1155 U.N.T.S. 331. *Compare with*

Pacta tertiis (nec nocent nec prosunt) and **Res inter alios acta alteri nocere non debet.**

Pacta quae turpem causam continent non sunt observanda. pak´ta kwī tūr´pām kô´sam kōntē´nānt nōn sūnt ōbsārwan´da. pâk´tu kwā tɜr´pem kă´zum kan´tinent nan sunt absɜrvân´du. "Agreements that embrace a corrupt objective are not recognized." A maxim meaning that treaties or contracts embracing illegal or immoral objectives may be considered legally void or unenforceable. *See also* **Ex turpi causa non oritur actio.**

Pacta sunt servanda. pak´ta sūnt sārwan´da. pâk´tu sunt sɜrvan´du. "Treaties are observed." A maxim meaning that every treaty in force binds the parties to that treaty to perform their obligations in good faith until their adherence to the treaty has been lawfully terminated (and afterward in the case of obligations that continue after termination of the treaty). Concomitantly, the breach of a treaty obligation violates international law except with the consent of the other parties or, in some cases, under an established rule of customary international law. *E.g.*, "The Court would set a precedent with disturbing implications for treaty relations and the integrity of the rule *pacta sunt servanda* if it were to conclude that a treaty in force between States, which the parties have implemented in considerable measure and at great cost over a period of years, might be unilaterally set aside on grounds of reciprocal non-compliance." *Gabcíkovo-Nagymaros Project* (Hung. v. Slovk.), 1997 I.C.J. Rep. 7, ¶ 114. *See* the Vienna Convention on the Law of Treaties art. 26, May 23, 1969, 1155 U.N.T.S. 331.

Pacta tertiis (nec nocent nec prosunt). pak´ta tār´tē-ēs (nāk nō´kānt nāk prō´sūnt). pâk´tu tɜr´šis (nek nō´sent nek prō´zunt). "Treaties (neither harm nor benefit) third parties." A maxim meaning that nonparties to a treaty cannot claim benefits under, or complain of violations of, the treaties of others except under limited circumstances. Neither can a treaty dispose of a right of a nonparty to the treaty or otherwise operate to the prejudice of a nonparty's existing legal rights. *See* the Vienna Convention on the Law of Treaties arts. 34–36, May 23, 1969, 1155 U.N.T.S. 331. An alternative phrase is **Pacta tertiis (non nocent).** *Compare with* **Res inter alios (acta) (alteri nocere non debet)** and **Pacta non obligant nis gentes inter quas inita.**

Pacta tertiis (non nocent). pak´ta tār´tē-ēs (nōn nō´kānt). pâk´tu tɜr´šis (nan nō´sent). "Agreements (do not harm) third parties." An alternative phrase for **Pacta tertiis (nec nocent nec prosunt).**

Pactio. pak´tēō. pâk´šō. *n.* [*pl.* **Pactiones.** paktēō´nās. pâkšō´nēz.] "Agreement." (1) A class of peace treaties used by the Romans permitting innocent passage of persons and vessels of each state through the territory of the other. (2) The process of negotiating an agreement (*pactum*). *Compare with* **Foedera**, **Pactum**, and **Sponsio**.

P

Pactum. pak´tūm. pâk´tum. *n.* [*pl.* **Pacta**. pak´ta. pâk´tu.] "Agreement." (1) A binding treaty, convention, or other agreement. (2) A binding contract. (3) A nonbinding agreement. *Compare with* **Foedus**, **Pactiones**, and **Sponsio**.

Pactum agendo. pak´tūm agān´dō. pâk´tum ujen´dō. *n.* "Treaty of agenda." A treaty, the terms of which express an expectation that the parties will agree on a future course of action. Compare with **Pactum de contrahendo**.

Pactum conventum. pak´tūm kōnwān´tūm. pâk´tum kanven´tum. *n.* [*pl.* **Pacta conventa**. pak´ta kōnwān´ta. pâk´tu kanven´tu.] "Agreed upon pact." (1) An agreement between a sovereign ruler and the people he or she governs that formally limits the ruler's power. (2) A municipal constitution or bill of rights.

Pactum de compromittendo. pak´tūm dā kōmprōmēttān´dō. pâk´tum dā kamprumiten´dō. *n.* "Agreement of submission." An agreement to submit disputes to third-party arbitration; a *compromis*. *E.g.*, "As regards the *pactum de compromittendo*, international law has made certain progress in developing the formulas regulating passage from arbitration *in potentia* to arbitration *in actu*, particularly in respect of the appointment of arbitrators by the act of a third party." *Advisory Opinion on Interpretation of Peace Treaties with Bulgaria, Hungary, and Romania*, 1950 I.C.J. Rep. 221, 248 (Judge Azevedo, dissenting).

Pactum de contrahendo. pak´tūm dā kōntrahān´dō. pâk´tum dā kantruhen´dō. *n.* "Agreement to bargain." (1) A binding agreement to conclude a more detailed treaty or agreement with the other party to the agreement. (2) A binding agreement to arbitrate future disputes; a *compromis*. (3) A binding agreement having some details left to further negotiation in the expectation that the parties are legally bound to work out a compromise. *Compare with* **Pactum agendo**. *Contrast with* **Punctationes**.

Pactum de negotiando. pak´tūm dā nāgōtē-an´dō. pâk´tum dā negōšē-ân´dō. *n.* "Agreement on conducting business." (1) An agreement on trade, commerce, or financial dealings between the parties. (2) An agreement on the manner in which the parties will conduct future business. Note that the Latin verb *negotiare* is a *faux ami* to the English verb "to negotiate."

P

Pactum illicitum. pak´tūm ēllē´kētūm. pâk´tum ili´situm. *n.* "Illicit agreement." An agreement that is invalid due to the illegality of the subject matter or the obligations imposed on one or more of the parties.

Pandectes. pandāk´tās. pândek´tēz. *adj. Gr.* (commonly used as a *n.*) "All received." (1) A collection of all statutes and laws of a particular country or region. (2) An encyclopedic work. (3) A book that contains all available information on its subject. Often anglicized as "pandect."

Par. par. par. *n.* "An equal." (1) An equal, equivalent, or cognate. (2) Something equivalent in magnitude, intensity, or value. *E.g.*, "Eritrea responded with declarations from public officials and hospital medical directors contending that Ethiopians received medical treatment throughout the conflict on *par* with Eritreans." *Civilian Claims—Ethiopia's Claim 5* (Eth. v. Eri.), Perm. Ct. Arb., Eth.-Eri. Cl. Comm'n, Partial Award of Dec. 17, 2004, ¶ 58, 44 I.L.M. 630, 641 (2005).

Par delictum. par dālēk´tūm. par dulik´tum. *n.* "An equal offense." One who is equal in wrongfulness to another; one who bears liability for a harm that is equal with the liability of another. *Compare with* **In pari delicto.**

Par in parem imperium non habet. par ēn pa´rām ēmpār´ē-ūm nōn ha´bāt. par in pa´rem impē´rē-um nan hâ´bet. "Equals have no sovereignty over each other." An alternative formulation of **Par in parem non habet imperium.**

Par in parem non habet imperium. par ēn pa´rām nōn ha´bāt ēmpār´ē-ūm. par in pa´rem nan hâ´bet impē´rē-um. "Equals have no sovereignty over each other." A maxim meaning that sovereign states may not exercise prescriptive, executive, or adjudicative jurisdiction over another sovereign, because such exercises unacceptably imply that the states do not benefit from equal dignity. An alternative formulation is **Par in parem imperium non habet.** *See also* **Iurisdictio inhaeret, cohaeret, adhaeret imperio; par in parem non habet iudicium** and **Par in parem non habet iurisdictionem.**

Par in parem non habet iurisdictionem. par ēn pa´rām nōn ha´bāt yūrēsdēktēō´nām. par in pa´rem nan hâ´bet jɜrisdikšō´num. "Equals have no jurisdiction over each other." A maxim meaning that no state's courts may exercise jurisdiction over a foreign sovereign. This doctrine was formerly cited to sustain the absolute sovereign immunity of states from the judicial jurisdiction of other states. This principle has been successfully challenged by states adopting a restrictive theory of sovereign immunity that permits the exercise of judicial jurisdiction over a limited class of acts by a foreign state (*acta iure gestionis*). *Compare with* **Rex extra territorium suum privatem.** *See also*

P

Iurisdictio inhaeret, cohaeret, adhaeret imperio; par in parem non habet iudicium and **Par in parem non habet imperium.**

Parens patriae. pa´rāns pa´trē-ī. pa´renz pât´rē-ā. *n.* "Parent of the country." (1) A doctrine by which the state has standing to act on behalf of its population generally or of specific citizens; the state acting in such capacity. Generally, a state government is considered empowered to act as *parens patriae* in the international arena on behalf of the state's citizens to protect their rights when they have no standing or ability to do so themselves. *E.g.*, "Croatia requests the Court to adjudge and declare…that the Federal Republic of Yugoslavia has an obligation to pay the Republic of Croatia, in its own right and as *parens patriae* for its citizens, reparations for damages to persons and property…caused by the foregoing violations of international law in a sum to be determined by the Court." *Application of the Convention on the Prevention and Punishment of the Crime of Genocide* (Croat. v. Serb.), I.C.J. No. 118, Judgment of Nov. 18, 2008, at 6, ¶ 20. (2) More generally, the state or its government in its capacity as sovereign, acting as guardian or representative of its population generally or of specific citizens in need of protection or representation. *E.g.*, "Mention may be made in this connection, as emphasizing this aspect of guardianship (which is exemplified, in its wider sense, in the system of protective upbringing), of the fact that in English law the Crown as the *parens patriae*—the parent of the country as a whole—is the supreme guardian of infants and, through its Courts, exercises its authority in this respect, at every stage, with total disregard of any artificial formalities of the law." *Application of the Convention of 1902 Governing the Guardianship of Infants* (Nether. v. Swed.), 1958 I.C.J. Rep. 55, 90 (separate opinion of Judge Lauterpacht). *Compare with* **Ex relatione** and **In loco parentis.**

Pari passu. pa´rē pas´sū. pa´rī pâ´sū. *n.* (commonly used as an *adv.*) "Equal pace." (1) Simultaneously. (2) Proceeding together in synchronization; at an equal pace. *E.g.*, "*Pari passu* with the breaking down of isolation, [which] makes a common public opinion possible, the building up of standards of conduct is being accomplished by the formulation and establishment of rules that are being gradually taken out of the domain of discussion into that of general acceptance." Elihu Root, *Address of the President of the Society*, 2 Am. Soc'y Int'l L. Proc. 14, 18 (1908).

Pari ratione. pa´rē ratēō´nā. pa´rī râšō´nē. *adv.* "By equal reasoning." By the same or similar reasoning as that relied upon previously. *E.g.*, "The rules regulating [the ordering of payments of debts owed by a decedent], in common with all other incidents attending to the *administration* of a decedent's estate, are those prescribed by the law of the place where the assets administered are situated (*lex fori et situs*)....*Pari ratione*, the *lex fori et situs* will determine the nature of the assets there situated, as whether they are to be deemed real or personal, legal or equitable." Raleigh C. Minor, Conflict of Laws; or, Private International Law 245–46, § 111 (1901).

P

Parte inaudita. par´tā ēnôdē´ta. par´tē inā´ditu. *adv.* "One party being unheard." An alternative term for **Inaudita altera parte.**

Passim. pas´sēm. pâ´sim. *adj.* "Here and there." A signal often used in citations to indicate that evidence to support the cited assertion is found throughout the referenced work, so that citation to specific pages would be unhelpful.

Paterfamilias. pa´tārfamē´lē-as. pa´tɜrfâmē´lē-us. *n.* "Father of the family." (1) The head of the household. In this sense, the term is sometimes used metaphorically to denote the leader of a small group. (2) A guardian. (3) An independent person. In Roman times, it connoted a relatively unrestrained autocratic power over one's family and children in particular. *See also* **Bonus paterfamilias.**

Patientia. patē-ān´tē-a. pâšen´šē-u. *n.* "Toleration." (1) Toleration. (2) Forbearance. Grotius used this term to indicate the international responsibility incurred by a sovereign for failing to prevent internationally illegal acts by his or her citizens or officials when such acts were both preventable and reasonably foreseeable or actually detected. *See* Hugo Grotius, 2 De Jure Belli ac Pacis ch. 21, para. 2 (1625). *Compare with* **Receptus.**

Patria. pat´rē-a. pât´rē-u. *n.* "Fatherland." (1) The state or its territory. (2) A person's state of nationality.

Pax. paks. pâks. *n.* "Peace." (1) The absence of any armed conflict of significant intensity. (2) The period of time between major wars. (3) Generally friendly or otherwise nonhostile relations between or among states.

Pax Americana. paks amārēka´na. pâks amārikâ´nu. *n.* "American Peace." A term sometimes used to denote a period of relative worldwide geopolitical stability sustained by American power, lasting from 1945 to the present. *Compare with* **Pax Europeana.**

Pax Britannica. paks brētan´nēka. pâks britâ´niku. *n.* "British Peace." A term sometimes used to denote a period of relative geopolitical stability in Europe sustained by British naval power and the defeat of the French armies at Waterloo, lasting from 1815 to 1870.

Pax Europeana. paks āūrōpā-a´na. pâks yɜrōpē-â´nu. *n.* "European Peace." A term sometimes used to denote a period of geopolitical stability in Western

Europe reinforced by the political and military power of European Communities and the North Atlantic Treaty Organization, lasting from 1945 to the present. *Compare with* **Pax Americana.**

Pax in maribus. paks ēn ma´rēbūs. pâks in ma´ribus. *n.* "Peace on the seas." The absence of war or other armed conflict on the high seas. Even during a general war, vessels of an innocent neutral or civilian on the high seas, and hospital ships, must be respected. *See, e.g.*, Hague Convention (III) for the Adaptation to Maritime Warfare of the Principles of the Geneva Convention of August 22, 1864, arts. 1–2, 6, July 29, 1899, 32 Stat. 1827; Geneva Convention (II) for the Amelioration of the Condition of Wounded, Sick, and Shipwrecked Members of Armed Forces at Sea art. 22, Aug. 12, 1949, 75 U.N.T.S. 31. *See also* **Occupatio non praecedit nisi in re terminata.**

Pax in terris. paks ēn tār´rēs. pâks in te´ris. *n.* "Peace on the lands." (1) The absence of armed conflict on the land (as opposed to the sea). (2) Worldwide peace.

Pax Romana. paks rōma´na. pâks rōmâ´nu. *n.* "Roman Peace." A term sometimes used to denote a period of relative geopolitical stability in most of Europe, North Africa, and the Middle East sustained by Roman power from approximately 27 BCE to 180 CE.

Pendente bello. pāndān´tā bāl´lō. penden´tā be´lō. *adv.* "During war." (1) While engaged in a formal war. (2) During the course of an armed conflict. *E.g.*, "The dispossession of the lawful government by the invader *pendente bello* is no more than an incident of military occupation." Hersch Lauterpacht, *Recognition of States in International Law*, 53 YALE L.J. 385, 412 n.63 (1944).

Pendente lite. pāndān´tā lē´tā. penden´tā li´tā. *adv.* "During the lawsuit." During the prosecution or pendency of a lawsuit, as opposed to before the lawsuit has been instituted or after a final judgment has been entered. *E.g.*, "These interim measures will cease to have effect as from the date of the present Judgment, since the power of the Court to indicate interim measures under Article 41 of the Statute of the Court is only exercisable *pendente lite*." *Fisheries Jurisdiction* (F.R.G. v. Ice.), 1974 I.C.J. Rep. 175, ¶ 70 (Merits). *Compare with* **Ad litem.** *See also* **Lis pendens.**

Pendente litis. A common misspelling of **Pendente lite.**

Per ambages. pār amba´gās. pɜr âm´bugēz. *adv.* "By evasions." (1) Furtively; evasively. (2) Indirectly.

Per analogiam. pār analō´gē-am. Pɜr ânulō´jum. *adj.* "By analogy." By inference from a different principle or scenario having sufficient similarities to the matter at hand to instruct its resolution. *E.g.*, "A measure taken by an official outside the sphere of competence of that official is by definition a non-existent measure, a measure limited to the factual sphere as it is devoid of legal effect. In that respect the qualification contained in the commentary on Article 8 of the Convention on the Law of Treaties is applicable *per analogiam*." *Application of the Convention on the Prevention and Punishment of the Crime of Genocide* (Bosn. & Herz. v. Yugo.), 1996 I.C.J. Rep. 595, 705, ¶ 39 (Judge *ad hoc* Kreća, dissenting).

Per annum. pār an´nūm. pɜr â´num. *adv.* "By the year." On an annual basis; every year. *E.g.*, "At the expiration of said periods, the said sum will bear interest at the rate of 6 per cent. *per annum*, the legal rate of interest in Portugal." *The Expropriated Religious Properties Cases* (Gr. Brit. v. Port.), Perm. Ct. Arb., Award of Sept. 2, 1920, ¶ 2, H.C.R. (2d series), at 8 (Scott 1932).

Per capita. pār kapē´ta. pɜr kâ´pitu. *adv.* "By head-count." Based on the number of relevant individuals; on a per-person basis. *E.g.*, "[A]s *per capita* income [in Turkey] has been gradually increasing since the 2001 financial crisis, the demand for importation of goods, including rice, has also increased." *Turkey—Measures Affecting the Importation of Rice*, WTO Doc. WT/DS334/R, at 222 (Sept. 21, 2007).

Per consequens. pār kōn´sākwāns. pɜr kan´sekwens. *adv.* "By consequence." Consequently; therefore. *Compare with* **Ergo** and **Ideo**.

Per contra. pār kōn´tra. pɜr kan´tru. *adv.* "By the opposite." (1) To the contrary; in contradiction. *E.g.*, "[C]ounsel for Respondent considered that a competency to grant a 'request' for the ending of the Mandate 'is totally unrelated to the subject of a supervisory power.' *Per contra*, the correct conclusion is that such a 'competency' is one of the highest manifestations of supervisory power." *South West Africa Cases* (Eth. v. S. Afr.; Liber. v. S. Afr.), 1966 I.C.J. Rep. 6, 388 (Judge Jessup, dissenting). (2) On the other hand; in contrast. *E.g.*, "[T]here have certainly been cases in which a claim has been pronounced to be inadmissible, even though the objections on the score of jurisdiction had not been fully disposed of, so that strictly the court might not be competent to act at all. *Per contra*, there have been cases in which a court has found itself to be competent, yet has refused to proceed any further, on what were essentially grounds of propriety." *Northern Cameroons Case* (Camer. v. U.K.), 1963 I.C.J. Rep. 15, 102 (separate opinion of Judge Fitzmaurice).

Per curiam. pār kū´rē-am. pɜr kyū´rē-um. *adv.* "By the court." Having been written by a tribunal unanimously, without any specific designated author. *Compare with* **Tota curia**.

Per definitionem. pār dāfēnētēō´nām. p3r definišō´num. *adv.* "By way of definition." In the way of a definition; as a definition. *E.g.*, "Aggression *per definitionem* is the 'use of armed force *by a state* against the sovereignty, territorial integrity or political independence of *another state*, or in any other manner inconsistent with the Charter of the United Nations.'" *Application of the Convention on the Prevention and Punishment of the Crime of Genocide* (Bosn. & Herz. v. Yugo.), 1996 I.C.J. Rep. 595, 690 (Judge *ad hoc* Kreća, dissenting).

P

Per dictum. pār dēk´tūm. p3r dik´tum. *adv.* "By saying." By way of a *dictum*; as a *dictum*. *E.g.*, "[Judge] Shahabuddeen nevertheless noted *per dictum* that Yugoslavia might have a duty to exercise due diligence." Jan Arno Hessbruegge, *The Historical Development of the Doctrines of Attribution and Due Diligence in International Law*, 36 INT'L L. & POL. 265, 304 (2004). *See* **Dictum.**

Per diem. pār dē´ām. p3r dē´um. "By the day." (1) *adv.* Daily. *E.g.*, "The Commission observes that the No. 1 diet is set out in the Schedule to the Prison Rules (Northern Ireland) 1954 and, when awarded for a period of three days, consists of the following: '12 ozs. bread and 8 ozs. potatoes *per diem* with water and 1 pint of tea morning and night and 1 pint soup midday.'" *McFeeley v. United Kingdom*, 3 E.H.R.R. 161, ¶ 74 (Eur. Comm'n Hum. Rts. 1981). (2) *adv.* Based on the number of days, as in the average number of cases heard by a tribunal *per diem*. (3) *n.* An amount of money allocated daily to an employee, contractor, or agent for quotidian expenses.

Per expressum. pār āksprās´sūm. p3r ekspre´sum. *adv.* "Expressly." Explicitly; in clear and direct language.

Per facta concludentia. pār fak´ta kōnklūdān´tē-a. p3r fâk´tu kanklūden´šu. *adv.* "By tacit deed." By implicit or tacit consent. *E.g.*, "The Permanent Court attached no importance to the form in which consent to its jurisdiction was given; this could be effected merely *per facta concludentia*. But the three States have not accepted the jurisdiction of the Court in any form." *Advisory Opinion on Interpretation of Peace Treaties with Bulgaria, Hungary, and Romania*, 1950 I.C.J. Rep. 65, 96 (Judge Winiarski, dissenting). *See also* **Facta concludentia.**

Per fas aut nefas. pār fas ôt nā´fas. p3r fâs ăt ne´fâs. *adv.* "By what is proper or improper." By any means, regardless of legality or ethics.

Per feloniam. pār fālō´nē-am. p3r felō´nē-um. *adv.* "By criminality." With criminal intent.

Per fraudem. pār frô´dâm. p3r fră´dum. *adv.* "By fraud." By means of fraud or deception.

Per incuriam. pār ēnkū´rē-am. p3r inkyū´rē-um. *adv.* "By way of neglect." (1) Having occurred through neglect or negligence. (2) Having incorrect or faulty reasoning.

P

Per insidias et industriam. pār ēnsē´dē-as āt ēndūs´trē-am. p3r insi´dē-us et indus´trē-um. *adv.* "By artifices and effort." Designedly; by careful planning with foresight.

Per legem. pār lā´gām. p3r le´jum. *adv.* "By law." According to or under the law.

Per legem terrae. pār lā´gām tār´rī. p3r le´jum te´rā. *adv.* "By the law of the land." According to the domestic law of the state concerned.

Per minas. pār mē´nas. p3r mī´nus. *adv.* "By threats." Occurring by threats of violence, extortion, or other coercion.

Per modum exceptionis. pār mō´dūm āks-kāptēō´nēs. p3r mō´dum eksepšō´nis. *adv.* "By means of exception." By way of exception; as an exception.

Per procurationem. pār prōkūratēō´nām. p3r prakyūrāšō´nem. *adv.* "By the agency." Through the intercession of one's agent; by proxy.

Per quod. pār kwōd. p3r kwad. *prep.* + *pro.* (sometimes used as an *adj.*) "By which." (1) By or through which. (2) Based on facts or a legal theory that proves an otherwise incomplete case. Historically, at common law, libel *per quod* was an indirect libel, the defamatory character of which was not apparent except by reference to facts known to the reader and not explicitly stated. *See* William L. Prosser, *Libel* Per Quod, 46 VIR. L. REV. 839 (1960).

Per saltum. pār sal´tūm. p3r sal´tum. *adv.* "By a leap." All at once; instantly rather than gradually.

Per se. pār sā. p3r sā. *adj.* or *adv.* "By itself." (1) In and of itself. (2) Alone. (3) Inherently. *E.g.*, "A weapon that is already unlawful *per se*, whether by treaty or custom, does not become lawful by reason of its being used for a legitimate purpose under the [UN] Charter." *Advisory Opinion Concerning the Legality of the Threat or Use of Nuclear Weapons*, 1996 I.C.J. Rep. 226, ¶ 39.

Per universitatem. pār ūnēwārsēta´tām. p3r yūniv3rsitā´tem. *adv.* "Universally." (1) Universally; by all relevant persons. (2) Unanimously. *Compare with* **Nemine contra dicente** and **Una voce**.

Perduellio. pārdūāl´lēō. p3rdū-e´lēō. *n.* "Treason." (1) An offense against the state's sovereignty, independence, or political integrity committed by its own citizen; treason. (2) In Roman law, a crime that, at various points in history, ranged from treason to any conduct that harmed Rome. *Compare with* **Crimen laesae maiestatis** and **Crimen maiestatis**. *See also* **Laesa maiestas**.

P

Perseverare diabolicum. pārsāwāra´rē dē-abō´lēkūm. pɜrsevɜra´rē dīuba´likum. An abbreviated form of **Errare humanum est, (sed) perseverare diabolicum.**

Persona. pārsō´na. pɜrsō´nu. *n.* "Mask." (1) An individual person. (2) Legal personality.

Persona ficta. pārsō´na fēk´ta. pɜrsō´nu fik´tu. *n.* [*pl.* **Personae fictae**. pārsō´nī fēk´tī. pɜrsō´nā fik´tā.] "Fictitious person." A fictitious person created under law (under either the municipal law of a state or international law) and endowed with legal personality. A corporation, a nonprofit organization, and an intergovernmental organization can all be *personae fictae*. Alternative terms are **Persona iuridica** and **Persona moralis**.

Persona grata. pārsō´na gra´ta. pɜrsō´nu gra´tu. *n.* [*pl.* **Personae gratae**. pārsō´nī gra´tī. pɜrsō´nā gra´tā.] "Welcome person." A diplomat accredited to and accepted by the receiving state. *Contrast with* **Persona non grata**.

Persona iuridica. pārsō´na yūrē´dēka. pɜrsō´nu jɜri´diku. *n.* "Juridical person." An alternative term for **Persona ficta**.

Persona moralis. pārsō´na mōra´lēs. pɜrsō´nu mōrâ´lis. *n.* "Moral person." An alternative term for **Persona ficta**.

Persona non grata. pārsō´na nōn gra´ta. pɜrsō´nu nan gra´tu. *n.* [*pl.* **Personae non gratae**. pārsō´nī nōn gra´tī. pɜrsō´nā nan gra´tā.] "Unwelcome person." (1) A term used to designate a diplomat or member of a mission staff whose request to be posted in a receiving state or whose continued presence in a receiving state is rejected by the receiving state. If the diplomat is present in the receiving state, he or she must return to the sending state upon designation as *persona non grata*. *E.g.*, "The receiving State may at any time and without having to explain its decision, notify the sending State that the head of the mission or any member of the diplomatic staff of the mission is *persona non grata* or that any other member of the staff of the mission is not acceptable." Vienna Convention on Diplomatic Relations art. 9(1), Apr. 18, 1961, 500 U.N.T.S. 95. (2) Generally, a person whose presence is unwelcome or unwanted. *Contrast with* **Persona grata**. *See also* **Non grata**.

Persona standi in iudicio. pārsō´na stan´dē ēn yūdē´kēō. pɜrsō´nu stân´dī in jūdi´šēō. *n.* "Person of standing in a court." (1) A person having standing to appear before a tribunal to represent himself or his or her principal. (2) The right or capacity of standing to appear before a tribunal.

Petitio principii. pātē´tēō prēnkē´pē-ē. peti´šō prin´sipī. *n.* "A laying claim to the premise." A fallacious argument that begs the question, or assumes the very premise, it is supposed to prove. *E.g.*, "In order to assert its view, the Belgian Government has repeatedly referred to a figurative concept of 'piercing the veil' of corporate personality. So far as this slogan is concerned, however, it simply means that the shareholders must be protected by their national State regardless of the juridical personality of the corporation. It is a *petitio principii* and nothing more." *Barcelona Traction, Light, and Power Co., Ltd.* (Belg. v. Spain), 1970 I.C.J. Rep. 3, 120 (separate opinion of Judge Tanaka).

Petitum. pātē´tūm. peti´tum. *n.* "Claim." (1) A claim at law. (2) A complaint. (3) A petition for relief. *See also* **Petitus.**

Petitus. pātē´tūs. peti´tus. *n.* "The claimed thing." The subject matter of a claim, complaint, or petition for relief. *See also* **Petitum.**

Pirata est hostis humani generis. pēra´ta āst hōs´tēs hūma´nē gā´nārēs. pī´retu est has´tis hyū´munī je´nuris. "A pirate is the enemy of humankind." A maxim, sometimes attributed to Cicero (*De Officiis* III.107) and also found in Edward Coke's *Institutes of the Laws of England* (3:113), meaning that one who engages in piracy has set himself or herself in opposition to the interests of every state and peoples. He is, therefore, an enemy to humankind and a criminal subject to universal jurisdiction. During much of the sixteenth through eighteenth centuries, a privateer in time of war carrying a lawful letter of marque was not, however, considered a pirate in spite of depredations on the merchant shipping of another state. *See also* **Hostis humani generis.**

Pirata non mutat dominium. pēra´ta nōn mū´tat dōmē´nē-ūm. pī´retu nan myū´tât dumi´nē-um. "A pirate does not change ownership." A maxim meaning that the unlawful capture of a vessel (*viz.*, by piracy) cannot constitute a lawful prize or otherwise result in a change of ownership of the vessel. After recapture, the vessel must be restored to its last owner (a right sometimes called *le droit de rescousse*, or "right of rescue").

Placita iuris. pla´kēta yū´rēs. plâ´situ j3´ris. *n. pl.* "Pleas of law." (1) General principles of law, as opposed to conclusions of law based on specific facts. (2) A statement of positive law.

Plenitudo potestatis. plānētū´dō pōtāsta´tēs. plenitū´dō pōtestā´tis. *n.* "Fullness of power." (1) Full sovereign power. (2) Unlimited power. *E.g.*, "In contrast to the classical and medieval legalists, the canonists did not think the papal *plenitudo potestatis* could have been granted by the Christian people. The pope received his authority from God." J.D. Watt, *Spiritual and Temporal Powers*, *in* Cambridge History of Medieval Political Thought 433 (J.H. Burns ed., 1988).

P

Pleno iure. plā´nō yū´rā. plē´nō jɜ´rē. *adv.* "In full right." Having an unrestricted right to something.

Portus. pōr´tūs. pōr´tus. *n.* "Port." (1) Port. (2) Harbor.

Positivi iuris. pōsētē´wē yū´rēs. paziti´vī jɜ´ris. *adj.* "Of positive law." Deriving from or relating to the positive law, as opposed to natural right or ethics. *E.g.*, "That the correspondence of the institution [of adoption] in all its main particulars, as it prevailed in the three countries of India, Greece, and Italy, was the result of communication, and not a coincidence, is inferable, considering that adoption, like inheritance, is an affair *positivi juris*, instead of depending upon those fundamental and universal principles, which, animating the breasts, and influencing the conduct of mankind in general, produce, in various subjects of familiar intercourse, an identity of rule." Thomas Strange, Hindu Law 95 (5th ed. 1875).

Possessio. pōssās´sēō. puze´šō. *n.* "Possession." Actual possession of personal property or occupation of territory. *E.g.*, "Immemorial possession *sive indefinita* manifests itself as a present and evident fact the commencement of which is unknown. It requires the fulfilment of two conditions. One condition is positive: proof of a peaceful *possessio* during the critical period, exercised for so long that there is no longer any memory of a time when it did not exist." *Advisory Opinion on Western Sahara*, 1975 I.C.J. Rep. 12, 154 (separate opinion of Judge De Castro).

Possessio ad interdicta. pōssās´sēō ad ēntārdēk´ta. puze´šō âd intɜrdik´tu. *n.* "Possession for interdiction." Occupation of territory or territorial waters for the purpose of blockading the territory and preventing trade or maritime communication therewith.

Possessio ad usucapionem. pōssās´sēō ad ūsūkapēō´nām. puze´šō âd yūzūkâpēō´nem. *n.* "Possession for the purpose of acquiring ownership." Adverse possession of territory or territorial waters for the purpose of annexation or claiming ownership of the territory or waters.

Possessio longi temporis. pōssās´sēō lōn´gē tām´pōrēs. puze´šō laŋ´ī tempō´ris. *n.* "Possession for a long period of time." A claim to sovereignty over a territory by virtue of long occupation and administration without significant interruption or consistent opposition from any other interested state. *E.g.*, "In its opinion Norway can justify the claim that these waters are territorial or internal on the ground that she has exercised the necessary jurisdiction over them for a long period without opposition from other States, a kind of *possessio longi temporis*." *Fisheries Case* (U.K. v. Nor.), 1951 I.C.J. Rep. 116. *See also* **Uti possidetis (iuris).**

P

Possessio nec vi nec clam nec precario. pōssās´sēō nāk wē nāk klam nāk prāka´rēō. puze´šō nek vī, nek klâm, nek preke´rēō. *n.* "Possession neither by force, nor secretly, nor by entreaty." (1) Adverse possession of property. (2) Peaceful occupation of territory obtained in a lawful manner without the use of force, fraud, or by gratuitous revocable loan by the owner or previous possessor. *See also* **Uti possidetis (iuris).**

Post. pōst. pōst. *adv.* "Later." Later; subsequently. The term *post* is sometimes used as a citation signal to indicate that the cited reference appears later in the same document. *E.g.*, "The dissenting opinion argues that our conclusion that *Wilko* is inapplicable to the situation presented in this case will vitiate the force of that decision....' *Post*, at 2461." *Scherk v. Alberto-Culver Co.*, 417 U.S. 506, 517 n.11 (1974). *Compare with* **Infra (citatum).** *Contrast with* **Ante.**

Post factum. pōst fak´tūm. pōst fâk´tum. *adj.* "After the fact." Afterward; after the event in question. *Compare with* **Ex post facto.**

Post hoc. pōst hōk. pōst hak. *adj.* "After this." Occurring retrospectively; after the event in question. *E.g.*, "[The Claimants argue] that the Respondent did not rely on the Convention when it cancelled the project, and that the Respondent has only invoked the Convention as a *post hoc* rationalization for an act of expropriation which in fact had nothing to do with the Convention." *Southern Pacific Properties (Middle East) Ltd. v. Egypt*, ICSID Case No. ARB/84/3, Award of May 20, 1992, ¶ 153. *Compare with* **Ex post facto** and **Nunc pro tunc.** *Contrast with* **Ante factum** and **Ante hoc.**

Post hoc ergo propter hoc. pōst hōk ār´gō prōp´tēr hōk. pōst hak ɜr´gō prap´tɜr hak. "After this, therefore because of this." An expression of the logical fallacy wherein one infers from the fact that a later event follows a prior event that the prior event must therefore have caused the later one. *E.g.*, "It is incorrect to claim that the United States is applying the suspension of concessions or other obligations 'with respect to a new measure' just because the United States continues to apply multilaterally authorized suspension of concessions or other obligations on a date after the EC unilaterally announced its compliance. This is the classic *post hoc, ergo propter hoc* (after, therefore because) fallacy." *United States—Continued Suspension of Obligations in the EC—Hormones Dispute*, Panel Report of Mar. 31, 2008, WTO Doc. No. WT/DS320/R, Annex B-3, ¶ 5.

P

Post mortem. pōst mōr´tām. pōst mōr´tum. "After death." (1) *adj.* Occurring after death. *E.g.*, "The remains of members of the force, the civilian component, and dependents who die in Spanish territory may be claimed, given *post mortem* examination, embalmed and transported outside such territory upon authorization of the appropriate Spanish authorities." Agreement on Friendship, Defense, and Cooperation (U.S.-Spain), Annex 1, art. 9, July 2, 1982, 34 U.S.T. 3885. (2) *adj.* Occurring after the demise, dissolution, or negation of a thing or concept. (3) *n.* An examination or analysis of a previously existing thing or concept. *E.g.*, "Korea, however, has not studied the detail of the ASI report, which was submitted to a different panel in a different case, and is concerned with a market in a different country. It is therefore unable to comment on the merits of the ASI study. Moreover, Korea doubts the value of a *post-mortem* on...the ASI study itself." *Korea—Taxes on Alcoholic Beverages*, Panel Report of Sept. 17, 1998, WTO Doc. No. WT/DS75/R, at 148, ¶ 7.24.

Post partum. pōst par´tūm. pōst par´tum. *adj.* "After separation." Occurring after a separation. The term is often used to refer to the period immediately after a woman has given birth, but can be applied to any period or event following the separation of two formerly united or affiliated entities. *E.g.*, "[T]he author does not attempt in this thin volume to describe the...*post-partum* depressions or raging fevers [of countries that had recently achieved independence from colonial powers]." Willard Barber, *Review of Philip C. Jessup, The Birth of Nations*, 71 AM. POLI. SCI. REV. 846, 847 (1977).

Post tantum temporis. pōst tan´tūm tām´pōrēs. pōst tân´tum tem´p3ris. *adv.* "After so long a time." After a very long time; following a long delay.

Postliminium. pōstlēmē´nē-ūm. pōstlimi´nē-um. *n.* "A return to one's threshold." (1) The right under international law, after a belligerent occupation has ended and the occupied state has regained an independent government, to invalidate acts (such as transfers of property) performed by the occupying belligerent in the occupied state's territory. (2) A Roman legal doctrine whereby Roman soldiers captured by an enemy are regarded as having died freemen before capture, thereby suspending their civil and property rights. Upon their return to Rome, the liberated soldiers reassumed the suspended civil and property rights. *See also* **Infra praesidium**.

P

Potentia debet sequi iustitiam, non antecedere. pōtăn´tē-a dā´bāt sā´kwē yūstē´tē-am, nōn antākā´dārā. pōten´šu de´bet se´kwī justi´šum, nan ântēsē´dɜrē. "Force should follow justice, not precede it." A maxim meaning that the use of armed force should only proceed in the service of a just cause, contrary to the maxim "might makes right."

Potestas gladii. pōtās´tas gla´dē-ē. pōtes´tus glâ´dī. *n.* "Power of the sword." (1) Military power; armed force. (2) In Roman law, the power of the government to enforce the laws and administer justice and punishment, including the death penalty. This was also termed *ius gladii* ("the right of the sword").

Potestas stricte interpretatur. pōtās´tas strēk´tā ēntārprāta´tūr. pōtes´tus strik´tē intɜrpretā´tɜr. "Power is interpreted narrowly." A principle of agency law to the effect that the scope of the agency should be interpreted conservatively in the absence of a clear mandate.

Potestas terrae finitur, ubi finitur armorum vis. pōtās´tas tār´rī fēnē´tūr, ū´bē fēnē´tūr armō´rūm wēs. pōtes´tus te´rā fi´nitɜr, ū´bē fi´nitɜr armō´rum vis. "Power over the land ends wherever the force of arms ends." An expression of the "cannon-shot rule," which was used to establish each state's maritime territorial boundaries by the maximum distance of a cannon shot from shore aimed seaward in a direction perpendicular to the shore. The cannonshot rule was superseded by developments in customary maritime law and, ultimately, the rule codified in the UN Convention on the Law of the Sea, which established territorial sea boundaries generally at twelve nautical miles from the littoral baseline. *See* the UN Convention on the Law of the Sea art. 3, Dec. 10, 1982, 21 I.L.M. 1245 (1982). An alternative formulation is **Terrae dominium finitur, ubi finitur armorum vis.**

Praedium. prī´dē-ūm. prā´dē-um. *n.* "Tenement." (1) An estate; real property. (2) Land or territory generally.

Praedium dominans. prī´dē-ūm dō´mēnans. prā´dē-um da´minânz. *n.* "Dominant tenement." Territory or property that benefits from an easement or servitude. *E.g.*, "[A] servitude in international law predicates an express grant of a sovereign right and involves an analogy to the relation of a *praedium dominans* and a *praedium serviens*; whereas by the Treaty of 1818 one State grants a liberty to fish, which is not a sovereign right, but a purely economic right, to the inhabitants of another state." *The North Atlantic Coast Fisheries Arbitration* (U.K. v. U.S.), 11 R.I.A.A. 167 (1910). *Contrast with* **Praedium serviens.**

Praedium serviens. prī´dē-ūm sār´wē-āns. prā´dē-um sɜr´vē-enz. *n.* "Servient tenement." Territory or property that is burdened by an easement or other right held by a state other than the territory's or property's owner. *Contrast with, and* see *the example of usage in,* **Praedium dominans.**

Praescriptio. prīskrēp´tēō. prēskrip´čō. *n.* "Prescription." (1) A principle that supports a state's claim to annexation or acquisition of territory through its undisputed exercise of sovereignty over it. (2) A defensive plea or objection in a case being heard before a tribunal.

P

Praescriptio fori. prīskrēp´tēō fō´rē. prēskrip´čō fō´rī. *n.* "Prescription of the forum." A formal objection to a claim against a person based on the tribunal's lack of jurisdiction over the person objecting.

Praesumptio iuris (et de iure). prīsūmp´tēō yū´rēs (āt dā yū´rā). prēzump´čō jɜ´ris et dā jɜ´rē. *n.* "Presumption of law (and by law)." A presumption as a matter of law that applies by default. In some cases, the presumption is irrebuttable; in others, it may be defeated by a showing of sufficient contrary evidence. An alternative spelling is **Presumptio iuris (et de iure).**

Presumptio iuris (et de iure). An alternative spelling of **Praesumptio iuris (et de iure).**

Praeter legem. prī´tār lā´gām. prā´tɜr le´jem. "Apart from the law." Relating to a matter not clearly addressed by the law, as in **Aquitas praeter legem.** *Compare with* **Contra legem.** *Contrast with* **Infra legem.**

Praetor inter peregrinos. prī´tōr ēn´tār pārāgrē´nōs. prā´tɜr in´tɜr perugri´nōs. *n.* "The magistrate between aliens." An alternative term for **Praetor peregrinus.**

Praetor peregrinus. prī´tōr pārāgrē´nūs. prā´tɜr perugri´nus. *n.* "The magistrate for aliens." A Roman magistrate who administered the *ius gentium*, or law relating to the treatment of foreign citizens and their relations with each other and with Roman citizens within the Roman Empire. An alternative term is **Praetor inter peregrinos.**

Prece partium. prā´kā par´tē-ūm. pre´sē par´tē-um. *n.* "At the request of the parties." Done at the request of one or more parties to a dispute.

Pretium. prā´tē-ūm. pre´šum OR prē´šum. *n.* "Price." (1) Reward. (2) Price; value. (3) Fee. (4) Amount.

Pretium doloris. prā´tē-ūm dōlō´rēs. pre´šum- OR prē´šum dulō´ris. *n.* "Price of pain." Intangible or "moral" damage caused by a wrongful act, such as mental anguish. *E.g.*, "Hungary…referred to reparation of the damage to the fauna, the flora, the soil, the sub-soil, the groundwater and the aquifer, the damages suffered by the Hungarian population on account of the increase in the uncertainties weighing on its future (*pretium doloris*), and the damage arising from the unlawful use, in order to divert the Danube, of installations over which the two Parties exercised joint ownership." *Gabcíkovo-Nagymaros Project* (Hung. v. Slovk.), 1997 I.C.J. Rep. 7, ¶ 127.

P

Prima facie. prē´ma fa´kē-ā. prī´mu fâ´šu. *adj.* or *adv.* "At first sight." Superficial; according to the initial impression made. A *prima facie* case is a claim, the evidence or arguments supporting which are sufficiently convincing to allow the claim to proceed to further evaluation. *E.g.*, "In contemporary international law, the State which first undertakes specified unprovoked, unlawful uses of force against another State—such as substantial involvement in the sending of armed bands onto its territory—is, *prima facie*, the aggressor." *Military and Paramilitary Activities in and Against Nicaragua* (Nicar. v. U.S.), 1986 I.C.J. Rep. 13, 271–72, ¶ 14 (Judge Schwebel, dissenting). *Compare with* **Primo fronte** and **Ictu oculi**. *See also* **Ex facie**.

Primo. prē´mō. prē´mō. *adv.* "At first." First in numerical order. *E.g.*, "The differences between [*ius standi* and personal jurisdiction], however, are considerably greater, making them distinct processual conditions. *Primo*, they reflect the different aspects of the legal nature of the Court." *Application of the Convention on the Prevention and Punishment of the Crime of Genocide* (Bosn. & Herz. v. Yugo.), I.C.J. No. 91, Judgment of Feb. 26, 2007, at 17, ¶ 35 (separate opinion of Judge *ad hoc* Kreća). *Compare with* **Semel**. *See also* **Primus**.

Primo fronte. prē´mō frōn´tā. prē´mō frun´tē. *adv.* "At first sight." (1) Superficially. (2) Evidently. *Compare with* **Prima facie** and **Ictu oculi**.

Primo loco. prē´mō lō´kō. prē´mō lō´kō. *adv.* "In the first place." (1) As first in order. (2) In the first location.

Primo prosequi, secundo dedere. prē´mō prō´sākwē, sākūn´dō dā´dārā. prē´mō pra´sekwī, sekun´dō de´dɜrē. *adv.* + *v.* "First to prosecute, second to deliver." A variant of the *aut dedere aut iudicare* principle espoused by some publicists according to which the state's primary obligation is to try a person shown to have committed a national or international crime in another state's territory or, if it declines, to extradite the individual to the offended state. *E.g.*, "Article 146 of the IVth Geneva Convention...according to some authors even prioritizes prosecution over extradition: *primo prosequi, secundo dedere*. Even if one adopts the doctrinal viewpoint that the notion of universal jurisdiction assumes the presence of the offender, there is nothing in Article 146 that warrants the conclusion that this is an actual requirement." *Arrest Warrant of 11 April 2000* (Congo v. Belg.), 2002 I.C.J. Rep. 3, 175, ¶ 62 (Judge Van den Wyngaert, dissenting). *Compare with* **Aut dedere aut iudicare**.

P

Primum decretum. prē´mūm dākrā´tūm. prī´um dekrē´tum. *n.* "First decree." In maritime law, a provisional order or decree.

Primum mobile. prē´mūm mō´bēlā. prī´mum mō´bilē. *n.* "First mover." The first or main cause of something.

Primus. prē´mūs. prī´mus. *adj.* "First." First in numerical order. *See also* **Primo** and **Semel.**

Primus in tempore potior (est) in iure. prē´mūs ēn tām´pōrā pō´tēōr (āst) ēn yū´rā. prī´mus in tem´pōrē pō´šɜr (est) in jɜ´rē. "The first in time (is) the more powerful in right." A maxim meaning that the first to acquire possession of property may claim a superior right to the property relative to others who acquire possession later in time.

Primus inter pares. prē´mūs ēn´tār pa´rās. prī´mus in´tɜr pa´rēz. *n.* "First among equals." One who, although formally equal to his or her peers, informally possesses greater power or stature. *E.g.*, "The Presidency of the Republic of Bosnia and Herzegovina taken as a whole, as a collegium, is the organ of representation according to the Constitution. The President of the Presidency as the *primus inter pares* does not exercise any independent political powers." *Application of the Convention on the Prevention and Punishment of the Crime of Genocide* (Bosn. & Herz. v. Yugo.), 1996 I.C.J. Rep. 595, 695, ¶ 29 (Judge *ad hoc* Kreća, dissenting).

Princeps legibus solutis. prēn´kāps lā´gēbis sōlū´tēs. prin´seps le´jibus salū´tis. "The sovereign can do no wrong." A largely defunct maxim meaning that a sovereign state or its government may not be hailed before a tribunal to answer for its actions or policies.

Prior in tempore, potior in iure. prē´ōr ēn tām´pōrā, pō´tēōr ēn yū´rā. prī´ɜr in tempō´rē, pō´tēɜr in jɜ´rē. "First in time, greater in right." A maxim meaning that the law favors those who establish their rights earlier rather than later. This principle is often cited in private law to support the claims of prior creditors over later creditors. An alternative phrase is **Qui prior est tempore potior est iure.**

Pro. prō. prō. *prep.* "For." (1) For the purpose of. (2) In preparation of. (3) In favor of. (4) Because of; due to.

Pro bono. prō bō´nō. prō bō´nō. *adj.* or *adv.* "For the good." (1) For the good (of something). (2) An abbreviation of **Pro bono publico.**

Pro bono et malo. prō bō´nō āt ma´lō. prō bō´nō et mâ´lō. *adj.* or *adv.* "For good and ill." For whatever the consequences may be, whether beneficial or harmful.

Pro bono publico. prō bō´nō pū´blēkō. prō bō´nō pub´likō. *adj.* or *adv.* "For the good of the public." Done or performed on behalf of the good of society and not for the gain of the person performing the work. The term is generally used with respect to an attorney's services on behalf of the indigent or unrepresented. Commonly abbreviated **Pro bono.**

Pro facto. prō fak´tō. prō fâk´tō. *adv.* "For the fact." Considering or assuming a stated proposition as if it were fact.

Pro forma. prō fōr´ma. prō fōr´mu. *adj.* or *adv.* "For form." For the sake of appearances or formal procedures only; without substantive import. *E.g.*, "Throughout, one finds that the important…instructions issued from Great Britain, the United States and Belgium and Spain itself, but rarely if ever from Canada. The general meetings of shareholders held in Toronto seem to have been *pro forma* affairs." *Barcelona Traction, Light, and Power Co., Ltd.* (Belg. v. Sp.), 1970 I.C.J. Rep. 3, 190, ¶ 49 (separate opinion of Judge Jessup).

Pro foro externo. prō fō´rō ēkstār´nō. prō fō´rō ekstɜr´nō. *adj.* "On behalf of a foreign forum." With respect to external matters. In international relations, matters *pro foro externo* relate to foreign, as opposed to domestic, affairs. *Contrast with* **Pro foro interno.**

Pro foro interno. prō fō´rō ēntār´nō. prō fō´rō intɜr´nō. *adj.* "On behalf of the internal forum." With respect to internal matters. In international relations, matters *pro foro interno* relate to domestic, as opposed to foreign, affairs. *Contrast with* **Pro foro externo.**

Pro foro interno et externo. prō fō´rō ēntār´nō āt ākstār´nō. prō fō´rō intɜr´nō et ekstɜr´nō. *adj.* "On behalf of the internal and foreign forum." Both within and outside the state; in both the state's municipal and foreign relations spheres. *E.g.*, "The notion of sovereignty appears in international law under two aspects: (*a*) as the doctrine of a rigid positivism according to which only rules expressly recognised by international custom and treaties are the exclusive sources of international law; (*b*) as the conception of the State as an entity of absolute legal and moral value, for which international law exists lawfully only so far as it is subservient to its self-preservation and development. The first is a formal statement to the effect that the will of the State is the ultimate and exclusive source of law *pro foro interno et externo*." Hersch Lauterpacht, PRIVATE LAW SOURCES AND ANALOGIES OF INTERNATIONAL LAW 43 (1927).

Pro futuro. prō fūtū´rō. prō fyū´čɜrō. *adv.* "For the future." (1) Beginning at present and extending indefinitely into the future. *E.g.*, "[I]t is quite realistic to expect that the Republic of Croatia will *pro futuro* cooperate with the

Tribunal as it has already done in surrendering Mr. Aleksovski to the Tribunal." *Prosecutor v. Aleksovski*, ICTY Case No. IT-95-14/1, Transcript of Dec. 2, 1998 (statement of Mr. Mikulicic, Defense Counsel). (2) To occur at some time in the future. *Compare with* **De futuro** and **In futuro**.

P

Pro gravitate admissi. prō grawēta´tā admēs´sē. prō grâvitā´tē âdmi´sī. *adv.* "For the gravity perpetrated." According to the gravity of the offense or harm. *Compare with* **Pro modo admissi.**

Pro hac vice. prō hak wē´kā. prō hâk vīs OR -vī´su OR -vē´čā. *adj.* or *adv.* "For this turn." (1) For or on a specific occasion only. (2) A permission given by a tribunal for a person who would not normally be entitled to appear before the tribunal to enter a special appearance, for example, as an agent or counsel for one of the parties to the dispute.

Pro indefenso. prō ēdāfān´sō. prō indufen´sō. *adv.* "For the lack of defense." With reference to one lacking in or not offering a defense.

Pro loco et tempore. prō lō´kō āt tām´pōrā. prō lō´kō et tempō´rē. *adv.* "For the place and time." For or relating to the location and time that an event has occurred or is expected to occur.

Pro maiori cautela. prō mayō´rē kôtā´la. prō mujō´rī kă´telu. *adv.* "For greater caution." An alternative phrase for **Ob maiorem cautelam.**

Pro modo admissi. prō mō´dō admēs´sē. prō mō´dō âdmi´sī. *adv.* "For the manner perpetrated." According to the kind or magnitude of the offense or harm. *Compare with* **Pro gravitate admissi.**

Pro parte. prō par´tā. prō par´tē. *adv.* "For the part." Partly; in part.

Pro patria (et rege). prō pat´rē-a (āt rā´gā). prō pât´rē-u (et re´jē). *adv.* "For country (and king)." An expression of willingness to serve or sacrifice for the good of one's country.

Pro per. prō pār. prō pɜr. (1) An abbreviation of **Pro persona.** (2) An abbreviation of **Propria persona.**

Pro persona. prō pārsō´na. prō pɜrsō´nu. *adj.* or *adv.* "For the person." An alternative term for **Pro se.** Sometimes abbreviated **Pro per.**

Pro posse suo. prō pōs´sā sū´ō. prō pa´sē sū´ō. *adv.* "To one's ability." To the extent of one's power or ability.

Pro rata. prō ra´ta. prō râ´tu OR -rā´tu. *adj.* or *adv.* "At the rate." At the given rate or in the given proportion. *E.g.*, "[I]n any case, and alternatively, 'Impregilo could certainly not claim more damages than its *pro rata* shares with joint ventures.'" *Impregilo S.p.A. v. Pakistan*, ICSID Case No. ARB/03/3, Award of Apr. 22, 2005, ¶ 98.

Pro rata temporis. prō ra´ta tām´pōrēs. prō râ´tu tempō´ris. *adj.* "At the rate for the time." At a rate (of interest, growth, etc.) proportional to the time allotted.

Pro re nata. prō rā na´ta. prō rā nā´tu. *adv.* "For the born matter." Because of an emergency or immediate need.

Pro se. prō sā. prō sā. *adj.* or *adv.* "For oneself." On behalf of one's self. A criminal defendant or civil litigant who appears *pro se* is representing himself rather than relying on representation by counsel. In criminal cases, courts are generally not bound to honor a defendant's wish to represent himself if the absence of professional counsel would prejudice his chances of a full and fair hearing. *E.g.*, "In the words of the [U.S.] Supreme Court, 'Courts, of course, may still exercise their discretion to allow a lay person to proceed *pro se*.' Courts continue to be entitled to exercise that discretion by virtue of their inherent and overriding responsibility to be fair." *Prosecutor v. Krajisnik*, I.C.T.Y. Case No. IT-00-39-A, Decision of Apr. 18, 2008, ¶ 14 (separate opinion of Judge Shahabuddeen). An alternative term is **Pro persona.**

Pro solido. prō sō´lēdō. prō sa´lidō. *adv.* "For the whole." For the whole; for the entirety.

Pro tanto. prō tan´tō. prō tân´tō. *adv.* "For so much." To a certain or limited extent; insofar. *E.g.*, "Mr. Giuseppe Bisconti also addressed the Court on behalf of the United States; since he had occasion to refer to matters of fact within his knowledge as a lawyer acting for Raytheon Company, the President of the Chamber acceded to a request by the Agent of Italy that Mr. Bisconti be treated *pro tanto* as a witness." *Case Concerning Elettronica Sicula S.p.A. (ELSI)* (U.S. v. Italy), 1989 I.C.J. Rep. 15, 18, ¶ 8. An alternative term is **In tantum.**

Pro tem. prō tem. An abbreviation of **Pro tempore.**

Pro tempore. prō tām´pōrā. prō tem´pərā OR -tempō´rē. *adj.* or *adv.* "For the time." (1) For the moment or a limited time; during an interim; temporarily. Someone holding an official position *pro tempore* is not intended to occupy the position permanently or indefinitely, but merely until a more suitable long-term replacement can be found. (2) Tentatively. *E.g.*, "According to Judge Higgins's opinion, the only way in which it can be determined whether a claimant's claims are sufficiently plausibly based upon the facts is to accept *pro tempore* the facts as alleged by the claimant to be true and to see whether on the basis of these claims of fact there could occur a violation of one or more of the relevant legal provisions." *Industria Nacional de Alimentos SA v. Peru*, ICSID Case No. ARB/03/4, Decision of Sept. 5, 2007, ¶ 118. Sometimes abbreviated **Pro tem.**

Pro veritate accipitur. prō wārēta´tā akkē´pētūr. prō veritā´tē usi´pit3r. *adj.* "It is accepted as truth." Considered to be an established fact or truth. *E.g.*, "The primary effect of *res judicata* in the procedural sense is claim preclusion…, whereas the effect of *res judicata* in the substantive sense is mainly related to the legal validity of the Court's decision as an individualization of objective law in the concrete matter—*pro veritate accipitur*—and, also, to the exclusion of the application of the principle of *stare decisis.*" *Application of the Convention on the Prevention and Punishment of the Crime of Genocide* (Bosn. & Herz. v. Yugo.), I.C.J. No. 91, Judgment of Feb. 26, 2007, at 1, ¶ 3 (separate opinion of Judge *ad hoc* Kreća).

Probandum. prōban´dūm. prōbân´dum. *n.* [*pl.* **Probanda**. prōban´da. prōbân´du.] "Thing needing to be proved." A fact that must be proved by the party alleging the fact.

Proiectio. prōyāk´tēō. prōjek´tēō. *n.* "A throwing forward." Alluvion; earth, silt, or other material deposited on a shore by the sea over time, causing gradual accretion to the landmass on which the material is deposited.

Propria persona. prōp´rē-a pārsō´na. prap´rē-u p3rsō´nu. *adj.* or *adv.* "In one's own person." An alternative term for **Pro se.** Sometimes abbreviated **Pro per.**

Proprio (suo) motu. prōp´rēō (sū´ō) mō´tū. prap´rēō (sū´ō) mō´tū. *adv.* "From its own motion." An abbreviated form of **Ex proprio (suo) motu.** *E.g.*, "The Tribunal regrets that Jamaica has failed to appear and to bring forward any objections to the jurisdiction of the Centre and the competence of the Tribunal which it might entertain. The Tribunal nevertheless, decided to examine its own jurisdiction *proprio motu* and in doing so to consider any objections which might be raised against its jurisdiction." *Kaiser Bauxite Co. v. Jamaica*, ICSID Case No. ARB/74/3, Decision of July 6, 1975, ¶ 10 (Jurisdiction). An alternative formulation is **Motu proprio.**

Proprio vigore. prōp´rēō wēgō´rā. prap´rēō vi´g3rē OR -vigō´rē *adv.* "By its own strength." Automatically and independently; by its own force.

Propter hoc. prōp´tēr hōk. prap´t3r hak. *adj.* "Because of this." Because of the previously stated reason. *See also* **Post hoc ergo propter hoc.**

Prorogatio fori. prōrōga´tēō fō´rē. prōrōgā´šō fō´rī. *n.* "Prerogation of the forum." (1) The presumption that an assumption of jurisdiction over a given dispute falls within the discretion of the tribunal petitioned to hear it, especially when the tribunal has been chosen by parties to a contract containing a forum selection clause designating that tribunal. (2) A designation in an agreement of a specific tribunal to hear a dispute arising under or relating to that agreement.

P

Prorogatio de loco in locum. prōrōga´tēō dā lō´kō ēn lō´kūm. prōrōgā´šō dā lō´kō in lō´kum. *n.* "Prorogation from one place to another." The dismissal of a case upon agreement of the parties to pursue it in another jurisdiction (which, absent such agreement, might not otherwise be competent to hear the case). *See also* **Prorogatio de tempore in tempus.**

Prorogatio de tempore in tempus. prōrōga´tēō dā tāmpō´rā ēn tām´pūs. prōrōgā´šō dā tempō´rē in tem´pus. *n.* "Prorogation from one time to another." A delay in litigation upon agreement of the parties to a time, such as when parties agree to toll a statute of limitations pending negotiation of a settlement of the dispute. *See also* **Prorogatio de loco in locum.**

Protectio trahit subiectionem et subiectio protectionem. prōtāk´tēō tra´hēt sūbyāktēō´nām āt sūbyāk´tēō prōtāktēō´nām. prōtek´tēō trā´hit subjekšō´nem et subjek´tēō prōtekšō´nem. "Protection brings subjugation, and subjugation brings protection." A maxim meaning that a sovereign state has the duty to protect its citizens, while the citizens owe a concomitant duty of loyalty to the protecting sovereign of allegiance.

Provisione legis. prōwēsēō´nā lā´gēs. prōvižō´nē le´jis. *adv.* "By provision of law." As provided for by law.

Publici iuris. pūb´lēkē yū´rēs. pub´likī j3´ris. *adj.* "By public right." Relating to or deriving from what is publicly owned or owned in common. *See also* **Iura communis.**

Q

Q.E.D. An abbreviation of **Quod erat demonstrandum.**

q.v. An abbreviation of **Quod vide.**

Qua. kwa. kwā. *prep.* "As." As; due to the role or capacity of. *E.g.*, "[Israeli Defense Force] soldiers are categorically forbidden to use civilians, *qua* civilians, as a 'live shield' or as 'hostages.'" *Adalah v. GOC Central Command, IDF*, Sup. Ct. Isr., Oct. 6, 2005, 45 I.L.M. 491, 496, ¶ 16 (2006).

Quacunque via data. kwakūn´kwā wē´a da´ta. kwakun´kwē vī´u dā´tu. *adv.* "Whatever way given." However it is understood; in whatever way it is taken.

Quae ab hostibus capiuntur, statim capientium fiunt. kwī ab hōs´tēbūs kapē-ūn´tūr, sta´tēm kapē-ān´tē-ūm fē´ūnt. kwā âb has´tibus kâ´pē-untɜr, stā´tim kâpē-en´tē-um fī´unt. "What is taken from the enemy immediately becomes property of the captor." An alternative phrase for **Item quae ex hostibus capiuntur, iure gentium statim capientium fiunt.** This maxim was formerly used by both civil law and common law courts to justify the expropriation of the property of domestic "enemies of the state" (especially criminals such as highwaymen and rebels).

Quae ab initio erant voluntatis ex post facto sunt necessitatis. kwī ab ēnē´tēō ā´rant wōlūnta´tēs āks pōst fak´tō sūnt nākāssēta´tēs. kwā âb ini´šō e´runt valuntā´tis eks pōst fâk´tō sunt nesesitā´tis. "Whoever was willing at the beginning is constrained after the event." A maxim meaning that persons will be held to their legally binding commitments even though they may later discover disadvantages to performance and seek to renege. *E.g.*, "The specific performance of preliminary contracts does not affect the sovereignty even of the State which rightfully alienated it to the extent necessary to permit a replacement of its own choice—*quae ab initio erant voluntatis ex post facto sunt necessitatis.*" *Advisory Opinion on Interpretation of Peace Treaties with*

Bulgaria, Hungary, and Romania, 1950 I.C.J. 221, 249 (Judge Azevedo, dissenting). *But see* **Clausula rebus sic stantibus.**

Quaelibet iurisdictio cancellos suos habet. kwī´lēbāt yūrēsdēk´tēō kankāl´lōs sū´ōs ha´bāt. kwā´libet jɜrisdik´šō kân´selus sū´ōs hâ´bet. "Any jurisdiction has its own boundaries." A maxim meaning that every sovereign state self-imposes at least some limitations on its own prescriptive, enforcement, and judicial jurisdiction, at a minimum to the extent mandated by international law.

Q

Quaeritur. kwī´rētūr. kwā´ritɜr. *v.* (commonly used as a *n.*) "It is asked." That which is in question; the subject under consideration. In Roman law, the term *quaeritur* was used to introduce a difficult legal problem for consideration.

Quaestio vexata. kwīs´tēō wāksa´ta. kwes´tēō veksa´tu. *n.* "Troublesome question." An alternative formulation of **Vexata quaestio.**

Quam primum. kwam prē´mūm. kwam prī´mum. *adv.* An alternative formulation of **Quamprimum.**

Quamprimum. kwamprē´mūm. kwamprī´mum. *adv.* "As soon as possible." At the first possible opportunity; as soon as possible. An alternative formulation is **Quam primum.**

Quandocunque. kwandōkūn´kwā. kwandōkun´kwē. *adv.* "Whenever." Whenever; at any time.

Quantum. kwan´tūm. kwan´tum. *n.* "So much as." (1) Quantity. (2) Amount, as in the *quantum* of compensation owed by the respondent to the claimant.

Quantum damnificatus. kwan´tūm damnēfēka´tūs. kwan´tum dâmnifikā´tus. *n.* "As much as the injury." The amount of damages suffered by a claimant.

Quantum meruit. kwan´tūm mār´ūēt. kwan´tum mā´rūit. *n.* "As much as he has earned." The amount of compensation or damages calculated according to the market value of a benefit conferred under a contract implied in law, especially for unpaid services rendered without an express agreement. At common law, *quantum meruit* was the remedy sought in an *assumpsit* action based on services performed. In modern times, when a tribunal awards damages in *quantum meruit*, it is usually applying an equitable remedy as opposed to a remedy at law. *E.g.*, "It is not entirely clear whether this constituted an award of salvage. If it did not but was simply some form of *quantum meruit*, then of course it affords no assistance on the topic one way or the other. But given the reference to the value of the vessel, it may well be that this was an award of salvage remuneration." *The Owners of the Vessel "Voutakos," Her Bunkers, Stores, and Cargo v. Tsavliris Salvage (International), Ltd.*,

Q

[2008] EWHC 1582, ¶ 36 (Comm.) QBD (Adm.) (U.K.). *Compare with* **Quantum valebat.** *See also* **In quantum meruit** and **Quasi ex contractu.**

Quantum valebat. kwan´tūm walā´bat. kwan´tum vâ´lebât. *n.* [*pl.* **Quantum valebant.** kwan´tūm walā´bant. kwan´tum vâ´lebunt.] "As much as it was worth." The amount of compensation or damages calculated according to the market value of merchandise delivered in the absence of an express contract. At common law, *quantum valebat* was the remedy sought in an *assumpsit* action based on unjust enrichment. In modern times, when a tribunal awards damages in *quantum valebat*, it is usually applying an equitable remedy as opposed to a remedy at law. *Compare with* **Quantum meruit.** *See also* **In quantum valeabat** and **Quasi ex contractu.**

Quare. kwa´rā. kwe´rē. *adv.* "On account of what [thing]." Why; for what reason.

Quare impedit. kwa´rā ēmpā´dēt. kwe´rē impē´dit. *n.* "Why he hinders." (1) In Canon law, a writ directing the sheriff to require a person to show cause why he has obstructed a patron's right to appoint his choice of clerk to occupy a vacant benefice. (2) Generically, a writ directing someone impeding another's assumption or possession of a right or title to show valid legal cause to justify the hindrance. The *quare impedit* was formerly an English writ but is now obsolete.

Quasi. kwa´sē. kwa´zē OR kwā´zī. *adj.* or *adv.* "As if." Almost; similar either by direct comparison or by analogy. *E.g.*, "The Security Council and the General Assembly, in so far as they, too, are competent to settle disputes, are only *quasi*-judicial organs of the United Nations." Hans Kelsen, THE LAW OF THE UNITED NATIONS 466–67 (1950).

Quasi ex contractu. kwa´sē āks kōntrak´tū. kwa´zē- OR kwā´zī eks kantrâk´tū. "As if from a contract." An equitable theory that finds an obligation to compensate or restore a benefit conferred on another unfairly in the absence of an express agreement to do so, usually to avoid the receiving party becoming unjustly enriched by the benefit conferred by the giving party. *See also* **Quantum meruit** and **Quantum valebat.**

Quasi in rem. kwa´sē ēn rām. kwa´zē- OR kwā´zī in rem. *adj.* "As if in the thing." *Quasi in rem* jurisdiction is obtained over a person by virtue of the presence of the person's property in the jurisdiction. It may also be exercised based on an event conferring legal status, such as a marriage in the jurisdiction. *E.g.*, "In divorce causes, the actual subject-matter of the litigation is the marriage status itself.... Hence they partake of the nature of proceedings *in rem* rather than of proceedings *in personam*, the *res* being the status.... At the same time these causes cannot be said to be altogether proceedings *in rem*. There is a personal element that enters into them, not found in suits instituted merely to subject or affect property.... Hence they are often very properly denominated proceedings *quasi in rem*." Raleigh C. Minor, CONFLICT OF LAWS; OR, PRIVATE INTERNATIONAL LAW 191–92, § 87 (1901). *Contrast with* **In rem** and **In personam.**

Quater. kwa´tār. kwa´t3r. *adv.* "Fourthly." An adverbial number (the fourth) usually inserted into a consecutively numbered series by way of amendment. An alternative spelling is **Quatt(u)or.** *See* the Appendix for a list of Latin adverbial numbers commonly used in international law. *See also* **Bis** and **Semel.**

Quaterdecie(n)s. kwa´tārdākē-ā(n)s. kwa´t3rdesē(n)z. *adv.* "Fourteenthly." An adverbial number (the fourteenth) usually inserted into a consecutively numbered series by way of amendment. An alternative spelling is **Quatt(u)ordecies.** *See* the Appendix for a list of Latin adverbial numbers commonly used in international law. *See also* **Bis** and **Semel.**

Quatt(u)or. kwat´t(ū)ōr. kwa´t3r. An alternative spelling of **Quater.**

Quatt(u)ordecie(n)s. kwatt(ū)ōrdē´kē-ā(n)s. kwatōr´desē(n)z. An alternative spelling of **Quaterdecie(n)s.**

Qui desiderat pacem, praeparet bellum. kwē dāsē´dārat pa´kām, prī´parāt bāl´lūm. kwē- OR kwī dezi´d3rât pâ´kum, prepa´ret be´lum. "May he who desires peace prepare for war." A maxim justifying arms escalation as a means of deterrence in opposition to theories equating disarmament with greater prospects for peace. An alternative phrase is **Si vis pacem, para bellum.**

Qui facit per alium, facit per se. kwē fa´kēt pār a´lē-ūm, fa´kēt pār sā. kwē- OR kwī fâ´sit p3r ā´lē-um, fâ´sit p3r sā. "Whoever acts through another, acts himself." A maxim meaning that a principal may be held liable for the wrongdoing of an agent acting on his or her behalf. Alternative phrases are **Qui mandat ipse fecisse videtur** and **Qui per alium facit per se ipsum facere videtur.** *See also* **Iniuria servi dominum pertingit** and **Respondeat superior.**

Qui in culpa non est, natura ad nihil tenetur. kwē ēn kūl´pa nōn āst, natū´ra ad nē´hēl tānā´tūr. kwē- OR kwī in k3l´pu nan est, nā´č3ru âd nī´hil te´nut3r. "Whoever is lacking in fault, nature holds nothing against him." A maxim of Roman civil law, adapted by Grotius to international law in *De Iure Belli ac Pacis*, meaning that under principles of natural law, there can be no liability without some wrongful act.

Qui in territorio meo est, etiam meus subditus est. kwē ēn tārrētō´rēō mā´ō āst, āt´ē-am mā´ūs sūbdē´tūs āst. kwē- OR kwī in teritō´rēō mē´ō est, e´tē-um mē´us subdi´tus est. "Whoever is in my territory is indeed my subject." A principle of private international law whereby a sovereign state exercises jurisdiction over all persons within its territory, regardless of any individual's nationality. *Compare with* **Quidquid est in territorio, est etiam de territorio.**

Q

Qui mandat ipse fecisse videtur. kwē man´dat ēp´sā fākēs´sā wēdā´tūr. kwē- OR kwī mân´dât ip´sē fesi´sē vi´det3r. "Whoever commands is considered to have acted." An alternative phrase for **Qui facit per alium, facit per se.**

Qui non prohibet quod prohibere potest, assentire videtur. kwē nōn prō´hēbāt kwōd prōhēbā´rā pō´tāst, assāntē´rā wēdā´tūr. kwē- OR kwī nan prōhi´but kwad prōhi´b3rē pō´test, asen´tirē vi´det3r. "Whoever does not prohibit that which he can prohibit is considered as assenting." A common law maxim meaning that one who has the lawful authority to prevent an act or wrongdoing by another (such as his subordinate or agent) will be legally bound by the act or liable for the wrongdoing if he fails to prevent it. An alternative phrase is **Qui potest et debet vetare et non vetat iubet.** *See also* **Respondeat superior.**

Qui per alium facit per se ipsum facere videtur. kwē pār a´lē-ūm fa´kēt pār āt nōn wā´tat sā ēp´sūm fa´kārā wēdā´tūr. kwē- OR kwī p3r â´lē-um fâ´sit p3r sā ip´sum fâ´s3rē vi´det3r. "Whoever acts through another is considered to act himself." An alternative phrase for **Qui facit per alium, facit per se.**

Qui potest et debet vetare et non vetat iubet. kwē pō´tāst āt dā´bāt wāta´rā āt nōn wā´tat yū´bāt. kwē- OR kwī pō´test et de´bet veta´rē et nan ve´tât jū´bet. "Whoever is able and should forbid and does not forbid commands." An alternative phrase for **Qui non prohibet quod prohibere potest, assentire videtur.**

Qui prior est tempore potior est iure. kwē prē´ōr āst tāmpō´rā pō´tēōr āst yū´rā. kwē- OR kwī prī´3r est tem´p3rē pō´tē-3r est j3´rē. "Whoever is earlier in time is stronger in right." An alternative phrase for **Prior in tempore, potior in iure.**

Qui tacet consentire videtur (ubi tractatur de eius commodo). kwē ta´kāt kōnsāntē´rā wēdā´tūr (ū´bē trakta´tūr dā ā´yūs kōm´mōdō). kwē- OR kwī tâ´set kansenti´rē vi´det3r (ū´bi trâktā´t3r dā ē´jus kō´mudō). "Whoever says nothing appears to agree (when that which is being discussed concerns his interest)." A generally obsolete maxim meaning that one who fails to deny or object to a claim, accusation, or statement of fact relevant to his interests must implicitly have done so because of its truth or validity, and it is therefore proper to construe the failure to deny or object as an admission. Sometimes abbreviated **Consentire videtur qui tacet.**

Qui tam. kwē tam. kwē- OR kwī tâm. *pro. + adv.* (commonly used as an *adj.*) "Who so much as." An abbreviation of the phrase: *Qui tam pro domino rege quam pro se ipso in hac parte sequitur*, meaning: "Who so much as sues on behalf of the king sues as well on behalf of himself in this matter." A legal claim brought by a person who seeks to recover for himself as well as the state. The claimant and state may share in the damages or penalties recovered in the *qui tam* action.

Qui tardius solvit minus solvit. kwē tar´dē-ūs sōl´wēt mē´nūs sōl´wēt. kwē- OR kwī tar´dē-us sal´vit mī´nus sal´vit. "Whoever pays rather tardily, pays less." An alternative formulation of **Minus solvit qui tardius solvit**.

Qui utuntur communi iure gentium. kwē ūtūn´tūr kōmmū´nē yū´rā gān´tē-ūm. kwē- OR kwī ūtun´tɜr kamyū´nī jɜ´rē jen´tē-um. *n. pl.* "Those who use the common law of peoples." Those who comply with international law. This term is often used in the specific sense of those who comply with *lex mercatoria. E.g.*, "Intimation [i.e., notice of a legal obligation and warning of failure to comply with it] being by our proper custom so necessary a solemnity, it holds not in the orders which stand for assignations among merchants, strangers especially, *qui utuntur communi jure gentium.*" *Cuthbertson v. Wallace*, Scot. Ct. Sess., July 8, 1658, *quoted in* William Galbraith Miller, THE LAW OF NATURE AND NATIONS IN SCOTLAND 108 (1896).

Quia timet. kwē´a tē´māt. kwī´u ti´met. *adj.* "Because he fears." Brought by one threatened with injury. A *quia timet* action may be commenced by a person threatened with an illegal act to have the act enjoined or declared invalid by a tribunal before the anticipated injury occurs.

Quid. kwēd. kwid. *n.* "What." (1) Something; a matter. (2) Anything.

Quid pro quo. kwēd prō kwō. kwid prō kwō. *n.* "What for what." An exchange of one thing or favor for another; the thing or favor so exchanged. The term is sometimes used to imply a surreptitious or questionable exchange of favors, but may also be used to describe the mutual consideration promised or exchanged in the formation of a binding contract. *E.g.*, "In order to sustain the necessary compromissory equilibrium, or what Elias called "fair balance," in this case, each of the Parties must be seen to carry out all its part of the obligations. Libya cannot pick and choose which obligations it would perform, neither can France. The fundamental considerations in this Treaty of 1955, the *quid pro quo*, are the issue of France's evacuation from Fezzan and the issue of Libya accepting…the Libyan southern boundary with Chad." *Territorial Dispute* (Libya v. Chad), 1994 I.C.J. Rep. 6, 73, ¶ 84 (separate opinion of Judge Ajibola).

Quidquid ab initio vitiosus est, non potest tractu temporis convalescere. kwēd´kwēd ab ēnē´tēō wētēō´sūs āst, nōn pō´tāst trak´tū tām´pōrēs kōnwalās´kārā. kwid´kwid âb ini´šō višō´zus est, nan pō´test trâk´tū tempō´ris kanvule´sɜrē. "Whatever is depraved from the outset cannot become valid by the carriage of time." A maxim meaning that the passage of time does not vitiate a violation of law. One who has committed especially deplorable crimes cannot achieve exoneration from the mere failure of authorities to apprehend or punish the person for a long period following crime. It follows that one who commits crimes against humanity, for example, would not benefit from a statute of limitations. *E.g.*, "Norms of *jus cogens* do not tolerate derogation, so any concurrent regime or situation, whether it be established by way of a bilateral or unilateral act, cannot acquire legal force due to the peremptoriness of *jus cogens*—more specifically, this act or acts remains in the sphere of simple facts. One could say that this is a classic example of application of the general principle of law expressed in the maxim *quidquid ab initio vitiosus est, non potest tractu temporis convalescere.*" *Application of the Convention on Prevention and Punishment of Genocide* (Bosn. & Herz. v. Yugo.), 1996 I.C.J. Rep. 595, 754–55, ¶ 90 (Judge *ad hoc* Kreća, dissenting).

Quidquid est in territorio, est etiam de territorio. kwēd´kwēd āst ēn tārrētō´rēō, āst ā´tē-ām dā tārrētō´rēō. kwid´kwid est in teritō´rēō, est e´tē-um dā teritō´rēō. "Whatever is in the territory is indeed of the territory." A principle of jurisdiction whereby a sovereign exercises jurisdiction over all real and personal property within its territory, regardless of the nationality of the property owner. *Compare with* **Qui in territorio meo est, etiam meus subditus est.**

Quidquid iudicii placuit, habet legis vigorem. kwēd´kwēd yūdē´kē-ē pla´kūēt, ha´bāt lā´gēs wēgō´rām. kwid´kwid jūdi´šī plâ´kwit, hâ´bet le´jis vi´gɜrum. "Whatever pleases the judiciary, has the force of law." A maxim meaning that the judiciary has broad discretion to interpret and fill in gaps in the law, and that its judgment in such matters is authoritative. *E.g.*, "The [Court majority's] reasoning suggests that *quidquid judicii placuit, habet legis vigorem.* It reflects the anachronistic and totally unacceptable idea that the Court is not the guardian but the creator of legality and, in fact, that the Court makes decisions independently from objective law established by its Statute." *Application of the Convention on the Prevention and Punishment of the Crime of Genocide* (Bosn. & Herz. v. Yugo.), I.C.J. No. 91, Judgment of Feb. 26, 2007, at 30, ¶ 59 (separate opinion of Judge *ad hoc* Kreća).

Quieta non movere. kwē-ā´ta nōn mōwā´rā. kwī-e´tu nan mō´vɜrē. "Do not move settled things." (1) A maxim counseling conservatism when a factual or legal homeostasis has emerged. *E.g.*, "Perhaps this decision of the Court, with its judicial flavour of *quieta non movere*, was aimed at ensuring finality and certainty on any dispute presented to it, and thereby preventing protracted and endless litigation which at times provoke hostilities and armed conflict." *Territorial Dispute* (Libya v. Chad), 1994 I.C.J. Rep. 6, ¶ 57 (Jurisdiction) (separate opinion of Judge Ajibola). (2) The principle that settled law should not be lightly disturbed. *Compare with* **Stare decisis.**

Quindecie(n)s. kwēndā´kē-ā(n)s. kwinde´sē(n)z. *adv.* "Fifteenthly." An adverbial number (the fifteenth) usually inserted into a consecutively numbered series by way of amendment. *See* the Appendix for a list of Latin adverbial numbers commonly used in international law. *See also* **Bis** and **Semel.**

Quinquie(n)s. kwēn´kwē-ā(n)s. kwin´kwē(n)z. *adv.* "Fifthly." An adverbial number (the fifth) usually inserted into a consecutively numbered series by way of amendment. *See* the Appendix for a list of Latin adverbial numbers commonly used in international law. *See also* **Bis** and **Semel.**

Quo animo? kwō a´nēmō. kwō â´nimō? "With what intention?" An interrogative inquiring into the motive or intentions of an actor.

Quo iure? kwō yū´rā. kwō j3´rē? "By what right?" An interrogative demanding the source of authority to support a claimed legal right. In medieval English practice, a *quo jure* writ ordered the possessor of land to show evidence of his title to the land.

Quo vadis? kwō wa´dēs. kwō va´dis? "Where are you going?" An interrogative asking what will be the likely outcome or future of an identified subject. The term is especially popular in article and book titles because of its brevity. *E.g.*, M. Cherif Bassiouni, *The ICC—Quo Vadis?*, 4 J. INT'L CRIMIN. JUST. 421 (2006).

Quoad. kwō´ad. kwō´âd. *prep.* "So long as." With regard to; in relation to. *E.g.*, "[T]he Brussels Court of Appeal…did not reverse the Commercial Court's finding on 15 November 1982 that AMP was an independent middleman, and not a mere sales agent deprived of any autonomy *quoad* the publishers." *S.A. Binon & Cie v. S.A. Agence et Messageries de la Presse*, E.C.J. Case No. 243/83, [1985] 3 C.M.L.R. 800, 806.

Quoad defunctum. kwō´ad dāfūnk´tūm. kwō´âd dēfunk´tum. *adj.* or *adv.* "So long as deceased." As a matter of, or with respect to, the demise or death of a person, thing, or concept. *E.g.*, "It seems, however, that the importance of the *dictum* that whereas in private law succession takes place *quoad defunctum*, in international law it does this *quoad iura* only, has been grossly exaggerated." Hersch Lauterpacht, PRIVATE LAW SOURCES AND ANALOGIES OF PUBLIC INTERNATIONAL LAW 131 (1927).

Quoad hoc. kwō´ad hōk. kwō´âd hak. *adj.* or *adv.* "So long as this." As to this; with regard to this; in this respect; as such. *E.g.*, "That the principle '*la robe ennemie confisque le vaisseau ami*' was at this time accepted seems clear from case No. 27. The Treaty of Breda had, in the interest of the Dutch carrying-trade, reversed it, and in the present case it was questioned whether the Hamburgers had adhered to it, and whether it was still valid, *quoad hoc*." Thomas Baty, *Scottish Prize Decisions of the Seventeenth and Eighteenth Centuries*, 27 YALE L.J. 453, 464 (1918).

Quoad iura. kwō´ad yū´ra. kwō´âd jɜ´ru. *adj.* or *adv.* "So long as the right." As a matter of, or with respect to, the assumption of a right. *E.g.*, "It seems, however, that the importance of the *dictum* that whereas in private law succession takes place *quoad defunctum*, in international law it does this *quoad iura* only, has been grossly exaggerated." Hersch Lauterpacht, PRIVATE LAW SOURCES AND ANALOGIES OF PUBLIC INTERNATIONAL LAW 131 (1927).

Quoad imperium. kwō´ad ēmpā´rē-ūm. kwō´âd impē´rē-um. *adj.* "So long as authority." With regard to, or during the term of, one's authority or sovereignty. *E.g.*, "[I]n relation to co-ordinated units, of which each in turn exercises an equal right over its territory, the right *quoad imperium* exhibits, *pro foro externo*, those formal characteristics which we attribute to *dominium* in private law." Hersch Lauterpacht, PRIVATE LAW SOURCES AND ANALOGIES OF PUBLIC INTERNATIONAL LAW 95 (1927).

Quoad potest. kwō´ad pō´tāst. kwō´âd pō´test. *adv.* "As far as one can." To the extent of one's ability; to the degree it is within one's power.

Quod enim nullius est id ratione naturali occupanti conceditur. kwōd ā´nēm nūllē´ūs āst ēd ratēō´nā natūra´lē ōkkūpan´tē kōnkā´dētūr. kwad e´nim nɜ´lē-us est id râšō´nē nâčɜrâ´lī akyūpan´tī kansē´ditɜr. "For whatever belongs to no one, by natural reason becomes property of the first taker." A maxim, originating in Justinian's *Digest* (41.1.3), meaning that the first occupant of land having no owner or sovereign rightfully belongs to the first occupant. *See also* **Res nullius** and **Terra nullius.**

Quod non. kwōd nōn. kwad nan. "Which not." Which it does not; a denial of the truth or persuasiveness of an assertion. *E.g.*, "[E]ven if the trick to change a contract for regular coastal service into a concession for exclusive navigation succeeded (*quod non*), in the face of absolute equity the trick of making the same contract a chain for one party and a screw-press for the other never can have success." *The Orinoco Steamship Company Case* (U.S. v. Venez.),

U.S.-Venez. Cl. Comm'n, Award of Feb. 22, 1904, H.C.R. (Series 1), at 266 (Scott, 1916).

Quod vide. kwōd wē´dā. kwad vi´dē. "Which see." A citation signal referring the reader to a source of authority appearing elsewhere in the same work. Abbreviated **q.v.**

Quod erat demonstrandum. kwōd ā´rat dāmōnstran´dūm. kwad e´rât demunstrân´dum. *n.* "[That] which was to be demonstrated." As was proved or explained previously. Commonly abbreviated **Q.E.D.**

Quod necessitas cogit, defendit. kwōd nākās´sētas kō´gēt, dāfān´dēt. kwad nuse´sitas kō´jit, dufen´dit. "Whatever necessity compels, it justifies." An alternative phrase for **Necessitas non habet legem.**

Quod (si) quis ex culpa sua sentit, non intelligitur damnum sentire. kwōd (sē) kwēs āks kūl´pa sū´a sān´tēt, nōn ēntāllē´gētūr dam´nūm säntē´rā. kwad (sē) kwis eks k3l´pu sū´u sen´tit, nan inteli´jit3r dâm´num senti´rē. "He who suffers damage by his own fault, has no right to complain." A maxim attributable to Pomponius (*Digest*, "De regula juris," 50,17,203) asserting that a claimant should be deprived of his right to reparation if the claimant can be accused of having contributed to his own injury. This maxim has been interpreted in several ways. In one interpretation, it is a crude statement of contributory negligence on the common law model. In another, it denies a remedy to a claimant who suffers injury in the course of wrongdoing even though the wrongdoing was not the immediate cause of the injury.

Quod vanum et inutile est, lex non requirit. kwōd wa´nūm āt ēnū´tēlā āst, lāks nōn rākwē´rēt. kwad vâ´num et inyū´tilē est, leks nan rekwī´rut. "The law does not look after what is vain and useless." An alternative phrase for **Lex neminem cogit ad vana seu impossibilia.**

Quod vero naturalis ratio inter omnes homines constituit, id apud omnes peraeque custoditur vocaturque ius gentium. kwōd wā´rō natūra´lēs ra´tēō ēn´tār ōm´nās hō´mēnās kōnstē´tūēt, ēd a´pūd ōm´nās pārī´kwā kūstō´dētūr wōkatūr´kwā yūs gān´tē-ūm. kwad ve´rō nâč3râ´lis rā´šō in´t3r am´nēz ha´minēz kansti´čwit, id ā´pud am´nēz pē´rekwē custō´dit3r vōkut3r´kwē jus jen´tē-um. "But the law that natural reason has established among all persons, that law is observed uniformly among all, and is called the law of peoples." A maxim, originating in Justinian's *Digest* (1:1.1.9), positing that "natural reason" is the basis for a universal law applicable to all persons of whatever nationality. *See also* **Ius gentium.**

Quoties in verbis nulla est ambiguitas, ibi nulla expositio contra verba expressa fienda est. kwō´tē-ās ēn wär´bēs nūl´la āst ambē´gūētas, ē´bē nūl´la ākspōsē´tēō kōn´tra wär´ba ākspräs´sa fē-ān´da āst. kwō´tēz in vɜr´bis nɜ´lu est âmbigyū´itus, i´bē nɜ´lu ekspōzi´šō kan´tru vɜr´bu ekspre´su fē-en´du est. "So long as there is no ambiguity in the words, there should be no interpretation contrary to the words." A maxim, originating in Justinian's *Digest* (32.25.1), meaning that the plain language of a legal instrument (such as a contract or treaty) should govern the interpretation unless the meaning of a provision is unclear. *See* the Vienna Convention on the Law of Treaties arts. 31–32, May 23, 1969, 1155 U.N.T.S. 331.

Quovis modo. kwō´wēs mō´dō. kwō´vis mō´dō. *adv.* "In whatever manner." In any manner whatsoever.

Q

R

R. (1) An abbreviation of **Regina.** (2) An abbreviation of **Rex.**

Ratio. ra´tēō. rā´šō. *n.* "Reason." (1) Logic. (2) Reason. (3) Basis. (4) An abbreviation of **Ratio decidendi.**

Ratio decidendi. ra´tēō dākēdān´dē. rā´šō desiden´dī. *n.* "Reason of the decision." The legal basis or reasoning underlying a judicial or administrative decision, award, or judgment.

Ratio impertinens. ra´tēō ēmpār´tēnāns. rā´šō impɜr´tinenz. *n.* "Out of place reasoning." An argument not germane to the issue at hand.

Ratio legis. ra´tēō lā´gēs. rā´šō le´jis. *n.* "Reason for the law." The policy reason or underlying purpose for a specific norm, rule, treaty provision, act of legislation, or tribunal decision. *E.g.*, "Despite uncertainties that may exist concerning the definition of universal jurisdiction, one thing is very clear: the *ratio legis* of universal jurisdiction is based on the international reprobation for certain very serious crimes such as war crimes and crimes against humanity." *Arrest Warrant of 11 April 2000* (Congo v. Belg.), 2002 I.C.J. Rep. 3, 166, ¶ 46 (Judge Van den Wyngaert, dissenting).

Ratio scripta. ra´tēō skrēp´ta. rā´šō skrip´tu. *n.* "Written reason." (1) The written opinion of a tribunal explaining its decision in a case before it. (2) A written or codified law.

Ratione cessante (cessat ipse lex). ratēō´nā kāssan´tā (kās´sat ēp´sā lāks). rāšō´nē sesan´tē (se´sât ip´sē leks). "When the reason ceases, the law itself ceases." An alternative phrase for **Cessante ratio, cessat etiam lex.**

Ratione contractus. ratēō´nā kōntrak´tūs. rāšō´nē kantrâk´tus. *adv.* "By reason of the contract." Based on or because of the relevant binding agreement.

Ratione delicti. ratēō´nā dālēk´tē. rāšō´nē dulik´tī. *adv.* "By reason of the wrongdoing." Because of the wrongful act.

Ratione domicilii. ratēō´nā dōmēkē´lē-ē. rāšō´nē damisi´lī. *adv.* "By reason of domicile." Because of the person's place of domicile. A finding of judicial jurisdiction may be made *ratione domicilii* under principles of private international law.

R

Ratione fori. ratēō´nā fō´rē. rāšō´nē fō´rī. *adv.* "By reason of the forum." Because of the jurisdiction of the relevant forum. *E.g.*, "*Ratione fori* jurisdiction relates to the nomination of the court or tribunal for settling a dispute between States Parties.... The dominant underlying principle of *ratione fori* jurisdiction is the conventional rule of public international law whereby applicant States are free to choose the court or tribunal before which they wish a dispute to be heard." Jean-René Dupuy and Daniel Vignes, 2 HANDBOOK ON THE NEW LAW OF THE SEA 1366 (1991).

Ratione loci. ratēō´nā lō´kē. rāšō´nē lō´sī. *adv.* "By reason of the place." Because of the relevant place or territory. *E.g.*, "[T]here can be no dispute as to the Court's jurisdiction *ratione loci* on account of internationally wrongful acts allegedly committed by one State on the territory of another, even in the case of human rights violations." *Armed Activities on the Territory of the Congo* (Congo v. Rwanda), 2002 I.C.J. Rep. 219, 284, ¶ 47 (separate opinion of Judge Mavungu). An alternative term is **Ratione territoriae.**

Ratione materiae. ratēō´nā matā´rē-ī. rāšō´nē mutē´rē-ā. *adv.* "By reason of the matter." Because of the nature of the relevant subject matter. The immunity of a diplomat or head of state to most criminal and civil actions brought in the courts of the receiving state based on the official's acts on behalf of the sending state is immunity *ratione materiae* and outlives the official's tenure in office. *E.g.*, "Where, as in this case, there is a general submission to the Court's jurisdiction, followed by particular exceptions, the general part states the principle underlying the declaration, namely, the principle of submission. That general part sets the framework within which the Court's jurisdiction is accepted. It constitutes, *inter alia*, a submission to the general *corpus* of international law and, in particular, to its ruling principles. The reservations constitute exceptions—in this case *ratione materiae*—to that jurisdiction." *Fisheries Jurisdiction* (Spain v. U.K.), 1998 I.C.J. Rep. 432, 502, ¶ 24 (Jurisdiction) (Judge Weeramantry, dissenting). *Compare with* **Ratione personae.**

Ratione personae. ratēō´nā pārsō´nī. rāšō´nē pɜrsō´nā. *adv.* "By reason of the person." Because of the nature or position of the relevant person. The immunity of a diplomat or head of state to most criminal and civil actions brought in foreign courts while the diplomat or head of state remains in office is immunity *ratione personae* and expires upon the individual relinquishing his or her official position. *E.g.*, "India has repeatedly made clear that it wishes to limit in this manner the scope *ratione personae* of its acceptance of the Court's jurisdiction [to exclude disputes with any other state that 'is or has been a Member of the Commonwealth of Nations']." *Aerial Incident of 10 August 1999* (Pak. v. India), 2000 I.C.J. Rep. 12, 31, ¶ 44 (Jurisdiction). *Compare with* **Ratione materiae.**

Ratione rei sitae. ratēō´nä rä´ē sē´tī. räšō´nē rā si´tā. *adv.* "By reason of the position of the thing." By reason of the location (*situs*) of property in dispute. *See also* **Situs.**

Ratione soli. ratēō´nä sō´lē. räšō´nē sō´lī. *adv.* "By reason of the land." Because of the ownership or possession of the land or territory itself, ownership of the fruits of land (*e.g.*, wild fauna and flora, natural minerals) is also claimed.

Ratione temporis. ratēō´nä täm´pōrēs. räšō´nē tem´pōris. *adv.* "By reason of time." Because of the relevant timing or period of time pertaining to the subject under consideration. *E.g.*, "Germany contends that the key issue for the purpose of applying Article 27(a) is not the date when this dispute arose, but whether the dispute relates to facts or situations that arose before or after the critical date. Only if these facts or situations took place after the critical date, that is after 1980, would the Court have jurisdiction *ratione temporis* under Article 27(a). But since, in Germany's view, this dispute relates to facts and situations that predate 1980, the Court lacks the requisite jurisdiction." *Certain Property* (Liecht. v. Ger.), 2005 I.C.J. Rep. 6, 20, ¶ 30.

Ratione territoriae. ratēō´nä tärrētō´rē-ī. räšō´nē teritō´rē-ā. *adv.* "By reason of the territory." An alternative term for **Ratione loci.**

Rationes obligandi. ratēō´näs ōblēgan´dē. räšō´nēz abligân´dī. *n. pl.* "Bases of duty." The grounds upon which an obligation rests.

Rebus sic stantibus. rä´būs sēk stan´tēbūs. rē´bus sik stân´tibus. An abbreviation of **Clausula rebus sic stantibus.**

Receptus. räkäp´tūs. rēsep´tus. *n.* "Received (person or thing)." (1) An arbitrator appointed by agreement of the disputing parties. (2) A term used by Grotius to indicate a sovereign's denial of encouragement of or complicity in the illegal acts of his or her officials or citizens, usually as evidenced through the domestic trial or extradition for foreign trial of the accused person. *See* Hugo Grotius, 2 De Jure Belli Ac Pacis ch. 21, paras. 3–4 (1625). *Compare with* **Patientia.**

R

Reddendo singula singulis. rāddān´dō sēn´gūla sēn´gūlēs. ruden´dō siŋ´yūlu siŋ´yūlis. "By assigning each one to each one." A principle of legal instrument construction whereby each term or phrase is interpreted to refer to its corresponding object in the text. *E.g.*, "It is one of the best-settled rules of construction, that words in different parts of a statute must be referred to their appropriate connection; giving to each in its place its proper force, *reddendo singula singulis*, and if possible rendering none of them useless or superfluous." *McIntyre v. Ingraham*, 35 Miss. 25 (1858) (U.S.).

Reductio ad absurdum. rādūk´tēō ad absūr´dūm. reduk´tēō âd âbsɜr´dum. *n.* "Reduction to the absurd." (1) An argument that, if followed to its logical conclusion, would prove nonsensical. (2) A rhetorical argument disproving the opposing argument by following its reasoning to a nonsensical conclusion.

Reformatio in peius. rāfōrma´tēō ēn pā´yūs. rēfōrmā´šō in pe´jus. *n.* "A change toward the worse." A change for the worse.

Reges ac magistratus. rā´gās ak magēstra´tūs. re´jēz âk mâjistrā´tus. *n. pl.* "Kings and magistrates." Public or government officials.

Regina. rāgē´na. rejī´nu. *n.* "Queen." (1) A female monarch. (2) Metonymically, the sovereign or state. *Compare with* **Rex**.

Regula. rā´gūla. re´gyūlu. *n.* "Rule." (1) A rule; a regulation. (2) A procedural law.

Rei turpis nullum mandatum est. rā´ē tūr´pēs nūl´lūm manda´tūm āst. rā tɜr´pis nɜ´lum mândā´tum est. "There is no mandate in connection with an immoral matter." A maxim meaning that a provision of an agreement requiring the parties to act immorally or illegally can create no legal obligation; that provision or the agreement as a whole is void.

Relegatio. rālāga´tēō. relugā´šō. *n.* "Banishment." In Roman law, the banishment of a citizen from Rome and his native province, either for a fixed period or indefinitely, as punishment for the commission of a serious crime. Although the citizen retained Roman citizenship and property rights, return prior to the lifting of the *relegatio* would result in capital punishment.

Remissio iniuriae. rāmēs´sēō ēnyū´rē-ī. rumi´sēō injɜ´rē-ā. *n.* "Forgiveness of injury." The forgiveness of an injury or offense without seeking punishment or compensation.

Res. rās. res. *n.* [*pl.* **Res.** rās. res.] "Thing." (1) Thing. (2) Property. (3) Subject or matter.

R

Res accendent lumina rebus. rās akkān´dānt lū´mēna rā´būs. res asen´dent lū´minu rē´bus. "One thing throws light upon others." The resolution of one issue assists the resolution of others.

Res adiudicata. rās adyūdēka´ta. res âdjūdika´tu. *n.* "Adjudicated thing." An alternative term for **Res iudicata.**

Res alicuius. rās alēkū´yūs. res âlikū´yus. *n.* "Another person's thing." Property owned by another person. An alternative term is **Res aliena.** *Contrast with* **Res sua.**

Res aliena. rās alē-ā´na. res ālē-e´nu. *n.* "Foreign thing." An alternative term for **Res alicuius.**

Res alienari prohibita. rās alē-āna´rē prōhē´bēta. res ālē-ena´rī prōhi´bitu. *n.* "A thing that may not be alienated." Property, title to which may not lawfully or ethically be transferred to another.

Res communes (omnium). A common misspelling of **Res communis (omnium).**

Res communis (omnium). rās kōmmū´nēs (ōm´nē-ūm). res kamyū´nis (am´nē-um). *n.* "Thing of the (entire) community." (1) The common heritage of all humankind, not subject to the appropriation by or sovereignty of any state or group of states, such as the high seas, Antarctica, or celestial bodies. *E.g.*, "Trinidad and Tobago's position is that Barbados could not acquire fishing rights by virtue of the long and continuous artisanal fishing practices of Barbardian nationals in waters near Tobago because those waters formerly had the status of high seas and were *res communis.*" *Barbados v. Republic of Trinidad & Tobago*, Permanent Ct. of Arb., Award of Apr. 11, 2006, ¶ 144, 45 I.L.M. 800, 823 (2006). (2) In civil law, a public good that cannot be subject to private ownership, such as the air. *Compare with* **Res universitatis.** *See also* **Terra communis.**

Res controversa. rās kōntrōwār´sa. res kantruv3r´su. *n.* [*pl.* **Res controversae.** rās kōntrōwār´sī. res kantruv3r´sā.] "Thing in controversy." (1) The point at issue; the property or matter that is the subject of dispute. (2) A question for determination.

Res coronae. rās kōrō´nī. res kurō´nā. *n.* "The crown's thing." Property or rights belonging to the monarch or, by extension, the state. Historically in English law, a royal manor or estate, or a royal prerogative, could be *res coronae* and heritable to the royal line. *Compare with* **Res publicae.** *Contrast with* **Res privatae.**

Res corporale. rās kōrpōra´lā. res kōrpɜrâ´lē. *n.* [*pl.* **Res corporales.** rās kōrpōra´lās. res kōrpɜrâ´lēz.] "Corporeal thing." A tangible thing; tangible property. *Contrast with* **Res incorporale.**

Res derelicta. *n.* rās dārālēk´ta. res derulik´tu. *n.* [*pl.* **Res derelictae.** rās dārālēk´tī. res derulik´tā.] "Abandoned thing." Property abandoned by its erstwhile owner and currently belonging to no one, such as the wreck of a sunken vessel after any interest in the wreck has been renounced by its owner.

Res exincta. rās ākstēnk´ta. res ekstink´tu. *n.* "Extinct thing." Something formerly existing that has been extinguished. This term usually refers to an extinct legal right or the basis for such a right.

Res extra commercium. rās āks´tra cōmmār´kē-ūm. res eks´tru kumɜr´šum. *n.* "Thing outside of commercial intercourse." Things not subject to ownership, commerce, or trade, such as the high seas or air.

Res fungibiles. rās fūngē´bēlās. res funji´bilēz. *n. pl.* "Fungible things." Goods that are interchangeable for all relevant purposes. In a commercial context, restitution of damaged property could satisfy the tortfeasor's liability if the property was *res fungibiles*, such as common livestock, grain, or lumber.

Res furtivae. rās fūrtē´wī. res fɜrti´vā. *n.* "Furtive thing." Property taken by theft. In Roman law, an escaped or stolen slave could be considered *res furtivae*.

Res gestae. rās gās´tī. res jes´tā. *n. pl.* "Things done." (1) Matters or events occurring contemporaneously. (2) Matters or events directly at issue. At common law, *res gestae* encompassed subsidiary or connected facts so tied to a principal fact as to constitute a single matter, event, or transaction that should be considered as a whole. Evidence that might not otherwise be admitted under the rules of evidence was, accordingly sometimes admitted as *res gestae*. For example, a hearsay statement might be admitted as *res gestae* under an accepted exception (such as an excited utterance or present sense impression), and statements directly connected with this admissible hearsay might be admitted as well.

Res habiles. rās ha´bēlās. res hâ´bilēz. *n. pl.* "Manageable things." Things to which lawful title may be acquired by ordinary prescription.

Res immobiles. rās ēmmō´bēlās. res imō´bilēz. *n. pl.* "Immovable things." Buildings or other immovable property attached to land. *Contrast with* **Res mobiles.**

Res in transitu. rās ēn tran´sētū. res in trân´zitū. *n.* "Thing in transit." Property currently being transported from one place to another.

Res incorporale. rās ēnkōrpōra´lā. res inkōrpɜrâ´lē. *n.* [*pl.* **Res incorporales.** rās ēnkōrpōra´lās. res inkōrpɜrâ´lēz.] "Incorporeal thing." Intangible property; things imperceptible by the tactile and visual senses. *Contrast with* **Res corporale.**

R

Res integra. rās ēntāg´ra. res integ´ru. *n.* "Whole matter." (1) A point of law on which neither a decision nor *obiter dicta* has been pronounced. (2) A matter of first impression. (3) An undecided point of law. *Compare with* **Res nova.**

Res inter alios (acta) (alteri nocere non debet). rās ēn´tār a´lēōs (ak´ta) (altā´rē nō´kārā nōn dā´bāt). res in´tɜr â´lēōs (âk´tu) (al´tɜrī nō´sɜrī nan de´bet). "A matter (acting) between others (should not harm third parties)." (1) **Res inter alios (acta).** *n.* A matter or rule not legally relevant to a specific person or entity; a matter creating no third-party rights or duties. *E.g.*, "Boundary and territorial treaties made between two parties are *res inter alios acta* vis-à-vis third parties." *Eritrea v. Yemen*, Permanent Ct. of Arb., Award of Oct. 9, 1998, ¶ 153, 40 I.L.M. 900 (2001). (2) **Res inter alios (acta) alteri nocere non debet.** A maxim meaning that treaties, agreements, or other legal instruments cannot derogate from the rights of, or create obligations for, nonparties to the instrument. *See* the Vienna Convention on the Law of Treaties arts. 34–36, May 23, 1969, 1155 U.N.T.S. 331. *Compare with* **Pacta non obligant nisi gentes inter quas inita** and **Pacta tertiis (nec nocent nec prosunt).**

Res ipsa loquitur. rās ēp´sa lō´kwētūr. res ip´su lō´kwitɜr. "The thing speaks for itself." (1) A maxim meaning that the answer to a question or cause of an effect is self-evident; no explanation other than the obvious one is possible. (2) A doctrine according to which a factual scenario that admits of only one logical explanation (usually, the negligence or wrongdoing of the defendant) is considered sufficient to establish that explanation's validity.

Res iudicata. rās yūdēka´ta. res jūdikā´tu. *n.* "Adjudicated thing." A matter upon which a final and binding judgment has already been passed, thereby precluding any later, conflicting judgment on the same matter. In some legal systems, an estoppel by *res iudicata* arises only when the prior judgment applied to the same parties that are now involved in the dispute. *E.g.*, "Germany contended that the Tribunal had no jurisdiction on the ground that, in view of the confirmation by the German Prize Court of the seizure and of the destruction of the vessel, the matter was *res judicata*." *The Cysne* (Port. v. Ger.), 2 R.I.A.A. 1053 (1930). An alternative term is **Res adiudicata.** *See also* **Res iudicata pro veritate habetur.**

Res iudicata pro veritate habetur. rās yūdēka´ta prō wārēta´tā habā´tūr. res jūdikā´tu prō veritā´tē hâ´butɜr. "An adjudicated thing is regarded as the truth." A maxim meaning that a matter upon which a binding judgment has already been passed will be upheld and not questioned later by the same or a different tribunal, with certain exceptions in case of corruption, manifest disregard of the law, *excès de pouvoir*, etc. *See also* **Res iudicata.**

Res mobiles. rās mō´bēlās. res mō´bilēz. *n. pl.* "Movable things." Personal property; goods capable of being moved from place to place. *Contrast with* **Res immobiles.**

Res nova. rās nō´wa. res nō´vu. *n.* "New matter." (1) A new case or question. (2) A matter not yet the subject of precedential authoritative opinion. *Compare with* **Res integra.**

Res noviter (veniens). rās nō´wētār (wā´nē-āns). res nō´vitɜr (vē´nē-enz). *n.* "Newly (arriving) thing." An unforeseen but fundamental change in circumstances, which in some cases may be argued to excuse contractual, treaty, or other legally binding obligations that were undertaken before the change arose if the change substantially deprives one or more parties of the value of the agreement. *E.g.*, "But, though the changes thus effected in diplomatic intercourse must more and more deprive States of the apology which they once possessed for not notifying their treaties, examples of ratification being withheld on the ground of *res noviter veniens*, are not awanting in recent times." 1 James Lorimer, The Institutes of the Law of Nations 265–66 (1883). This phrase is sometimes seen in the misspelled form *res novitur veniens*. *Compare with* **Clausula rebus sic stantibus.**

Res nullius. rās nūllē´ūs. res nɜ´lē-us. *n.* "Nobody's thing." (1) A thing without substance or otherwise lacking a relevant and important quality. (2) Property currently unowned by any person or by any sovereign power. (3) Property incapable of ownership by any person. *Contrast with* **Res privatae.** (4) A thing or person lacking rights or obligations. *Compare with* **Bona vacantia, Res derelictae,** and **Terra nullius.** *See also* **Res nullius naturaliter fit primi occupantis.**

Res nullius naturaliter fit primi occupantis. rās nūllē´ūs natūra´lētār fēt prē´mē ōkkūpan´tēs. res nɜ´lē-us nâčɜrâ´litɜr fit prē´mī akyūpân´tis. "Nobody's thing naturally belongs to the first occupier." A maxim, originating in Justinian's *Digest* (41.1.3), meaning that the first person to lay proper claim to unowned or unoccupied property becomes its legal owner. Proper claim generally includes at least occupation and making use of the property. This principle follows from the position that all property is subject to private ownership. *See* Justinian's *Institutes* (2.1 § 12). *See also* **Ius primi occupatis** and **Res nullius.**

Res perit domino. rās pā´rēt dō´mēnō. res pe´rit da´minō. "The property is lost to the owner." A judgment of nonliability for the loss of or damage to the property of another.

R

Res petita. rās pātē´ta. res putē´tu. *n.* "Petitioned thing." The property or subject matter that is the object of a complaint, claim, or petition.

Res privatae. rās prēwa´tī. res pruvā´tā. *n.* "Private thing." (1) Personal or real property owned by private persons. (2) Personal or real property capable of ownership by private persons. *Contrast with* **Res coronae**, **Res nullius**, **Res publicae**, and **Res universitatis**.

Res publicae. rās pūb´lēkī. res pub´likā. *n.* "Public thing." Personal or real property owned by the government or the public as a whole, such as public parks, major bodies of water, or highways. *Compare with* **Res universitatis**. *Contrast with* **Res privatae**. *See also* **Res coronae**.

Res publicae res nullius (est). rās pūb´lēkī rās nūllē´ūs (āst). res pub´likā res nɜ´lē-us (est). *n.* "A public thing (is) nobody's thing." A maxim meaning that property belonging to the public does not in effect belong to any specific person, and so no person may claim the right to exclude others from using the property or otherwise to treat the property as his or her own.

Res quotidianae. rās kwōtēdē-a´nī. res kwōtidē-â´nā. *n. pl.* "Daily matters." In civil law, familiar or common matters or points of law.

Res sua. rās sū´a. res sū´u. *n.* "One's own thing." One's own property. *Contrast with* **Res alicuius** and **Res aliena**.

Res transit cum suo onere. rās tran´sēt kūm sū´ō ō´nārā. res trân´zit kum sū´ō a´nɜrē. "A thing passes away with its burden." A maxim meaning that all debts, servitudes, and other third-party rights attached to territory or property are transferred with the sovereignty or title to the territory or property itself. Thus, if a small state is absorbed into a new, larger state, the rights and obligations of the predecessor state may devolve upon the successor state. *Compare with* **Nemo plus iuris transfere quam ipse habet**.

Res universitatis. rās ūnēwārsēta´tēs. res yūnivɜrsitā´tis. "Universal thing." A thing owned by the community for public purposes and that cannot be acquired by any individual or subgroup. *Compare with* **Res communis (omnium)** and **Res publicae**. *See also* **Terra communis**.

Reservatio mentalis. rāsārwa´tēō mānta´lēs. rezɜrvā´šō mentâ´lis. *n.* "Mental reservation." An unexpressed reservation or belief. A mental reservation to a legally binding agreement has no legal effect if not shared by all parties to the agreement or reasonably inferable. *E.g.*, "A mental reservation (*reservatio mentalis*) regarding old claims to be worked out only in the future—which neither party may mention just now because both are too exhausted to continue the war—with the ill will to make use of the first favorable opportunity for this end belongs to jesuitical casuistry and is beneath the dignity of a ruler." Immanuel Kant, *Toward Perpetual Peace: A Philosophical Project*, *in* IMMANUEL KANT, PRACTICAL PHILOSOPHY 317, 317–18 (Mary J. Gregor trans., 1999) (1795).

R

Respectu totius generis humani. rāspā´ktū tō´tē-ūs gā´nārēs hūma´nē. respek´tū tō´šus je´nɜris hyūmâ´nī. *adj.* or *adv.* "Concerning all humankind." Pertaining or relevant to the entire human race. *E.g.*, "[T]he exalted conception of the father of international law and of other publicists of the classical period which regarded nations as moral individuals *respectu totius generis humani*, is still an ideal worthy of pursuance." Hersch Lauterpacht, PRIVATE LAW SOURCES AND ANALOGIES OF PUBLIC INTERNATIONAL LAW 305 (1927).

Respondeat superior. rāspōn´dā-at sūpā´rēōr. respan´dē-ât sūpē´rēōr. *v. imp.* "Let the master respond." A doctrine by which a supervisor, commander, employer, manager, or other superior in military or civilian hierarchical rank or office answers and assumes responsibility for the wrongdoing of his or her inferior. In the international law of war, criminal liability can arise under *respondeat superior* only if the military commander had reason to know of the crimes of his or her subordinates, was in a position to prevent or mitigate them, and failed to do so. *See* Protocol (I) Additional to the Geneva Conventions of 12 August 1949, and Relating to the Protection of Victims of International Armed Conflicts art. 87, June 8, 1977, 1125 U.N.T.S. 3. The doctrine does not operate as a defense to a charge of having committed a grave breach of international humanitarian law. *See also* **Idem est facere et nolle prohibere cum possis**, **Iniuria servi dominum pertingit**, and **Qui facit per alium, facit per se.**

Responsa. rāspōn´sa. ruspan´su. *n. pl.* [*s.* **Responsum.** rāspōn´sūm. ruspan´sum.] "Answers." A body of written opinions by authoritative legal scholars in response to specific questions addressed to them. *Responsa* make up a substantial portion of the body of religious law, especially in Judaism and Islam. *See also* **Responsa prudentium.**

Responsa prudentium. rāspōn´sa prūdān´tē-ūm. ruspan´su prūden´šum. *n. pl.* "The opinions of the learned." The considered opinions of jurists, legal scholars, and other technical experts. *Responsa prudentium* were one of the authoritative sources of Roman law. *See also* **Responsa.**

R

Restitutio. rästētū´tēō. restitū´šō. *n.* "Restitution." Restoration to the previous condition, as by the restoration of a thing taken (or a comparable substitute) to its previous owner. In modern times, when restoration is not possible, monetary compensation has generally been considered an adequate substitute. *See also* **Restitutio in integrum** and **Restitutio in pristinum.**

Restitutio ad integrum (statum). rästētū´tēō ad ēntäg´rūm (sta´tūm). restitū´šō âd integ´rum (stâ´tum). *n.* "Restoration to a former (state)." An alternative term for **Restitutio in integrum.**

Restitutio in integrum. rästētū´tēō ēn ēntäg´rūm. restitū´šō in integ´rum. *n.* "Full restitution." Restitution of a damaged or taken thing to its previous condition, as by the restoration of the thing (or a comparable substitute) to the owner who has been deprived of it. In modern times, the term has sometimes been used to refer to the payment of full compensation for the loss sustained in the event that restoration or replacement of the thing damaged or taken is not feasible (for example, when it has been depleted or destroyed). This term differs from simple **Restitutio** merely in emphasizing that the restoration must be complete as opposed to partial. *E.g.*, "The Party who has been dispossessed has a choice of remedies. He may claim restitution of the property taken. This is what is meant by *restitutio in integrum*. He may on the other hand abandon any claim to restitution of the actual property and claim damages instead." *Factory at Chorzów*, P.C.I.J. Ser. A, No. 17, 1928, at 70 (Merits) (Judge Finlay, dissenting). *See* International Law Commission, Draft Articles on State Responsibility art. 35, UN GAOR 56th Sess., Supp. No. 10, at 155–68, UN Doc. A/56/10 (2001). An alternative term is **Restitutio ad integrum (statum).** *Compare with* **Restitutio in pristinum.**

Restitutio in genere. rästētū´tēō ēn gā´nārā. restitū´šō in je´nɜrē. *n.* "Restitution in kind." Substitute restitution; compensation for damages by supplying goods or other restitution of a kind similar to what was lost by reason of the wrongdoing. *E.g.*, "Principle VII…excludes the possibility of retaining cultural objects which 'may never be retained as war reparations.' In other words, the Declaration aims to exclude restitution in kind (*resitutio in genere*) and the duty to redress damage, in the area of culture in this case, by the States responsible for the outbreak of the Second World War." UNESCO, Report by the Director General on the Preparation of a Draft Declaration of Principles Relating to Cultural Objects Displaced in Connection with the Second World War, Doc. 177 EX/17 (Sept. 17, 2007), Annex II (Doc. 34 C/22), at 3. *See also* **In genere.**

Restitutio in pristinum. rāstētū´tēō ēn prēstē´nūm. restitū´šō in pristē´num. *n.* "Restoration to the original." Restoration of an injured entity or person to its condition before an event (such as an injury) occurred that altered that condition. *Compare with* **Restitutio in integrum.**

Reus in excipiendo actor est. rā´ūs ēn āks-kēpē-ān´dō ak´tōr āst. rā´us in eksipē-en´dō âk´tɜr est. "The defendant, in making a legal defense, is a plaintiff." A maxim, derived from Ulpian's *Disputations*, meaning that one interposing a positive defense must adduce sufficient evidence to carry the burden of proving the defense valid. The maxim assumes that the plaintiff has already carried the initial burden of presenting a *prima facie* valid claim.

Revisio in iure. rāwē´sēō ēn yū´rā. revi´zēō in jɜ´rē. *n.* "Revisitation of law." The hearing of an appeal from a legal decision without reconsidering the facts as found by the lower tribunal or other fact-finder.

Rex. rāks. reks. *n.* "King." (1) A male monarch. (2) Metonymically, the sovereign or state. Sometimes abbreviated **R.** *Compare with* **Regina.**

Rex extra territorium suum privatem. rāks āks´tra tārrētō´rē-ūm sū´ūm prēwa´tūm. reks eks´tru teritō´rē-um sū´um prīvā´tum. *n.* "A king outside his own private territory." A maxim referring to the immunity of a sovereign in foreign courts. *Compare with* **Par in parem non habet iurisdictionem.**

Rigor iuris. rē´gōr yū´rēs. ri´gɜr jɜ´ris. *n.* "Strictness of law." The strict or literal interpretation of the law.

Rusticum iudicium. rūs´tēkūm yūdē´kē-ūm. rus´tikum jūdi´šum. *n. Neo.* "Rough judgment." The division of liability for an accident so that the respondent pays only a portion (usually, half) of the claimant's loss because of the equal fault of the parties. This practice arose in the seventeenth-century English Admiralty Courts to resolve disputes relating to maritime accidents and was sometimes applied by common law courts to tort cases as a kind of comparative negligence rule to mitigate the harsh effects of the traditional contributory negligence rule. *See also* **Rusticum ius.**

Rusticum ius. rūs´tēkūm yūs. rus´tikum jus. *n. Neo.* "Rough law." A rule of liability by which all parties share liability in proportion to their fault for the damages resulting from an accident. *See also* **Rusticum iudicium.**

S

S.J.D. An abbreviation of **Scientiae iuris doctor**.

Salvo iure. sal´wō yū´rā. sâl´vō jɜ´rē. *adv.* "Saving the rule." Without prejudice to the rights (of any person). The term may also be used with a possessive pronoun, *e.g.*, *salvo iure meo* ("without prejudice to my rights"), *salvo iure cuiuslibet* ("without prejudice to anyone's rights"), or *salvo iure regis* ("without prejudice to the sovereign's rights").

Scandalum magnatum. skan´dalūm magna´tūm. skân´dalum mâgnā´tum. *n.* "The stumbling block of great persons." (1) Something that creates confusion or error in even the most skillful, knowledgeable, or intelligent persons. (2) In English common law, the defamation of a state official, aristocrat, or other person of high office, rank, or social standing, giving rise to civil and criminal liability in order to censor criticism of the state, its government, and its privileged classes. *E.g.*, "Words spoken in derogation of a peer, a judge, or other great officer of the realm, which are called *scandalum magnatum*, are held to be still more heinous; and, though they be such as would not be actionable in the case of a common person, yet when spoken in disgrace of such high and respectable characters, they amount to an atrocious injury, which is redressed by an action on the case founded on many ancient statutes; as well on behalf of the crown, to inflict the punishment of imprisonment on the slanderer, as on behalf of the party, to recover damages for the injury sustained." 3 William Blackstone, COMMENTARIES ON THE LAWS OF ENGLAND 123–24 (1768).

Scienter. skē-ān´tār. sē-en´tɜr OR sī-en´tɜr. *adv.* (commonly used as a *n.*) "Knowingly; skillfully." (1) The kind of intent or degree of knowledge prerequisite to civil or criminal liability for an act committed with this intent or knowledge. *Compare with* **Animus malus**, **Dolus malus**, and **Mens rea**. (2) An intent to commit a harmful act. (3) Generally, consciousness or knowledge.

Scientiae iuris doctor. skē-ān´tē-ī yū´rēs dōk´tōr. sī-en´tē-ā jɜ´ris dak´tɜr. "Doctor of juridical science." An alternative formulation of **Iuris scientiae doctor.** Abbreviated **S.J.D.**

Scripto. skrēp´tō. skrip´tō. *adv.* "By writing." Done by writing or in written form.

Se defendendo. sā dāfāndān´dō. sā dufenden´dō. *adv.* "In defending oneself." In self-defense.

Secundum aequum et bonum. sākūn´dūm ī´kwū-ūm āt bō´nūm. sekun´dum e´kwum et bō´num. *adv.* "According to what is just and good." An alternative phrase for **Ex aequo et bono.** This phrase is commonly misspelled *secundum aequo et bono*, *secundum aequum et bono*, or some variation thereon.

Secundum allegata et probata. sākūn´dūm allāga´ta āt prōba´ta. sekun´dum âlegā´tu et prōba´tu. "According to the claims and proof." Based on the claims and evidence presented by the parties (the tribunal will arrive at its judgment). *E.g.*, "The parties put forward facts and submit the evidence that they consider favourable to their claims, and the court takes them into consideration when making its decision (*secundum allegata et probata*)." *Advisory Opinion on the Western Sahara*, 1975 I.C.J. Rep. 12, 138 (separate opinion of Judge De Castro).

Secundum artem. sākūn´dūm ar´tām. sekun´dum ar´tum. *adv.* "According to the craft." In accordance with common trade or industry usages.

Secundum bonos mores. sākūn´dūm bō´nōs mō´rās. sekun´dum bō´nōs mō´rēz. *adv.* "According to good customs." According to established custom; in compliance with proper industry or trade usages.

Secundum bonum et aequum. sākūn´dūm bō´nūm āt ī´kū-ūm. sekun´dum bō´num et e´kwum. *adv.* "According to what is good and just." An alternative phrase for **Ex aequo et bono.**

Secundum legem domicilii vel loci contractus. sākūn´dūm lā´gām dōmēkē´lē-ē wāl lō´kē kōntrak´tūs. sekun´dum le´jum damisi´lī vel lō´sī kantrâk´tus. *adv.* "According to the law of domicile or place of contracting." According to the law of the place where one or both parties were domiciled or, alternatively, the place in which the contract was concluded. This maxim has sometimes been used to establish a general rule dictating which forum or fora may assume jurisdiction over a dispute under private international law. *See also* **Lex loci contractus.**

Secundum regulam. sākūn´dūm rā´gūlam. sekun´dum re´gyūlum. *adv.* "According to the rule." (1) As a rule. (2) In compliance with the rule.

S

Secus. sā´kūs. se´kus. *adv.* "Otherwise." (1) The legal position is different or otherwise. (2) The contrary is true. *Compare with* **Contra.**

Sed quaere. sād kwī´rā. sed kwē´rē. *v. imp.* "But ask!" (1) But is it true?; but are they true? The term is often used as a shorthand for doubting or questioning the accuracy of an assertion. *E.g.*, "It is suggested that [the Decision to transfer all chauffeurs from employment by members of the European Court of Auditors to the President's Department] was taken in the interests not only of the service but of the drivers themselves and examples have been given which it is said support the latter justification (*sed quaere*)." Opinion of Advocate General Slynn, *Rousseau v. Court of Auditors of the European Communities*, [1988] E.C.R. 2705. (2) But one might ask the question...; But one might or should inquire...

Sedente curia. sādān´tā kū´rē-a. seden´tē kyū´rē-u. *adv.* "The court sitting." While the tribunal is in session.

Sedes materiae. sā´dās matā´rē-ī. se´dēz mutē´rē-ā. *n.* (sometimes used as an *adv.*) "The seat of the matter." (1) (Regarding) the jurisdiction or venue in which a legal issue is decided. (2) (Regarding) the main substance or key point of a matter. *E.g.*, "While the Respondent argues that what is involved is a humanitarian intervention provoked by the 'human tragedy and the enormous suffering,' the Applicant finds that *sedes materiae* the underlying reasons are to be sought elsewhere—in the support to the terrorist organization in Kosovo and in the political aim of secession of Kosovo and Metohija from Yugoslavia." *Legality of the Use of Force* (Yugo. v. Port.), 1999 I.C.J. Rep. 656, 757, ¶ 15 (Provisional Measures) (Judge *ad hoc* Kreća, dissenting).

Sedes personae. sā´dās pārsō´nī. se´dēz pɜrsō´nā. *n.* (sometimes used as an *adv.*) "The seat of the person." (Regarding) a person's residence or domicile, which may be used for determining jurisdiction under private international law.

Semel. sā´māl. se´mul. *adv.* "Firstly." An adverbial number (the first) usually inserted into a consecutively numbered series by way of amendment. In amending or supplementing a treaty or other legal document, the drafters may choose to append *semel* and other adverbial numbers to the old article numbers rather than renumber the articles. For example, in introducing a new article into a treaty between current articles 6 and 7, the drafters may rename article 6 to article 6*semel* and designate the newly added article as article 6*bis*. *See* the Appendix for a list of Latin adverbial numbers commonly used in international law. *Compare with* **Primo.** *See also* **Bis** and **Primus.**

Semel civis semper civis. sā´māl kē´wēs sām´pār kē´wēs. se´mul si´vis sem´pɜr si´vis. "Once a citizen, always a citizen." A maxim of the Roman civil law, adopted for a time in the English common law, meaning that, once someone has acquired citizenship, it cannot be renounced or lost through the acquisition of a new nationality. This principle was not, however, strictly followed; instances of changing nationality occurred even in the Roman Empire, and it has never been successfully asserted to represent international law. *Compare with* **Nemo patriam (in qua natus est) exuere potest (nec ligeantiae debitum eiurare possit).**

Seminaufragium. sāmēnôfra´gē-ūm. semīnăfrā´jum. *n.* "Half-shipwreck." (1) Cargo (jetsam) cast into the sea to prevent a complete shipwreck. (2) A state of damage to a seagoing vessel caused by such events as severe weather, collision, or disrepair that render repairs to a seaworthy state more expensive than the vessel's value.

Semper. sām´pār. sem´pɜr. *adv.* "Always." Always; permanently; continually; at all times.

Semper ubique et ab omnibus. sām´pār ūbē´kwā āt ab ōm´nēbūs. sem´pɜr ubi´kwē et âb am´nibus. *adj.* or *adv.* "Always everywhere and by everyone." Universally accepted, agreed upon, or practiced. *E.g.*, "There is a concealed, half conscious battle on the question of legislative policy, and if any one thinks that it can be settled deductively, or once for all, I only can say that I think he is theoretically wrong, and that I am certain that his conclusion will not be accepted in practice *semper ubique et ab omnibus.*" Oliver Wendell Holmes, *The Path of the Law*, 10 Harv. L. Rev. 457 (1897).

Sensu stricto. sān´sū strēk´tō. sen´sū strik´tō. *adv.* "In the strict sense." Speaking or writing literally and without exaggeration or approximation. Sometimes misspelled *sensu strictu*. An alternative formulation is **Stricto sensu**. *Contrast with* **Sensu latu.**

Sensu latu. sān´sū lā´tū. sen´sū lâ´tū. *adj.* "In the broad sense." Speaking or writing using an expansive or figurative meaning. *Contrast with* **Sensu stricto.**

Sententia. sāntān´tē-a. senten´šu. *n.* "Judgment." (1) A judicial opinion or judgment. (2) An expert or technical opinion. (3) Sense; meaning; signification.

Sententia non fertur de rebus non liquidis. sāntān´tē-a nōn fār´tūr dā rā´būs nōn lē´kwēdēs. senten´šu nan fɜr´tɜr dā rē´bus nan li´kwidis. "Judgment is not born from unclear matters." A doctrine preventing a tribunal from rendering judgment where the facts do not permit adequate certainty about the proper decision.

This doctrine is not generally applied in international practice. *Compare with* **Non liquet.**

Separatim. sāpara´tēm. sepɜrā´tim. *adv.* "Separately." Separately; severally.

Septie(n)s. sāp´tē-ā(n)s. sep´tē(n)z. *adv.* "Seventhly." An adverbial number (the seventh) usually inserted into a consecutively numbered series by way of amendment. *See* the Appendix for a list of Latin adverbial numbers commonly used in international law. *See also* **Bis** and **Semel.**

Seriatim. sārē-a´tēm. sērē-â´tim. *adj.* or *adv. Med.* "In series." (1) In a consecutive series; successively; one by one. *E.g.*, "After various observations on the facts and the law, New Zealand sets out, *seriatim*, in the concluding paragraph of her Application five separate categories of rights which she claims to be violated by France's atmospheric nuclear tests." *Nuclear Tests* (N.Z. v. Fr.), 1974 I.C.J. Rep. 457, 511, ¶ 33 (Judge Onyeama, dissenting). (2) Word for word. *E.g.*, "The applicant's claims are set out *seriatim* and every one of them is thus mentioned [in the judgment given in this case]." *Advisory Opinion on the Application for Review of Judgment No. 158 of the United Nations Administrative Tribunal*, 1973 I.C.J. Rep. 166, 211, ¶ 96. *Compare with* **Verbatim.**

Sexie(n)s. sā´ksē-ā(n)s. se´ksē(n)z. *adv.* "Sixthly." An adverbial number (the sixth) usually inserted into a consecutively numbered series by way of amendment. *See* the Appendix for a list of Latin adverbial numbers commonly used in international law. *See also* **Bis** and **Semel.**

Si omnes. sē ōm´nās. sē am´nēz. "If all…" An abbreviation of a Latin phrase that translates to: "If all relevant parties are not bound by the treaty, then the treaty is not binding upon any of the parties." *See* **Clausula si omnes.**

Si quid universitati debetur singulis non debetur, nec quod debet universitas singuli debent. sē kwēd ūnēwārsēta´tē dābā´tūr sēn´gūlēs nōn dābā´tūr, nāk kwōd dā´bāt ūnēwār´sētas sēn´gūlē dā´bānt. sē kwid yūnivɜrsitā´tī de´betɜr siŋ´gyūlis nan de´betɜr, nek kwad de´bet yūnivɜr´situs siŋ´yūlī de´bent. "If something is owed to the whole, it is not owed each to each, nor do each individually owe what the whole owes." A maxim, originating in Justinian's *Digest* (3.4.7.1), meaning that a debtor or injured party may not retaliate for a wrong or collect a debt against one not directly responsible for the injury or debt. The maxim has been used to explain why creditors of a limited liability company cannot recover against the company's owners.

Si vis pacem, para bellum. sē wēs pa´kām, pa´ra bāl´lūm. sē vis pâ´kem, pa´ru be´lum. "If you want peace, prepare for war." An alternative phrase for **Qui desiderat pacem, praeparet bellum.**

Sic. sēk. sik. *adv.* "Thus." So written or stated in the original. The term is often used in brackets to indicate that an error or idiosyncrasy in quoted text originates in the text itself and not in the person quoting the text. *E.g.*, "At approximately 7 a.m. Eastern Daylight Time on 19 October 1987, United States naval vessels destroyed the Iranian military ocean platform at Rashadat [*sic*] (also known as Rostam) in international waters of the Persian Gulf." *Oil Platforms Case* (Iran v. U.S.), 2003 I.C.J. 161, 185, ¶ 48.

Sic et simpliciter. sēk ät sēmplē´kētär. sik et simpli´sitɜr. *adv.* "Thus and simply." Without further complication or elaboration. *E.g.*, "[T]he principle of fiscal territoriality, which the court has recognised in respect of the rules on free movement of persons and freedom of establishment, cannot be transposed *sic et simpliciter* to freedom of services." Opinion of Advocate General Tesauro, *Safir v. Skattemyndigheten I Dalarnas Län*, [1998] 3 C.M.L.R. 739, 754, ¶ 25.

Sic interpretandum est ut verba accipiantur cum effectu. sēk ēntärprätan´dūm äst ūt wär´ba akkēpē-an´tūr kūm äffäk´tū. sik intɜrpretân´dum est ūt vɜr´bu usi´pē-ântɜr kum efek´tū. "So should words be understood such that they are construed as to their effect." A maxim originating in Edward Coke's *Institutes of the Laws of England* (3:80) meaning that, where the provisions of a contract or other legal instrument are unclear, they should be interpreted in a manner that will make the instrument legally binding and effective to its purpose.

Sic subscribitur. sēk sūbskrē´bētūr. sik subskri´bitɜr. "Thus it is written." A phrase indicating that the writer or speaker witnessed the execution of a document, after which the witness signs his or her own name in attestation thereof.

Sic utere tuo ut alienum non laedas. sēk ū´tärā tū´ō ūt alē-ā´nūm nōn lī´das. sik yū´tɜrē tū´ō ūt ālē-e´num nan lā´dus. "Use your own in such a way that you do not harm that which belongs to another." A maxim enjoining all who own or possess property or territory to enjoy it in such a way that it causes no harm to others. This principle has been incorporated into several instruments and decisions relevant to the international environmental responsibilities of states. *See, e.g.*, Stockholm Declaration of the United Nations Conference on the Human Environment, Principle 21, 11 I.L.M. 1416 (1972); Rio Declaration on Environment and Development, Principle 2, 31 I.L.M. 874 (1992); *Advisory Opinion on the Legality of the Threat or Use of Nuclear Weapons*, 1996 I.C.J. Rep. 226, 241–42, ¶ 29. Sometimes abbreviated **Sic utere tuum.**

Sic utere tuum. sēk ū´tärā tū´ūm. sik yū´tɜrē tū´um. "Use your own thus." An abbreviation of **Sic utere tuo ut alienum non laedas.**

Silent leges inter arma. sē´lānt lā´gās ēn´tār ar´ma. sī´lent le´jēz in´tɜr ar´mu. "Among arms, laws are silent." An alternative formulation of **Inter arma silent leges.**

Simplex. sēm´plāks. sim´pleks. *adv.* "Simple." (1) Pure; sheer; unadulterated. (2) Uncomplicated; straightforward.

S

Simpliciter. sēmplē´kētār. simpli´sitɜr. *adj.* "Simply." (1) Unconditionally and absolutely. *E.g.*, "Article 2(4) [of the UN Charter] does not forbid the 'threat or use of force' *simpliciter*; it forbids it only when directed 'against the territorial integrity or political independence of any state, or in any other manner inconsistent with the Purposes of the United Nations.'" Julius Stone, AGGRESSION AND WORLD ORDER 95 (1958). (2) Purely; without qualification or complication. *E.g.*, "And consent to jurisdiction cannot be established, even *prima facie*, when it is clear from the terms of the declarations themselves that the necessary consent is not *prima facie* present, or simply is not present, *simpliciter*." *Legality of Use of Force* (Yugo. v. Belg.), 1999 I.C.J. Rep. 124, 168, ¶ 26 (separate opinion of Judge Higgins). (3) By itself; alone. *E.g.*, "It is true that there is a significant measure of overlap between what the Applicant sought, and to some extent obtained, in its [two requests for provisional measures.] But whatever may be the degree of overlap—and it is not total—the question is not really *simpliciter* whether the subject-matter of the first request may be revisited." *Application of Convention on Prevention and Punishment of Crime of Genocide* (Bosn. & Herz. v. Yugo.), 1993 I.C.J. Rep. 325, 411, ¶ 12 (separate opinion of Judge Lauterpacht).

Sine. sē´nā. si´nē OR si´nā. *prep.* "Without." Without.

Sine die. sē´nā dē´ā. si´nē- OR si´nā dē´ā. *adv.* "Without a day." (1) Lacking the designation of a specific day. (2) Indefinitely. *E.g.*, "[T]he Agents of the two Parties jointly informed the Court that their Governments had 'entered into negotiations that may lead to a full and final settlement of the case' and requested the Court 'to postpone *sine die* the opening of the oral proceedings,' for which it had been fixed the date of 12 September 1994." *Aerial Incident of 3 July 1988* (Iran v. U.S.), 1996 I.C.J. Rep. 9, 10.

Sine mora. sē´nā mō´ra. si´nē- OR si´nā mō´ru. *adv.* "Without delay." (1) Immediately. *Compare with* **Statim.** (2) Without undue delay.

Sine qua non. sē´nā kwa nōn. si´nē- OR si´nā kwā nan. *adj.* (commonly used as a *n.*). "Without which…not." An abbreviation of **Condicio sine qua non.** *E.g.*, "An active involvement on the part of the parents…needed to be promoted as a condition *sine qua non* for the overall improvement of the education situation of the Roma." *D.H. v. Czech Rep.*, Eur. Ct. Hum. Rts. App. No.

57325/00, Judgment of Nov. 13, 2007, ¶ 76, 47 I.L.M. 38. *See also* **Causa sine qua non.**

Situs. sē´tūs. sī´tus OR si´tus. *n.* "Physical position or site." The position or location of property. *See also* **Lex situs.**

Sive indefinita. sē´wā ēndāfēnē´ta. si´vē indefini´tu. *adj.* "Whether or not indefinite." As to whether the matter is indefinite or unknown. *E.g.*, "Immemorial possession *sive indefinita* manifests itself as a present and evident fact the commencement of which is unknown." *Advisory Opinion on Western Sahara*, 1975 I.C.J. Rep. 12, 154 (separate opinion of Judge De Castro).

Societas navalis. sōkē´ātas nawa´lēs. sōsī´etus nā´vulis. *n. Med.* "Naval partnership." (1) In European law, a partnership in a seagoing vessel, the vessel being treated as capital divided into tradable shares. (2) A group of seagoing vessels sailing together for mutual protection. An alternative term is **Admiralitas.**

Soluta legibus scelera sunt. sōlū´ta lā´gēbūs skā´lāra sūnt. salū´tu le´jibus se´lзru sunt. "Crimes are committed with impunity." A condemnation of the nonenforcement or underenforcement of law, written by Seneca in *De beneficiis* in the first century CE.

Solutio. sōlū´tēō. sulū´tēō OR salū´šō. *n.* "Payment." Performance or payment in satisfaction of an obligation.

Solve et repete. sōl´wā āt rā´pātā. sal´vē et rupē´tē. *v. imp.* "Pay and seek again." A doctrine by which a party wrongfully adjudged liable for an injury must pay the victorious party before seeking restitution of the wrongfully disbursed award.

Specialia generalibus derogant. spākē-a´lē-a gānāra´lēbūs dā´rōgant. spešâ´libus jenзrâ´libus de´rōgent. "The specific derogates from the general." (1) When both general and specific rules may apply to a legal issue, the more specific rules prevail on the understanding that they are considered exceptions to or special applications of the general rule. (2) When a legal instrument contains multiple clauses relating to an issue, the more specific provisions and terms apply even in contradiction to the more general ones. *E.g.*, "Sir Gerald Fitzmaurice makes a forceful argument against any 'too rigid and sweeping' application of the continuity rule, but I believe his illustrative situation...may be covered by another rule deriving from the law of State succession, and on that basis would escape the application of the continuity rule for international claims which I consider to be generally binding—*specialia generalibus derogant*." *Barcelona Traction, Light, and Power Co., Ltd.* (Belg. v. Sp.), 1970

I.C.J. Rep. 3, 202, ¶ 73 (separate opinion of Judge Jessup). *Compare with* **Generalia specialibus non derogant** and **Generalis clausula non porrigitur ad ea quae antea specialiter sunt comprehensa.**

S

Spes recuperandi. spās rākūpāran´dē. spes rukūpзrân´dī. *n.* "Hope of recovery." The expectation or hope of recovering a seagoing vessel captured as prize. Between belligerents in an armed conflict, the title to a vessel and its cargo taken as prize passes to the capturing belligerent the moment that the vessel passes beyond any hope of recovery (as when it enters a heavily defended friendly port). *See also* **Infra praesidia.**

Spolia. spō´lē-a. spō´lē-u. *n. pl.* [*s.* **Spolium.** spō´lē-ūm. spō´lē-um.] "Booty." (1) In Roman practice, weapons and armor taken as spoils from defeated enemy soldiers. (2) More generally, anything taken in plunder from an enemy during an armed conflict. In either meaning, the plural form is more commonly used than the singular.

Spolium. *See* **Spolia.**

Sponsio. spōn´sēō. span´sēō. *n.* [*pl.* **Sponsiones.** spōnsēō´nās. spansēō´nēz.] "Promise." (1) Generally, any promise intending to be binding on the promisor. (2) A class of treaties of alliance accompanied by religious rituals, sometimes used in the Roman Empire, in which the more powerful party bound itself to defend its less powerful ally. *Compare with* **Foedera, Pactiones,** and **Pactum.**

Sponsio iudicialis. spōn´sēō yūdēkē-a´lēs. span´sēō jūdšâ´lis. *n.* "Judicial wager." A frivolous or groundless lawsuit, prosecution, or argument.

Sponsiones. *See* **Sponsio.**

Sponte sua. spōn´tā sū´a. span´tē sū´u. An alternative formulation of **Sua sponte.**

Stare decisis. sta´rā dākē´sēs. sta´rē desī´sis. *v. inf.* (commonly used as a *n.*) "To abide by settled matters." A common law doctrine holding that a point of law already decided by a tribunal will be followed and not normally called into question by another tribunal of identical jurisdiction. *E.g.*, "It is my view that, while the Judgment in the *Right of Passage* case bears on the present case, it should not have controlled its outcome, as it would seem to have done. Moreover, it is an important principle of this Court that it does not recognize the principle of *stare decisis*—the principle of binding precedent does not apply in the Court." *Land and Maritime Boundary Between Cameroon and Nigeria* (Camer. v. Niger.), 1998 I.C.J. Rep. 275, 380 (Preliminary Objections) (Judge Koroma, dissenting). *Compare with* **Non quieta movere.**

Statim. sta´tēm. stâ´tim. *adv.* "Immediately." (1) Immediately. *Compare with* **Sine mora.** (2) At the earliest possible or legally permissible moment.

Status iure. sta´tūs yū´rā. stâ´tus jз´rē. *n.* "Status with respect to the law." Legal status; status under the law. *E.g.*, "The absence of that *joint will* [to dispose of jointly owned territory] is equivalent to the omission of an empowering formality, since the Government of Nicaragua lacks the legal capacity to alter by itself the *status jure* existing in the Gulf." Hersch Lauterpacht, Private Law Sources and Analogies of Public International Law 289 (1927).

Status libertatis. sta´tūs lēbārta´tēs. stâ´tus libзrtā´tis. *n.* "A state of freedom." (1) A state of freedom from constraint or limitation. (2) A negative obligation; An obligation not to act in a certain, defined manner. *E.g.*, "The individual freedoms place purely negative duties on the government authorities [not to interfere with any person's education]...(negative status, *status libertatis*)." *Belgian Linguistics Case*, 1 E.H.R.R. 252, ¶ 1 (1968). *See also* **In statu libertatis.**

Status mixtus. sta´tūs mēks´tūs. stâ´tus miks´tus. *n.* "Mixed status." (1) A half-hearted or desultory war. (2) A state of armed conflict not rising to war but short of neutrality or peace.

Status quo. sta´tūs kwō. stâ´tus kwō. *n.* "The condition in which." The state of things existing at the moment. The term was historically sometimes used to denote the current state of a sovereign power's possession of territory acquired by conquest or occupation. *E.g.*, "Guyana contends that the activities it authorized in the disputed maritime area were in line with a *status quo* represented by 40 years of oil practice by the Parties." *Guyana v. Suriname*, Perm. Ct. Arb., Award of Sept. 17, 2007, ¶ 267, 47 I.L.M. 166 (2008). *Contrast with* **Status quo ante.** *See also* **In statu quo.**

Status quo ante. sta´tūs kwō an´tā. stâ´tus kwō ân´tē. *n.* "The condition in which before." The state of things as they existed before a specific event, especially one of legal significance, occurred. *E.g.*, "The concept of restitution is not uniformly defined. According to one definition, restitution consists in re-establishing the *status quo ante*, i.e. the situation that existed prior to the occurrence of the wrongful act." International Law Commission, Draft Articles on State Responsibility art. 35, cmt. 2, UN GAOR 56th Sess., Supp. No. 10, at 155–68, UN Doc. A/56/10 (2001). *Contrast with* **Status quo.** *See also* **In statu quo ante.**

Status quo ante bellum. sta´tūs kwō an´tā bāl´lūm. stâ´tus kwō ân´tē be´lum. *n.* "The condition in which before war." The situation as it existed before an armed conflict occurred, usually with reference to the situation existing before one belligerent seized and occupied foreign or disputed territory. *E.g.*, "In case of a conflict between two or more American States...the High Contracting Parties, meeting in consultation shall call upon the contending States to suspend hostilities and restore matters to the *status quo ante bellum*." Inter-American Treaty of Reciprocal Assistance art. 7, Sept. 2, 1947, 21 U.N.T.S. 77. *Contrast with* **Status quo post bellum.**

S

Status quo de facto. sta´tūs kwō dā fak´tō. stâ´tus kwō dā fâk´tō. *n.* "The condition in which in fact." The situation as it exists in fact, as opposed to in theory or as required by law. *Contrast with* **Status quo de iure.**

Status quo de iure. sta´tūs kwō dā yū´rā. stâ´tus kwō dā jū´rē. *n.* "The condition in which in law." The situation as the law requires it to be at present, as opposed to the what the situation actually is. *Contrast with* **Status quo de facto.**

Status quo post bellum. sta´tūs kwō pōst bāl´lūm. stâ´tus kwō pōst be´lum. *n.* "The condition in which after war." The situation as it exists after an armed conflict has terminated, usually with reference to the situation existing after a belligerent seized and occupied foreign or disputed territory. *Contrast with* **Status quo ante bellum.**

Statuta suo clauduntur territorio (nec ultra territorium disponunt). statū´ta sū´ō klôdūn´tūr tārrētō´rēō (nāk ūl´tra tārrētō´rē-ūm dēspō´nūnt). stâ´čūtu sū´ō klă´dunt3r teritō´rēō (nek 3l´tru teritō´rē-um dispō´nunt). "Statutes are confined to their territory (nor do they apply extraterritorially)." A common law maxim meaning that the laws of a state are presumed to apply only to conduct and persons within the state's borders and not to those outside of them. In most common law countries, this presumption is rebuttable on a showing of legislative intent for the law to apply extraterritorially.

Stet. stāt. stet. *v. imp.* "Let it stand." In copy editing, this term is commonly used to indicate that a proposed alteration in a text, such as the correction of a putative error, should be ignored so that the text should stand as originally written.

Stet processus. stāt prōkēs´sūs. stet prases´us. *v. imp.* "Halt the proceeding." (1) An order, usually issued by a tribunal, to stop a legal process such as a trial or the enforcement of an order. (2) An agreement to put such a process on hold.

Stricti iuris. strē´ktē yū´rēs. strik´tī j3´ris. *adj.* or *adv.* "Of strict right." (1) In strict accordance with the law or the rights of relevant parties, without variation or expansion in interpretation. (2) Conferred by grant and not by entitlement. Rights obtained *strici iuris* (by license or governmental grant, for example) are narrowly construed. An alternative formulation is **Ius strictum**. *Compare with* **Strictissimi iuris.**

Strictissimi iuris. strēktēs´sēmē yū´rēs. strikti´simī jɜ´ris. *adj.* or *adv.* "Of the strictest right." By the positive law construed as strictly and literally as possible; by the strictest or narrowest interpretation of a party's rights. *Compare with* **De rigor iuris, Ius strictum,** and **Stricti iuris.**

Stricto iure. strēk´tō yū´rā. strik´tō jɜ´rē. *adj.* or *adv.* "In strict law." According to a technical point of positive law, as opposed to equity. *Compare with* **De rigor iuris** and **Strictum ius.** *See also* **Actio stricti iuris** and **Ius strictum.**

Stricto sensu. strēk´tō sān´sū. strik´tō sen´sū. *adj.* or *adv.* "In the strict sense." (1) Literally and without exaggeration or approximation. (2) In a technical sense. *E.g.*, "In the view of Nicaragua, '*stricto sensu*, the military and paramilitary attacks launched by the United States against Nicaragua do not constitute a case of civil strife. They are essentially the acts of the United States.'" *Military and Paramilitary Activities in and Against Nicaragua* (Nicar. v. U.S.), 1986 I.C.J. Rep. 14, ¶ 114. An alternative formulation is **Sensu stricto.** *Contrast with* **Lato sensu.**

Strictu sensu. A misspelling of **Stricto sensu.**

Strictum ius. strēk´tūm yūs. strik´tum jus. *n.* "Exact law." An alternative formulation of **Ius strictum.**

Sua sponte. sū´a spōn´tā. sū´u span´tē. *adv.* "On one's own initiative." (1) Done on one's own initiative, without external prompting. In judicial and arbitral practice, any procedure undertaken by a tribunal *sua sponte* is done at the tribunal's own behest and in the absence of any motion by any party before the tribunal. *E.g.*, "[T]he Court is always free, *sua sponte*, to examine into its own jurisdiction." *South West Africa Cases* (Eth. v. S. Afr.; Liber. v. S. Afr.), 1966 I.C.J. Rep. 6, 333 (separate opinion of Judge Jessup). *Compare with* **Ex proprio vigore.** (2) Spontaneously. Alternative terms are **Ex mero motu, Ex proprio (suo) motu, Mero motu,** and **Sponte sua.**

Sub colore iuris. sūb kōlō´rā yū´rēs. sub kulō´rē jɜ´ris. *adv.* "Under color of right." Done with the appearance of a legal right, regardless of whether the actor in fact possessed the legal right. *Compare with* **Colore officii.**

Sub colore officii. sūb kōlō´rā ōffē´kē-ē. sub kulō´rē ōfi´šī. *adv.* "Under color of office." An alternative term for **Colore officii.**

Sub disiunctione. sūb disyūnktēō´nā. sub disjunkšō´nē. *adv.* *Neo.* "Under disjunction." In the alternative.

S

Sub iudice. sūb yū´dēkā. sub jū´disē. *adj.* "Under the judge." Under active consideration by a tribunal, judge, or arbitrator. *E.g.*, "[T]he situation during the period in which a case is not yet before a tribunal is not the same as the situation during the period in which that case is *sub judice.* So long as a dispute has not been brought before the tribunal…the period of negotiation is not over." *Air Services Agreement of 27 March 1946* (U.S. v. Fr.), 18 R.I.A.A. 415, ¶ 95 (1979). *See also* **Lis sub iudice.**

Sub modo. sūb mō´dō. sub mō´dō. *adj.* or *adv.* "Under the method." (1) Subject to a condition. (2) Subject to a qualification.

Sub nom. An abbreviation of **Sub nomine.**

Sub nomine. sūb nō´mēnā. sub na´minē. *adj.* or *adv.* "Under the name." Under the specific name. This term is commonly used as a designation for a change of a case name or other title, as in the following example of a case citation: "*Gilmore Steel Corp. v. United States*, 585 F. Supp. 670 (Ct. Int'l Trade 1984), *aff'd sub nom. Oregon Steel Mills v. United States*, 862 F.2d 1541 (Fed. Cir. 1988) (U.S.)." Commonly abbreviated **Sub nom.**

Sub poena. sūb pœ´na. sub pē´nu. An abbreviation of **Sub poena duces tecum** or **Sub poena ad testificandum.**

Sub poena ad testificandum. sūb pœ´na ad tāstēfēkan´dūm. sub pē´nu âd testifikân´dum. *v. ger.* (commonly used as a *n.*) "Being required to testify under penalty." An order from a tribunal to testify under threat of penalty.

Sub poena (duces tecum). sūb pœ´na (dū´kās tā´kūm). sub pē´nu (dū´sēz te´kum). *v. imp.* (commonly used as a *n.*). "Bring with you under penalty." An order from a tribunal to produce documents under threat of penalty.

Sub potestate. sūb pōtāsta´tā. sub pōtesta´tē. *adv.* "Under the protection." Under the protection or power of another, usually of a sovereign. Every state has the duty to try to attempt to protect its citizens, who are said to be *sub potestate*, from the denial of human rights or other maltreatment by other states.

Sub rosa. sūb rō´sa. sub rō´zu. *adj.* or *adv.* "Under the rose." Furtive(ly); confidential(ly). *E.g.*, "It would be absurd if the Court were to afford 'just satisfaction to the injured party' and then *sub rosa* acquiesce to the continuation of the *status quo* which the offending state would not be obliged…to remedy in its essential aspects." *Broniowski v. Poland*, 40 E.H.R.R. 21, ¶ O-I8 (2005) (Judge Zupancic, concurring). *Compare with* **Sub silentio.**

Sub silentio. sūb sēlān´tēō. sub silen´šō. *adj.* or *adv.* "Under silence." (1) Furtive(ly); covert(ly). (2) On pledge of secrecy or discretion. (3) Without express mention or notice. *Compare with* **Sub rosa.**

Sub spe rati. sūb spā ra´tē. sub spā rā´šī. *adj.* "Under hope of ratification." In the hope or expectation of ratification. A legal instrument signed *sub spe rati* remains nonbinding until ratified by the sovereign whom the signer represents. A treaty *sub spe rati* is ineffective and nonbinding unless ratified by the signatory states. *E.g.*, "*Sub spe rati* may be explained to indicate that the agent is himself inclined to favor the proposal, but there is no reason why he should compromise either himself or his government." Ernest Satow, A Guide to Diplomatic Practice 110, § 175 (Neville Bland ed., 4th ed., 1957). *Compare with* **Ad referendum.**

Sub specie aeternitatis. sūb spā´kē-ā ītārnēta´tēs. sub spē´šē ētɜrnitā´tis. *adj.* or *adv.* "Under the pretense of eternity." Universally true or binding without regard to individual or cultural differences, time, or place. A rule, principle, or assertion *sub specie aeternitatis* is considered universally and always true and valid, regardless of any contrary reality or subjective norm.

Sub specie (legis) ferendae. sūb spā´kē-ā (lā´gēs) fārān´dī. sub spē´šē (le´jis) fɜren´dā. *adj.* or *adv.* "Under pretense of [what is to be] proposed (as law)." Done with intent to improve or otherwise alter the current law, as opposed to merely acknowledging or restating the legal *status quo*. *E.g.*, "In the circumstances, the Court, as a court of law, cannot render judgment *sub specie legis ferendae*, or anticipate the law before the legislator has laid it down." *Fisheries Jurisdiction* (U.K. v. Ice.), 1974 I.C.J. Rep. 3, 23–24, ¶ 53. *Compare with* **De lege ferenda.**

Subditus. sūb´dētūs. subdi´tus. *n.* "Subject." One who is formally under another's power; a vassal; a subject.

Sublata causa tollitur effectus. sūbla´ta kô´sa tōl´lētūr āffāk´tūs. sublâ´tu kă´zu ta´litɜr efek´tus. "Upon removal of the cause, the effect is removed." A maxim meaning that the cessation of a continuing harmful act or situation puts an end to the resulting injury (without necessarily remedying any past injury).

Sublato fundamento, cadit opus. sūbla´tō fūndamān´tō, ka´dēt ō´pūs. sublâ´tō fundumen´tō, kâ´dit ō´pus. "Upon removal of the foundation, the work collapses." A maxim meaning that, once the foundation of some thing or idea (an argument or a government, for example) is sufficiently undermined, the entire thing or idea loses its validity or is destroyed.

Sufferentia pacis. sūffărăn´tē-a pa´kēs. suf3ren´šu pâ´kis. *n.* "Toleration of peace." (1) A truce; an armistice. (2) A treaty of peace.

S

Sui generis. sū´ē gă´nărēs. sū´ē je´n3ris. *adj.* "Of its own kind." A type of subject matter that is treated differently than other types due to some idiosyncrasy of the subject matter or a perception of the subject matter. *E.g.*, "General Assembly resolution 55/12 of 1 November 2000 [approving UN membership of the Federal Republic of Yugoslavia] cannot have changed retroactively the *sui generis* position which the FRY found itself in *vis-à-vis* the United Nations over the period 1992 to 2000 [its continuance of the defunct Yugoslavia's legal personality being contested], or its position in relation to the Statute of the Court." *Application of the Convention on the Prevention and Punishment of the Crime of Genocide* (Bosn. & Herz. v. Yugo.), 2003 I.C.J. Rep. 7, 31, ¶ 71 (Application for Revision of the Judgment of 11 July 1996).

Sui iuris. sū´ē yū´rēs. sū´ē j3´ris. *adj.* "Of its own right." (1) Independent. (2) Having full legal capacity to act on one's own behalf. *E.g.*, "Every natural person, free and *sui juris*, may change his domicil at pleasure." Raleigh C. Minor, CONFLICT OF LAWS; OR, PRIVATE INTERNATIONAL LAW 72, § 30 (1901). (3) Not subordinate or subject to any law; dictatorial. Cicero describes Verres, the tyrannical dictator of Sicily, as a *homo sui juris* ("a man of his own law"), meaning that he is subject to no law and his word is law for others. (Cicero, *Verres* 2.1.7.18). *Contrast with* **Alieni iuris.**

Summa cum laude. sūm´ma kūm lô´dā. su´mu kum lăd OR -lă´dē. *adj.* or *adv. Neo.* "With highest praise." With the greatest distinction or honors. The term is commonly applied to a graduating student who has achieved the highest academic distinction. *See also* **Cum laude** and **Magna cum laude.**

Summa iniuria. sūm´ma ēnyū´rē-a. su´mu inj3´rē-u. *n.* "The greatest injury." A greatest possible injury or injustice.

Summa necessitate. sūm´ma nākăssēta´tā. su´mu nusesitā´tē. *n.* "The greatest necessity." The greatest possible necessity.

Summo iure. sūm´mō yū´rā. su´mō j3´rē. *adv.* "In the greatest right." Having the greatest right.

Summum bonum. sūm´mūm bō´nūm. su´mum bō´num. *n.* "The greatest good." The greatest possible good. *Contrast with* **Summum malum.**

Summum imperium. sūm´mūm ēmpā´rē-ūm. su´mum impē´rē-um. *n.* "The greatest authority." The full or maximum sovereign power (usually, of a state).

S

Summum ius (summa iniuria) (est). sūm´mūm yūs (sūm´ma ēnyū´rē-a) (āst). su´mum jus (su´mu inj3´rē-u) (est). "The greatest right (is) (the greatest injury)." A maxim meaning that granting a party the maximum extent of its rights may do an extreme injustice to the party against whom the right is asserted. *E.g.*, "What is just is however not always equitable, witness the well-known adage: *summum jus summa injuria*. And it is in order to mitigate this inconvenience of strict justice that recourse may be had to equity whose role is to moderate the rigour of law." *North Sea Continental Shelf* (F.R.G. v. Den.; F.R.G. v. Nether.), 1969 I.C.J. Rep. 3, 132 (separate opinion of Judge Ammoun).

Summum malum. sūm´mūm ma´lūm. su´mum mâ´lum. *n.* "The greatest evil." The greatest possible wrong or injury. *Contrast with* **Summum bonum.**

Suo motu. sū´ō mō´tū. sū´ō mō´tū. *adj.* "Its own motion." An abbreviation of **Proprio suo motu.** *See also* **Proprio motu.** *Compare with* **Sua sponte** and **Ex priorio vigore.**

Suo nomine. sū´ō nō´mēnā. sū´ō na´minē. *adv.* "In its own name." In one's own name; on one's own behalf.

Super altum mare. sū´pār al´tūm ma´rā. sū´p3r âl´tum ma´rē. *adj.* or *adv.* "On the high seas." On the high seas; beyond the territorial seas of any state. *See also* **Altum mare.**

Super eisdem deductis. sū´pār ā´yūsdām dādūk´tēs. sū´p3r e´jusdem dēduk´tis. *adv.* "Brought upon the same grounds." Brought on the same grounds or basis, as when multiple cases are brought based on the same facts or claims.

Supra (citatum). sūp´ra (kēta´tūm). sūp´ru (sītā´tum). *adj.* "(Cited) above; (cited) formerly." A citation signal used today, as in antiquity, to direct a reader to a reference earlier in the same writing. *E.g.*, "The matter was put as follows by the Court in the *Nottebohm* case, *supra*, where it said...." *Oil Platforms Case* (Iran v. U.S.), 2003 I.C.J. Rep. 161, 277, ¶ 17 (separate opinion of Judge Buergenthal). *Compare with* **Ante** and **Opera citato.** *Contrast with* **Infra (citatum).**

Suum cuique (tribuere). sū´ūm kwē´kwā (trēbū´ārā). sū´um kwi´kwā (tri´bw3rē). "To each (allot) his own." (1) A general expression advising to do justice or give just deserts to each person. (2) In prize law, the principle that contraband on board a vessel may be subject to capture even if the vessel itself is immune to capture.

T

Tabula rasa. ta´būla ra´sa. tâ´byūlu ra´zu. *n.* (also commonly used as an *adv.*). "Scraped slate." Generally, something started anew, without regard for or knowledge of prior events or conditions. In international law, the term has been used as a shorthand for the theory that a successor state does not automatically inherit all of the treaty obligations or rights of its predecessor. *E.g.*, "[T]he rule on automatic succession of multilateral treaties—*lex ferenda*, as matters now stand—has not been accepted in positive international law. However, it would be wrong to conclude from this that a new State begins life in the international community as a *tabula rasa*, a newborn in a legal vacuum deprived of all treaty rights and obligations." *Application of Convention on Prevention and Punishment of Genocide* (Bosn. & Herz. v. Yugo.), 1996 I.C.J. Rep. 595, 781, ¶ 112 (Judge *ad hoc* Kreća, dissenting). *See generally* the Vienna Convention on the Succession of States in Respect of Treaties, Aug. 23, 1978, 1946 U.N.T.S. 3.

Tacito consensu. ta´kētō kōnsān´sū. tâ´sitō kansen´sū. *adv.* "With tacit consent." Done with the unexpressed but presumed consent of a principal party.

Talis qualis. ta´lēs kwa´lēs. tâ´lis kwâ´lis. *adj.* "Such like." Such as it is; in the currently existing condition, with all imperfections or qualifications. An alternative term is **Tantum et tale**.

Tanquam quilibet. tan´kwam kwē´lēbāt. tân´kwum kwī´libet. *adj.* or *adv.* "Like anyone else." In the same manner as any ordinary person. Historically, this term was sometimes applied to acts of the sovereign of a kind in which a private person could have engaged. *Compare with* **Iure gestionis**.

Tantum et tale. tan´tūm āt ta´lā. tân´tum et tâ´lē. *adv.* "So much and of such kind." An alternative term for **Talis qualis**.

T

Tantum quantum. tan´tūm kwan´tūm. tân´tum kwan´tum. *adv.* "Just as much." In the same or similar quantities.

Tempus. tām´pūs. tem´pus. *n.* "Time." (1) Time. (2) A specific period of time.

Tempus commisi delicti. tām´pūs kōmmē´sē dālēk´tē. tem´pus kumi´sī dulik´tī. *n.* "The time when the delict was committed." The moment of the commission of a wrong.

Tempus fugit. tām´pūs fū´gēt. tem´pus fyū´jit. "Time flees." An expression of the ephemeral nature of life and all things human. The phrase derives from a line in Virgil's *Georgics*, in which the poet remarks upon how time passes swiftly for a farmer lovingly devoted to his work. The expression became a commonplace in antiquity.

Tempus regit factum. tām´pūs rā´gēt fak´tūm. tem´pus re´jit fâk´tum. "Time rules events." A maxim meaning that the legality of an act or legal consequences of an event can only be judged according to the law in effect at the time the act or event occurred. *E.g.*, "The generally accepted principle of intertemporal law, which is contained in the rule *tempus regit factum*, should therefore be considered as a recognized principle of international law. Consequently, the creation of ties with or titles to a territory must be determined according to the law in force at the time. The same law will also determine the nature and validity of the ties at that time. The rule *tempus regit factum* must also be applied to ascertain the legal force of new facts and their impact on the existing situation. New facts will be subject to the rules of law in force at the time when they occur." *Advisory Opinion on the Western Sahara*, 1975 I.C.J. Rep. 12, 169 (separate opinion of Judge De Castro).

Tempus utile. tām´pūs ū´tēlā. tem´pus yū´tilē. *n.* "Useful time." The period of time during which one may exercise his or her legal rights before they expire. A statute of limitations, for example, specifies the terminal point of a *tempus utile* for commencing an action.

Ter. tār. tɜr. *adv.* "Thirdly." An adverbial number (the third) usually inserted into a consecutively numbered series by way of amendment. Treaty drafters inserting several new articles into an existing treaty by amendment commonly designate the second inserted article by *ter*, so that the original article (*e.g.*, article 6) either remains the same or becomes article 6*semel*, the first inserted article becomes article 6*bis* and the second becomes article 6*ter*. *See* the Appendix for a list of Latin adverbial numbers commonly used in international law. *See also* **Bis** and **Semel**.

Terminus a quo. tăr´mēnūs a kwō. t3r´minus a kwō. *n.* "End from which." (1) The beginning. (2) The starting point of a stated period or event. *Compare with* **Dies a quo.** *Contrast with* **Terminus ad quem.**

T

Terminus ad quem. tăr´mēnūs ad kwăm. t3r´minus âd kwem. *n.* "End to which." (1) The finish. (2) The end point of a stated period or thing. *E.g.*, "Starting from the point indicated in the previous paragraph, the envisaged segment of the delimitation line crosses George Bank between points on the 100-fathoms depth line.…As for the *terminus ad quem* of this final segment of the delimitation line, a point has to be situated within the triangle defined by the Special Agreement between the Parties." *Delimitation of the Maritime Boundary in the Gulf of Maine* (Can. v. U.S.), 1984 I.C.J. Rep. 246, ¶¶ 227–28. *Compare with* **Dies ad quem.** *Contrast with* **Terminus a quo.**

Terminus technicus. tăr´mēnūs tăk´nēkūs. t3r´minus tek´nikus. *n.* "Technical term." A technical term; a term of art. *Compare with* **Vox signata.**

Terra communis. tăr´ra kōmmū´nēs. te´ru kumyū´nis. *n.* "Common land." Land that no one owns or over which no state exercises sovereignty and that is theoretically available on equal terms for all to use. In international practice, Antarctica is one of the few examples of *terra communis*. *See also* **Res communis (omnium), Res universitatis,** and **Terra nullius.**

Terra firma. tăr´ra fēr´ma. te´ru f3r´mu. *n.* "Solid land." (1) Solid ground. (2) Land of the kind that forms territory subject to state sovereignty. *E.g.*, "It has never been disputed that islands constitute *terra firma*, and are subject to the rules and principles of national acquisition." *Maritime Delimitation and Territorial Questions* (Qatar v. Bahr.), 2001 I.C.J. Rep. 102, ¶ 206 (Judgment). (3) Figuratively, a sound basis to support an argument, interpretation, or other abstract edifice.

Terra incognita. tăr´ra ēnkōg´nēta. te´ru inkagnē´tu. *n.* "Unknown land." (1) An unexplored or unknown territory or region. *E.g.*, "The knowledge and objectivity of the cartographers of Africa are not in doubt. It is true that there was in the interior of Africa a *terra incognita*, but the situation of the territories near the coasts was well known." *Advisory Opinion on Western Sahara*, 1975 I.C.J. 12, 153 (separate opinion of Judge De Castro). (2) Figuratively, a concept or idea not fully known or considered. *E.g.*, "The separability of void or invalid reservations from declarations accepting the Court's compulsory jurisdiction is still in most ways *terra incognita*." *Aerial Incident of 10 August 1999* (Pak. v. India), 2000 I.C.J. Rep. 12, 53, ¶ 21 (Jurisdiction) (Judge Al-Khasawneh, dissenting).

Terra nullius. tär´ra nūllē´ūs. te´ru nɜ´lē-us. *n.* [*pl.* **Terrae nullius.** tär´rī nūllē´ūs. te´rā nɜ´lē-us.] "Nobody's land." Land or territory over which no state exercises sovereignty but that is open to claims of exclusive rights or peaceful occupation by any state with the intention of acquiring sovereignty over it. The continued viability of this concept has been brought into question by modern state practice, at least with respect to lands considered *terra communis* and lands occupied by indigenous peoples. *E.g.*, "In the view of the Court…a determination that Western Sahara was a '*terra nullius*' at the time of colonization by Spain would be possible only if it were established that at that time the territory belonged to no-one in the sense that it was then open to acquisition through the legal process of 'occupation.'" *Advisory Opinion Concerning the Western Sahara*, 1975 I.C.J. Rep. 3, ¶ 79. The plural form should be avoided as nonidiomatic. An alternative term is **Territorium nullius.** *See also* **Res nullius** and **Terra communis.**

Terrae dominium finitur, ubi finitur armorum vis. tär´rī dōmē´nē-ūm fēnē´tūr, ū´bē fēnē´tūr armō´rūm wēs. te´rā dumi´nē-um fi´nitɜr, ū´bē fi´nitɜr armō´rum vis. "The ownership over land ends where the force of arms ends." An alternative phrase for **Potestas terrae finitur, ubi finitur armorum vis.**

Terrae imperii. tär´rī ēmpä´rē-ē. te´rā impē´rī. *n. pl.* "The lands of the empire." The lands subject to the sovereignty of a state or other authority.

Territorium nullius. tärrētō´rē-ūm nūllē´ūs. teritō´rē-um nɜ´lē-us. *n.* "Nobody's territory." An alternative term for **Terra nullius.** *E.g.*, "Consequently, there is ground to admit that, when…France proclaimed her sovereignty over Clipperton, that island was in the legal situation of *territorium nullius*, and, therefore, susceptible of occupation." *Sovereignty over Clipperton Island Case* (Fr. v. Mex.), Award of Jan. 28, 1931, 26 AM. J. INT'L L. 390, 393 (1932).

Territorium serviens. tärrētō´rē-ūm sär´wē-āns. teritō´rē-um sɜr´vē-enz. *n.* "The serving territory." Territory belonging to one state that is subject to some servitude or right of usage by another state or group of states. Classic examples are Hong Kong, over which the United Kingdom exercised a long-term lease for many years, and the United Nations Headquarters on Manhattan Island, which is for most purposes considered outside of U.S. jurisdiction.

Terrus nullius. A common misspelling of **Terra nullius.**

Tertium non datur. tär´tē-ūm nōn da´tūr. tɜr´šum nan dā´tɜr. "There is no third [option]." A statement asserting that a dichotomy defines the universe of possibilities. *E.g.*, "The essential difference between law and politics or administration lies in the fact that law distinguishes in a categorical way what is right and just from what is wrong and unjust, while politics and

T

administration, being the means to attain specific purposes, and dominated by considerations of expediency, make a distinction between the practical and the unpractical, the efficient and the inefficient. Consequently, in the judgment of law there is no possibility apart from what is just or unjust (*tertium non datur*), in the case of politics and administration there are many possibilities of choice from the viewpoint of expediency and efficiency." *South West Africa* (Eth. v. S. Afr.; Liber. v. S. Afr.), 1966 I.C.J. Rep. 6, 283 (Second Phase) (Judge Tanaka, dissenting).

Tertium quid. tär´tē-ūm kwēd. tɜr´šum kwid. *n.* "Third thing." (1) Something that escapes classification in either of two mutually or more exclusive and supposedly exhaustive categories. (2) A third party, often of ambiguous status.

Tertius. tär´tē-ūs. tɜr´šus. *n.* "The third." (1) A third party. (2) A nonparty to a treaty or other agreement.

Thesauri. *See* **Thesaurus.**

Thesaurus. t-hāsô´rūs. θe´sărus. *n.* [*pl.* **Thesauri.** t-hāsô´rē. θe´sărī.] "Treasure." Treasure or valuable goods, especially precious metals and money. The term has sometimes been used to mean treasure that has been abandoned or hidden by an unknown person and then discovered by someone else. *See also* **Occultatio thesauri inventi**, **Thesaurus absconditus**, and **Thesaurus inventus.**

Thesaurus absconditus. t-hāsô´rūs abskōn´dētūs. θesă´rus âbskan´ditus. *n.* "Hidden treasure." Hidden or buried treasure. *See also* **Occultatio thesauri inventi** and **Thesaurus.**

Thesaurus inventus. t-hāsô´rūs ēnwān´tūs. θesă´rus inven´tus. *n.* [*pl.* **Thesauri inventio.** t-hāsô´rē ēnwān´tēō. θesă´rī inven´tēō OR -inven´šō.] "Discovery of treasure." The discovery of treasure or valuable goods; treasure trove. In Roman law, the discoverer of *thesaurus inventus* might acquire a full or partial ownership interest in the treasure. In medieval European law, the principle was sometimes invoked, as by Grotius, to justify the feudal lord's accession to all treasure of unknown ownership found in his territory. *See also* **Occultatio thesauri inventi** and **Thesaurus.**

Tota curia. tō´ta kū´rē-a. tō´tu kyū´rē-u. *n.* (commonly used as an *adv.*) "Entire court." (By) the entire tribunal, as opposed to a panel, majority, or minority.

Totidem verbis. tō´tēdām wār´bēs. tō´tidem vɜr´bis. *adv.* "In so many words." (1) Literally; in the precise words used; word for word. (2) In express language, as opposed to being implicit. *E.g.*, "But if the voluntary law of nations derives all its obligatory force from the general usage of nations, as inferring or implying general consent, it is neither more nor less, than what is generally understood by the terms consuetudinary law of nations; which rests upon the general consent of nations, as being, though not *totidem verbis*, yet virtually expressed by their conduct for ages, and as being in fact the practical realization or adoption in practice of the natural law of nations." James Reddie, INQUIRIES INTO INTERNATIONAL LAW, PUBLIC AND PRIVATE 125 (1851). *Compare with* **De verbo in verbum**, **In haec verba**, **Ipsis verbis**, **Ipsissima verba**, and **Verbatim**. *Contrast with* **Non totidem verbis**.

T

Toties quoties. tō´tē-ās kwō´tē-ās. tō´tēz kwō´tēz. *adv.* "As often as." (1) As often as; occurring equally often. (2) Whenever the same thing occurs. *E.g.*, "I take the fair and proper meaning of the words used, having due regard to the context, to be that, so often as every first eleven years of the term of twenty-one years...shall expire, the lessors will grant a similar new lease upon the surrender of the old lease, and so on *toties quoties*." *Wynn v. Conway Corp.*, [1914] 2 Ch. 705, 710 (Judge Joyce) (U.K.).

Toto caelo. tō´tō kī´lō. tō´tō sē´lō OR -kā´lō. *adj.* "Throughout the entire sky/heavens." Completely; entirely; to the greatest extent possible.

Toto caelo errare. tō´tō kī´lō ārra´rā. tō´tō sē´lō- OR -kā´lō era´rē. *v. inf.* "To be mistaken throughout the entire heavens." To be entirely mistaken; to be as mistaken as anyone could possibly be.

Tredecie(n)s. trādā´kē-ā(n)s. trē´desē(n)z. *adv.* "Thirteenthly." An adverbial number (the thirteenth) usually inserted into a consecutively numbered series by way of amendment. *See* the Appendix for a list of Latin adverbial numbers commonly used in international law. *See also* **Bis** and **Semel**.

Treuga dei. trā-ū´ga dā´ē. trū´gu dā. *n.* "Truce of God." A customary war practice of suspending hostilities during religious holidays. This practice was only observed when the belligerents both espoused the same religion, and even then observance was inconsistent.

Tu quoque. tū kwō´kwā. tū kwō´kwā. *n.* "You also." (1) A legal doctrine of reciprocality, according to which a violation by one party of its duties justifies a violation of the duties of its counterpart. (2) An argument that is undermined by contradiction through the arguer's own actions or other arguments; an inconsistent argument. *E.g.*, "Let it be assumed...that a purely '*tu quoque*' argument might have some validity on a sort of preclusive basis. Accordingly, it is said, the Belgian case must concede what it claims: just as it claims that the Canadian nationality of the Barcelona Company is not conclusive, so must it also concede that the ostensibly Belgian nationality of Sidro-(Sofina) is not conclusive as to that entity's true character, which must in consequence be established by reference to the underlying shareholding interests in it." *Barcelona Traction, Light, and Power Co., Ltd.* (Belg. v. Sp.), 1970 I.C.J. Rep. 3, 92, ¶ 46 (separate opinion of Judge Fitzmaurice). (3) A legal argument to the effect that, because others have not been prosecuted for similar international crimes, this attests to the invalidity or demise of the legal rule such that the defendant should be exempt from prosecution as well. *E.g.*, "[T]his Tribunal does not recognise *tu quoque* as a valid defence and has accepted, but only to a very limited extent, evidence relating to crimes allegedly committed by other parties to the conflict. As a consequence, the Trial Chamber may disallow questions which are irrelevant either because they are beyond the Indictment's temporal scope or are unrelated to the specific facts of the violations alleged in the Indictment." *Prosecutor v. Delic*, I.C.T.Y. Case No. IT-04-83-T, Decision of July 24, 2007, ¶ 9.

Tuum. tū´ūm. tū´um. *adj.* (often used as a *n.*) "Your." Yours; that which belongs to you. *Contrast with*, and *see* the example of usage in, **Meum**.

U

Uberrimae fidei. ūbär´rēmī fē´dā-ē. ūbɜ´rimā fī´dē. *n.* "[Having the quality of] the utmost faith." The greatest candor and good faith. In common law jurisdictions, *uberrimae fidei* is a duty owed by an insured to the insurer to voluntarily and fully disclose all facts material to the calculation of insurance risk. A misrepresentation relating to the risk of an adventure, or failure to disclose information material to risk even if not inquired about by the insurer, may constitute a breach of the obligation of *uberrimae fidei*. Information is generally considered "material" if it would influence the insurer in determining whether he would accept the risk. *E.g.*, "Under *uberrimae fidei*, a material misrepresentation on an application for marine insurance is grounds for voiding the policy." *HIH Marine Services, Inc. v. Fraser*, 211 F.3d 1359, 1363 (11th Cir. 2000).

Ubi ius ibi remedium (est). ū´bē yūs, ē´bē rāmā´dē-ūm (āst). ū´bē jus, i´bē remē´dē-um (est). "Wherever there is a right, there is a remedy." A maxim meaning that every legal right implies some form of remedy to rectify the consequences of a transgression of the right. *Compare with* **Lex dabit remedium** and **Ubicunque est iniuria, ibi damnum sequitur.**

Ubi lex non distinguit, nec nos distinguere debemus. ū´bē lāks nōn dēstēn´gū-ēt, nāk nōs dēstēngū´ārā dābā´mūs. ū´bē leks nan distiŋ´it, nek nas distiŋ´ɜrē de´bemus. "Where the law does not distinguish, neither should we distinguish." A maxim meaning that new legal distinctions should not be recognized based on novel facts to justify departing from or creating a new exception to an established legal rule.

Ubi societas, ibi ius. ū´bē sōkē´ātas, ē´bē yūs. ū´bē susī´etus, i´bē jus. "Wherever there is society, there is law." A maxim meaning that law may be found in all forms of stable political organization arising from social collaboration. The maxim suggests that the term "law" applies to processes more general than impartial decision by a court or other authoritative tribunal. *E.g.*, "In turning away from [morality], international law condemns itself to sterility in face of a society bubbling over with life. The normative school and its pure theory of law, in rejecting the moral, social, and political elements, described as metajuridical, become isolated from international realities and their progressive institutions: *ubi societas, ibi jus.*" *North Sea Continental Shelf* (F.R.G. v. Den.; F.R. G. v. Nether.), 1969 I.C.J. Rep. 3, 137 (separate opinion of Judge Ammoun).

U

Ubi te invenero, ibi te iudicabo. ū´bē tā ēnwā´nārō, ē´bē tā yūdēka´bō. ū´bē tā inve´nɜrō, i´bē tā jūdika´bō. "Wherever I find you, there I shall judge you." A principle according to which jurisdiction may be asserted over a person whenever found within the territory of the forum.

Ubicunque est iniuria, ibi damnum sequitur. ūbēkūn´kwā āst ēnyū´rē-a, ē´bē dam´nūm sā´kwētūr. ūbikun´kwē est injɜ´rē-u, i´bē dâm´num se´kwitɜr. "Wherever there is a legal wrong, there the penalty follows." A common law maxim meaning that every wrongful act entails a remedy, usually in the form of monetary damages to the injured party. *Compare with* **Lex dabit remedium** and **Ubi ius ibi remedium (est).**

Ultima ratio. ūl´tēma ra´tēō. ɜl´timu rā´šō. *n.* "Last basis." (1) The primary, best, or most important basis or reasoning for an argument. (2) The last resort. (3) By ironical analogy, the use of force to resolve a dispute.

Ultra fines compromissi. ūl´tra fē´nās kōmprōmēs´sē. ɜl´tru fīnz- OR –fī´nēz kamprumi´sī. *adj.* "Beyond the limits of the *compromis.*" Outside the scope of the agreement to submit disputes to arbitration; beyond the powers conferred on the arbitral tribunal by the parties to resolve the dispute. *Compare with* **Ultra vires compromissi.**

Ultra fines mandati. ūl´tra fē´nās manda´tē. ɜl´tru fīnz- OR -fī´nēz mândā´tī. *adj.* "Beyond the limits of the mandate." Outside the scope of the authority's or agent's mandated powers. *Compare with* **Ultra vires.**

Ultra licitum. ūl´tra lē´kētūm. ɜl´tru li´situm. *adj.* "Beyond what is legal." Beyond what is legal or permitted.

Ultra mare. ūl´tra ma´rā. ɜl´tru ma´rē. *adj.* "Beyond the sea." (1) Literally, overseas. (2) Outside of the jurisdiction or territory of a state.

Ultra petita. ūl´tra pātē´ta. ɜl´tru putē´tu. *adv.* "Beyond the petition." Greater in amount or scope than the complaint, claim, or petition requested. *E.g.*, "[T]he Court has never declared itself competent to change the subject-matter of a dispute, and if it had ever sought to do so, such a decision would have been without legal foundation and *ultra petita.*" *Fisheries Jurisdiction*

Case (Spain v. Can.), 1998 I.C.J. Rep. 432, 554, ¶ 4 (Jurisdiction) (Judge Ranjeva, dissenting). *See also* **Non ultra petita (partum).**

Ultra posse nemo tenetur. ūl´tra pōs´sā nā´mō tānā´tūr. ɜl´tru pa´sē nē´mō te´netɜr. "Nobody is held beyond his ability." A maxim meaning that the law will not require someone to perform an act beyond his or her objective capabilities. *Compare with* **Impossibilium nulla obligatio est, Impotentia excusat legem, Lex neminem cogit ad vana seu impossibilia,** and **Lex non cogit impossibilia.**

U

Ultra valorem. ūl´tra walō´rām. ɜl´tru vâlō´rum. *adj.* "Beyond the value." Greater than the value.

Ultra vires. ūl´tra wē´rās. ɜl´tru vī´rēz. *adj.* (sometimes used as an *adv.*) "Beyond the powers." Outside the scope of the authorized powers of the actor. In general, the fact that the organ or agent of a state acted *ultra vires* is not considered to relieve the principal state of liability for the organ or agent's acts so long as the organ or agent had apparent authority to act. *E.g.*, "The case of purely private conduct should not be confused with that of [a state] organ functioning as such but acting *ultra vires* or in breach of the rules governing its operation. In this latter case, the organ is nevertheless acting in the name of the State." Draft articles on *Responsibility of States for Internationally Wrongful Acts, with Commentaries* art. 4 cmt. 13, UN GAOR 56th Sess., Supp. No. 10, UN Doc. A/56/10 (2001). See *id.* art. 7. *Compare with* **Ultra fines mandati.** *See also* **Respondeat superior.**

Ultra vires compromissi. ūl´tra wē´rās kōmprōmēs´sē. ɜl´tru vī´rēz kamprumi´sī. *adj.* "Beyond the powers of the *compromis.*" Outside the scope of the authority in the submission to arbitration delegated to an arbitral tribunal to decide a dispute. *Compare with* **Ultra fines compromissi.**

Una testis, nulla testis. ū´na tās´tēs, nūl´la tās´tēs. ū´nu tes´tis, nɜ´lu tes´tis. "If one is a witness, no one is a witness." An alternative formulation of **Unus testis, nullus testis.**

Una voce. ū´na wō´kā. ū´nu vō´sē. *adv.* "In one voice." Unanimously; without expressed dissent. *Compare with* **Nemine contra dicente** and **Per universitatem.**

Undecie(n)s. ūndā´kē-ā(n)s. undē´se(n)z. *adv.* "Eleventhly." An adverbial number (the eleventh) usually inserted into a consecutively numbered series by way of amendment. *See* the Appendix for a list of Latin adverbial numbers commonly used in international law. *See also* **Bis** and **Semel.**

U

Unicum. ū´nēkūm. yū´nikum. *adj.* "Unique." Of unique character or facts for which no general rule of law or precedent provides a clear resolution. In a case characterized as *unicum*, a judgment of *non liquet* may in some limited circumstances result.

Universitatis iuris. ūnēwārsēta´tēs yū´rēs. yūnivɜrsitā´tis jɜ´ris. *n.* "Totality of right." The totality of the rights of a state, entity, or person. *Compare with* **Universum ius.**

Universum ius. ūnēwār´sūm yūs. yūnivɜr´sum jus. *n.* "Entire right." The totality of the rights of a state, entity, or person. *Compare with* **Universitatis iuris.**

Uno actu. ū´nō ak´tū. ū´nō âk´tū. *adv.* "By one act." By a single act. *E.g.*, "Annexation turns the conquest into subjugation. It is the very annexation which *uno actu* makes the vanquished State cease to exist, and brings the territory under the conqueror's sovereignty." Lassa Oppenheim, INTERNATIONAL LAW: A TREATISE 395 (3d ed., Ronald F. Roxburgh ed. 1921).

Uno animo. ū´nō a´nēmō. ū´nō â´nimō. *adv.* "With one mind." With unanimous intent.

Uno ictu. ū´nō ēk´tū. ū´nō ik´tū. *adv.* "With one blow." Occurring all at once; simultaneously; collectively. *E.g.*, "Thus the Commission claims that the succession here occurred in the relations between the SFRY as the predecessor-State and the newly-independent republics as the successor-States. In other words, it did not take place *uno ictu*; rather, what is known as succession is in fact a set of successions which occurred one after another between 8 October 1991 and 27 April 1992." *Application of the Convention on Prevention and Punishment of Genocide* (Bosn. & Herz. v. Yugo.), 1996 I.C.J. Rep. 595, 706, ¶ 40 (Judge *ad hoc* Kreća, dissenting).

Unus testis, nullus testis. ū´nūs tās´tēs, nūl´lūs tās´tēs. ū´nus tes´tis, nɜ´lus tes´tis. "One witness is no witness." A principle of evidence that the uncorroborated evidence of a single witness will be discounted due to presumed unreliability. This principle has been rejected by the International Criminal Court. *See Prosecutor v. Seromba*, Case No. ICTR-2001-66-A, Appeals Judgment of Mar. 12, 2008, ¶¶ 91–92. An alternative formulation is **Una testis, nulla testis.** Mixtures of these declensions (*e.g.*, *una testis, nullus testis* or *unus testis, nulla testis*) are grammatically incorrect.

Urbi et orbi. ūr´bē āt ōr´bē. ɜr´bī et ōr´bī. *adv.* "To the city and to the world." To everyone; to all; with universal effect. *E.g.*, "Evidence to this effect is found in the fact that the addressee of the Note was the Secretary-General, who was requested to circulate the Declaration and the Note as an official document of the General Assembly, whereas the Declaration as such was addressed *urbi et orbi*." *Application of the Convention on the Prevention and Punishment of the Crime of Genocide* (Bosn. & Herz. v. Yugo.), I.C.J. No. 91, Judgment of Feb. 26, 2007, at 32, ¶ 67 (separate opinion of Judge *ad hoc* Kreća).

U

Usque ad coelum (et ad inferos). ūs´kwā ad kœ´lūm (āt ad ēn´fārōs). yūs´kwē âd sē´lum (et âd in´fɜrōs). *adv.* "All the way to heaven (and all the way to hell)." An abbreviation of the maxim **Cuius est solum eius est usque ad coelum (et ad inferos).**

Usque ad filum aquae. ūs´kwā ad fē´lūm a´kwī. yūs´kwē âd fī´lum a´kwā. *adv.* "Up to the middle of the stream." A measure for the delimitation of territorial boundaries using the geographical middle of the watercourse as the basis for the delimitation. *See also* **Medium filum acquae.**

Usucapio. ūsūka´pēō. yūzūkā´pēō. *n.* "Acquisition by use." The long-term settlement or exploitation of land to establish sovereignty or a right of possession. To acquire land through *usucapio* in Roman law, it was necessary to begin possession in good faith and to continue that possession for ten years for land. It was also theoretically possible to acquire title to personal property in the same way after three years of continuous possession.

Usura. ūsū´ra. yū´žɜru. *n.* [*pl.* **Usurae**. ūsū´rī. yū´žɜrā.] "Interest." Monetary interest; A standard measure of the time value of money for its use or a debt owed.

Usus ancipites. ū´sūs ankē´pētās. yū´zus ânsi´pitēz. *n. pl.* "Ambiguous uses." (1) Property of uncertain (specifically, whether civilian or military) use. (2) Goods that can be used for either civilian or military purposes; dual-use goods. (3) In war, goods whose status as either contraband or legitimate trade goods is unclear. Sometimes misspelled *usus ancipitus*. *See also* **Usus bellici.**

Usus bellici. ū´sūs bāl´lēkē. yū´sus be´likī. *n.* "Warlike use." A practical use in warmaking. Usually, the term applies not to arms and distinctively military items, but rather to items with a dual military and civilian use that may be considered contraband if delivered to a belligerent power. *E.g.*, "It is the *usus bellici* which determine an article to be contraband, and as articles come into use as implements of war which were before innocent, there is truth in the remark, that as the means of war vary and shift from time to time, the law shifts with them." James Kent, COMMENTARY ON INTERNATIONAL LAW 336 (2d ed., J.T. Abdy ed. 1878). *See also* **Usus acipites.**

Usus fit ex iteratis actibus. ū´sūs fēt āks ētāra´tēs ak´tēbūs. yū´zus fit eks itɜrā´tis âk´tibus. "Usage is made by repeated acts." A maxim meaning that customs either binding on the parties or useful for interpreting legal instruments between them arise from a repeated course of conduct by the parties or their relevant community or industry.

Usus in bello. ū´sūs ēn bāl´lō. yū´zus in be´lō. *n.* "Usage in war." A now obsolete term for the customary laws of war. *See* **Ius in bello.**

Ut currere solebat. ūt kūr´rārā sōlā´bat. ūt kɜ´rɜrē sō´lebât. *adv.* "As it was accustomed to run." Referring to a watercourse, the usual course followed in the absence of diversion by human intervention. *See also* **Aqua currit et debet currere ut currere solebat.**

Ut infra. ūt ēn´fra. ūt in´fru. *adv.* "As below." As provided or stated below or subsequently. *Contrast with* **Ut supra.**

Ut res magis valeat quam perat. ūt rās ma´gēs wa´lā-at kwam pā´rat. ūt res mâ´jis vâ´lē-ât kwam pe´rât. "So that the matter may flourish rather than perish." A principle of legal instrument construction dictating that one should avoid reading the instrument in a manner that would render language in the instrument redundant, void, or ineffective. It follows that a tribunal will interpret ambiguous, vague, or apparently conflicting provisions of a legal instrument in a manner that best sustains the validity and enforceability of the instrument. This may result in a broader or narrower reading than the plain language of the instrument seems to indicate. *E.g.*, "*Lex specialis* is not explicitly included as such in the VCLT [Vienna Convention on the Law of Treaties], but it is consonant with the principles of *effective treaty interpretation* (*ut regis valeat quam paereat*), which provides the cornerstone of the VCLT: were one not to start from the rule that specifically regulates a particular transaction (and were one to privilege, instead, the application of the more general rule), one risks making such specific rules redundant." Petros C. Mavroidis, *No Outsourcing of Law? WTO Law as Practiced by WTO Courts*, 102 Am. J. Int'l L. 421, 444 (2008).

Ut supra. ūt sūp´ra. ūt sūp´ru. *adv.* "As above." As provided or stated above or previously. *Contrast with* **Ut infra.**

Uti possidetis, ita possideatis. ū´tē pōssēdā´tēs, ē´ta pōssēdā-a´tēs. ū´tē pōside´tis, i´tu pōsidē-â´tis. "As you possess, so may you possess." An archaic maxim meaning that a state that has acquired possession of territory with intent to annex it has thereby established sovereignty over that territory. The maxim has been used by some publicists (*e.g.*, Memorandum on *Uti Possidetis: Costa Rica–Panama Arbitration*, 1911, *in* 3 Collected Papers of John Bassett Moore 328–30 (1944)) to justify the application of the Roman civil law concept of *interdictum uti possidetis* to establish the legality of a *status quo post bellum*. *Compare with* **Uti possidetis (iuris).**

Uti possidetis (iuris). ū´tē pōssēdā´tēs (yū´rēs). ū´tē pōside´tis (jɜ´ris). *adv.* (commonly used as a *n.*) "So that you may (rightly) possess." (1) A modern principle according to which a change in sovereignty over a territory, especially due to independence following decolonization, does not *ipso facto* alter that territory's administrative boundaries as established by colonial authorities out of respect for succession to legal title by the new sovereign. The doctrine has often been invoked to prevent a change in land and maritime boundaries of former colonies when they become independent states, especially in favor of the sovereignty of aboriginal populations over lands historically occupied by them, and has sometimes been applied aggressively in recent successionist controversies. The *uti possidetis iuris* doctrine has sometimes been contrasted with *uti possidetis de facto*, under which principle the operative boundaries are not the boundaries delimited by the colonizing states or their administrations but rather those actually administered by the colonial and post-colonial authorities. *E.g.*, "[*U*]*ti possidetis juris* is essentially a retrospective principle, investing as international boundaries administrative limits intended originally for quite other purposes." *Land, Island, and Maritime Dispute* (El Salv. v. Hond.; Nicar. Intervening), 1992 I.C.J. Rep. 351, 388, ¶ 43; "It is a general principle, which is logically connected with the phenomenon of the obtaining of independence, wherever it occurs. Its obvious purpose is to prevent the independence and stability of new States being endangered by fratricidal struggles provoked by the challenging of frontiers following the withdrawal of the administering power.... The essence of the principle lies in its primary aim of securing respect for the territorial boundaries at the moment when independence is achieved." *Frontier Dispute* (Burk. Faso v. Mali), 1986 I.C.J. Rep. 554, ¶¶ 20, 23. (2) An archaic doctrine according to which a belligerent state acquires sovereignty over all territory claimed and occupied by it at the termination of an armed conflict. (3) More generally, the well-established possession of property. (4) In Roman law, a kind of preliminary injunction (*interdictum uti possidetis*) ordering the party in possession of disputed land or buildings who has not obtained such possession by force, fraud, or gratuitous revocable loan (*nec vi nec clam nec precario*) to remain in such possession without interference until the dispute over possession is resolved by the court. *Compare with* **Uti possidetis, ita possideatis.** *Contrast with* **Uti possidetis de facto.** *See also* **Nec vi nec clam nec precario** and **Possessio longi temporis.**

Uti possidetis de facto. ū´tē pōssēdā´tēs dā fak´tō. ū´tē pōside´tis dā fâk´tō. *adv.* (commonly used as a *n.*) "So that you may possess in fact." A principle that

U

was formerly invoked on occasion by postcolonial states to the effect that the boundaries of newly independent states upon decolonization should be defined by the limits of the territory actually administered by the colonial authorities and/or newly independent state rather than the administrative boundaries delimited by the colonizing states. A major basis of this claim was that, in some cases, and especially in Central and South America, colonial authorities would often exercise *de facto* governmental power over territory that was technically beyond their administrative competence. *See* Suzanne Lalonde, DETERMINING BOUNDARIES IN A CONFLICTED WORLD 31–35 (2002). *Contrast with* **Uti possidetis (iuris)**. *See also* **Possessio longi temporis**.

Utile. ū´tēlā. yūti´lē. *n.* "That which is useful." (1) A useful thing. (2) The use to which something can be or is put.

V

v. An abbreviation of **Versus**.

Vacantia bona. wakan´tē-a bō´na. vukân´šu bō´nu. *n. pl.* "Unowned goods." An alternative formulation of **Bona vacantia**.

Vacuum iuris. wa´kū-ūm yū´rēs. vâ´kyū-um jз´ris. *n.* "Absence of law." A situation in which no applicable law clearly dictates the status, rights, or obligations of the relevant actors. *E.g.*, "[B]efore independence, the present boundaries of Quebec are guaranteed by the Constitution....After independence, these boundaries will be secured by the principles governing the territorial integrity of States and the stability of frontiers. Between these two situations there is no room for a *vacuum juris* and one can hardly see at what moment this protection would cease." Thomas M. Franck, Rosalyn Higgins, Alain Pellet, Malcolm N. Shaw, and Christian Tomuschat, *The Territorial Integrity of Québec in the Event of the Attainment of Sovereignty*, *in* COMMISSION D'ÉTUDE DES QUESTIONS AFFÉRENTES À L'ACCESSION DU QUÉBEC À LA SOUVERAINETÉ: PROJET DE RAPPORT, annex § 2.39 (1992).* *Compare with* **Dubii iuris** and **Non liquet**. *But see* **Iudex decidere debet**.

Vacuus. wa´kū-ūs. vâ´kyū-us. *adj.* "Empty." Empty; vacant.

Vade mecum. wa´dā mā´kūm. va´dē mē´kum. *v. imp.* (commonly used as a *n.*) "Go with me." (1) The standard in a field. (2) The most highly respected or often used reference or precedent. *E.g.*, "The decision of the Court in the present case, provides a *vade mecum* and precedent for those who might wish to delay United Nations action by a miasma of legalistic activity." *Questions of Interpretation and Application of the 1971 Montreal Convention Arising from*

* The use of this quotation as an example is not intended to endorse the stated reasoning or its conclusion.

the Aerial Incident at Lockerbie (Libya v. U.K.), 1998 I.C.J. Rep. 9, 113 (Judge Jennings, dissenting).

Valeat quantum (valere potest). wa´lā-at kwan´tūm (walā´rā pō´tāst). vâ´lē-ât kwan´tum (vâ´lɜrē pō´test). "(Let it be worth) as much as it is worth." The Latin equivalent of the idiom: "Take it for what it's worth."

Valuta. walū´ta. valū´tu. *n. Ital.* "Value." Value. The term is most commonly used to refer to the value of one country's currency relative to that of a foreign currency.

Vel. wāl. vel. *conj.* "Or." Or (conjunctive). *Vel* is used when one or more options are simultaneously possible—a concept sometimes awkwardly rendered in English as "and/or." *Contrast with* **Aut.**

Vel non. wāl nōn. vel nan. "Or not." Or not; including the opposite alternative; or its absence. *E.g.*, "More fundamental and difficult than the previous issue is that concerning the existence *vel non* of a 'dispute' within the meaning of Article 27 and Article 32 [of the UN Charter]." *Advisory Opinion on Legal Consequences of the Continued Presence of South Afirca in Namibia (South West Africa) Notwithstanding Security Council Resolution 276*, 1971 I.C.J. Rep. 16, 153 (separate opinion of Judge Dillard).

Venire contra factum proprium (non valet). wānē´rā kōn´tra fak´tūm prōp´rē-ūm (nōn wa´lāt). veni´rē kan´tru fâk´tum prap´rē-um (nan vâ´let). "To come against one's own fact (is not allowed)." A maxim of customary international law meaning that one may not set one's self in contradiction to one's own previous conduct. For example, a state may be estopped from claiming to be contrary to international law the acts of another state, if the claimant earlier declared those same acts were permissible when the claimant itself performed them.

Verba. wār´ba. vɜr´bu. *n. pl.* [*s.* **Verbum.** wār´būm. vɜr´bum.] "Words." Words; the language of a text.

Verba accipienda ut sortiantur effectum. wār´ba akkēpē-ān´da ūt sōrtē-an´tūr āffāk´tūm. vɜr´bu âksipē-en´du ūt sōr´tē-untɜr efek´tum. "Words are to be construed so that they obtain effect." A maxim, the purport of which originates in Justinian's *Digest* (2.2.1), meaning that terms in a legal instrument should not be construed as useless or redundant, but should instead be interpreted in a manner to effectuate the purposes of the instrument. Alternative phrases are **Verba aliquid operari debent, Verba cum effectu accipienda sunt, Verba debent intelligi cum effectu,** and **Verba quae aliquid operari possunt non debent esse superflua.** *See also* **Verba intentioni, non e contra, debent inservire.**

Verba aliquid operari debent. wār´ba a´lēkwēd ōpāra´rē dā´bānt. vɜr´bu â´likwid apɜra´rī de´bent. "Words should have some effect." An alternative phrase for **Verba accipienda ut sortiantur effectum.**

Verba cum effectu accipienda sunt. wār´ba kūm āffāk´tū akkēpē-ān´da sūnt. vɜr´bu kum efek´tū âksipyen´du sunt. "Words are to be construed as to their effect." An alternative phrase for **Verba accipienda ut sortiantur effectum.**

Verba debent intelligi cum effectu. wār´ba dā´bānt ēntāl´lēgē kūm āffāk´tū. vɜr´bu de´bent inte´lijī kum efek´tū. "Words should be understood as to their effect." An alternative phrase for **Verba accipienda ut sortiantur effectum.**

Verba intentioni, non e contra, debent inservire. wār´ba ēntāntēō´nē, nōn ā kōn´tra, dā´bānt ēnsārwē´rā. vɜr´bu intenšō´nī, nan ē kan´tru, de´bent insɜrvī´rē. "Words should serve intentions, not the reverse." A maxim meaning that any vague or ambiguous provisions of a legal instrument should be construed in a manner to give effect to the intentions of the drafters or negotiators; an interpretation of a legal instrument should effectuate rather than subvert its purpose. *Compare with* **Verba sunt indices animi.** *See also* **Verba accipienda ut sortiantur effectum.**

Verba quae aliquid operari possunt non debent esse superflua. wār´ba kwī a´lēkwid ōpāra´rē pōs´sūnt nōn dā´bānt ās´sā sūpār´flūa. vɜr´bu kwā â´likwid apɜra´rī pō´sunt nan de´bent e´sē sūpɜr´flū-u. "Words that can have some effect should not be superfluous." An alternative phrase for **Verba accipienda ut sortiantur effectum.**

Verba solemnia. wār´ba sōlām´nē-a. vɜr´bu salem´nē-u. *n. pl.* "Solemn words." Formal words, such as those used to express a binding commitment.

Verba sunt indices animi. wār´ba sūnt ēn´dēkās a´nēmē. vɜr´bu sunt in´disēz â´nimī. "Words are indicators of intention." A maxim meaning that the terms of a legal instrument are to be interpreted in light of the intentions of its drafters and not as a purely intellectual exercise. *Compare with* **Verba intentioni, non e contra, debent inservire.** *See also* **Verba accipienda ut sortiantur effectum.**

Verbatim. wārba´tēm. vɜrbā´tim. *adv. Med.* "Word by word." (1) Literally. (2) In his/her/its precise words; word for word. *E.g.*, "In its request for provisional measures, Germany asked the Court for an Order that tracked *verbatim* the language of the Court's Order of 9 April 1998 in the *Breard* case." *LaGrand Case* (Ger. v. U.S.), 2001 I.C.J. Rep. 466, 555, ¶ 20 (Judge Buergenthal, dissenting). *Compare with* **De verbo in verbum, In haec verba, Ipsis verbis, Ipsissima verba,** and **Totidem verbis.**

Verbis expressis. wār´bēs ākspräs´sēs. vɜr´bis ekspre´sis. *adv.* "In express words." An alternative formulation of **Expressis verbis.**

Verbum. *See* **Verba.**

Veritas. wā´rētas. ve´ritus. *n.* "Truth." (1) Abstract truth. (2) Honesty; integrity. (3) Fact. (4) An abbreviation of Bureau Veritas Group, a multinational enterprise founded in 1828 to assess the seaworthiness of merchant vessels for maritime insurance purposes. The organization, now based in Paris, has expanded its mandate since that time to encompass standards inspection and verification of industrial equipment, construction sites, environmental quality, and other business assets and practices.

Vero. wā´rō. vē´rō. *adv.* "Truly; however; even." (1) In truth. (2) Extremely. This term has multiple other meanings in Latin that are obsolete in modern legal usage.

Versa vice. wār´sa wē´kā. vɜr´su vī´su OR -vīs. An alternative formulation of **Vice versa.**

Versus. wār´sūs. vɜr´suz. *prep.* "Against." (1) In contrast to. (2) In opposition to. *Versus* is often used in case names to indicate the parties in opposition to each other, equivalent to the French "*c.*" or *contre.* Commonly abbreviated as *v.* or *vs. Compare with* **Adversus.**

Verus. wā´rūs. ve´rus. *adj.* "True." True; genuine; truthful.

Vetus ius. wā´tūs yūs. ve´tus jus. *n.* "Old law." (1) Ancient law; longstanding law. (2) A law adopted prior to the adoption of another, subsequent law. *Compare with* **Lex posterior.** (3) In Roman practice, the earliest surviving civil code of the Romans, enacted in the fifth century BCE and inscribed on twelve tables (hence the popular name Twelve Tables, or *Lex Duodecim Tabularum*). The *vetus ius* continued to be considered a binding part of Roman law at least until Justinian's *Code* (534 CE).

Vexata quaestio. wāksa´ta kwīs´tēō. veksa´tu kwes´tēō. *n.* "Troubled question." A difficult or bothersome question or issue; a matter often debated but never satisfactorily settled. A point of law decided differently by different tribunals is commonly considered a *vexata quaestio.* An alternative formulation is **Quaestio vexata.**

Vi aut clam. wē ôt klam. vī- OR vē ăt klâm. *adv.* "By force or secretly." By physical or military force on one hand or by covert action or subterfuge on the other.

Vi et armis. wē āt ar´mēs. vī- OR vē et ar´mis. *adv.* "By force and arms." By physical or military force. *E.g.*, "Believing firmly in the sovereignty of the State, there was never an idea among the masses of the people of the South that secession would entail war.... Coercion, '*vi et armis*,' was not dreamed of." Joseph Wheeler, *Alabama*, *in* 7 CONFEDERATE MILITARY HISTORY 1, 22 (Clement A. Evans ed. 2004) (1899).

V

Vi et metu. wē āt mā´tū. vī- OR vē et me´tū. *adv.* "By force or fear." By physical or military force on one hand or by intimidation on the other.

Via iuris. wē´a yū´rēs. vī´u jɜ´ris. *adv.* "By the path of the law." By legal means; through the use of legal procedures.

Vis legibus est inimica. wēs lā´gēbūs āst ēnēmē´ka. vis le´jibus est ini´miku. "Force is hostile to the law." A maxim of Edward Coke's *Institutes* (3: 176) meaning that the law is designed to restrain the use of force and concentrate its power in the hands of legitimate authorities; therefore, any private and unauthorized use of force even in a rightful cause violates the law.

Vice versa. wē´kā wār´sa. vī´su- OR vīs vɜr´su. *adv.* "Reversely." Reversely; the other way around. The phrase is used when the reverse of a proposition is true. *E.g.*, "[T]here was a natural reluctance on the part of courts and tribunals to give preference to those elements [bearing on delimitation] more closely connected to the continental shelf over those more closely related to the EEZ or *vice versa*." *Barbados v. Republic of Trinidad & Tobago*, Permanent Ct. of Arb., Award of Apr. 11, 2006, ¶ 228, 45 I.L.M. 800, 837. By Roman authors, the phrase was more commonly written **Versa vice.**

Vide. wē´dā. vi´dē. *v. imp.* "See." A citation signal instructing the reader to see the named source of authority. *E.g.*, "The law of war applies, of course, even in regard to an internal war (*vide* Geneva Convention 1977, Protocol II)." *Application of the Convention on the Prevention and Punishment of the Crime of Genocide* (Bosn. & Herz. v. Yugo.), 1996 I.C.J. Rep. 595, 651 (separate opinion of Judge Weeramantry).

Videlicet. wēdālē´kāt. vidēlī´set. *v.* "It is permitted to see." (1) That is to say. (2) Namely; to wit. Commonly abbreviated **Viz.**

Vigilantibus iura sunt scripta. wēgēlan´tēbūs yū´ra sūnt skrēp´ta. vijulân´tibus jɜ´ru sunt skrip´tu. "The laws of the vigilant are written." A maxim meaning that a treaty or other agreement should set forth its terms in writing, with the implication that one should be reluctant to infer unwritten terms into a written agreement.

Vigilantibus non dormientibus subvenit lex. wēgēlan´tēbūs nōn dōrmē-ān´tēbūs sūbwā´nēt lāks. vijulân´tibus nan dōrmyen´tibus sub´vēnit leks. "The law supports the waking, not the sleeping." A maxim meaning that the law favors those who do not sleep on their rights but instead seek to enforce them vigilantly—which is to say, in a timely manner. Alternative phrasings include substituting for "*subvenit lex*" any of the following verb-object combinations: **subveniunt leges, serviunt leges, subveniunt jura**, and **succurrit lex**. All mean essentially the same thing.

V

Vinculum iuris. wēn´kūlūm yū´rēs. vin´kyūlum jɜ´ris. *n.* "Chain of law." (1) A reference to the binding nature of law. (2) A specific, legally binding obligation.

Vires. *See* **Vis.**

Vis. wēs. vis. *n.* [*pl.* **Vires.** wē´rās. vī´rēz.] "Force." (1) Physical force; violence. (2) Metaphorically, any kind of power, such as official power or jurisdiction. *E.g.*, "'[C]ompetence' is a loose and undefined concept in Russian administrative law, and the Russian legal system at the moment offers no judicial means of resolving issues of *vires* either between departments of the state and/or state corporations." William E. Butler, *Treaty Capacity and the Russian State Corporation*, 102 AM. J. INT'L L. 310, 313 (2008). *See also* **Intra vires** and **Ultra vires.**

Vis armata. wēs arma´ta. vis arma´tu. *n.* "Armed force." Military or armed force or compulsion.

Vis clandestina. wēs klandāstē´na. vis klândes´tinu. *n.* "Clandestine force." Force used covertly, as through sabotage or clandestine attack.

Vis inertiae. wēs ēnār´tē-ī. vis inɜr´šē-ā. *n. Neo.* "The force of inactivity." Inertia, either literal (physical) or metaphorical. *E.g.*, "Florence Nightingale was fortunate in her personal associations with men in positions of responsibility, who gave her support against obscurantism and the appalling *vis inertiae* prevailing at the time." M.C.S.P., *A Bio-Bibliography of Florence Nightingale*, 1963 INT'L REV. RED CROSS 106, 107.

Vis maior. wēs ma´yōr. vis mā´jɜr. *n.* "Greater force." (1) An unforeseeable intervening event that purportedly excuses treaty or contractual obligations with which the event interferes. (2) A *force majeur* or act of nature.

Viva voce. wē´wa wō´kā. vē'vu vō´sē OR -vō´čā. *adj.* or *adv.* "With a living voice." (1) Out loud. (2) Verbal(ly); oral(ly). *E.g.*, "Court may also permit the giving of *viva voce* (oral) or recorded testimony of a witness by means of video or audio technology, as well as the introduction of documents or written transcripts, subject to this Statute and in accordance with the Rules of Procedure and Evidence." ROME STATUTE OF THE INTERNATIONAL CRIMINAL COURT art. 69(2), UN Doc. No. A/CONF.183.9 (July 1, 1998). (3) Live; In person. *E.g.*,

"A Letter of Request shall…either be accompanied by a list of interrogatories to be put to the witness or witnesses, or…request the competent authority to allow such questions to be asked *viva voce* as the parties or their representatives shall desire to ask." Convention Regarding Legal Proceedings in Civil Matters art. 10 (G.D.R.–U.K.), Feb. 28, 1980, 20 I.L.M. 929, 932.

Viz. An abbreviation of **Videlicet.**

Voces signatae. *See* **Vox signata.**

Volenti non fit iniuria. wōlān´tē nōn fēt ēnyū´rē-a. vulen´tī nan fit injɜ´rē-u. "To the willing comes no injury." A maxim meaning that one who has agreed that another will perform a specific course of conduct may not later advance a legal claim for damages if the other performs the conduct as agreed.

Votum separatum. wō´tūm sāpara´tūm. vō´tum sepɜrā´tum. *n.* "Separate vote." The right of individual members of a tribunal to issue or publish separate concurring or dissenting opinions.

Vox populi. wōks pō´pūlē. vaks pa´pyūlī. *n.* "Voice of the people." (1) The popular sentiment. (2) The common sentiments or demands of the population of a region or state.

Vox signata. wōks sēgna´ta. vaks signā´tu. *n.* [*pl.* **Voces signatae.** wō´kās sēgna´tī. vō´sēz signa´tā.] "Prescribed voice." The preferred technical term. *Compare with* **Terminus technicus.**

Vs. An abbreviation of **Versus.**

APPENDICES

ADVERBIAL NUMBERS

LATIN	ENGLISH
semel	firstly
bis	secondly
ter	thirdly
quater *or* quattor	fourthly
quinquie(n)s	fifthly
sexie(n)s	sixthly
septie(n)s	seventhly
octie(n)s	eighthly
novie(n)s	ninthly
decie(n)s	tenthly
undecie(n)s	eleventhly
duodecie(n)s	twelfthly
tredecie(n)s	thirteenthly
quaterdecie(n)s *or* quattordecie(n)s	fourteenthly
quindecie(n)s	fifteenthly

CARDINAL NUMBERS

LATIN	ENGLISH
unus	one
duo	two
tres	three
quattuor	four
quinque	five
sex	six
septem	seven
octo	eight
novem	nine
decem	ten
undecim	eleven
duodecim	twelve
tredecim	thirteen
quattuordecim	fourteen
quindecim	fifteen

ORDINAL NUMBERS

LATIN	ENGLISH
primus	first
secundus	second
tertius	third
quartus	fourth
quintus	fifth
sextus	sixth
septimus	seventh
octavus	eighth
nonus	ninth
decimus	tenth
undecimus	eleventh
duodecimus	twelfth
tertius decimus	thirteenth
quartius decimus	fourteenth
quintus decimus	fifteenth